D0206018

# TREATING
# STRESS in
# FAMILIES

# Brunner/Mazel Psychosocial Stress Series
## Charles R. Figley, Ph.D., Series Editor

1. *Stress Disorders Among Vietnam Veterans*, Edited by Charles R. Figley, Ph.D.
2. *Stress and the Family Vol. 1: Coping with Normative Transitions*, Edited by Hamilton I. McCubbin, Ph.D., and Charles R. Figley, Ph.D.
3. *Stress and the Family Vol. 2: Coping with Catastrophe*, Edited by Charles R. Figley, Ph.D., and Hamilton I. McCubbin, Ph.D.
4. *Trauma and Its Wake Vol. 1: The Study and Treatment of Post-Traumatic Stress Disorder*, Edited by Charles R. Figley, Ph.D.
5. *Post-Traumatic Stress Disorder and the War Veteran Patient*, Edited by William E. Kelly, M.D.
6. *The Crime Victim's Book, Second Edition*, By Morton Bard, Ph.D., and Dawn Sangrey
7. *Stress and Coping in Time of War: Generalizations from the Israeli Experience*, Edited by Norman A. Milgram, Ph.D.
8. *Trauma and Its Wake Vol. 2: Traumatic Stress Theory, Research, and Intervention*, Edited by Charles R. Figley, Ph.D.
9. *Stress and Addiction*, Edited by Edward Gottheil, M.D., Ph.D., Keith A. Druley, Ph.D., Steven Pashko, Ph.D., and Stephen P. Weinstein, Ph.D.
10. *Vietnam: A Casebook*, By Jacob D. Lindy, M.D., in collaboration with Bonnie L. Green, Ph.D., Mary C. Grace, M.Ed., M.S., John A. MacLeod, M.D., and Louis Spitz, M.D.
11. *Post-Traumatic Therapy and Victims of Violence*, Edited by Frank M. Ochberg, M.D.
12. *Mental Health Response to Mass Emergencies: Theory and Practice*, Edited by Mary Lystad, Ph.D.

BRUNNER/MAZEL PSYCHOSOCIAL STRESS SERIES No. 13

# TREATING STRESS in FAMILIES

*Edited by*

## Charles R. Figley, Ph.D.

BRUNNER/MAZEL, *Publishers* • New York

**Library of Congress Cataloging-in-Publication Data**

Treating stress in families.

(Brunner/Mazel psychosocial stress series ; no. 13)
Includes bibliographies and indexes.
1. Family psychotherapy.   2. Stress (Psychology)
3. Family—Mental health.   I. Figley, Charles R.,
1944–     . II. Series.   [DNLM: 1. Family Therapy.
2. Stress, Psychological—therapy.   W1 BR917TB no.13 /
WM 430.5.F2 T7837]
RC488.5.T719   1989      616.89′156      88–8554
ISBN 0–87630–530–3

Copyright © 1989 by Charles R. Figley

*Published by*
BRUNNER/MAZEL, INC.
19 Union Square
New York, New York 10003

MANUFACTURED IN THE UNITED STATES OF AMERICA

10   9   8   7   6   5   4   3   2   1

To Ann Alhadeff
whose life blessed
so many of us
in so many ways . . .

# Contents

# Contributors

**Marcia D. Brown-Standridge, Ph.D.**
Assistant Professor of Marriage and Family Therapy, Department of Human Development and Family Studies, Texas Tech University, Lubbock, Texas

**Cassandra A. Erickson, M.S.**
Research Assistant, Marriage and Family Therapy Doctoral Program, Department of Child Development and Family Studies, Purdue University, West Lafayette, Indiana

**Charles R. Figley, Ph.D.**
Professor of Family Therapy and Psychology, Department of Child Development and Family Studies, Purdue University, West Lafayette, Indiana

**Judith L. Fischer, Ph.D.**
Professor of Human Development and Family Studies, Department of Human Development and Family Studies, Texas Tech University, Lubbock, Texas

**Arthur Freeman, Ed.D.**
Associate Professor and Director of Professional Education, Center for Cognitive Therapy, Department of Psychiatry, University of Pennsylvania School of Medicine, Philadelphia, Pennsylvania

**J. Scott Fraser, Ph.D.**
Clinical Associate Professor, School of Professional Psychology, Wright State University, and Director, Crisis/Brief Therapy Center, Good Samaritan Medical Center, Dayton, Ohio

**Bernard G. Guerney, Jr., Ph.D.**
Professor of Human Development and Psychology, Department of Individual and Family Studies, Pennsylvania State University, University Park, Pennsylvania

**Gary Hardley, Ed.D.**
President, Relationship Enhancement Institute, Charlottsville, Virginia

**Hamilton I. McCubbin, Ph.D.**
Dean of the School of Family Resources and Consumer Sciences, and Professor of Family Studies, University of Wisconsin, Madison, Wisconsin

**Marilyn A. McCubbin, R.N., Ph.D.**
Assistant Professor, School of Nursing, and Research Associate, Family Stress, Coping and Health Project, University of Wisconsin, Madison, Wisconsin

**Thorana S. Nelson, Ph.D.**
Assistant Professor of Family Therapy, Department of Child Development and Family Studies, Purdue University, West Lafayette, Indiana

**William C. Nichols, Ed.D.**
Editor, *Journal of Contemporary Family Therapy*, Tallahassee, Florida

**Fred P. Piercy, Ph.D.**
Associate Professor of Family Therapy, Department of Child Development and Family Studies, Purdue University, West Lafayette, Indiana

**Terry S. Trepper, Ph.D.**
Associate Professor of Psychology and Director, Family Studies Center, Department of Behavioral Sciences, Purdue University Calumet, Hammond, Indiana

**Everett L. Worthington, Jr., Ph.D.**
Associate Professor, Department of Psychology, Virginia Commonwealth University, Richmond, Virginia

**Flora Zaken-Greenberg, Ph.D.**
Director, Florida Center for Cognitive Therapy, Ft. Myers, Florida

# Introduction

This book builds on the important, ground-breaking contributions of another multiauthored set of books, *Stress and the Family*, which I co-authored with my long-time collaborator and friend, Hamilton McCubbin (McCubbin & Figley, 1983; Figley & McCubbin, 1983). The focus of those volumes was on the functional and dysfunctional methods by which families attempted to cope with the stress of normative transitions (Volume I) and catastrophes (Volume II). Consistent with the previous two volumes, the purpose of this book is to *organize a compendium of empirically based observations about the ways families produce, are exposed to, and cope with stress, and the most effective ways of helping families master stress.*

Whereas the initial volumes emphasized how families managed to utilize their own resources, rarely seeking outside, professional assistance, this present volume will discuss how to intervene with help-seeking families. The editor and contributors hope that this book will serve as an important resource to practicing clinicians, and that it will be adopted as a textbook for courses and training programs in the area of stress and the family in departments of psychology, counseling psychology, nursing, social work, psychiatry, family medicine, child development, and family studies.

In addition, this book is designed to serve as a single reference guide to practitioners in the above specialties. Finally, it can be useful to scholars interested in the study of families from a stress and coping perspective.

## OBJECTIVES

Specifically, the objectives of *Treating Stress in Families* incorporate and expand those of the first two family stress volumes. They are:

1. to clearly define and provide a framework for viewing the family system as both a stress absorber and a stress producer;

2. to explicate the key concepts and variables associated with this framework;
3. to identify the important areas of research inquiry that converge into the family stress area of study;
4. to facilitate the development of a discrete set of axioms toward which a theory of family stress can be built;
5. to identify the sources of stress, stress reactions of family members, stress-coping resources, repertoire, and behaviors;
6. to note the effective strategies of intervention used by professionals to either mitigate or ameliorate the impairments of family stress;
7. to expand and apply the family stress concept emerging from empirically based theory to effective professional intervention;
8. to expand and apply the individual-centered stress management and intervention approaches to include relationships and families;
9. to identify and discuss the most valid and reliable instruments available to detect and quantify family stress reactions;
10. to identify, discuss, and provide detailed guidance for the use of various intervention programs proven to be effective in preventing or ameliorating family distress (a) from particularly stress sources; (b) with particularly innovative methods; or (c) a combination of the two.

## ORGANIZATIONAL STRUCTURE AND CONTENT

This volume includes 10 chapters divided among three sections. Section I, *Theoretical Orientations*, comprises two chapters which summarize the scientific literature and introduce the reader to both conceptual and clinical orientations to family stress and coping. Chapter 1, written by Marilyn and Hamilton I. McCubbin, provides a comprehensive review of the scientific literature on family stress and coping. Based on this literature, the authors promote a Typology Model of Family Adjustment and Adaptation. They first describe and then utilize this model as a framework for discussing the characteristic ways in which families cope successfully or unsuccessfully with various stressors.

What is especially important to this volume is McCubbin and McCubbin's discussion of targeting intervention to family types suggested by their model and associated measures. They briefly describe various dimensions of regenerative, resilient, and rhythmic families. They then discuss the various measures available to measure and treat these types of families. The final section discusses some applications of their family typology model to crisis and health care intervention, therapy, and education.

Everett Worthington, Jr., in Chapter 2, maintains that family therapy will meet with greater success if the therapist employs the treatment theory that best matches the client family's characteristics. He identifies three variables that affect the family's response to life transitions, the degree of time schedule disruption, the number of new decisions involving initial disagreement, and the level of pretransitional conflict. Then, the author explains how those three dimensions will affect the probable success of each of six fundamental family therapy treatment theories. While the relationship between those six types of family therapy and the three types of family characteristics has not yet been tested empirically, it does provide a systematic and theoretically sound way to match client families with an appropriate therapist or therapeutic technique.

Section II, *Treatment Approaches*, includes four chapters which present different and competing methods of preventing and treating family stress. Each are written by well-known authorities on the approach they discuss. Each author was asked to follow a common outline in order to ensure continuity among the chapters in this section.

1. *Case example:* Each chapter begins with a case study that describes a typical family seeking treatment. The case is discussed throughout the chapter as a means of illustrating the author's approach.
2. *Theoretical overview:* discusses treatment orientation, history, basic assumptions, major axioms, uniqueness of the approach, how its use has evolved over time and contexts, who has used the approach, with what types of clients/problems, and why it is appropriate for use with families attempting to cope with extraordinary stress.
3. *Assessment and diagnosis:* covers formal and informal methods of determining the precise problem, and method(s) of approach are presented.
4. *Treatment process:* presents step-by-step discussion of methods of intervention. Such detail, we hope, will facilitate adaptation by trained clinicians.

Chapter 3, by William C. Nichols, is the first in this section. He focuses on the way family systems therapy can be used to help families deal effectively with the stress of marital breakup. First, Nichols provides a brief history of family systems therapy, identifying the key characteristics of the systems approach that distinguish it from individual therapy approaches. Then, using a case study situation involving a separated couple and their three children, Nichols takes the reader through a step-by-step description of the family systems therapy process.

Moreover, Nichols discusses the creation of a family assessment that includes a demographic profile, a history of the family's development, the presenting complaint and an early clinical assessment of the spouses as individuals, the interpersonal dynamics, the extended family system, and the family's social network. Based on that assessment, the chapter describes a hypothetical series of therapy visits with members of the case study family in which the therapist treated the couple as spouses, the couple as parents, the individual adult when the marriage relationship breaks down, and the sibling subsystem. At each step in the therapeutic process, the family members are seen as part of a system in which each person's actions are reflected in the other family members' well-being.

Cognitive Therapy (CT), a technique originally developed to treat individual depression, can be effectively used to treat family problems. Arthur Freeman and Flora Zaken-Greenberg, in Chapter 4, explain the theoretical underpinnings of CT, the conceptual framework for developing cognitive-behavioral strategies, and intervention techniques adapted for use with families. CT assumes that clients can develop more successful ways of responding by understanding the idiosyncratic ways in which they perceive themselves, the world and experience, and prospects for the future. The therapist helps clients list and prioritize problems, dispute distortions and the schemata underlying them, and build new behavioral patterns. Freeman and Zaken-Greenberg use a case example of a single-parent family presenting with a problem of teenage disobedience and show how the cognitive therapy approach can be used to help the family members develop more successful methods of interacting.

J. Scott Fraser has developed an emergency, family stress treatment approach, discussed in Chapter 5, which he calls the Strategic Rapid Intervention (SRI). This approach is based on the assumption that crises provide a "window of opportunity" to effect family system change. Some families in crisis are able to successfully assimilate changes brought about by the crisis. Others get caught in vicious cycles caused by the family's coping mechanisms that lead to system deterioration and escalation of the problem. Using the SRI approach, the therapist can move the family system to a more adaptive set of mutually supportive coping patterns. The therapist does this by introducing second-order changes or paradoxical interventions.

Using the case of a family that experiences a terrifying home burglary on top of several preexisting stressors, Fraser takes the reader through a six-phase treatment model that typically takes one-to-ten sessions. In the first three phases the therapist establishes a relationship with the clients by joining the system, gathers information, and helps the family reach consensus regarding formulation of the problem. The assessment that takes place at this point focuses on the nature of the crisis, the family's generic and specific response patterns, and identification of any dysfunctional solutions generated by the family. The fourth phase is a break or recess from therapy during which the family and the therapist review the problems. At this point the therapist develops a treatment plan, sometimes relying on the input of a therapy team or colleague who is monitoring the case. The final two phases involve problem solving and closure.

In Chapter 6, Gary Hardley and Bernard G. Guerney, Jr., present the psychoeducational model of crisis intervention. This model goes beyond the traditional model of diagnosis and cure to a transfer of psychotherapeutic skills to the clients so they might better resolve their own problems. Hardley and Guerney use the Relationship Enhancement approach, which emphasizes skill training, to illustrate how the psychoeducational model effectively helps a case study family deal with a crisis situation that includes mutual spouse abuse; a hyperactive, violent child; a spontaneous miscarriage; premenstrual syndrome; and negative extended family interactions.

First, the therapist helps the family identify its stressors and family problems. If the family is in the midst of a major crisis, the therapist uses psychotherapeutic skills to solve that immediate problem, thereby clearing the air so the clients can concentrate on their lesser problems. The bulk of the therapy, however, focuses on teaching the clients skills in expression, empathy, discussion/negotiation, conflict resolution, self-change, helping others change, generalization, and skill maintenance. The therapist explains the purpose of these skills and the attitudes necessary to use them effectively and then provides behavior guidelines, coaching the clients in the practice of the skills. The clients start using their new-found skills to solve their less emotionally intense problems until the core skills are mastered sufficiently to be used with more serious problems.

Section III, *Treating Specific Family Stressors*, the final section of the book, includes four chapters which identify and discuss different major sources of stress that impact the family. Several stressors discussed here typically emerge gradually within the family system, whereas others overwhelm the family with little or no warning.

As with the previous section, each author was asked to follow an identical outline in order to provide continuity among chapters. This outline is as follows:

1. *Case example:* begins with a case study that describes a typical family seeking treatment for a particular family stressor. The case is discussed throughout the chapter as a means of illustrating the author's approach.

2. *Introduction:* focuses on a particular stressor affecting the family. Early in each chapter the authors discuss the stressor in some detail. They note why it is important for the reader to be concerned and the general impact of the stressor on individuals and families. This section also introduces the reader to the author's theoretical and/or intervention orientation to the stressor being discussed.

3. *Description of the stressor:* reviews the literature on the incidence and prevalence of the stressor, if available, and its typical impact on families is discussed.

4. *Primary sources of stress for the family:* lists and discusses the specific individual and systemic consequences of the stressor, citing the relevant scientific literature is found here.

5. *Functional family coping:* lists and briefly discusses the ways families effectively deal with the stressor and thereby preclude the need for professional services. It gives the "success stories": how families are able to utilize their own resources and pull together to overcome extraordinary circumstances. Moreover, this section provides, in effect, the model family functioning family clinicians attempt to foster.

6. *Dysfunctional family coping:* lists and briefly discusses the way families *ineffectively* deal with the stressor and thereby *require* professional services. It presents the "failure stories": how families are *unable* to utilize their own resources and pull together to overcome extraordinary circumstances. Moreover, this section provides, in effect, the model of a typical client family seeking treatment to overcome the particular stressor being discussed throughout the chapter.

7. *Overview of this approach to treatment:* presents a brief overview of the general approach to helping families to cope more effectively with the stressor. It introduces the reader to the

methods of assessment, diagnosis, and treatment, which are discussed in much greater detail below.

8. *Assessment methods:* includes a description of the procedures for assessment, including a detailed description of any suggested instruments, along with a report of any published estimates of reliability and validity.

9. *Diagnosis and treatment plan:* discusses data interpretation from the assessment/diagnosis, differential diagnosis, goals, and general approach to treatment/intervention.

10. *Treatment approach details:* provides the step-by-step methods of treatment/intervention from first to last session. The case study introduced at the beginning of the chapter and discussed throughout is utilized here extensively.

11. *Signs of treatment completion/effectiveness:* discusses outcomes, indications of success, completion of treatment/intervention, and issues of follow-up and referral.

12. *Conclusion:* briefly summarizes the approach and discusses the need for further development through research and practice.

The first chapter in this section—Chapter 7, by Terry S. Trepper— focuses on perhaps the least understood family stressor. Trepper discusses the application of family therapy techniques to a unique family problem, intrafamily sex abuse. The multiple systems model discussed here assumes that all families have differing degrees of vulnerability to intrafamily sexual abuse. Certain factors increase vulnerability, but intrafamily abuse also requires precipitating events and impairment in family coping mechanisms for the abuse to take place. Using the case of a family in which the father sexually abused the 11-year-old daughter, Trepper explains how the interaction of these factors can develop into a situation where the normal prohibitions against intrafamily sexual abuse break down.

The remainder of the chapter describes the therapeutic approach used by Trepper to treat families in which sexual abuse is the presenting problem. The therapeutic goals of the model are: (1) to protect the child from further abuse; (2) to change the family structure; (3) to decrease family vulnerability; (4) to increase family coping strategies; and (5) to encourage victim assertiveness. First, the therapist assesses the family's vulnerability to incest on the basis of the socioenvironment, the family system, individual personalities, the families of origin, precipitating episodes, and the normal coping mechanisms used by the family. The treatment program involves creating a context for change, challenging existing patterns and expanding alternatives, and consolidating the changes that have taken place to assure that the sexual abuse does not have a good chance of recurring.

Chapter 8 describes a family therapy model useful in treating problems of adolescent substance abuse. Fred Piercy and Thorana Nelson describe an integrated treatment model they developed that synthesizes compatible skills borrowed from structural, strategic, functional, and behavioral family therapy approaches. The goals of the integrated treatment model are: (1) to decrease family resistance to treatment; (2) to restrain immediate change; (3) to establish appropriate parental influence; (4) to make a systemic assessment of the presenting problem; (5) to interrupt dysfunctional sequences of behavior; and (6) to provide assertiveness training that will help the children resist pressures to use drugs.

Piercy and Nelson use the case study of a teenage drug abuser to illustrate how an adolescent's drug use interacts with other family stressors and problems with coping. They describe two types of assessment methods: one that uses a battery of instruments on a set timetable and another, more informal method that determines the nature and extent of drug use, assesses family functioning, and assesses larger system issues such as peer group relations, interactions with social agencies, and the school and work environments. Then they take the case study family through a four-phase, 12-week, integrated family therapy program that helps the family develop more functional methods of dealing with their family interactions and that discourages further adolescent substance abuse.

In Chapter 9, Judith L. Fischer and Marcia Brown-Standridge use the clinical transcripts from a particularly poignant case to illustrate contextual family therapy, an approach that takes into account multiple layers of systemic and intrapsychic patterns. The presenting problem, a sudden decline in the young adolescent son's academic work, is relatively easily solved by establishment of a more functional balance between parental and child responsibility. However, discussion of the presenting problem revealed several unresolved issues within the family system that set the context for the son's academic problems. Since the family was unwilling to deal with those issues, further therapy was put off until a new problem arose.

When the family again sought therapy to solve the problem of the wife's compulsive spending, the therapist was finally able to lead the family into issues they did not dare to address on their own. The wide scope of the contextual family therapy approach allows the therapist to look well beyond the immediate family problems presented to treat long-standing problems that would most likely otherwise continue to manifest themselves in ever new problems. Fischer and Brown-Standridge show how the therapist can help relieve the burden of parental experiences and expectations on the children without undue strain on the parents.

The final chapter focuses on one of the newest and perhaps the most troublesome category of family stressor, that which results in traumatic stress. In Chapter 10, Cassandra Erickson describes her innovative methods for helping families of rape victims. The case example describes a young woman who is raped on the way to her car after attending a university class. The victim begins to withdraw and her family reacts with concern that soon develops into more serious manifestations of *family traumatic stress reactions*. Rape is described as a crisis that is *shared* by the victim and her family. The victim and her family often experience a series of trauma-related symptoms that characterize the rape trauma syndrome of the victim and secondary catastrophic stress responses of her family.

Erickson describes a step-by-step treatment approach in which she borrows from, modifies, and adapts Williamson's *consultation process* for helping young adults to terminate the intergenerational hierarchical boundary with their parents. In this approach, the therapist initially works with the victim and her family separately in order to prepare them for sharing their experiences and perceptions of the impact of the rape. The therapist then works with the victim in a formal ritual to invite the family to join her in confronting the trauma and its aftermath. A three-day consultation follows in which the victim and her family confront first those issues that pertain only to the victim, then those issues related to the other family members. Finally, the issues related to the family as a whole are confronted. The therapist helps family members to learn new methods of coping in a healthy, supportive environment. The ultimate goal of treatment is to facilitate integration of the trauma of the rape experience into the family system.

Finally, it should be useful to the reader to note that a rather detailed glossary of terms in the area of family stress treatment can be found in the Appendix. As far as we know, this is the first published glossary of its kind. We hope that among other things, it will help bring some degree of order and much needed conceptual uniformity in this growing area of interest.

## A FINAL NOTE

Nearly all of the contributors to this volume are leading experts in their areas of specialization. Most of us have had many years of experience working with families who are struggling to cope with enormous stress.

We have been impressed with the extraordinary power of the family—as a system of both destruction and healing. The clinical literature, however, generally has represented the family only in terms of the former—as a victimizing system (Figley, in press). Unfortunately, by focusing on family or family-induced psychopathology and dysfunction, the family system has become the bane of mental health. Certainly the family psychology/family therapy movement is attempting to change this view.

Pilisuk and Parks (1986), however, challenge this view and suggest that *families in particular and social support networks and groups in general provide a vital and often-overlooked function in fostering mental health and well-being.* They urge clinicians to assume that the family was functioning acceptably well for all its members prior to the impact of the traumatic event. By intervening at the family systems level, many believe that not only will the pain and suffering of members be alleviated but, as a result of the intervention, the family will be more equipped to cope effectively with future challenges.

Be they victims, patients, or clients, those exposed to highly stressful events require the best intervention services possible. The effective and efficient treatment requires careful attention to many factors. One of the most important factors is the client's access to an effective social support system.

For those clients who *do* have access to social support, particularly intact systems such as a family, the system itself may require professional assistance. Just as family therapy emerged as a result of clinicians' struggling with efforts to cure individuals with major mental illness, family-centered treatment should be the treatment of choice for stress-related problems.

We are impressed with the ability of individuals and the intimate systems within which they live to spring back from adversity. We have witnessed how families, devastated by traumatic events, drug abuse, parent-child conflict, and more mundane but highly stressful challenges of life were able to not only recover from their difficulties, but become strengthened by them and better prepared for future hardships. We hope that the clinical approaches to treating stress in families presented here will be a valuable addition to the libraries of anyone responsible for the welfare of individuals and families.

*Charles R. Figley, Ph.D.*
*West Lafayette, Indiana*

## REFERENCES

Figley, C. R., & McCubbin, H. I. (Eds.) (1983). *Stress and the family, Volume II: Coping with catastrophe.* New York: Brunner/Mazel, pp. 3–20.

Figley, C. R. (in press). Victims, victimization, and traumatic stress. *Counseling Psychologist.*

McCubbin, H. I., & Figley, C. R. (1983). Introduction. In *Stress and the family, Volume I: Coping with normative transitions.* New York: Brunner/Mazel.

Pilisuk, M., & Parks, S. H. (1986). *The healing web: Social networks and human survival.* Hanover, NH: University Press of New England.

# Acknowledgments

As with every important effort in life, this volume is the product of a large and extraordinary group of people. Certainly the Editorial Board of the Series was instrumental in approving and guiding this project and its various elements. The members of the Board are listed at the beginning of the book. The staff of Brunner/Mazel always deserves special praise for their work: Bernard Mazel and Ann Alhadeff were continual sources of support and encouragement. They reminded me of the success of *Stress and the Family, Volumes 1 and 2*, and were confident that this one would be well received.

My colleagues at Purdue continually provide the intellectual stimulation and social support that allow me to develop and complete projects such as this. Dr. Donald Felker, Dean of the School of Consumer and Family Sciences, Dr. Wallace Denton, Head, Department of Child Development and Family Studies, and Dr. Douglas H. Sprenkle, Director, Marriage and Family Therapy Program, are gratefully acknowledged for their genuine interest and support of my work.

Several of my students were very helpful at various phases of this project: C. J. Harris, Mitchell Young, Dr. Kathy Gilbert, Dr. Shirley Segel, Dr. Richard Kishur, and, particularly Cassandra Erickson. As my research assistant, Cassandra helped me to keep the project on track and in touch with the contributors and critically reviewed several of the manuscripts, including my own. Perhaps the most critical Purdue colleague, however, is Phoebe Herr. As editorial assistant she provided all of the necessary clerical and administrative tasks to insure that this and many other projects were completed promptly and with the highest quality.

Finally, I am indebted to my immediate family: my wife, Dr. Marilyn Reeves, who helped write some of the sections of this book, and my daughters, Jessica and Laura, who *inspired* the writing of parts of this book. Their support, encouragement, and just being themselves make treating stress in our family unnecessary.

Charles R. Figley, Ph.D.
West Lafayette, Indiana

# TREATING STRESS in FAMILIES

# SECTION I

# Theoretical Orientations

# 1

# Theoretical Orientations to Family Stress and Coping

## MARILYN A. McCUBBIN and HAMILTON I. McCUBBIN

*Jennifer Williams, a Black woman 36 years of age, is a single parent, currently living with a white male, James, who is 28. They share in the responsibility for raising Jennifer's daughter, Claudia, age 16. Claudia is struggling academically and appears to be involved with a group of teenagers who are heavily involved in smoking and alcohol use and, in some reported cases, substance abuse. Tension between mother and daughter has increased in recent months around Claudia's friends, and James has entered the conflict by siding with Claudia. Jennifer has sought the help of the school counselors, one of whom is a family therapist.*

*Through clinical interviews and the application of standardized, family-focused, self-assessment measures, the social worker evaluated the family unit, including James, and discovered the following: During the past eight months Claudia has grieved over two suicides in her peer group coupled with the pileup of other life events, including an unreported (to mother) confrontation with the law around accusations of shoplifting in which her friend was the perpetrator, a grandparent's illness, and racial tensions in school which have hurt Claudia. She feels supported and protected by her friends who are predominantly Black teens.*

This project was funded in part by a grant to the senior author from the Graduate School, University of Wisconsin-Madison and a grant to the second author from the Agricultural Experiment Station, University of Wisconsin-Madison. The authors would like to thank Assistant Dean, Anne Thompson, for her support of and investment in this effort, and Kim Guenther, who played a significant role in the preparation of this chapter.

3

Jennifer has not been able to be home much because she is going to
school (technical school) and works full time, thus causing her to return
home between 9 P.M. and 10 P.M., often to an empty apartment. She has
recently been diagnosed as hypertensive (high blood pressure). She has
been advised to lose weight, alter her diet, and reduce the stress in her
living situation. James arrives home after 10 P.M. due to his late working hours.

The relationship between Jennifer and James is rocky at best; she
feels used and that he doesn't really care about her and Claudia. James
has a steady job and wants to marry, but Jennifer is not comfortable
with such long-range plans. Jennifer distrusts James and feels that
something may be going on between him and her daughter, although
nothing could be offered to confirm or support even a suspicion of this.
The systemic assessment revealed that the family unit of three members
could be classified as a vulnerable type, that is, being low on family
hardiness and coherence. They cope with family problems by getting
upset, indicating less respect for one another, blaming other people or
other family members, as well as showing less caring and understanding.
They appear to have a lower sense of purpose and less sense of being
valued or appreciated. They repeat the same patterns over and over;
there is little desire to do something new or to encourage others to be
different. Furthermore, after examining the family's routine patterns of
behavior, the family unit can be classified as an intentional type. The
members of this family carry on their lives with little emphasis on the
actual practice of family time and routines. They express the desire to
establish more family routines of togetherness, but they are not able to
conduct even the most routine of activities such as eating or talking
together. They feel guilty about this but have reconciled themselves to
believing that this is the best they can do. Claudia has expressed
repeatedly the desire for a little more quality time with her mother as
she struggles to gain a fuller understanding of herself and the meaning
of their personal struggles and feelings.

The family has numerous strengths, however. A systematic review of
the family unit reveals love and caring among all members. Their concern for each other appears to be real. Adult members contribute their
income to making the financial struggles less of a burden; they feel they
can depend on each other to be there in times of need; they also seek new
ways to be together and to gain greater control over their lives. They
both have relatives in town who make themselves available for assis-

*tance and listening. Jennifer and James value their relatives and the*
*support they receive from them.*

*The school social worker agrees to see the family as a unit on a*
*weekly basis for four weeks with all members agreeing to participate.*
*The plan of intervention includes (a) focusing upon the accumulation of*
*life events and changes and their impact upon Claudia and her feelings,*
*with an eye toward including adult members in being more sensitive to*
*Claudia's struggles; (b) diffusing the misplaced emphasis upon Claudia's*
*friends which seems to be a smoke screen for other struggles; (c)*
*building upon the family's existing strengths both in the quality of the*
*relationships that already exist and the unit that has already formed;*
*and (d) making efforts to encourage the family unit to build in quality*
*time for the developing young adult and for the family as a unit.*

Family scholars have struggled with the design of research and the
development of theories aimed toward uncovering why some families are
better able to negotiate their way through transitions and tragedies and to
cope with and even thrive on life's hardships, whereas other families, faced
with similar if not identical stressors or family transitions, give up or are
easily exhausted. Family stress theory has been advanced and adapted to
guide this line of scientific inquiry and family system interventions. The
importance of family stress theory to the study of normative family transitions and adaptation to major life changes and illnesses is based on the
central roles that family type and family strengths and capabilities play in
understanding and explaining family behavior. Family stress theory highlights the complex but meaningful role which certain family typologies
such as the Balanced family type (Lavee, 1985; M. A. McCubbin, 1986;
Olson, McCubbin, Barnes, Larsen, Muxen, & Wilson, 1983), Resilient,
Regenerative, or Rhythmic family types (McCubbin, Thompson, Pirner,
& McCubbin, 1988) play in buffering the impact of stressful life events and
and in facilitating family adaptation following a crisis situation. In contrast to family frameworks which underscore the deficiencies and dysfunctional aspects of family systems, family stress theory sharpens its focus on
and targets the strengths and resistance resources families have as part of
their innate abilities to endure hardships. The purpose of this chapter is to
introduce the Typology Model of Family Adjustment and Adaptation as a
specific evolution of family stress theory and to focus upon family assessment strategies based on this model as critical components of family crisis
interventions and long-term family systems interventions.

## THE TYPOLOGY MODEL OF FAMILY
## ADJUSTMENT AND ADAPTATION

The Typology Model of Family Adjustment and Adaptation has been based on nine fundamental assumptions about family life and intervention in family life:

1. Families face hardships and changes as a natural and predictable aspect of family life over the life cycle.
2. Families develop basic strengths and capabilities designed to foster the growth and development of family members and the family unit and to protect the family from major disruptions in the face of family transitions and changes.
3. Families also face crises that force the family unit to change its traditional mode of functioning and adapt to the situation.
4. Families develop basic and unique strengths and capabilities designed to protect the family from unexpected or nonnormative stressors and strains and to foster the family's adaptation following a family crisis or major transition and change.
5. Families benefit from and contribute to the network of relationships and resources in the community, particularly during periods of family stress and crisis.
6. Family functioning is often characterized as predictable with shaped patterns of interpersonal behavior, which in turn are molded and maintained by intergenerational factors, situational pressures that have evolved over time, the personalities of the family members, and the normative and nonnormative events that punctuate family life throughout the life cycle.
7. Family interventions can be enhanced and families supported by both a diagnostic and an evaluation process which takes the strengths in the family system as well as the deficiencies of the family system into consideration.
8. Family functioning can be enhanced by interventions that target both the vulnerabilities and dysfunctional patterns of the family unit and the family's interpersonal capabilities and strengths which, if addressed, can serve as a catalyst for other family-system, wellness-promoting properties.
9. Families develop and maintain internal resistance and adaptive resources, which vary in strength and resiliency over the family

life cycle, but which can be influenced and enhanced to function more effectively. These resources can play a critical role in fostering successful family adjustments and adaptations even after the family unit has deteriorated to the point of exhibiting major difficulties and symptoms of dysfunction.

Family stress theory and particularly the Typology Model of Family Adjustment and Adaptation may be described as attempting to describe families as two related but discernible phases in their response to life changes and catastrophes. The first phase is the *adjustment phase* and the second the *adaptation phase*. Realizing that not all transitions or changes create family crises or call for major shifts in the family's rules or patterns of behavior, the Typology Model of Family Adjustment and Adaptation focuses first upon those family types and strengths and capabilities that explain why some families are better suited than others to adjust to minor changes. It is also true that some transitions such as the death of a family member or a divorce or separation, which are also demands on family life in modern America, call for a major shift in the way the family unit normally operates, and thus a crisis emerges. The Typology Model also focuses upon the second phase of family adaptation. Here the theoretical framework attempts to guide research and intervention as to what family types, strengths, and capabilities are needed, called upon, or created in order to manage a major transition and change calling for family reorganization and systemic change.

THE ADJUSTMENT PHASE

The earliest conceptual foundations for research to examine the variability in family adjustment responses were the Hill (1949, 1958) ABCX family crisis model and McCubbin and Patterson's Double ABCX Model (McCubbin & Patterson, 1981c, 1983a, 1983b). Their formulations focused upon the stressor, the family's resistance resources, and the family's appraisal of the stressor event. Recent investigations have encouraged us to expand upon these formulations and introduce the Typology Model with the inclusion of *family types and levels of vulnerability*. The adjustment phase in the Typology Model and its components, outlined in Figure 1, may be stated as:

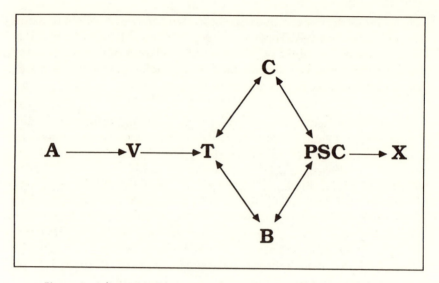

Figure 1.  Adjustment Phase, Typology Model of Family Adjustment
and Adaptation.

*The level of family adjustment and/or the family's transition into a*
*crisis situation (X)* (and into the adaptation phase or exhaustion) in
response to a stressor event or transition is determined by: *A* (the
stressor event or transition and its level of severity)—interacting
with the *V* (the family's vulnerability determined in part by the
concurrent pileup of demands—stressors, transitions, and strains
and by the pressures associated with family's life-cycle stage)
—interacting with *T* (the family's typology—regenerative, resilient,
rhythmic, balanced, etc.)—interacting with *B* (the family's resistance
resources)—interacting with *C* (the appraisal the family makes of
the event)—interacting with *PSC* (the family's problem-solving and
coping repertoire and capabilities).

### Stressor/Transition: Demands (A Factor)

A stressor is defined as a life event or transition (e.g., death, purchase of
a home, parenthood) impacting upon or within the family unit which
produces, or has the potential of producing, change in the family social
system. This change may be in various areas of family life, such as the
health status of one of its members, family system boundaries, goals, pat-

terns of interaction, or values. The *severity of a stressor or transition* is determined by the degree to which the event or transition threatens or disrupts the family's stability, or places demands on the family's resources or capabilities, the result of which could also threaten the family's stability (see Comeau, 1985; M. A. McCubbin, 1986).

*Family Vulnerability: Pileup and Family Life-Cycle Stage (V Factor)*

Vulnerability, the V factor, is defined as the interpersonal and organizational condition of the family system shaped, in part, by: (1) the pileup of demands on or within the family unit co-occurring at the onset or impact of another stressor or transition; and (2) the family's life-cycle stage with all of its normative demands and variability in resources and strengths. For example, the impact of an economic stressor event is likely to be more problematic for families in the adolescent or launching stage of the family life-cycle because of the accumulation of life changes and strains as well as the depletion of family interpersonal, social, and economic resources (see Olson et al., 1983).

*Family Type: Profile of Family Functioning (T Factor)*

A family's typology is defined as a set of basic attributes about the family system which characterizes and explains how a family system typically appraises, operates, and/or behaves. These are predictable and discernible patterns of family behavior. Balanced families (Lavee, 1985) respond more supportively and with greater ease to normative transitions. In the face of a severe chronic illness situation, balanced families indicate more positive health outcomes for the chronically ill child (M. A. McCubbin, 1986; 1988). In the face of normative transitions, regenerative families (i.e., those with strengths of family hardiness and coherence) are better able to manage hardships and promote other family strengths of bonding, flexibility, and predictability, as well as marital and family satisfaction (McCubbin, Thompson, Pirner, & McCubbin, 1988).

*Resistance Resources: Capabilities and Strengths (B Factor)*

The B factor, the family's resources for meeting the demands of stressor events and hardships, has been described at the adjustment phase as the family's ability to prevent an event or a transition in the family from creating a crisis or disruption and to facilitate the family's problem solving, coping, and adjustment (Burr, 1973). Resources or family strengths then become part of the family's capabilities for resisting crisis and promoting family adjustment.

The research and theory-building literature on family resources and family strengths (referred to here as resistance or adjustment resources because they play a role in resisting changes, buffering the impact of a stressor or change on family life and promoting adjustment) has flourished in recent years (e.g., Curran, 1983; Stinnet & DeFrain, 1985). This focus is reflected in the annual efforts of the University of Nebraska in their Family Strengths Conference. This renewed emphasis on family strengths falls into the mainstream of research designed to determine what it is about families that fosters their continuity and stability in the face of a host of normal and demanding changes and adversities which seem to impact on families.

*Family Management: Problem Solving and Coping (PSC Factor)*

The PSC factor in the Typology Model is the family's management of the stressful situation through its problem-solving and coping skills. Problem solving refers to the family's ability to define the stressor and the situation into manageable components, to identify alternative courses of action, to initiate steps to resolve the discrete issues, and ultimately to resolve the problem. Coping refers to the family's strategies, patterns, and behaviors designed to maintain and/or strengthen the organization and stability of the family unit, maintain the emotional stability and well-being of family members, obtain and/or utilize family and community resources to manage the situation, and initiate efforts to resolve the family hardships created by the stressor/transition.

*Family Appraisal: Focus on Stressor (C Factor)*

The family's subjective definition of the stressor, accompanying hardships, and their effect on the family unit comprises the C factor in the Typology Model. Although there are objective cultural definitions of the seriousness of life events and transitions representing the collective judgment of the community, this factor represents how the family defines the seriousness of the experienced stressor. The family's values and previous experience in managing change and handling crises are also reflected in this subjective meaning. The family's appraisal of the situation can range from interpreting a stressor as uncontrollable and contributing to the family's disintegration to viewing the situation as a challenge to be met with growth producing outcomes (McCubbin & Patterson, 1983d).

**Family Response: Stress and Distress.** Stressor events, transitions, and related hardships produce tension which calls for management (Antonovsky, 1979). Stress emerges when this tension is not overcome. A state of tension, characterized as family stress rather than stressor, arises when there is an actual or perceived imbalance between the demands (e.g., challenge or threat) placed on the family and the capabilities (e.g., resources, coping) of the family. Family stress is then depicted as a nonspecific demand for adjustment or adaptive behavior. A state of hyperstress occurs when the imbalance is due to the demands exceeding the family's resources; when these resources exceed the demands, there is a state of hypostress in the family. Therefore, the amount of stress in a family can vary depending upon the nature of the situation, the resources and capabilities of the family unit, and the psychological and physical well-being of its members. Family distress implies a negative state in which the family defines the demands-resources imbalance as unpleasant. In contrast, eustress is a positive state characterized by the family's defining the demands-resources imbalance as desirable and a challenge which family members appreciate and accept (McCubbin & Patterson, 1983d).

**The Family Adjustment Process.** Family functioning is assumed to be relatively stable prior to the occurrence of a stressor event or transition. However, there can be some preexisting and disturbing conflicts in family interaction (e.g., marital, sibling, parent-child subsystems). Consequently, the family can actually be at any point from low to high on the vulnerability continuum. Families faced with a stressor event or transition must simultaneously manage a cluster of demands. In addition to the specific event, families must also deal with the direct hardships associated with the situation and any preexisting strains already present in the family system. These prior strains are frequently exacerbated by the stressor or transition. The family moves through a roller coaster course of adjustment during this time. Initially, the family is resistant to change and tries to maintain established patterns of interaction with minimal disruption of the family's established behavior and structure. By maintaining established patterns, the family makes an effort to protect itself from change (McCubbin & Patterson, 1983d). For example, Claudia's transition into young adulthood brings a demand for greater independence which includes the selection of friends. Previous tensions and strains between Claudia, her mother, and James are also increased as a result. Initially, Jennifer and James may be reluctant to increase Claudia's independence since they need to be away from home all day and into the evening. Finally, rather than demand total adherence to rigid rules calling for minute-by-minute accounting developed when Claudia was young, the Williams' family may change its pattern of interaction and institute the practice of signing in and out, which minimizes parental lecturing and nonverbal expressions of concern or discomfort with Claudia's increasing independence.

### Adjustment Coping Strategies

Avoidance, elimination, and assimilation are three basic adjustment coping strategies which can be used alone or in combination by the family to achieve family adjustment (McCubbin & Patterson, 1983d). Family efforts to deny or ignore the stressor and other demands in the hope that they will go away or resolve themselves are characterized as avoidance coping strategies. Active family efforts to remove all the demands of the stressor or alter the definition of the stressor are elimination coping strategies. These two coping strategies promote the maintenance of the existing structure and interaction in the family and protect the family from making any modifications in their patterns of behavior. The third coping strategy, assimilation, is used when the family accepts the demands created by the stressor or transition into its present structure and interaction. Only minor changes within the family unit are made during this process. When the family unit has an adequate and appropriate supply of existing resources (e.g., flexibility and hardiness) that may be employed or re-allocated, minimal change and disruption occurs. These resources also influence the selection of coping strategies and the definition and appraisal of demands by the family.

Many family life changes, transitions, and demands are adequately managed by the short-term response of adjustment. However, families can encounter other occasions where adjustment coping strategies are inadequate or unsatisfactory. These situations would include: (a) structural changes in the family system (e.g., parenthood, divorce, death); (b) depletion of the family's existing resources as a result of the number, nature, and duration of experienced demands (e.g., loss of financial well-being due to long-term care of chronically ill member); (c) overtaxing of the family's resources due to continued unresolved strains (e.g., ongoing conflict with a former spouse); (d) insufficient resources and capabilities to meet the demands (e.g., lack of income to cover child care or maintain single household); and (e) overt or covert action to bring about structural change in the family unit by allowing or facilitating a demand-capability imbalance or family crisis (e.g., allowing unresolved marital conflict to dissolve the marriage). Thus, the family moves toward or into a state of crisis when the demand-capability imbalance continues or increases (McCubbin & Patterson, 1983d).

*Family Adjustment, Maladjustment, and Crisis:*
*Demand for Change (X Factor)*

Some stressful life events and transitions do not create major hardships for the family system given the family's type, resources, and coping and problem-solving abilities, appraisals, and vulnerabilities. In these cases, the family moves through the situation with relative ease, which leads to a positive outcome involving minor adjustments or changes in the family system. However, in some situations, the resulting hardships are numerous and severe, demanding more substantial changes in the family system— its rules, boundaries, and overall patterns of behavior. These families, in this type of situation, are not likely to achieve stability with ease and without making substantial changes in the family system. Consequently, they will experience maladjustment and the resulting state of crisis.

*Family crisis* has been conceptualized as a continuous variable denoting the amount of disruptiveness, disorganization, or incapacitation in the family social system (Burr, 1973). Crisis is a state of family system disorganization whereas family stress is a state of tension brought about by the demand-capability imbalance in the family. Families in crisis have a situational inability to restore stability, undergo cyclical trial-and-error struggles to reduce tensions, and try to make changes in the family's structure and patterns of interaction (McCubbin & Patterson, 1983d). Although these attempts at change contribute to the family's instability, the crisis state is a transitional one and represents the family's efforts to achieve adaptation to the stressors and demands from both within and outside the family unit.

As previously noted, crisis denotes family disorganization and a demand for changes in order to restore stability to the previous level of functioning or at another higher or lower functioning level. This movement to initiate change in the family unit marks the beginning of the adaptation phase of the Typology Model of Adjustment and Adaptation. It is very important to note that a family " 'in crisis' does not carry the stigmatizing value judgment that somehow the family has failed, is dysfunctional, or is in need of professional counseling" (McCubbin & Patterson, 1983d, p. 22). In order to cope with developmental changes in family members and the family system, many, if not most, family crises are normative and expected.

Other family crises are brought about by conscious family decisions to make structural changes (e.g., separation, engaging in dual career lifestyle, a reentry into the work force) or alter core family values or goals as a planned step to improve family conditions, reduce financial or emotional strains, and enhance the overall functioning of the family unit. The process of family adaptation involves the integration and interaction of another set of family demands, capabilities, resources, appraisals, and coping strategies (McCubbin & Patterson, 1983d).

## THE FAMILY ADAPTATION PHASE

The assessment of family adaptation requires a more dynamic model that focuses upon family efforts over time to recover from a crisis situation. The Typology Model, which emerged from studies of war-induced family crises (McCubbin, Boss, Wilson, & Lester, 1980; McCubbin & Patterson, 1981c, 1982c, 1983a,b), expanded upon and redefined Hill's original ABCX Model and added postcrisis variables in an effort to describe: (a) the additional life stressors and changes that may influence the family's ability to achieve adaptation; (b) the critical psychological, family, and social factors that families call upon and use in adaptation; (c) the processes families engage in to achieve satisfactory adaptation; and (d) the outcome of these family efforts. The adaptation phase of the Typology Model of Family Adjustment and Adaptation is outlined in Figure 2.

*The level of family adaptation (XX) and/or the family's transition back into a crisis situation* (or exhaustion) in response to a crisis situation is determined by: *AA*, the pileup of demands on or in the family system created by the crisis situation, life-cycle changes, and unresolved strains—interacting with *R*, the family's level of regenerativity determined in part by the concurrent pileup of demands (stressors, transitions, and strains)—interacting with *T*, the family's typology (resilient, rhythmic, balanced, etc.)—interacting with *BB*, the family's strengths (the family's adaptive strengths, capabilities, and resources)—interacting with *CC*, the family's appraisal of the situation (the meaning the family attaches to the total situation) and *CCC*, the family's schema (i.e., world view and sense of coherence which shapes the family's situational appraisal and meaning)—interacting with *BBB*, the support from friends and the community (social support)—interacting with *PSC*, the family's problem-solving and coping response to the total family situation.

## *Family Adaptation (XX Factor)*

Family adaptation becomes the central concept in the adaptation phase and is used to describe the *outcome* of family efforts to achieve a new level of balance and fit in response to a family crisis. In crisis situations, the family unit struggles to achieve a *balance and fit at both the individual-to-family and the family-to-community levels of functioning.* Family efforts directed toward adaptation involve consideration and response to both levels of functioning since a change at one level affects the other. In addition, reciprocal relationships emerge where the demands at one level are met by the capabilities at another level. This brings about a simultaneous "balance and fit" at both levels of interaction.

A balance between individual family members and the family unit is sought at the first level of interaction. A demand-capability imbalance at this level brings about family stress or distress (McCubbin & Patterson, 1983d). In the case example at the beginning of the chapter, the demands related to Claudia's academic difficulties, her relationships with peers who are involved with alcohol and possibly drugs, and ongoing conflicts and strains between her mother and James, has brought about a demand-capability imbalance at the individual-to-family level of functioning. This has resulted in considerable stress for the family unit. At the second level

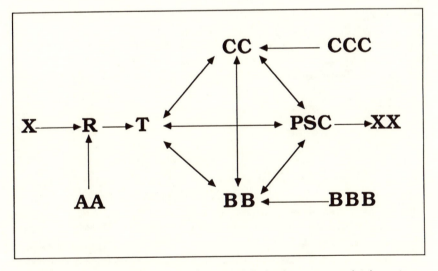

Figure 2. Adaptation Phase, Typology Model of Adjustment and Adaptation.

of functioning, a balance is sought between the family system and the community in which the family lives and participates. Two social institutions, the family unit and the workplace, frequently compete for the involvement of family members. In the Williams family, the work and school demands of the adult members have been in competition with the family's needs to spend more time together and establish more family routines of togetherness. Therefore, a demand-capability imbalance can also occur at this level of functioning and cause stress for the family.

*Family Demands: Pileup (AA Factor)*

Because family crises evolve and are resolved over a period of time, families are seldom dealing with a single stressor. Our research indicates that they experience a pileup of demands, particularly from a chronic stressor such as caring for a disabled or chronically ill family member or in the aftermath of a major stressor, such as a death, a major role change for one member, or a natural disaster (McCubbin & Patterson, 1983d). This pileup is referred to as the AA factor in the adaptation phase. The demands or needs of individuals, families, and society are not static but change over time. In the case example of the Williams family, the grandparent's illness, Claudia's school performance and peer relationships, adult members' long work hours and health problems, and ongoing unresolved tensions among family members are all stresses that call for family adjustment and adaptation, and represent cumulative sources of additional demands on the family unit.

There appear to be at least five broad types of stressors and strains contributing to a pileup in the family system in the adaptation phase: (a) the initial stressor and its hardships; (b) normative transitions; (c) prior strains; (d) the consequences of family efforts to cope; and (e) ambiguity, both intrafamily and social (McCubbin & Patterson, 1983d).

*Crisis and Its Hardships*

When the family experiences a crisis such as the birth of a child, a divorce, or the serious illness of a family member, there are inherent, specific hardships that increase or intensify the difficulties faced by the family (McCubbin & Patterson, 1983d). Additional hardships associated with a crisis can include ambiguity surrounding the diagnosis and course of an illness or treatment outcomes, increased marital or relationship strains, parent-child conflicts, and decreased emotional or financial resources.

## Normative Transitions

Predictable and expected transitions are experienced by the family unit as a result of the normal growth and development of child members (e.g., need for nurturance, supervision, or increasing independence and autonomy), of adult members (career advancement, return to school for more education), of the extended family (e.g., illness and death of grandparents), and family life-cycle changes (e.g., children entering school, adolescence). These transitions can occur at the same time as the crisis-precipitating event but can also be independent of the stressor (McCubbin & Patterson, 1983d). The simultaneous occurrence of a normative transition and a stressor event places additional demands on the family unit and necessitates an adaptation response.

## Prior Strains

In today's society, most family systems carry with them some residue of strain, which may be the result of unresolved hardships from earlier stressors or transitions or may be inherent in ongoing roles such as parent or employer (Pearlin & Schooler, 1978). These prior strains are exacerbated when a new stressor event is encountered by the family and contribute to the pileup of difficulties these families now face. Although the emergence and awareness of these strains are more insidious than a specific discrete event, these prior strains are a component of the accumulation of demands which a family must manage in a crisis situation (McCubbin & Patterson, 1983d).

## Consequences of Family Efforts to Cope

The fourth source of pileup includes stressors and strains which emerge from specific behaviors that the family may have used in the adjustment phase, such as increased rigidity or anger, or that the family uses currently in an effort to cope with the crisis situation (McCubbin & Patterson, 1983d). Sometimes the coping strategies, such as taking on a second job to handle a financial crisis or consuming alcohol which turns into a dependency, may produce additional unanticipated burdens on the already overtaxed family unit. These demands, created initially as a result of a positive effort, must be considered in the assessment of family pileup.

*Intrafamily and Social Ambiguity*

Every crisis situation has a certain amount of ambiguity and uncertainty associated with it. Any change and demand for adaptation has an element of uncertainty because the family is altering its structure, rules, roles, and responsibilities. Boss (1977, 1980) has suggested that boundary ambiguity within the family system is a major stressor, since a system needs to be sure of it components, that is, who is inside of the system boundaries, physically and psychologically, and who is outside. Additionally, given the expectation that society will offer guidelines or blueprints for families coping with crises, it is probable that families will face the added strain of social ambiguity in those situations where needed social prescriptions for crisis resolution and family adaptation are unclear or absent (McCubbin & Patterson, 1983c). Society's policies and programs play a major role in helping families to adapt to major crises and transitions. In the absence of such guidelines, family adaptation is oftentimes a trail-and-error process, again with deleterious side effects and additional demands on the family system. If the culture or community can provide the family with adequate solutions, the family's ability to manage the accumulation of demands will be enhanced; if the community is lacking or insufficient in its guidelines and supports, the family will face additional struggles in the adaptation process.

*Family Strengths, Resources, and Capabilities (BB Factor)*

In the Typology Model, a capability is defined as a potential the family has available to it for meeting demands. We emphasize two major sets of capabilities: resources and strengths, which are what the family has, and coping behaviors and strategies, which are what the family does as individual members in the family unit and what the family does collectively as a family unit. Just as there are three sources of demands identified in this phase, there are the same three potential sources of resources: individual family members, the family unit, and the community. An adaptive resource is a characteristic, trait, or competency of one of these systems. Resources may be tangible, such as money, or intangible, such as self-esteem. It becomes readily apparent that a listing of potential resources is nearly infinite. However, we would like to emphasize those that have emerged in the stress literature as most salient for meeting demands and that may be of particular relevance for family health and stress research and interventions.

*Personal resources.* Some of the important personal resources that may be used by the family in adaptation include (a) innate intelligence, which can enhance awareness and comprehension of demands and facilitate the family's mastery of these; (b) knowledge and skills acquired from education, training, and experience so one can gain employment and perform the tasks necessary for daily living; (c) personality traits (e.g., a sense of humor, extroversion), which may facilitate efficacious coping behaviors; (d) physical and emotional health, so that intact faculties and personal energy may be available for meeting family demands; (e) a sense of mastery, which is the belief that one has some control over the circumstances of one's life; and (f) self-esteem, that is , a positive judgment about one's self-worth. These latter two personal resources have been emphasized by many stress researchers as important factors in the stress process because their presence is one of the most critical for active, effective efforts at managing demands. Yet, they are the resources most readily threatened when the pileup of demands gets too large, particularly chronic strains which imply a failure at mastery. In fact, one of the important pathways which may link stressors and strains to negative outcomes, such as psychological depression, is through the diminishment of self-esteem (Pearlin, Menaghan, Lieberman, & Mullan, 1981). Time is an important resource which should not be overlooked. It is unique among family resources because all individuals and families have an equal amount of it. However, its allocation and use are important in the management of demands.

*Family system resources.* The identification of family resources in both family adjustment and adaptation is one of the most intensely studied domains of family research. As already described in the adjustment phase, scientists and lay persons alike are interested in knowing what the traits of "healthy, normal, invulnerable, resilient, well-functioning families" are. Many of the prominent family theoretical models are focused on variables that we would include as part of "family resources." Two of the most prominent family resources identified by several investigators (see review by Olson, Sprenkle, & Russell, 1979) are cohesion (i.e., the bonds of unity running through family life) and adaptability (i.e., the family's capacity to meet obstacles and shift course). Other aspects of cohesion that have been emphasized include trust, appreciation, support, integration, and respect for individuality (Stinnet & Sauer, 1977).

Family organization is another resource that has received attention (Hill, 1958; Moos, 1974) and includes agreement, clarity, and consistency (not to preclude fluidity) in the family role and rule structure. Shared parental leadership and clear family and generational boundaries are additional resources related to organization (Lewis & Looney, 1984). Communication skill is frequently identified as a critical family system resource. Different aspects of communication ability have received emphasis such as clear and direct messages (Satir, 1972), both instrumental and affective communication capability (Epstein, Bishop, & Baldwin, 1982), and verbal-nonverbal consistency (Fleck, 1980). Quality communication is of particular importance to stress management in families because it enables the group to coordinate their efforts to manage demands and because it helps to reduce ambiguity, which is part of what makes change so stressful.

Family hardiness is a stress resistance and adaptation resource in families. It is viewed as a buffer or mediating factor in mitigating the effects of stressors and demands, and as a facilitator of family adjustment and adaptation over time. Family hardiness specifically refers to the internal strengths and durability of the family unit and is characterized by a sense of control over the outcomes of life events and hardships, a view of change as beneficial and growth producing, and an active rather than passive orientation in adjusting to and managing stressful situations.

Family time together and the routines families adopt and practice are critically important and relatively reliable indices of family integration and stability which include effective ways of meeting common problems and the ability to handle major crises.

Family problem solving, which involves coping, is the hub of the process of family adaptation. It refers to the family's ability to identify, garner, and utilize personal, family, and community resources in a constructive way to manage tensions and strain, promote family well-being, and resolve conflicts, tensions, and problems.

*Community Resources and Supports (BBB Factor)*

Community-based resources are all of those characteristics, competencies, and means of persons, groups, and institutions outside the family that the family may call upon, access, and use to meet their demands. This includes a whole range of services, such as medical and health care services. The services of other institutions in the family's meso environment, such as schools, churches, and employers, are also resources to the family. At the macro level, government policies that enhance and support families can be viewed as community resources.

Of all the community resources referenced in the study of family adaptation, the one that has received the most attention in the stress literature is social support. It is most often viewed as one of the primary buffers or mediators between stress and health breakdown (see reviews by Cassel, 1976; Cassel & Tyroler, 1961; Cobb, 1976; Pilisuk & Parks, 1983). What is social support? There have been many conceptualizations of social support (see Caplan, 1974; Cassel, 1976; Granovetter, 1973; House, 1981; Pinneau, 1975), but we believe Cobb's (1976) definition to be most useful for consideration in the context of the Typology Model. Cobb (1976) defines social support as information exchanged at the interpersonal level which provides: (a) emotional support, leading the individual to believe that he or she is cared for and loved; (b) esteem support, leading the individual to believe he or she is esteemed and valued; and (c) network support, leading the individual to believe he or she belongs to a network of communication involving mutual obligation and mutual understanding. We have expanded on Cobb's three forms of support to include: (a) appraisal support, which is information in the form of feedback allowing the individual to assess how well he or she is doing with life's tasks; and (b) altruistic support, which is information received in the form of goodwill from others for having given something of oneself.

It is important to distinguish social support from social network, the latter being all the people one has contact with and from whom one potentially gets support but may, in fact, be more a source of demand than a source of support. In any case, social support implies more than superficial contact with people; rather, it involves a qualitative exchange of communication in an atmosphere of trust. Support may be available from intimate ties (e.g., a spouse) or weak ties (e.g., a neighbor). In fact, these may be differentially helpful depending upon the type of stressors and strains with which the family is struggling (Granovetter, 1973). Members of the family can get support from each other (which we would consider a family resource). In addition, the family unit and its members can get support from relatives, friends, neighbors, work associates, social or church groups, and self-help groups, as well as from more formal networks such as physicians and health care providers. There is some disagreement in the literature as to whether the latter should be considered social support since there is usually not mutuality or reciprocity implied (Gottlieb, 1983) and, in fact, exclusive reliance on formal networks could undermine development of mutually supportive networks. However, it is our view that even formal networks can be instrumental in providing esteem and appraisal support, especially if they are mindful not to undermine the person's own sense of control over one's life.

*Family Typologies and Family Strengths (T Factor)*

David Olson and his colleagues (Lavee, 1985; Olson, 1986; Olson, Lavee, & McCubbin, in press) have made a concerted effort to introduce and document the importance of family typologies, developed on the basis of family strengths, in explaining as well as predicting both family adjustment and family adaptation. By taking two family strength dimensions—family cohesion and family adaptability—these family researchers have tested an alternative version of the Circumplex Model consisting of four family types: flexibly connected, flexibly separated, rigidly connected, and rigidly separated. This four-cell typology proved to be helpful in identifying which families are better able than others to adapt to normative transitions (see Lavee, 1985; Lavee, McCubbin, & Olson, 1987; Olson, Lavee, & McCubbin, in press).

We can expect that this line of scientific inquiry, based upon family strength typologies, to advance our understanding of which family types with what other additional personal, family, and community strengths are better able to respond to different types of normative and nonnormative demands. The investigation reported on in this chapter attempts to expand upon this promising line of research and intervention in family stress by examining three family types which also build upon family strengths: Regenerative families, Resilient families, and Rhythmic families.

*Family Appraisals*

In the adjustment phase, the C factor was the family's definition of the stressor. In defining the Typology Model of Family Adjustment and Adaptation, we have expanded on this factor to include appraisals at three levels. At the first level, we refer to the family's *appraisal of the specific stressor event, strain, or transition* (the C factor). At the second level, we refer to *situational appraisals*, which include the family's subjective definitions of their demands, and their capabilities, and of these two factors relative to each other. At the third level, we emphasize *global appraisals*, which make up the family schema for how it views the relationship of family members to each other and the relationship of the family unit to the larger community.

*Situational Appraisals (CC Factor)*

When demands are experienced, they are consciously or unconsciously interpreted from the context of prior experience. The interpretation includes many components of the demand, such as valence, degree of controllability, and amount of change implied. In some instances, demands only exist by virtue of the perception, as in the case of role strain because one cannot meet the high expectations set for oneself, or when a patient believes he or she has a serious illness but there is no clinical evidence for it. Resources and coping behaviors are also evaluated through perceptions. When these are viewed as inadequate or insufficient relative to perceived demands, there is an imbalance, which is what produces tension and stress. In some instances, it is the lack of a clear definition about how to cope or conflicting definitions which create ambiguity. Although there is a certain amount of uncertainty and ambiguity inherent in all change and the management of stress involves reducing this, some strains exist primarily because this ambiguity is so difficult to resolve.

*Global Appraisals and Family Schemas (CCC Factor)*

At a supra or global (third) level, we believe that families hold a set of beliefs or assumptions, which we call a family schema, about themselves in relationship to each other and about their family in relationship to the community and systems beyond their boundaries. Our conceptualization of this global appraisal has been shaped by the work of Reiss and his colleagues (Reiss, 1981; Reiss & Oliveri, 1980), who have emphasized the importance of family paradigms in the stress process, and by other theorists concerned primarily about individual response to stress, who have emphasized the central importance of global orientations, as in the concept of coherence (Antonovsky, 1979) and hardiness (Kobasa, Maddi, & Kahn, 1982). The hierarchical ordering of these levels of appraisal was conceptualized, discussed, and partially tested through a LISREL analysis (Lavee & McCubbin, 1985).

A family schema is conceptualized as consisting of five dimensions: shared purpose, collectivity, frameability, relativism, and shared control (Patterson, in press). Families who reveal a strong family schema emphasize their investment in themselves, their values and goals, their investment in the family's collective "we" rather than "I," their sense of shared control and trust in others, as well as their optimistic view of life situations complemented by a relativistic view of life circumstances and willingness to accept less-than-perfect solutions to all their demands. The family schema, like the other constructs of the Typology Model, is not static and unchangeable over time. Rather, we believe it is shaped, molded, and remolded over time in response to stressful experiences, particularly crisis situations when family homeostasis is upset. However, we believe that it is more stable than situational appraisals and that it transcends and influences the latter.

Although appraisals are held individually, they can be shared by a group, like the family or the community, and, in fact, appraisals are formed and shaped by this social context. This process by which we develop meaning for experience and share, or do not share, these meanings with significant others is an important part of the stress process. Although beyond the scope of this chapter, we have attempted, in an earlier publication, to describe a family's internal efforts to develop shared perceptions and meanings as they make changes in their family system in response to crisis (McCubbin & Patterson, 1983b). In many instances, intrafamily strains are a result of discrepant perceptions between members. For example, parental perceptions of appropriate role behavior and rules for an adolescent are often different from those of the adolescent, and this creates conflict.

*Adaptive Coping (PSC Factor)*

The process of acquiring and allocating resources for meeting demands is a critical aspect of family adjustment and adaptation. Researchers who use management framework view resources, both human and material, as limited. Therefore, resources must be allocated among multiple goals to meet the needs of the family and its members (Deacon & Firebaugh, 1975; Paolucci, Hall, & Axinn, 1977). The family is seen as a resource exchange network. In the Typology Model, we view coping as the action for this exchange.

In the context of the Typology Model, we define a coping behavior as a specific effort (covert or overt) by which an individual (or a group of individuals such as the family) attempts to reduce or manage a demand on the family system. Specific coping behaviors can be grouped together into patterns, such as coping directed at "maintaining family integration and cooperation," which is one of the coping patterns that has emerged as important for families who have a chronically ill child (M. A. McCubbin, 1984). Coping patterns are more generalized ways of responding that transcend different kinds of situations. When coping is viewed in the context of multiple family demands (i.e., the pileup), it seems more useful and relevant to view coping as a generalized response rather than situation specific.

Although coping most often has been conceptualized at the individual level, we can also consider family and even community level coping if we think of collective group action to eliminate or manage demands. Family coping could be viewed as coordinated problem-solving behavior of the whole system (Klein & Hill, 1979), but it could also involve complementary efforts of individual family members which fit together as a synthetic whole. In our view, the function of coping is to maintain or restore the balance between demands and resources. We have identified four ways in which this can be accomplished by the family system:

1. Coping can involve direct action to reduce the number and/or intensity of demands. For example, a mother could refuse a job promotion that would require the family to move to another city. Or a family could decide to place their terminally ill grandmother in a nursing home rather than keep her at home with them any longer. At the community level, families could band together to eliminate a hazardous waste disposal site from their neighborhood.
2. Coping can involve direct action to acquire additional resources not already available to the family. Finding medical services for a member diagnosed with chronic illness or developing self-reliance skills when a spouse dies suddenly would be examples of coping to increase resources.
3. Managing the tension associated with ongoing strains is another function of coping which is necessary because of the inevitable residue of strain families have as part of their demands. Exercising is one of the commonly recognized coping mechanisms for managing tension. Taking time out for playing together as a family, using humor appropriately, and the open expression of emotion and affect in a responsible, nonblaming manner are other ways to release tension.
4. Coping can also involve appraisal to change the meaning of a situation to make it more manageable. This strategy for coping interacts very directly with what we have labeled "perceptions" in the Typology Model. It may be directed at changing the individual's or family's view of demands, such as reducing role strain by lowering performance expectations, or it may be directed at resources (e.g., seeing oneself or the family as capable and competent). Maintaining an optimistic outlook and acceptance that this is the best the family can do under the circumstances are other appraisal coping strategies.

## The Family Adaptation Process

Family adaptation is a process by which families experiencing excessive demands and depleted resources begin to understand that their ability to restore some functional stability and/or improve family satisfaction depends upon restructuring or making changes which include modifications in roles, rules, and/or patterns of interaction. After making some initial changes, families need to consolidate to bring about family unity and support for these initial efforts and subsequent changes which may be needed. This restructuring and consolidation is a process which evolves over time (McCubbin & Patterson, 1983d).

*System Strategies of Adaptive Coping*

Obtaining and using social support is a key component in lessening the strains associated with the family process of restructuring. Both resources and social support aid in the restructuring phase to buffer the impact of the pileup or accumulation of demands by providing sources of help to resolve problems, altering the appraisal of the situation (e.g., a more positive definition of the events or a sense of mastery) and by expanding the solutions available, such as the use of extended family members and professional assistance in the care for a disabled family member.

Adaptive coping strategies of synergizing, interfacing, and compromising also assist the family's efforts towards restructuring and consolidation (McCubbin & Patterson, 1983d). Synergizing indicates the family's ability to work together as a unit to achieve a lifestyle and orientation which cannot be attained by the efforts of only one member but which is achieved by the family's interdependence and mutuality. As family members work to synchronize their perceptions, needs, and resources, they become attuned to one another and become a more harmonious unit.

Families are also not confined to strictly internal changes. Since the family has daily transactions with other social institutions (workplace, school, etc.) and the community as a whole, the interfacing with the community to achieve a "better fit" is also part of the adaptive coping process. The family's internal restructuring may also necessitate a new set of rules and transactions for maintaining the complementary relationship between the family and the community.

It is almost impossible for families to attain a "perfect" intrafamily and family-to-community fit. Since all needs cannot be met, a compromise must be reached whereby there is a realistic appraisal of the family's situation and a willingness to accept a less than perfect resolution. Coping efforts directed at family system maintenance (i.e., integration, morale, and member self-esteem) are also critical to the process of successful adaptation. If these areas are ignored or not attended to, the family unit may undergo breakdown in spite of its efforts at restructuring and consolidation.

Finally, research with and observations of families who are managing an accumulation of stressors indicate that family system strategies of adaptive coping are not created instantly and not specifically directed at a single stressor. Coping strategies enhance both individual family member growth and development and the family's functioning as a coherent and organized unit. When the family is viewed as a system, coping strategies are utilized to manage several dimensions of family life simultaneously. These include creating and maintaining satisfactory internal conditions for communication, problem-solving and reorganization; promoting member autonomy and self-esteem; maintaining family coherence and unity; developing and maintaining social support; and ongoing efforts to control the impact of demands on the family unit and the amount of need change (McCubbin & Patterson, 1983d).

## FOCUSING ON FAMILY TYPES: TARGETS FOR INTERVENTION

The Typology Model of Family Adjustment and Adaptation brings family typologies to center stage as one of the major influential variables involved in the family processes of resistance, adjustment, accommodation, and adaptation. Family typologies are defined as a set of basic attributes about the family system which characterize and explain how a family system typically appraises, operates, and/or behaves. The predictable and discernible patterns of family life, which are reinforced by rules and norms and guided by family values and goals, play an important role in explaining family behavior in the face of stressful life events and transitions. Once identified and measured, these characteristics of family life may be used to classify each family unit. Once families are classified or placed within a typology, it is possible to use the typology to make predictions about a family unit, its capabilities, responses, and outcomes in the face of stressful life events and/or crisis situations. Thus family typologies play a vital role in family stress research.

### Typology of Regenerative Families

The Regenerative model of family system types is achieved by assigning two levels (low and high) to the Family Coherence dimension and to the Family Hardiness dimension and placing them in property-space (orthogonal) position (see Figure 3). The Family Coherence dimension is defined

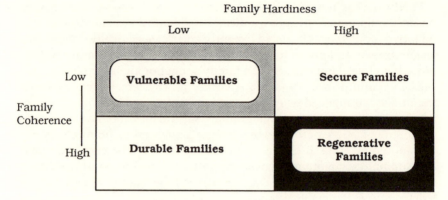

Figure 3. Regenerative Family Type.

as a fundamental coping strategy families employ in the management of family problems. Family Coherence is operationalized as the family's emphasis on acceptance, loyalty, pride, faith, trust, respect, caring, and shared values in the management of tension and strain.

The Family Hardiness dimension is defined as the family's internal strengths and durability characterized by an internal sense of control over life events and life's hardships, a sense of meaningfulness in life, involvement in activities, and a commitment to learn and to explore new and challenging experiences.

With two levels to each dimension, the Regenerative model enables one to identify and describe four types of family systems:

*1. Families with low Family Coherence and low Family Hardiness are named Vulnerable families.* These families indicate that they cope with family problems by getting upset, indicating less respect for one another, blaming other people or other family members, as well as showing less caring and understanding, less pride, less loyalty, and less acceptance of family hardships. Additionally, Vulnerable families indicate a lower sense of purpose, lower meaningfulness in life, and less sense of being appreciated. These families also feel less in control of what happens to them as a family; accidents, bad luck, and self-blame for mistakes characterize their accounting of the hardships they face. In general, Vulnerable families are more complacent, less likely to try new and exciting things, tending to do the same things over and over, and less likely to encourage each other to be active and to learn new things.

*2. Families with low Family Coherence and high Family Hardiness are named Secure families.* These families, like Vulnerable families, indicate that they cope with family problems by getting upset, indicating less respect for one another, blaming other people or other family members, as well as showing less caring and understanding, less pride, less loyalty, and less acceptance of family hardships. On the other hand, these families are secure in that their major strength is in their basic hardiness. These families indicate that they have a sense of purpose, of being able to plan ahead, of being valued for their efforts, and feeling that life is meaningful. They feel in control and have a sense that they can influence both good and bad things that happen; they are not just victims of life events. Additionally, Secure families are active; they try new things and encourage others to be active. In general, Secure families are active, in control, but when faced with difficulties are also less supportive of each other, less caring and loyal, and less tolerant of hardships.

*3. Families who are low on Family Hardiness but high on Family Coherence are named Durable families.* These families, like their vulnerable counterparts, indicate a lower sense of purpose, lower sense of meaningfulness in life, and lack of being appreciated. They also feel less in control of what happens to them as a family. They appear to be less active and are not very encouraging of family members' efforts to learn new things. In contrast, these families also have a positive regard for their ability to cope. They emphasize being less reactive and more caring as part of their coping repertoire. They underscore the importance of coherence through developing trust, respect, and maintaining calm and emotional stability. Additionally, these families cope through having faith, accepting the stressful life events, accepting difficulties, and working together as a family to solve problems. In general, Durable families may have less basic internal strengths, but they appear to compensate for this deficiency by having a strong coping repertoire characterized by caring, respect, trust, reduced tension, and calmness.

*4. Families who are high on Family Hardiness and high on Family Coherence are named Regenerative families.* These families indicate that they cope with family problems by cultivating trust, respect, and maintaining an emotional calm and stability. These families cope through having faith, accepting stressful life events, accepting difficulties, and working together to solve problems. Additionally, they are secure in their sense of purpose, of being able to plan ahead, of being valued for their efforts, and feeling that life is meaningful. These families feel in control and have a sense that they can influence both good and bad things that happen; they are not victims of circumstances. Additionally, Regenerative families are active; they try new things and encourage others to be active in addressing their problems and concerns. In general, Regenerative families are active, in control, and when faced with difficulties, are also more caring, more loyal, and more tolerant of hardships than Vulnerable, Secure, and Durable families.

*Typology of Resilient Families*

The Resilient model of family system types is achieved by assigning two levels (low and high) to the Family Bonding dimension and to the Family Flexibility dimension and placing them in property-space (orthogonal) position (see Figure 4). The Family Bonding dimension is defined as the degree to which the family is emotionally bonded together into a meaningful and integral family unit. The families scoring high on this dimension may be described as being open to discussion of problems, feeling close to family members, desirous of staying connected to other family members, and involved in doing things together as a family unit. The Family Flexibility dimension is defined as the degree to which the family unit is able to change its rules, boundaries, and roles to accommodate to changing pressures from within and outside of the family unit. The flexible family is described as having an open communication pattern, a willingness to compromise, experience in shifting responsibilities among family members, and active participation by family members in decision making. This typology assumes linearity of family bonding and family flexibility.

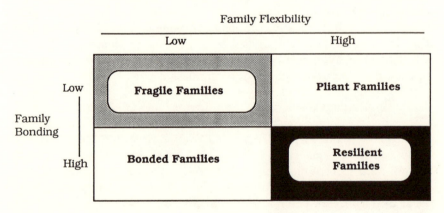

Figure 4.  Resilient Family Type.

This family typology is based upon the Circumplex Quadrant — Typology II (Lavee, 1985; Olson, Lavee, & McCubbin, in press; Lavee, McCubbin, & Olson, 1987) advanced by family researchers associated with The Family Wellness Project at the University of Minnesota. The labels used to describe the Resilient typology were modified, however, to emphasize the difference from the Circumplex typology. Specifically, the Circumplex Quadrant typology is assumed to encompass extreme family types (chaotic, disengaged, rigid, enmeshed) in its four quadrants. Given our emphasis upon treating the bonding and flexibility dimensions as linear variables, the Resilient family typology is based on the assumption that the extreme family types are not captured in this framework.

With two levels to each dimension, the Resilient model enables one to identify and describe four types of family systems:

*1. Families with low Family Bonding and low Family Flexibility are named Fragile families.* These families indicate that they are hesitant to depend upon the family for support and understanding, prefer to confide in persons outside the family, avoid other family members, have difficulty in doing things with the family, and feel that the family emphasizes members going their own way. Additionally, these families perceive themselves as being closed in their communication, resistant to compromise, set in their ways and inexperienced in shifting responsibilities among family members, and not involving all family members in making major decisions.

*2. Families with low Family Flexibility but high Family Bonding are named Bonded families.* These families indicate that they have a major strength in their sense of internal unity. These families are dependent upon each other for understanding and support, feel close to each other, are pleased to engage other family members, and have no difficulty deciding what to do as a family unit. However, Bonded families, like Fragile families, are low on flexibility in that they are resistant to compromising, are set in their ways and inexperienced in shifting responsibilities among family members, and do not involve all family members in making major decisions. These families are dependent upon their sense of unity and togetherness, as well as their resistance to change as their mode of managing tensions and strains.

*3. Families with low Family Bonding but high Family Flexibility are named Pliant families.* These families indicate that they do have a major strength in their ability to change. These families view themselves as being able to say what they want, as having input into major decisions, as being able to shape rules and practices in the family, and as being able to compromise; they are also experienced in shifting responsibilities in the family unit and are willing to experiment with new ways of dealing with problems and issues. However, these Pliant families, like their fragile counterparts, are limited in their sense of family bonding. They indicate that they are hesitant to depend upon the family for support and understanding, prefer persons outside the family to confide in, avoid other family members, have difficulty in doing things with the family, and feel that the family emphasizes members going their own way.

*4. Families with high Family Bonding and high Family Flexibility are named Resilient families.* They indicate that they have a major strength in their ability to change. These families view themselves as being able to say what they want, as having input into major decisions, as being able to shape rules and practices in the family, as well as being able to compromise; they are experienced in shifting responsibilities in the family unit and willing to experiment with new ways of dealing with problems and issues. These families also indicate that they have a major strength in their sense of internal unity. They are dependent upon each other for understanding and support, feel close to each other, were pleased to engage other family members, and have no difficulty deciding what to do as a family unit.

*Typology of Rhythmic Families*

The Rhythmic model of family system types is achieved by assigning two levels (low and high) to the Family Time and Routines dimension and placing them in a property-space (orthogonal) position (see Figure 5). The Family Time and Routines dimension is defined as those family behaviors and practices that families choose to adopt and maintain in an effort to orient and routinize family life into a predictable pattern of living. The Family Time and Routines dimension emphasizes the importance of routines to promote parent-child togetherness, husband-wife togetherness, family unit togetherness, and family-relative togetherness. The Valuing of Family Time and Routines dimension is defined as the meaning and importance families attach to the value of such practices designed to promote family unity and predictability.

With two levels to each dimension, the Rhythmic model enables one to identify and describe four types of family systems:

*1. Families with low Family Time and Routines and low Valuing of Family Time and Routines are named Unpatterned families.* These fami-

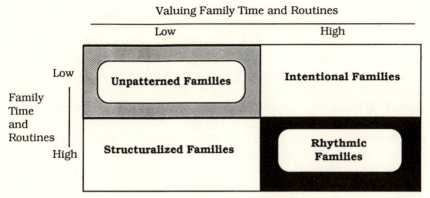

Figure 5. Rhythmic Family Type.

lies carry on their lives with little emphasis on family time or routines and place equally limited value on the importance of these routines or manifestations of investments in family life.

2. *Families with low Family Time and Routines but a high Valuing of Family Time and Routines are named Intentional families.* These families carry on their lives with little emphasis on the actual practice of family time and routines, but with a greater emphasis upon the value of family time and routines. Seemingly, Intentional families indicate a desiring and valuing of Family Time and Routines, but a reluctance or inability to practice these expressions of Family Time and Routines with any degree of regularity.

3. *Families with a strong emphasis on practicing Family Time and Routines but a low Valuing of these practices are called Structuralized families.* These families appear to carry on their lives with a heavy investment in regularized activities designed to promote family time together but with a reluctance to embrace these behaviors and practices as being desirable or even valued.

4. *Families with a strong emphasis upon Family Time and Routines as well as a strong investment in Valuing Family Time and Routines are named Rhythmic families.* These families foster development of predictable activities and routines within the family unit involving relatives and with an added emphasis upon valuing these patterns in an effort to foster a shared Rhythmic sense of purpose and meaning of family togetherness, regularity, and predictability.

The Regenerative, Resilient, and Rhythmic typologies represent an attempt to classify families into unique groups which we assume characterize how families function and suggest processes operative within the family system. The Regenerative family typology, based upon the family dimensions of Coherence and Family Hardiness, characterizes families along a continuum of having different degrees of resiliency, that is, of being capable of maintaining a sense of family integrity which serves them well in enduring hardships, stressors, and strains. The Resilient family typology, based upon the family dimensions of Bonding and Flexibility, characterizes families along a continuum of having different degrees of resiliency, that is, of being capable of unity and changeability which serves them well in recovering from the impact of stressors and strains. The Rhythmic family typology, based upon the family dimensions of Family Time and Routines and the Valuing of Family Time and Routines, classifies families along a continuum of having different degrees of family routinization, that is, of being capable of establishing and valuing a family pattern of predictability and stability. The current literature on family strengths (Curran, 1983; McCubbin, Patterson, & Lavee, 1983; Olson, McCubbin, Barnes, Larsen, Muxen, & Wilson, 1983; Stinnet & DeFrain, 1985) points to the importance of these family attributes: family integrity, unity and changeability, and predictability.

## FAMILY ASSESSMENT AND INTERVENTION AND THE TYPOLOGY MODEL

Research on families under stress will continue to move forward with the concerted efforts on the part of social, behavioral, and health scientists to advance theory building, measurement, and intervention. While we have witnessed a proliferation of theory-building efforts, some of which are creative and innovative, and others limited but interesting recapitulations of extant conceptualizations, we have only begun to advance the development of family-system-level measures which are needed for hypothesis testing, for assessment, and to guide interventions.

Although family scholars have examined families in both the adjustment (e.g., routine transitions) and the adaptation phases (e.g., crisis situations) of the Typology Model of Family Adjustment and Adaptation, family measures of stressors, pileup of demands, typologies, coping, family resources, problem solving, appraisal, coherence, community and social support, and adaptation, with a few exceptions to be noted, have not emerged with a separate emphasis on the different phases. This state of the art of family assessment is not altogether surprising in light of the obvious fact that family systems call upon and utilize their own internal strengths in both routine and crisis situations. Families may differ in the degree to which a family capability, coping strategy, or community support is used—in response to a normative transition and a major family crisis. Families also appear to differ on the degree to which they utilize community supports in response to the demands on the family system. Therefore, our brief presentation of family measures focuses upon those components of the Typology Model of Adjustment and Adaptation for which measures were developed, relatively independent of the phases of family adjustment and adaptation. The major family assessment measures related to the Model and its emphasis on family typologies are presented in Table 1.

TABLE 1
Family Assessment and Screening Strategy (FASS)
Typology Model of Family Adjustment and Adaptation

| Typology Model of Family Adjustment and Adaptation Family Dimensions | Primary Source | Number of Items | Concepts |
|---|---|---|---|
| Family Stressors (A/AA) | FILE | 10 | Pileup |
| Family Strains (A/AA) | FILE | 10 | Pileup |
| Relative and Friend Support (PSC) | FCOPES | 8 | Family Support |
| Social Support (BB/BBB) | SSI | 17 | Community Support |
| Family Coherence (C/CC/CCC) | FCOPES | 4 | Regenerative Type |
| Family Hardiness (C/CC/CCC) | FHI | 20 | Regenerative Type |
| Family Time and Routines (B/BB) | FTRI | 32 | Rhythmic Type |
| Valuing Family Time and Routines | FTRI | 32 | Rhythmic Type |
| Family Bonding (B/BB) | FACES IIA | 10 | Resilient Type |
| Family Flexibility (B/BB) | FACES IIA | 10 | Resilient Type |
| Self-Reliance Index (B/BB) | SRI | 9 | Co-Oriented Self-Reliant Family Type |
| Member Well-being (X/XX) | FWBI | 8 | Adjustment |
| Family Stress and Family Distress (X/XX) | FAC | 10 | Adaptation |

*The Family Stressor Index* (McCubbin, Patterson, & Wilson, 1982)
consists of 10 items selected to record those life events and changes
that can render a family vulnerable to the impact of a subsequent
stressor or change. The index includes the addition of a member,
changes in the work situation, illnesses, and deaths.

*The Family Strains Index* (McCubbin, Patterson, & Wilson, 1982)
consists of 10 items selected to record those interpersonal strains
that can render a family vulnerable to the impact of a subsequent
stressor or change. The index includes conflict between husband
and wife, conflict among and with children, financial hardships,
and the strains of caring for an ill family member.

*The Relative and Friend Support Index* (McCubbin, Larsen, & Olson,
1982) consists of 8 items selected to record the degree to which
families call upon relative and friend support as one of the strategies the family unit uses to manage its stressors and strains. *The
Social Support Index* (McCubbin, Patterson, & Glynn, 1982)
consists of 17 items selected to record the degree to which families
are integrated into the community, view the community as a
source of support, and feel that the community can provide
emotional, esteem, and network support.

*The Family Coherence Index* (McCubbin, Larsen, & Olson, 1982)
consists of 4 items selected to record the degree to which families
call upon their appraisal skills to manage stressful life events,
strains, and changes. This index includes the acceptance of stressful events, accepting difficulties, a positive appraisal of a problem,
and having faith in God.

*The Family Hardiness Index* (McCubbin, McCubbin, & Thompson,
1986a) was developed to measure the characteristic of hardiness
as a stress resistance and adaptation resource in families which
would function as a buffer or mediating factor in mitigating the
effects of stressors and demands, and a facilitation of family
adjustment and adaptation over time. The Family Hardiness Index
is a 20-item instrument consisting of four subscales (Co-oriented
Commitment, Confidence, Challenge, and Control) which calls
for the respondent to assess the degree to which (False, Mostly
False, Mostly True, True) each statement describes their current
family situation (see McCubbin & McCubbin, 1987).

*The Family Time and Routines Inventory (FTRI)* (McCubbin,
Thompson & McCubbin, 1987), a 32-item index, was designed to
measure family unity and related practices to promote family
integration and stability as well as meet common problems. The

index is designed to assess the type of activities and routines families use and maintain. Since the Valuing of Family Time and Routines is another component of the model, the inventory also records to what degree the family values its time together and routines.

*The Family Bonding Index (FBI)* (adapted from FACES II by Olson, Portner, & Bell, 1982), a 10-item scale, was designed to assess the degree to which the family is emotionally bonded together into a meaningful and integrated family unit.

*The Family Flexibility Index (FFI)* (adapted from FACES II by Olson, Portner, & Bell, 1982), a 10-item scale, was designed to assess the degree to which the family unit is able to change its rules, boundaries, and roles to accommodate to changing pressures from within and outside of the family unit.

*The Self-Reliance Index (SRI)* (McCubbin & Patterson, 1982b), a 9-item inventory, was developed as a reliable and valid index of the degree to which a family member felt capable of managing children, finances, decisions, and hardships in the absence of a military member.

*The Family Member Well-being Index (FWBI)*, an 8-item inventory, was developed as a reliable and valid index of the degree to which the family member is adjusted in terms of concern about health, tension, energy, cheerfulness, fear, anger, sadness, and general concern. This is a measure of the well-being of a family member in general and a measure of the Adjustment (X) or Adaptation (XX) factors.

*The Family Adaptation Checklist (FAC)* (McCubbin & Patterson, 1982d), a 10-item inventory, was developed as a reliable and valid index of the degree to which the family may be distressed. The checklist focuses upon hospitalization, the need for professional help, injury, separation or divorce, financial hardships, physical abuse, substance abuse, considered or attempted suicide, and conflict with the law. This is a measure of family adaptation as reflected in major indices of family deterioration or symptomatology indicating family members with difficulties.

The importance of indirect indices of family system adaptation is based upon two fundamental assumptions. First, the family system under stress, created in part by the pressures of family adaptation, will have a profound (negative and positive) impact upon the total family unit, its subsystems, and individual members. Second, *the negative consequences of family adaptation will present themselves through indices of deterioration or breakdown in the total family unit, the quality of the relationship within and among subsystems in the family unit, and/or in the psychological and physical health status of family members.*

## THE GESTALT OF STRESS THEORY'S CONTRIBUTIONS TO CRISIS AND HEALTH CARE INTERVENTION, THERAPY, AND FAMILY LIFE EDUCATION

The application of theory to both assessment and intervention is based on the belief that planful and focused analyses of family behavior will serve as a better guide to practitioners involved in influencing and shaping of family functioning. Under the watchful eye of the family theorist, family practitioners of all disciplines—social work, psychology, family science, the health sciences, and particularly nursing—have benefited from the conceptualization and systematic measurement of the complex properties of family life. We have come to believe that family crisis intervention and therapy will be enhanced by knowledge about how families behave under a wide range of stressful situations and in response to crises across stages of the family life cycle.

In the context of family stress theory, we are confronted by the realization that families negotiate change and stressful life events with an innate and not so surprising "knee jerk" reaction to fight to remain stable and resistant to systemic changes in the family's instituted patterns of behavior. Family adjustment, characterized by minor changes in the family system, is the predicted course of action. But we realize, too, that the family system must also change systemically, paradoxical as that may seem; by design, families are called upon to expand and contract, to incorporate and to launch, and to achieve stability while disrupting what is stable. In these struggles, families adapt by making major changes internal to the family and in the family's relationship to the outside world.

Family stress theory attempts to understand and explain this dynamic process by isolating those individual, family unit, and community properties that interact and shape the course of family behavior over time and in response to a wide range of circumstances. The Typology Model of Family Adjustment and Adaptation encourages the family practitioner, crisis counselor, health educator, and family life educator responsible for families under stress to recognize and appreciate the natural healing qualities of family life which, if understood, could become targets for intervention. Such interventions, however, would be different from the penetrating probes and strategic manipulations of the family therapist, at least in the beginning. In crisis situations, the emphasis would be upon family problem-solving strategies to release the blocks to the family's own natural healing abilities and upon family enhancement strategies to promote this natural process of family regenerativity.

The practitioner would be the catalyst for system response and change by dwelling upon the current issues affecting family life—the pressures, the pileup of stressors and strains, the normative transitions that disturb and disrupt the family's coping repertoire, and the family's innate abilities to find supports, to cope, and to adapt. The family health practitioner would accentuate what is happening in the family, here and now, and encourage families to initiate strategies that can help the family to better manage the current situation with ease and effectiveness. Sometimes hurdle help to overcome the immediate pressure may be all that is needed. Practical advice and concrete suggestions would be part of the practitioner's and educator's repertoire of intervention strategies, complemented, naturally, by efforts to foster the family's self-discovery of the truth and its own unique patterns of coping with the situation.

Family stress theory, as underscored by the Typology Model of Family Adjustment and Adaptation, emphasizes the importance of established patterns or typologies of family functioning which, if understood, can serve well the therapist, crisis manager, and educator. Helping families to move from being a Fragile family unit (i.e., low on Bonding and Flexibility) to being Resilient (i.e., high on Bonding and Flexibility) or moving the family from Intentional (i.e., high on Valuing Family Time and Routines but low on Family Routines) to being a Rhythmic family unit (i.e., high on Valuing Family Time and Routines and high on Family Routines), as in the case of Jennifer's family introduced at the beginning of the chapter, are legitimate and measurable objectives. Current research (McCubbin, Thompson, Pirner, & McCubbin, 1988) provide us with initial evidence that these family types—Resilient, Rhythmic, and Regenerative—may be at the hub of family functioning; if touched and improved upon, the family unit would then be in a better position to manage its own recovery and adaptation to stressful and crisis situations.

Interventions can be enhanced by systematic assessments. While the clinician may feel more comfortable and skilled with assessments by interview, current studies (see Olson et al., 1983; McCubbin & Thompson, 1987) suggest the emerging value of family-system-level assessments, particularly in the use of self-report measures, as part of therapy, health care intervention, crisis intervention, and family life education (McCubbin & McCubbin, 1988; McCubbin, Thompson, Pirner, & McCubbin, 1988).

A multidimensional strategy for family assessment, which draws from the current work at the Family Stress Coping and Health Project, is suggested in this chapter.

We have quite a way to go before we can fully appreciate and demonstrate the contribution of family stress theory to therapy, crisis intervention, health care intervention, and family life education. We remain convinced, however, that families are durable and resilient interpersonal and social systems. They have enduring qualities of bonding, flexibility, hardiness, coherence, and underlying patterns or types such as resilient or rhythmic, which are legitimate targets for catalytic change. Family stress theory encourages us to examine a host of strategies that can be employed in support of families under stress. Penetrating family therapy and its emphasis on structural change is but one among many alternatives available to the practitioner involved in supporting families under stress. We can be guided by systematic interventions but should not become slaves to empirical data. We can become diagnosticians but not become dependent upon our heuristic classifications. We can become educators, facilitators, and catalytic agents as part of our becoming therapists and change agents. Family stress theory and the Typology Model of Family Adjustment and Adaptation can steer and temper our approach to families and offer us tools to guide our probes and the depth of our interventions. In this regard, stress theory has already made a difference in our work with families.

## REFERENCES

Antonovsky, A. (1979). *Health, stress and coping.* San Francisco, CA: Jossey-Bass.
Boss, P. (1977). A clarification of the concept of psychological father presence in families experiencing ambiguity of boundary. *Journal of Marriage and the Family, 39,* 141–151.
Boss, P. (1980). Normative family stress: Family boundary changes across the life-span. *Family Relations, 29,* 445–450.
Burr, W. R. (1973). *Theory construction and the sociology of the family.* New York: John Wiley & Sons.
Caplan, G. (1974). *Support systems and community mental health.* New York: Behavioral Publications.
Caplan, G. (1976). The family as a support system. In G. Caplan & M. Killilea (Eds.), *Support systems and mutual help.* New York: Grune & Stratton.
Cassel, J. (1976). The contribution of the social environment to host resistance. *American Journal of Epidemiology, 104,* 107–123.
Cassel, J., & Tyroler, H. (1961). Epidemiological studies of culture change: 1. Health status and recency of industrialization. *Archives of Environmental Health, 3,* 25–33.
Cobb, S. (1976). Social support as a moderator of life stress. *Psychosomatic Medicine, 38,* 300–314.
Cobb, S. (1982). Social support and health through the life course. In H. I. McCubbin, A. E. Cauble, & J. M. Patterson (Eds.), *Family stress, coping and social support.* Springfield, Il: Charles C Thomas.

Comeau, J. (1985). *Family resources in the care of the spina bifida child.* Unpublished doctoral dissertation, University of Minnesota, Dissertation Abstracts, University of Michigan.

Curran, D. (1983). *Traits of a healthy family.* Minneapolis: Winston Press.

Deacon, R., & Firebaugh, F. (1975). *Home management context and concepts.* Boston: Houghton Mifflin.

Epstein, N., Bishop, D., & Baldwin, L. (1982). McMaster model of family functioning: A view of the normal family. In F. Walsh (Ed.), *Normal family processes.* New York: Guilford Press.

Epstein, N. B., Levin, S., & Bishop, D. S. (1976). The family as a social unit. *Canadian Family Physician 22,* 1411–1413.

Family Member Well-Being (1982). In H. I. McCubbin & A. Thompson (Eds.), *Family assessment inventories for research and practice.* Madison: University of Wisconsin, 1987.

Fleck, S. (1980). Family functioning and family pathology. *Psychiatric Annals, 10,* 46–57.

Gottlieb, B. (1983). *Social support strategies.* Beverly Hills, CA: Sage.

Granovetter, M. (1973). The strength of weak ties. *American Journal of Sociology, 78,* 1360–1380.

Hill, R. (1949). *Families under stress.* New York: Harper & Row.

Hill, R. (1958) Generic features of families under stress. *Social Casework, 49,* 139–150.

House, J. (1981). *Work stress and social support.* Reading, MA: Addison-Wesley.

Klein, D., & Hill, R. (1979). Determinants of family problem-solving effectiveness. In W. Burr, R. Hill, I. Reiss, & I. Nye (Eds.), *Contemporary theories about the family (Vol. I).* New York: The Free Press.

Kobasa, S., Maddi, S., & Kahn, S., (1982). Hardiness and health: A prospective study. *Journal of Personality and Social Psychology, 42,* 168–177.

Lavee, Y. (1985). *Family types and family adaptation to stress: Integrating the Circumplex model of family systems and the family adjustment and adaptation response model.* Unpublished doctoral dissertation, University of Minnesota-St. Paul.

Lavee, Y., & McCubbin, H. I. (1985). *Adaptation in stress theory: Theoretical and methodological considerations.* Paper presented at the Theory Construction and Research Methodology Workshop, National Council on Family Relations, Dallas (November).

Lavee, Y., McCubbin, H. I., & Olson, D. H. (1987). The effect of stressful life events and transitions on family functioning and well-being. *Journal of Marriage and the Family, 49,* 857–873.

Lavee, Y., McCubbin, H. I., & Patterson, J. M. (1985). The Double ABCX Model of Stress and Adaptation: An empirical test by analysis of structural equations with latent variables. *Journal of Marriage and the Family, 47,* 811–825.

Lewis, J., & Looney, J. (1984). *The long struggle: Well-functioning working-class black families.* New York: Brunner/Mazel.

McCubbin, H. I., Boss P., Wilson, L., & Lester, G. (1980). Developing family invulnerability to stress: Coping patterns and strategies wives employ. In J. Trost (Ed.), *The family and change.* Sweden: International Library Publishing.

McCubbin, H. I., Larsen, A., & Olson, D. H. (1982). F-COPES: Family Crisis Oriented Personal Scales. In H. I. McCubbin & A. Thompson (Eds.), *Family assessment inventories for research and practice.* Madison: University of Wisconsin, 1987.

McCubbin, H. I., & McCubbin, M. A. (1988). Family systems assessment in child oriented research. In P. Karoly (Ed.), *Handbook of child health assessment.* New York: John Wiley.

McCubbin, H. I., McCubbin, M. A., & Thompson, A. (1986a). Family Hardiness Index. In H. I. McCubbin & A Thompson (Eds.), *Family assessment inventories for research and practice.* Madison: University of Wisconsin, 1987.

McCubbin, H. I., McCubbin, M., & Thompson, A. (1986b). Family Time and Routines Scale. In H. I. McCubbin & A. Thompson (Eds.), *Family assessment inventories for research and practice.* Madison: University of Wisconsin, Madison, 1987.

McCubbin, H. I., & Patterson, J. M. (1981a). Family Distress Index. In H. I. McCubbin & A. Thompson (Eds.), *Family assessment inventories for research and practice*. Madison: University of Wisconsin, 1987.

McCubbin, H. I., & Patterson, J. M. (1981b). Family Stressors. In H. I. McCubbin & A. Thompson (Eds.), *Family assessment inventories for research and practice*. Madison: University of Wisconsin, 1987.

McCubbin, H. I., & Patterson, J. M. (1981c). *Systematic assessment of family stress, resources and coping: Tools for research, education and clinical intervention*. St. Paul, Minnesota, Department of Family Social Science.

McCubbin, H. I., & Patterson, J. M., (1982a). Family Strains. In H. I. McCubbin & A. Thompson (Eds.), *Family assessment inventories for research and practice*. Madison: University of Wisconsin, 1987.

McCubbin, H. I., & Patterson, J. M. (1982b). Self-Reliance Index. In H. I. McCubbin & A. Thompson (Eds.), *Family assessment inventories for research and practice*. Madison: University of Wisconsin, 1987.

McCubbin, H. I., & Patterson, J. M. (1982c). Family adaptation to crisis. In H. I. McCubbin, A. Cauble, J. M. Patterson (Eds.), *Family stress, coping and social support*. Springfield, IL: Charles C Thomas.

McCubbin, H. I., & Patterson, J. M. (1982d). Family adaptation checklist. In H. I. McCubbin & A. Thompson (Eds.), *Family assessment inventories for research and practice*. Madison: University of Wisconsin, 1987.

McCubbin, H. I., & Patterson, J. M. (1982e). Family changes and strains. In H. I. McCubbin & A. Thompson (Eds.), *Family assessment inventories for research and practice*. Madison: University of Wisconsin, 1987.

McCubbin, H. I., & Patterson, J. M. (1983a). The family stress process: The Double ABCX Model of adjustment and adaptation. In M. Sussman, H. I. McCubbin, & J. M. Patterson (Eds.), Social stress and the family: Advances and developments in family stress theory and research. *Marriage and Family Review*, Volume 6. Binghamton, NY: Haworth Press.

McCubbin, H. I., & Patterson, J. M. (1983b). The family stress process: The Double ABCX Model of adjustment and adaptation. In H. I. McCubbin, M. Sussman, & J. M. Patterson (Eds.), *Advances and developments in family stress theory and research*. New York: Haworth Press.

McCubbin, H. I., & Patterson, J. M. (1983c). Stress: The Family Inventory of Life Events and Changes. In E. Filsinger (Ed.), *Marriage and family assessments: A source book for family therapy*. Beverly Hills, CA: Sage.

McCubbin, H. I., & Patterson, J. M. (1983d). Family transitions: Adaptation to stress. In H. I. McCubbin & C. R. Figley (Eds.), *Stress and the family, Volume 1: Coping with normative transitions*. New York: Brunner/Mazel.

McCubbin, H. I., Patterson, J. M., & Glynn, T. (1982). Social Support Index (SSI). In H. I. McCubbin & A. Thompson (Eds.), *Family assessment inventories for research and practice*. Madison: University of Wisconsin, 1987.

McCubbin, H. I., Patterson, J. M., & Lavee, Y. (1983). *One thousand army families: Strengths, coping and supports*. St. Paul: University of Minnesota.

McCubbin, H. I., Patterson, J. M., & Wilson, L. (1979). *Family Inventory of Life Events (FILE)*. St. Paul: University of Minnesota.

McCubbin, H. I., Patterson, J. M., & Wilson, L. (1980). Family Inventory of Life Events and Changes (FILE) Form A. In H. I. McCubbin & A. Thompson (Eds.), *Family assessment inventories for research and practice*. Madison: University of Wisconsin, 1987.

McCubbin, H. I., Patterson, J. M., & Wilson, L. (1982). Family Strains Index. In H. I. McCubbin & A. Thompson (Eds.), *Family assessment inventories for research and practice*. Madison: University of Wisconsin, 1987.

McCubbin, H. I., & Thompson, A. (1987). *Family assessment inventories for research and practice*. Madison: University of Wisconsin.

McCubbin, H. I., Thompson, A., & McCubbin, M. A. (1987). Family Time and Routines

Inventory. In H. I. McCubbin & A. Thompson (Eds.), *Family assessment inventories for research and practice*. Madison: University of Wisconsin, 1987.

McCubbin, H. I., Thompson, A., Pirner, P., & McCubbin, M. A. (1988). *Family types and family strengths: A life-span and ecological perspective*. Minneapolis: Burgess Publishing.

McCubbin, M. A. (1984). Nursing assessment of parental coping with cystic fibrosis. *Western Journal of Nursing Research, 6*, 407–418.

McCubbin, M. A. (1986). *Family stress and family types: Chronic illness in children*. Doctoral dissertation, University of Minnesota.

McCubbin, M. A. (1988). Family stress, resources, and family types: Chronic illness in children. *Family Relations, 37*, 203–210.

McCubbin, M. A., & McCubbin, H. I., (1987). Family stress theory and assessment: The T-Double ABCX Model of Family Adjustment and Adaptation. In H. McCubbin & A. Thompson (Eds.), *Family assessment inventories for research and practice*. Madison: University of Wisconsin, 1987.

Moos, R. (1974). *Family environment scales*. Palo Alto: Consulting Psychologists Press.

Olson, D. H., (1986). Circumplex Model VII: Validation studies and FACES III, *Family Process, 25*, 337–351.

Olson, D. H., Lavee, Y., & McCubbin, H. I. (in press). Family types, stress, and adaptation. In J. Aldous & D. Klein (Eds.), *Family stress and development*. New York: Guilford Press.

Olson, D. H., McCubbin, H. I., Barnes, H., Larsen, A., Muxen, M., & Wilson, M. (1983). *Families: What makes them work*. Beverly Hills, CA: Sage.

Olson, D. H., Portner, J., & Bell, R. (1982). *FACES II: Family Adaptability and Cohesion Evaluation Scales*. St. Paul, MN: Family Social Science, University of Minnesota.

Olson, D. H., Sprenkle, D. H., & Russell, C. S. (1979). Circumplex model of marital and family systems, 1: Cohesion and adaptability dimensions, family types and clinical applications. *Family Process, 18*, 3–28.

Olson, D. H., Russell, C. S., & Sprenkle, D. H., (1983). Circumplex Model VI: Theoretical update. *Family Process, 22*, 69–83.

Paolucci, B., Hall, O., & Axinn, N. (1977). *Family decision making: An ecosystem approach*. New York: John Wiley.

Patterson, J. M. (in press). A family stress model for family medicine research: The family adjustment and adaptation response. In C. Ramsey (Ed.), *Family medicine research*. New York: Guilford Press.

Pearlin, L., Menaghan, E., Lieberman, M., & Mullan, J. (1981). The stress process. *Journal of Health and Social Behavior, 22*, 337–356.

Pearlin, L., & Schooler, C. (1982). The structure of coping. In H. I. McCubbin, A. E. Cauble, & J. M. Patterson (Eds.), *Family stress, coping, and social support*. Springfield, IL: Charles C Thomas.

Pilisuk, M., & Parks, S. (1983). Social support and family stress. In H. I. McCubbin, M. Sussman, & J. M. Patterson (Eds.), *Social stress and the family: Advances and developments in family stress theory and research*. New York: Haworth Press.

Pinneau, S. (1975). *Effects of social support on psychological and physiological stress*. Unpublished doctoral dissertation. University of Michigan.

Reiss, D. (1981) *The family's construction of reality*. Cambridge, MA: Harvard University Press.

Reiss, D., & Oliveri, M. E. (1980). Family paradigm and family coping: A proposal for linking the family's intrinsic adaptive capacities to its responses to stress. *Family Relations, 29*, 431–444.

Satir, V. (1972). *Peoplemaking*. Palo Alto: Science & Behavior Books.

Stinnet, H., & DeFrain, J. (1985). *Secrets of strong families*. Boston: Little, Brown.

Stinnet, N., & Sauer, K. (1977). Relationship characteristics of strong families. *Family Perspective, 11*(4), 3–11.

# 2

# Matching Family Treatment to Family Stressors

## EVERETT L. WORTHINGTON, JR.

Throughout life, families and individual family members encounter both normative and nonnormative life transitions, which sometimes result in considerable turmoil within the family. Many seek therapy in the midst of these upheavals. Others seem little affected by the life transitions. This chapter suggests that there are three important variables that account for most families' responses to life transitions: the degree of disruption of time schedules, the number of new decisions involving initial disagreement, and the level of pretransition conflict. It proposes simple means for assessing the three variables, and advocates that on the basis of the assessment, a family's likely response to the life transitions can be predicted. Treatment of families usually occurs within the boundaries of one of six schools of family therapy (see Levant, 1984). It is recommended that on the basis of the anticipated response of the family to the life transition, the family receive family treatment using a theory that is most likely to produce a successful outcome.

## THE FUNDAMENTAL ASSUMPTION

The assumption central to this chapter is that therapists should tailor their treatment of a family to their assessment of the family—not just within their favorite theory of therapy but to the extent of employing different theories of therapy with different clients. One can think of different metaphors to support this assumption. The story of Procrustes, the innkeeper who changed the height of his lodgers to fit the invariant size of his bed, can be stretched or shrunk to apply to this assumption. Or, the quote, "Give a boy a hammer and he will soon find that everything he meets wants hammering," can drive home the point. Unfortunately, I cannot with clear conscience employ such metaphors to motivate agreement with my central assumption. My belief is that all experienced therapists *do* already tailor their approach to fit each family they treat (with the possible exception of the "invariant prescription" [Simon, 1987]). The tenor of family therapy, though, is to work within one theory of family therapy, and tailor the interventions of that approach to each family.

For years, the primary goal of theorists of individual psychotherapy was to create a therapeutic approach powerful enough to account for all individual variance among clients. Regardless of the personality of the therapist or the client, regardless of the presenting problem or underlying personal dynamics, it was hoped that treatment would induce each client to give up the presenting problem and function well. *Within* psychoanalysis, rational emotive therapy, or any other theory of psychotherapy, the therapist tailored his or her approach to the client.

In 1966, Kiesler labeled this goal of a universally applicable theory as the "uniformity myth." This viewpoint has revolutionized individual psychotherapy, as illustrated by the two special issues on psychotherapy research published recently (Kazdin, 1986; Vanden Bos, 1986). Most researchers studying the effectiveness of psychotherapy now begin their study with an obligatory citation of the uniformity myth. Then, they direct their efforts toward identifying "which treatments apply to which clinical problems for what persons, and under what conditions" (Kazdin, 1986, p. 3). Adoption of this viewpoint has made researchers more specific and exact and has made practitioners more eclectic and integrative (albeit inexact about the decision rules that are employed to determine what treatment to apply in each case).

For family therapy, we may frame the nonuniformity hypothesis as follows: Which family-oriented interventions are effectively applied by what kinds of therapists for which presenting problems and for which family variables in what situations during what part of the family and individual life cycle? In family therapy, we have not been very sophisticated in answering this question with valid research findings. Little is known about the effectiveness of tailoring family-oriented interventions to any specific family variables apart from a few client diagnoses (for an exception see the Oregon group's research, e.g., Patterson, 1982). In 1981, Gurman and Kniskern identified success rates of family therapy for different diagnostic problems. Based on less than systematic comparative research, they concluded that (a) structural family therapy (Minuchin, Rosman, & Baker, 1978) was effective with psychosomatic problems and adult drug addiction; (b) operantly oriented behavioral treatment was appropriate for acting-out children (Patterson, 1982); and (c) functional family therapy was useful for soft juvenile delinquency (Alexander & Parsons, 1973). In the same review, there were almost embarrassingly few treatment factors, patient-family factors, and therapist factors that predicted positive outcomes in family therapy. Paucity of findings seems related to paucity of good outcome research.

Individual psychotherapies have been found to be more effective when matched to client problems than when a single theory has been applied to all clients regardless of their presenting problem. My suggestion in this chapter is that the same might be true of family therapies if we were to match treatments systematically to families. We should not do this just because individual therapists did it. Nor should we avoid doing it merely because the beginning of the family therapy movement involved strongly parochial presentations of theories and tempted us to claim universal applicability of our theories. Rather, we should match our theoretical treatment of families to the characteristics of the family because we care for our clients and set their needs above our theoretical allegiances.

Of course, I am not claiming that matching is more effective than nonmatching. There is little current empirical evidence that applies to the problem. I am suggesting that we scientifically investigate a matching model. That can only begin when we try it with our clients and impartially assess the outcomes.

Family therapy has been more resistant to this "matching" mentality than has individual psychotherapy for several reasons. Family therapy is newer and has not had as much time to become dissatisfied with the failures of uniformity theory. Further, there has been less theorizing about matching treatment to families than about matching treatment to individuals (for three exceptions, see Grunebaum & Chasin, 1982; Levant, 1984; Weltner, 1986). Finally, training generally occurs within theory-consistent training programs rather than in eclectic training programs such as occurs with most training in individual psychotherapy.

These resistances to matching families and treatments are formidable but not insurmountable—witness individual psychotherapy. To be sure, bastions of uniformity theory still remain, but most training in psychotherapy is now eclectic. Training programs hire faculty who propound divergent theoretical conceptualizations and teach different theoretical interventions. Internship and practicum sites offer a variety of theoretical approaches. Trainees are expected to be conversant, if not at least minimally proficient, in several major theoretical persuasions.

At present, few family therapists are disposed to and capable of employing different theoretical interventions with different families. I expect that such future constraints as government-organized investigations of the effectiveness of family therapy and the unabating pressure by the public and by insurance companies to reduce health care costs will eventually push family therapists increasingly toward eclecticism or integration (Lebow, 1987). However, the widespread acceptance of matching family treatment to problem is currently not on the horizon.

In this chapter I suggest a practical way in which interested family therapists can begin to tailor theoretical approaches to different family characteristics. At one extreme is the Renaissance therapist, who is a virtuoso at every theoretical approach to the family (and undoubtedly also has a perfect family and obedient dog). At the more common intermediate point is the mental health agency or consortium of private practitioners (of *different* theoretical persuasions). Such therapists might use intake assessment interviews to assign (or refer) families to the therapists with the highest likelihood of therapeutic success. At the other end of the spectrum is the therapist committed to using a particular theory of family therapy with most (if not all) of his or her clients. Such a therapist might still benefit from the following suggestions by more clearly identifying target areas for intervention within his or her theoretical approach.

The remainder of the chapter consists of four sections. First, three critical variables are identified as important to understanding family responses to life transitions. Second, some practical ways to assess the variables within a one- or two-session (intake) format are suggested. Third, the likely family response to a transition is predicted depending on the family's reaction to the three critical variables. Finally, six types of family treatment are evaluated in terms of which are likely to succeed with families that show particular response patterns to life transitions.

## THREE CRITICAL VARIABLES IN LIFE TRANSITIONS

### An Array of Potentially Important Variables

Whether an individual reacts to a life transition with aplomb, concern, or panic is dependent on a number of the characteristics of the life event. Danish, Smyer, and Nowak (1980) identified six characteristics of transitions that affected individuals' responses to transitions: (a) timing (on time, earlier than expected, or later than expected); (b) duration of transition relative to expectations; (c) sequencing relative to the societally expected order; (d) cohort specificity; (e) probability of event occurrence (normative or nonnormative); and (f) contextual purity of the event.

Pittman (1987), in an excellent theory of family therapy in crises, suggested other dimensions on which to evaluate life events. He stated that life events create different problems for families when stresses are overt rather than covert, permanent rather than temporary, real rather than imagined, specific to a family rather than universally experienced by families, and arising from perceived intrinsic forces in the family rather than from forces extrinsic to the family. Little of Pittman's intervention is based on the characteristics of the life events. Rather, most of his intervention depends on an assessment of "snag points," or areas where families resist change.

Family scholars (Hill, 1949; McCubbin & Figley, 1983; McCubbin & Patterson, 1983) have proposed other variables thought to be related to families' reactions to transitions. For the most part, these involve characteristics of family rather than of life events.

*What Makes a Variable Important?*

What one considers to be an important explanatory variable depends on the use one intends for the explanation. Haley (1976) has described theories as being of two types: theories primarily useful for research and theories primarily useful for therapy. The former are used to understand the complexities of phenomena and to account for large amounts of variance. They must be heuristic and internally consistent; they are necessarily complex and interrelate large numbers of variables. In comparison, theories for therapy are generally simpler, must be verifiable by most clients, and should use fewer explanatory variables than theories for research so that practitioners can easily remember and apply the theoretical precepts. Theories for therapy are less directed at accounting for variance than at enabling clients to take constructive actions to change their lives. The two types of theories are not incompatible. For example, psychoanalysis, which was originally proposed as a clinical theory, later became one of the most widely used explanatory theories for extratherapy phenomena. Behavioral marriage therapy (Jacobson & Holtzworth-Monroe, 1986; Jacobson & Margolin, 1979; Stuart, 1980) is compact and powerful in the clinic and has been heuristic in generating research and further theoretical ideas. Nonetheless, most theories have been used primarily in one type of setting—the laboratory or the clinic—with little cross-referencing.

A theory of the effects of transitions on the family that is useful in the clinic is needed. A complete understanding of the transition and its effects on individual family members, the marriage, the family as a whole, and the broader social matrix of the family requires a multidimensional integrative approach (e.g., Walker, 1985). In contrast, a clinically useful theory must choose from among the relevant variables to provide for powerful interventions (Haley, 1976).

I have proposed that three variables are critical to understanding the amount and types of distress a family will experience during a transition: disruption of time schedules, number of necessary new decisions involving initial disagreement, and pretransition conflict (Worthington, 1987; Worthington & Buston, 1986). The variables (somewhat artificially dichotomized into high and low values) can be used to predict eight ($2 \times 2 \times 2$) categories of family response to transition, which in turn can be used to match families to treatment.

## Disruption of Time Schedules

A transition can disrupt the time schedules of family members. Some transitions create massive reallocations of activities, whereas other transitions might scarely be noticed. Turmoil within the family is hypothesized to be directly proportional to disruption in the time schedules of individual family members. There are three possible reasons for this relationship.

First, new time schedules force family members to adjust their ways of meeting their needs for intimacy, distance, and coaction. Alexander and his colleagues (Alexander & Parsons, 1973; Barton & Alexander, 1981) have shown, in functional family therapy, that all activities function to balance a person's need for intimacy and distance. Some activities promote intimacy—such as making love, discussing values, sharing dreams and plans for the future, or reminiscing about the past. Other activities promote coaction, but do not necessarily build intimacy—such as playing board games as a family, playing tennis, attending a movie, or discussing the events of one's day. Still other activities promote distance—such as reading, watching television, listening to audiotapes on a walkman, or studying.

Each person attempts to fulfill his or her needs for intimacy, coaction, and distance within some acceptable range, which is individually determined. All daily activities contribute to the balance. Over time, family members adjust their time schedules within the context of the family so that family intimacy is regulated.

A transition might affect a family member's time schedule greatly, not at all, or anywhere between the two extremes. Generally, large changes are perceived as distressing. As the person negotiates the transition, he or she rearranges his or her time schedule to regain the lost balance among intimacy, coaction, and distance. The extent to which the person is able to readjust the time schedule depends on the flexibility of the person's time commitments outside of the family, on the person's resourcefulness in initiating changes, and on the reactions of people within and outside the family to the changes that are initiated.

For example, the Howe family is shocked to discover that their oldest daughter, Susan, has become pregnant at age 16. Abortion is thought to be morally wrong and the arrival of Susan's baby creates major reorganizations in the family. Mrs. Howe, having taken a job the year before, refuses to take over child care for Susan. Throughout the pregnancy, Susan had continued to attend high school classes at a school for pregnant teens. Now, she attends classes on mothering with her newly found friends; however, her old friendships have weakened because she is rarely able to see her former friends. Susan is lonely and depressed, which elicits concern from her mother (and incidentally requires time and emotional energy). Susan's depression also places more child-care burdens on Mrs. Howe, until at last Mrs. Howe's own mother offers to help with child rearing. She moves in with the Howes which further disrupts the family's time schedules. Mr. Howe feels extra financial pressure, so he takes a second job as a night watchman. The new job eases the financial strain, but requires Mr. Howe to sleep in the afternoon, which ends his coaching involvement with his son's soccer and basketball teams. The son feels isolated from family members because most of his family interactions had been with his older sister (who now has mothering responsibilities) and his father. The son attempts to fill his feelings of loss of intimacy by spending more time at friends' houses. Mr. Howe also finds that his partner on the night job talks incessantly, which makes Mr. Howe feel like escaping additional interpersonal interaction at home.

Eventually, the family arrives at a new balance of intimacy, coaction, and distance, but not without lengthy negotiation, numerous false starts at redressing the difficulties, and general turmoil, uncertainty, and interpersonal discomfort. Obviously, this family, functioning well before the adolescent pregnancy, might emerge from the transition functioning poorly —with family conflict, two new family members, a depressed teen, and, in the worst case, a son at risk for juvenile delinquency. Just as easily, the family could emerge with an increased sense of family unity and confidence that they could handle difficult life transitions. Their final level of functioning is not determined by the amount of turmoil experienced.

It is easy to imagine the same family but with fewer needs to rearrange their time schedules. For example, suppose the family had been secure financially so that Mr. Howe did not need to take a second job. Or imagine the family response if Mrs. Howe had not been employed prior to the pregnancy and if she had been willing to work closely with Susan to teach her to mother and to help out in child rearing when necessary. The pregnancy would still have required adjustment within the family; however, fewer needs to readjust time schedules would have created less turmoil in the family.

A second reason that rearranging time schedules has an impact on a family is that with any transition, new roles must be assumed. The role of caretaker of the baby, in the example above, was assumed by Susan and later by Susan's grandmother (the baby's great-grandmother). Susan might also have had to assume some of the cooking chores. Mrs. Howe assumed the role of the baby's grandmother. The adolescent son might have adopted the role of yard caretaker because Mr. Howe, working two jobs, could no longer care for the yard. These changes in roles introduce role strain (LaRossa, 1983), which increases the perceived stress of a transition. Again, one can imagine a transition in which few additional roles are necessary in a particular family, or in which adding new roles is balanced by giving up old roles.

A third reason that rearranging time schedules has an impact on the family is that *change* is necessary. Although change is part of life and can sometimes be perceived as exhilarating or stimulating, change is perceived by most people as introducing uncertainty or uncontrollability—both of which increase the subjective perception of stress. The way a transition is perceived may depend on the way a person construes change, the attributions he or she makes about the change, and the ability of the person to handle the change (Epstein & Bishop, 1981).

*New Decisions Involving Initial Disagreement*

Each phase of life necessitates new decisions among family members. Often spouses bring to marriage "blueprints" specifying how to behave during a new phase of life. For example, when a first child is born, the new mother and father must make numerous decisions ranging from who gets up for the 3 A.M. feeding to whether to buy a new house. Because the parents were raised in different homes and experienced different child-rearing practices from their own parents—to which they reacted, either positively or negatively—they could either agree or disagree initially on each new decision. Each decision that involves initial disagreement must be resolved, which calls into question the fundamental rules of the relationship.

Haley (1963) described relationship dynamics *as if* they were rule-governed. He identified three types of rules. *Overt rules* are usually explicit agreements. *Covert rules* are patterns of behavior that are usually not explicitly discussed, but if an observer points them out, the couple likely will agree that the patterns occur. *Power rules* describe who has the power to make decisions and how the decisions are made. These rules describe the "pragmatics of human communication" (Haley, 1963; Sluzki, 1978; Watzlawick et al., 1967). When a transition occurs, the power rules are tested and perhaps renegotiated through resolving disagreements. Greater initial disagreement — in level of discrepancy and in sheer number — will lead to greater turmoil in family relationships.

*Pretransition Conflict*

A family system that is in perpetual conflict prior to the transition is generally thought to have a family hierarchy or structure that is in question (Haley, 1976; Minuchin & Fishman, 1981). Further, conflict as a response to the transition can exacerbate the disturbance, called "positive feedback" because disturbances build. On the other hand, a system with low pretransition conflict is likely to be characterized by "negative feedback," which decreases perturbations over time.

Actually, the presence of high perpetual conflict does not necessarily indicate potential positive feedback in a conflict loop, just as not all families with low conflict are necessarily able to handle new conflict and change successfully. Nevertheless, the presence of high or low pretransition conflict is a reasonably accurate predictor of family functioning. Given the relative ease with which chronic conflict is assessed, it serves as a good diagnostic criterion.

## ASSESSMENT OF THE THREE FAMILY VARIABLES

Because this model is intended to be clinically useful, variables are conceptualized so they can be easily assessed. Disruption in time schedules may be assessed by direct inquiry concerning activities of each family member and concerning how those differ from activities prior to the transition. However, direct inquiry sometimes results in superficial responses. When sufficient time is available for assessment, I ask family members to describe systematically their use of time throughout the week. This often dramatizes how little or how much time they spend as couples, families, or parent-children units. Other information such as complaints about being overworked or bored or about loss of family unity or closeness may indicate that large disruptions in time schedules have been experienced. In marriage counseling, I use two inventories that assess intimacy and other aspects of the marriage: the Personal Report of Intimacy in Relationships (Schaefer & Olson, 1981) and the Couple's Pre-Counseling Inventory (Stuart & Jacobson, 1987).

The presence of new disagreements is determined by attending to presenting complaints. Most families who have sought counseling in the wake of a life transition readily discuss their differences of opinion. Sometimes, when a troubled child is the focus of concern, parents are somewhat reluctant to discuss their differences but can be persuaded to do so in the interest of "getting a thorough understanding of the problem" or after some other justification.

The chronicity of conflict can usually be assessed directly, especially if conflict is frequent and intense. Usually, I tape-record a 7–10 minute discussion by the family of some issue about which they disagree. I generally leave the room during that discussion. Despite the initial artificiality of "fighting on cue" in the presence of a tape recorder, most family members quickly uphold their points of view. Listening to the tape afterwards, I can identify many rehearsed conflictual patterns and persuasive strategies. While some therapists stay in the room when families are directed to argue, I have found that I can use that 10 minutes to review assessment forms that the family completed prior to the initial interview and to plan an intervention or homework task, if appropriate.

## FAMILY RESPONSES TO TRANSITIONS

By dichotomizing these three easily assessed variables, a $2 \times 2 \times 2$ (disruption of time schedules $\times$ new decisions involving initial disagreement $\times$ pretransition conflict) classification schema can be constructed. Admittedly, each dimension is continuous rather than dichotomous.

Each variable is hypothesized to affect family relationships differently. Disruptions in time schedules are thought to produce large upheavals in family relationships that require numerous adjustments over time as family members react to the transition and to the attempts of other family members to restructure roles and time commitments. New decisions involving initial disagreements produce discrete perturbations in the relationships as the issues are discussed and debated and as family members use various behavioral strategies to induce or coerce agreement from other family members. Pretransition conflict produces three effects: increased frequency of discrete conflicts as power rules become more openly contested, use of progressively more coercive compliance-gaining attempts, and a growing sense of dissatisfaction and discontent with family life.

These effects may be represented graphically (albeit somewhat abstractly) as in Figure 1. An eight-celled matrix is shown, and in each cell the (somewhat abstract) "collective sense of family turmoil" is graphed. This might be thought of as the total adrenaline output of all family members. Long, high curves represent protracted upheaval. Brief spikes represent abrupt disruptions, which are likely experienced as family conflict. Curves that return to the original level indicate that negative feedback is occurring; those that continue to rise suggest that positive feedback is operating.

If the effects of the three variables are superimposed on each other, eight distinct responses to transitions emerge. The top 2 × 2 matrix describes families that have low pretransition conflict, thus presumably low instability in their power rules. Families with few changes in their time schedules and few initial disagreements should be little affected by the transition. Families with low disruption in their time schedules but with many initial disagreements will experience episodic conflict, which should decrease over time. Families with highly disrupted time schedules but with few initial disagreements should experience protracted turmoil as they adjust their new time schedules to meet their needs and perform their roles. Families with high disruptions in their time schedules and many initial disagreements will experience both protracted turmoil and periodic conflict, which should eventually subside.

Families in the lower half of Figure 1, those who are involved in chronic conflict, will experience the same fundamental patterns as families with low conflict. The differences are that the families will tend to experience chronic difficulties and perhaps become progressively more disturbed, disorganized, and conflicted over time.

## TREATMENTS OF FAMILIES

Although there are many family treatments, I will consider only six fundamental classes of treatments. Levant (1980, 1984) has identified three types of family therapies: historical, structure/process, and experiential. Historical family therapies conceptualize the root of current family problems as being within the parents' families of origin. Within historical family therapies are psychodynamic, multigenerational, and intergenerational-contextual approaches. Structure/process family therapies emphasize current family interactions and the relations of those current interactions to symptomatic behavior. The most prominent structure/process theories include those of Minuchin, Haley, the Mental Research Institute, and the Milan group, as well as behavioral and functional family therapies. Expe-

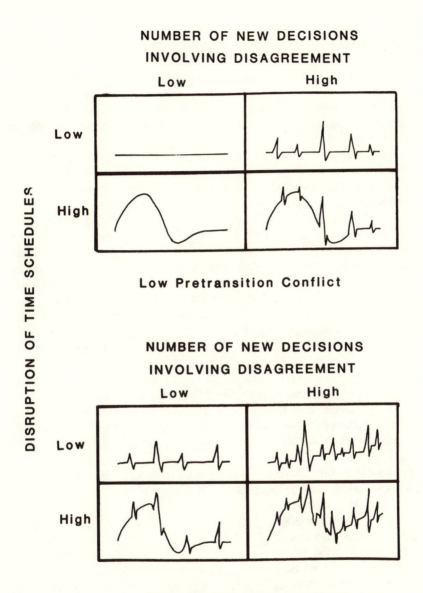

NUMBER OF NEW DECISIONS
INVOLVING DISAGREEMENT

Low Pretransition Conflict

NUMBER OF NEW DECISIONS
INVOLVING DISAGREEMENT

High Pretransition Conflict

*Figure 1.* Family disruption as a function of time schedules, new decisions involving disagreement, and level of pretransition conflict: A model for predicting family response during normative and nonnormative life transitions.

riential family therapies heighten the awareness of individual family members, focusing on individuals' phenomenology and on growth and fulfillment of human potential. Three schools of therapy compose this group: client-centered, Gestalt, and experiential (Napier & Whitaker, 1978) family therapies. This categorization of family therapies is given additional credence by its similarity to the categorization by Grunebaum and Chasin (1982).

There are three other categories of family treatment. First, psychoeducational approaches have evolved from the treatment of the chronically severely disturbed (McFarlane, 1983). These approaches generally accept the difficulty of the patient as being due to nonfamily causes. The family is supported in dealing with the chronic problem through social support groups and meetings in which families of similarly diagnosed patients learn about the problem and their alternatives for coping with the problem. Second, family crisis intervention has enjoyed limited attention among practitioners, but three versions have obtained some acceptance. Family crisis therapy (Langsley & Kaplan, 1978) uses a home visit and several office visits within three weeks; treatment identifies the crisis, defines it as a family problem, and prescribes actions to palliate the crisis. Multiple impact therapy (MacGregor, Ritchie, Serrano, & Schuster, 1964) created crisis teams that generally spent two full days with a family in multiple meetings with various combinations of family members. Pittman's (1987) turning points therapy assesses the stress on the family and the "snag points" (the aspects of the family's structure or functioning that resist change) and applies a seven-step method of moving the family through the crisis productively. The third nontherapy family treatment is family enrichment. This has been developed to help families avoid difficulties and develop positive aspects of their lives together (L'Abate & Weinstein, 1987; L'Abate & Young, 1987; Otto, 1976).

## MATCHING TREATMENT WITH FAMILY RESPONSE

It is assumed that not every treatment will be effective for every family in transition. Based on the pattern of disruption a family experiences during transition (see Figure 1) and on the characteristics of each of the six types of family treatment, I hypothesize a different likelihood of success for each method of treatment with families who exhibit each particular type of response to transition. In Table 1, the eight family responses to transition are listed and predictions are advanced about the likely success of each type of family treatment.

## TABLE 1
### Likelihood of Success of Six Therapeutic Treatments of Families During Normative and Life Transitions Based on Three Family Variables

| Group | | | Treatments | |
|---|---|---|---|---|
| Disruption of Time Schedules | Number Decisions with Initial Disagreement | Power Structure Instability | Likely Successful | Likely Unsuccessful |
| Low | Low | Low | Experiential FT<br>Enrichment | Structure/Process FT<br>Historical FT<br>Psychoeducational<br>Crisis Intervention |
| Low | High | Low | Enrichment<br>Experiential FT<br>Structure/Process FT<br>Historical FT | Psychoeducational<br>Crisis Intervention |
| High | Low | Low | Enrichment<br>Experiential FT<br>Crisis Intervention | Historical FT<br>Structure/Process FT<br>Psychoeducational |
| High | High | Low | Structure/Process FT<br>Experiential FT<br>Historical FT<br>Crisis Intervention | Psychoeducational<br>Enrichment |

(continued)

TABLE 1 (continued)
Likelihood of Success of Six Therapeutic Treatments of Families During Normative and
Life Transitions Based on Three Family Variables

| Group | | | Treatments | |
| --- | --- | --- | --- | --- |
| Disruption of Time Schedules | Number Decisions with Initial Disagreement | Power Structure Instability | Likely Successful | Likely Unsuccessful |
| Low | Low | High | Psychoeducational<br>Structure/Process FT<br>Historical FT<br>Experiential FT | Enrichment<br>Crisis Intervention |
| Low | High | High | Psychoeducational<br>Structure/Process FT<br>Historical FT<br>Experiential FT | Enrichment<br>Crisis Intervention |
| High | Low | High | Crisis Intervention<br>Psychoeducation<br>Structure/Process FT<br>Historical FT | Enrichment<br>Experiential FT |
| High | High | High | Crisis Intervention<br>Psychoeducation<br>Structure/Process FT<br>Historical FT | Enrichment<br>Experiential FT |

Note: FT = Family Therapy

## *Historical Family Therapies*

Given its emphasis on helping uncover long-term family or individual conflicts, historical family therapy is thought to be effective primarily for families with current or enduring conflict.

## *Structural/Process Family Therapies*

Most structure/process family therapies train families to communicate or help families resolve disagreements. They are consequently useful for families in conflict. In addition, they are generally concerned with the underlying structure of the family, with power hierarchies, and chronic conflict.

## *Experiential Family Therapies*

Experiential family therapies focus more on individual growth than do other family therapies. Thus, experiential family therapies are expected to be effective when family members do not perceive themselves as highly disturbed. Families high in pretransition conflict and simultaneously experiencing the turmoil of disrupted time schedules will generally perceive themselves in crisis, which will predispose them against experiential family therapy.

## *Psychoeducational Approaches*

Psychoeducational approaches are thought to be particularly effective with chronically disturbed families. However, for their use to be appropriate, the family should have a clearly identified patient with evidence that the malady is resistant to traditional family therapies.

## *Family Crisis Intervention*

Intensive intervention that treats a disturbance as a crisis is indicated when massive disruptions in time schedules are experienced by the family members. Probably, family crisis therapy (Langsley & Kaplan, 1978) will be effective with families who have very disrupted time schedules because it provides for about three weeks for the time schedule to stabilize. Multiple impact therapy (MacGregor et al., 1964) and turning points therapy (Pittman, 1987) are appropriate for discrete disturbances that are severe enough to propel the family into treatment.

*Enrichment*

Family enrichment is thought to be appropriate only when the disturb-ance in the family is low to moderate. Marriage enrichment is particularly ineffective for couples who have preexisting severe marital difficulties (Doherty, Lester, & Leigh, 1986). If an analogy between marriage enrich-ment and family enrichment holds, family enrichment should not be used when more than one difficulty exists simultaneously (e.g., time schedule changes at the same time that the family faces many disagreements that need resolution).

AN EXAMPLE

Suppose we return to the Howe family with their pregnant adolescent, Susan, new live-in grandmother, disengaged son, and father who takes on an extra job—reducing the intimate and coactive contact among family members.

In the initial therapeutic contact, the therapist assesses the disruption in the time schedules of family members through information spontaneously volunteered and through probes. Assessing the extent of distress the disruption has caused is also relatively easy. Family members are directed to discuss the impact of the changes on each of them while the therapist attends to the patterns of interaction—their intensity, their repetitive occurrence, and their apparent instability or stability. A family history reveals that the problem is acute rather than chronic and that pretransition conflict was low. The therapist concludes that the Howe family has highly disrupted time schedules but has infrequent ongoing conflict or crisis-specific conflict. The expected disruption is massive disorientation over several weeks to several months. The therapist checks on the validity of the expectation with the couple prior to deciding which type of treatment to employ. As shown in Table 1, enrichment, experiential family therapy and crisis intervention are anticipated to be more successful than histori-cal or structure/process family therapy or psychoeducational approaches. The therapist decides to present several options for the Howes to consider: referral to an ongoing enrichment group within the agency, crisis treat-ment focusing on time management, or experiential family therapy (which involves referral to a local therapist with that orientation).

## NEED FOR EMPIRICAL VALIDATION

In this chapter, a conceptualization of families during normative and nonnormative life transitions has been proposed and some hypotheses tentatively advanced that predict the success of different types of families with six types of current treatments for families. The usefulness of this conceptualization, obviously, depends on empirical investigation. Most family treatment practitioners would like to believe that they are effective with everyone with whom they work. The current schema predicts that treatment effectiveness is different and challenges practitioners to match treatment to ways that families respond to life transitions and to document outcomes.

Some family theories suggest interactions between life events and families with different characteristics (such as communication styles, power dynamics, cohesiveness, flexibility). The present proposal suggests an interaction at a more observable level—family *response* to life transitions. It directs therapeutic attention to disruptions in time schedules, initial topics of disagreement, and pretransition conflict level. These easily assessed dimensions can support divergent theoretical conceptualizations and thus provide a clinically useful level of intervention regardless of the practitioner's theory.

## REFERENCES

Alexander, J. F., & Parsons, B. V. (1973). *Functional family therapy.* Monterey, CA: Brooks/ Cole.

Barton, C., & Alexander, J. F. (1981). Functional family therapy. In A. J. Gurman & D. P. Kniskern (Eds.), *Handbook of family therapy* (pp. 403–442). New York: Brunner/Mazel.

Danish, S. J., Smyer, M. A., & Nowak, C. A. (1980). Developmental intervention: Enhancing life-event processes. In P. B. Baltes & O. G. Brim, Jr. (Eds.), *Life-span development and behavior, Vol. 3* (pp. 339–336). New York: Academic Press, 1980.

Doherty, W. J., Lester, M. E., & Leigh, G. (1986). Marriage encounter weekends: Couples who win and couples who lose. *Journal of Marital and Family Therapy, 12,* 49–62.

Epstein, N. B., & Bishop, D. S. (1981). Problem-centered systems therapy of the family. In A. S. Gurman & D. P. Kniskern (Eds.), *Handbook of family therapy* (pp. 444–482). New York: Brunner/Mazel.

Grunebaum, H., & Chasin, R. (1982). Thinking like a family therapist: A model for integrating the theories and methods of family therapy. *Journal of Marital and Family Therapy, 8,* 403–416.

Gurman, A. S., & Kniskern, D. P. (1981). Family therapy outcome research: Knowns and unknowns. In A. S. Gurman & D. P. Kniskern (Eds.), *Handbook of family therapy* (pp. 742–776). New York: Brunner/Mazel.

Haley, J. (1963). *Strategies of psychotherapy*, New York: Grune & Stratton, 1963.

Haley, J. (1976). *Problem solving therapy*. San Francisco: Jossey-Bass.

Hill, R. (1949). *Families under stress*. New York: Harper & Row.

Jacobson, N. S., & Holtzworth-Monroe, A. (1986). Marital therapy: A social learning-cognitive perspective. In N. S. Jacobson & A. S. Gurman (Eds.), *Clinical handbook of marital therapy* (pp. 29–70). New York: Guilford.

Jacobson, N. S., & Margolin, G. (1979). *Marital therapy: Strategies based on social learning and behavior exchange principles*. New York: Brunner/Mazel.

Kazdin, A. E. (Ed.) (1986). Special issue: Psychotherapy research. *Journal of Consulting and Clinical Psychology, 54*, 3–117.

Kiesler, D. J. (1966). Some myths of psychotherapy research and the search for a paradigm. *Psychological Bulletin, 65*, 110–136.

L'Abate, L., & Weinstein, S. (1987). *Structured enrichment programs for couples and families*. New York: Brunner/Mazel.

L'Abate, L., & Young, L. (1987). *Casebook: Structured enrichment programs for couples and families*. New York: Brunner/Mazel.

Langsley, D. G., & Kaplan, S. M. (1978). *The treatment of families in crisis*. New York: Grune & Stratton.

LaRossa, R. (1983). The transition to parenthood and the social reality of time. *Journal of Marriage and the Family, 45*, 579–589.

Lebow, J. L. (1987). Developing a personal integration in family therapy: Principles for model construction and practice. *Journal of Marital and Family Therapy, 13*, 1–14.

Levant, R. F. (1980). A classification of the field of family therapy: A review of prior attempts and a new paradigmatic model. *American Journal of Family Therapy, 8*(1), 3–16.

Levant, R. F. (1984). *Family therapy: A comprehensive overview*. Englewood Cliffs, NJ: Prentice Hall.

MacGregor, R., Ritchie, A. N., Serrano, A. C., & Schuster, F. P. (1964). *Multiple impact therapy with families*. New York: McGraw-Hill.

McCubbin, H. I., & Figley, C. R. (Eds.) (1983). *Stress and the family, Volume I: Coping with normative transitions*. New York: Brunner/Mazel.

McCubbin, H. I., & Patterson, J. M. (1983). Family transitions: Adaptation to stress. In H. I. McCubbin & C. R. Figley (Eds.), *Stress and the family, Volume I: Coping with normative transitions* (pp. 5–25). New York: Brunner/Mazel.

McFarlane, W. (1983). *Family therapy in schizophrenia*. New York: Guilford.

Minuchin, S., & Fishman, H. C. (1981). *Family therapy techniques*. Cambridge, MA: Harvard University Press.

Minuchin, S., Rosman, B. L., & Baker, L. (1978). *Psychosomatic families: Anorexia nervosa in context*. Cambridge, MA: Harvard University Press.

Napier, A. Y., & Whitaker, C. A. (1978). *The family crucible*. New York: Harper & Row.

Olson, D. H., Russell, C. S., & Sprenkle, D. H. (1983). Circumplex model VI: Theoretical update. *Family Process, 22*, 69–83.

Otto, H. A. (Ed.). (1976). *Marriage and family enrichment: New perspectives and programs*. Nashville, TN: Abingdon.

Patterson, G. R. (1982). *Coercive family process: A social learning approach*. Eugene, OR: Castalia Publishing Co.

Pittman, F. S., III. (1987). *Turning points: Treating families in transition and crisis*. New York: W. W. Norton.

Schaefer, M. T., & Olson, D. H. (1981). Assessing intimacy: The PAIR inventory. *Journal of Marital and Family Therapy, 7*, 47–60.

Sheehy, G. (1976). *Passages: Predictable crises of adult life*. New York: Dutton.

Simon, R. (1987). Good-bye paradox, hello invariant prescription: An interview with Mara Selvini-Palazzoli. *Family Therapy Networker, 11*(5), 16–33.

Sluzki, C. E. (1978). Marital therapy from a system theory perspective. In T. J. Paolino

& B. S. McCrady (Eds.), *Marriage and marital therapy* (pp. 366–394). New York: Brunner/Mazel.

Sprenkle, D., & Olson, D. (1978). Circumplex model of marital systems IV: Empirical study of clinic and non-clinic couples. *Journal of Marital and Family Therapy, 4*, 59–74.

Stuart, R. B. (1980). *Helping couples change: A social learning approach to marital therapy.* New York: Guilford.

Stuart, R. B., & Jacobson, B. (1987). *Couples Pre-Counseling Inventory, Revised edition, 1987.* Champaign, IL: Research Press.

Vanden Bos, G. R. (Ed.). (1986). Special issue: Psychotherapy research. *American Psychologist, 41*, 111–214.

Walker, A. J. (1985). Reconceptualizing family stress. *Journal of Marriage and the Family, 47*, 827–837.

Watzlawick, P., Beavin, J., & Jackson, D. D. (1967). *Pragmatics of human communication.* New York: Norton.

Weltner, J. S. (1986). A matchmaker's guide to family therapy. *Family Therapy Networker, 10*(2), 51–55.

Worthington, E. L., Jr. (1987). Treatment of families during life transitions: Matching treatment of family response. *Family Process, 26*, 295–308.

Worthington, E. L., Jr., & Buston, B. G. (1986). The marriage relationship during the transition of parenthood. *Journal of Family Issues, 7*, 443–473.

# SECTION II

# Treatment Approaches

# 3

# A Family Systems Approach

## WILLIAM C. NICHOLS

*Fashionably and expensively dressed, George and Joan Blake could have been the models in an advertisement for success. A tall handsome couple who wore their affluence well, the Blakes appeared to be moving toward middle age gracefully. The real picture was different.*

*When Joan Blake called for an appointment for herself and her husband, she made it clear that the cracks in the family portrait were deep. Things were at a difficult stage in the marriage. Although it was "not publicly known," she said, George had moved out of the home three months earlier, the second time in a 17-year marriage when the partners had separated. "The stress is beginning to get to both of us, and to our kids as well. My attorney — neither of us has filed for divorce, but I have seen an attorney and he strongly recommended that we try with you. And we've got three boys that I don't want to see messed up." Was her husband willing to come in? "Yes, he was last night, but we've tried before without getting very far, and George is just not intrigued with the idea of any kind of therapy."*

*As many other couples who seek professional help, the Blakes were far advanced in their marital discord and quite mixed in their motivations for making an appointment.*

## A FAMILY SYSTEMS APPROACH

The Blakes went to a therapist who worked with an integrative family systems approach (Nichols & Everett, 1986). Family systems therapy is defined here in broad terms as any form of family therapy that focuses on individuals in their primary context, the family, and is concerned with altering the family system. Rather than considering problematic/symptomatic behavior as stemming from the intrapsychic difficulties of individuals, family systems approaches take a larger contextual view. An individual is viewed in connection with the primary setting in which he or she is functioning, the family.

With respect to separation and divorce, for example, a family systems approach involves dealing with marital breakup and family reorganization in systemic terms, rather than as outcomes of individual neurosis. Individuals are regarded as members of a system, as part of an organized network that continues to exist in a changed form even though separation/divorce occur. Family systems theory helps with the recognition that separation/divorce disrupt but do not end the family system and that the various subsystems of the family—not merely the various individuals—are affected differently by the marital disruption.

Perceiving problems as arising in a system and not merely in individuals allows the family systems therapist to "deal with the structures." That is, the clinician can work with various parts of the family system to produce the desired change. One can intervene with subsystems in a family, including the couple, parental, sibling, individual, and transgenerational subsystems as indicated. Briefly, one works to alter the system and thereby to help the system help its members.

Family members do not necessarily have to be present in order to be affected by what occurs in therapy. Family systems therapy is characterized, therefore, not by the number of persons seen in interview situations but by the orientation of the clinician. One "thinks family," which means conceptualizing actions and meanings in terms of at least two and generally three generations, regardless of which family member or members are actually seen in therapy.

Accordingly, family systems therapy is not defined here in terms of technique. Schultz (1984), who also described family systems therapy primarily as a way of thinking about problems and only secondarily as a method of treatment, indicated that many family therapists have overemphasized technique. There are numerous techniques that can be used in attempting to fulfill the goal of altering the family system (Nichols & Everett, 1986). The particular form of integrative family therapy approach taken with the Blake family used several techniques and interventions in a flexible manner.

*History*

Strangely enough, family therapy and a family systems approach to human difficulties are rather recent newcomers to the general field of psychotherapy. Although some psychodynamically oriented therapists point to Sigmund Freud's handling of the case of Little Hans, in which the father of psychoanalysis treated a phobic youngster through the child's father, as a progenitor of family therapy, it would require a revisionist history of psychotherapy to reveal a genuine developmental link. On the contrary, those psychoanalytically oriented clinicians who began to work with couples and families often had to struggle mightily against the disapproval of their orthodox colleagues. The roots of family therapy lie primarily in public demands for marital assistance following World War I, the child guidance movement in the United States beginning in the 1920s, and in attempts to research and treat schizophrenia starting in the 1940s and 1950s (Nichols & Everett, 1986).

*Basic Assumptions*

Family therapy has been a rambunctious field, populated by strong, idiosyncratic, and often iconoclastic figures. The "basic assumptions" of a family systems approach still would be described differently by adherents of different schools of family therapy, including several varieties of family systems practitioners. One school would characterize them in one fashion and others quite differently. Even if family therapists were all gathered together and consensus sought, there would be dissenting reports. Hence, the description of concepts that follows will have to stand simply as one effort to provide an accurate and carefully constructed picture of axiomatic statements and basic assumptions underlying family systems work.

*Systems and organization.* Families are organized as systems. A system is "a set of elements standing in interaction" (von Bertalanffy, 1968). Human families are organized, as noted, so that what affects one member or part affects others. The parts are organized by the ongoing and consistent nature of the relationship between the parts, by the continuing patterns of interaction (Steinglass, 1978). A subsystem—an individual, the siblings, the spouses, or the parents and children, for example, in a family—is an element that carries out a particular process in a system (Miller, 1969). Subsystems, like the larger systems to which they belong, have their own interactive patterns, organization, and boundaries (Nichols & Everett, 1986).

*Key characteristics of system organization.* Wholeness, boundaries, and hierarchies have been described as the key concepts within the larger idea of organization (Gurman & Kniskern, 1981). Briefly, the idea of wholeness pertains to seeing patterns in behavior rather than reducing entities to their constituent parts in a reductive fashion. This concept has significant relevance for examining and working with families where there is marital discord, separation, and divorce. Affixing blame or assigning responsibility to one of the partners becomes an impossible and futile enterprise when the situation is viewed holistically. Fortunately, such reductionism is not necessary in order to work therapeutically with couples and families.

*Nonsummativity* is a concept that reinforces the idea of wholeness. The family cannot be understood merely by adding up its parts or characteristics. It is different from the sum of its parts. Rather, one must look at the pattern and not simply at the parts. Summarizing the personality attributes and characteristics of the spouses as individuals does not provide an accurate picture of their marriage, for example. Each partner may perform in one fashion in the work and/or social world and in a quite different manner in relation to the spouse. One must examine the marriage and the marital interaction, not the sum of the individuals as individuals.

Who is to be included within a given system and the interactive process and feedback of communication/information that occurs between that system and other related systems is described by the term *boundary*. Boundaries also form an important part of the interior of the family system, separating subsystems. Do the children belong in the spousal subsystem, for example?

Living systems, including families, are *hierarchically organized*, having several different levels. The concepts of hierarchy and boundary become particularly relevant when a therapist is working with family organization and reorganization (Aponte, 1976; Nichols, 1980). One of the significant issues that emerges with separation/divorce and the subsequent stages of single-parent living, remarriage, and stepfamily formation is the boundary question. What constitutes the family? Who is included? Not only the boundaries but also the power/authority hierarchy becomes disturbed under such circumstances. Particularly during periods of upset and maladjustment for one or both parents, dependency relationships may be reversed so that the child is called on to be a source of strength and support for the parent, sometimes even becoming a kind of "parent to the parent." Following divorce, families frequently become reorganized into what Ahrons (1979) has termed the "binuclear family," meaning that the children split their lives between the residences of their parents. When new live-in or marital partners for the parents enter the arena, the boundaries and hierarchies require further redefinition.

*Open systems and closed systems.* Systems theory holds that living systems are relatively open in nature. That is, they exchange information with other systems. Such interchange is necessary in order for the system to continue to function in an optimal or at least adequate fashion. Families that are too open and operate "centrifugally" so that the members define benefits and good things as coming from the exterior are disorganized or at least underorganized (Aponte, 1976). Families that are too closed and operate "centripetally" so that benefits and good things are viewed as existing only within the family unit are also dysfunctional.

*Feedback.* This concept means that systems have two channels of communication so that information is fed back into the system, thus affecting succeeding outputs from the system. One type of feedback (positive) increases change. Another type (negative) cancels errors and helps to decrease change and maintain a steady state in the system (Watzlawick, Beavin, & Jackson, 1967). Both of these concepts are useful tools and techniques for therapists in altering family systems.

*Equifinality.* This basic principle from General System Theory that similar outcomes may result from different origins (American Association for Marriage and Family Therapy, 1983; von Bertalanffy, 1974) differs from a simple A causes B, cause-and-effect relationship explanation for behavior. Equifinality not only has an explanatory function but also a practical use in therapy. If causality is circular rather than linear in nature, it becomes possible to intervene at any one of several points or stages, rather than having to work strictly on linear cause-effect factors. Many family systems therapists work without reference to history, for example. Others use the concept of equifinality as a basis for assuring clients that searching for "who is responsible" is futile and unnecessary.

*Communication.* All behavior is considered communication. One "cannot not communicate" (Watzlawick, Beavin, & Jackson, 1967) according to one of the axioms of communication theory that has become a staple of family systems approaches. Patterns of communication and the accompanying metacommunications (communications about how to receive and respond to the messages) define rules, roles, and relationships (including boundaries) within the family and between the family and external systems.

*Structure and process.* These two concepts overlap to some extent with some ideas already mentioned. Structure refers to the manner of organization of a system, the way the parts are arranged. Process is change over time and includes the current functioning and history of a system (Miller & Miller, 1980). The structure of a family will change across time.

The family life-cycle aspect of family development, for example, has become a widely used conceptual tool in family therapy (Carter & McGoldrick, 1980; Duvall, 1971; Howells, 1975; Nichols & Everett, 1986; Solomon, 1973).

The combination of structure and process becomes important for the therapist working with families undergoing the changes associated with separation and divorce. In recent decades many persons have become regularly affected by a series of structural changes in marital and family living. Rather than marrying and living in a marriage until parted by death, a significant number—although by no means the popularly cited "one in two marriages"—of couples go through a process that runs as follows: Dating/Courtship (with or without living together)—Engagement/Marriage—Marital Discord—Separation/Divorce—Single-Parent Living—Remarriage (again, with or without living together)—Stepfamily Living. The fact that this is a *process* for divorcing persons and their children and that they do not remain stuck in the early stage of tension, confusion, loss, and pain is pragmatically important for the individuals and for the therapist.

Separation, divorce, and remarriage all produce stress. Whether they develop to the stage of crisis for the family members depends on whether the family is able to use its available "resources and define the situation so as to resist systemic change and maintain family stability" (Ahrons & Rodgers, 1987, p. 44). An important aspect of this definition involves the recognition by the family that divorce signals a breakup of the marriage but a reorganization of the family.

## Usefulness of the Family Systems Approach

Family therapy in its various manifestations has not proven to be the panacea for schizophrenia that its early adherents thought it was. Used in combination with other modalities such as drug medication and family education (in the psychoeducational approach, e.g., Anderson, Reiss, & Hogarty, 1986), however, it still is effective and is a major form of treatment for the schizophrenias and related disorders.

Among the varied difficulties for which family therapy and working with the family system are used are anorexia nervosa (Andolfi, Angelo, Menghi, & Nicolo-Corigliano, 1983; Minuchin, Rosman, & Baker, 1978); drug abuse (Stanton, Todd, & Associates, 1982); alcoholism (Berenson, 1976); asthma (Liebman, Minuchin, Baker, & Rosman, 1976); sexual dysfunction (Jackman, 1976); marital problems (Beavers, 1985; Nichols, 1985; Sluzki, 1978), child and adolescent difficulties (Schaefer, Briemeister,

& Fitton, 1984; Mirkin & Koman, 1985); divorce and stepfamily issues (Bowen, 1978; Nichols, 1980, 1986); and a number of others.

*Appropriateness with Extraordinary Stress Situations*

Several factors already mentioned make a family systems approach especially appropriate for use with unusual and extraordinary family stress. Symptomatic behavior is considered reflective of family systems dislocations and difficulties and not merely as pathological reactions or problems of an individual. Problems arise in the system and not merely in the individual. Change in one part of the system affects other parts. Intervention with the various subsystems as indicated is possible with a family systems approach.

A family systems approach is particularly well suited for dealing with separation and divorce situations which, after all, involve the breakup of one family subsystem—the marriage or spousal subsystem—and the reorganization of the nuclear family system. Metaphorically, separation/divorce represent for many couples and their families a stream of prolonged emotional stress with alternating rapids and whirlpools. Ahrons (1983) emphasized the important point that clinicians can help families during the divorcing process only when they regard and assist client families to regard the divorced family as a continuing family system. While Ahrons focused on divorce as a normative, developmental change with some families, Sprenkle and Cyrus (1983) described it as a catastrophic source of upset when it is undesired and unexpected by one of the spouses. Both descriptions are accurate: separation and divorce are sources of family stress whether expected or unexpected.

The amount of stress occasioned by separation/divorce depends on several factors. These include not only whether the change is desired by the participants but also the stage in the family life cycle at which it occurs, for example. Beal (1980) has described the impact of divorce on families without children, with young children, with adolescents, and with adult children. The developmental issues for families and some tasks of the family life cycle when divorce occurs have been sketched by Carter and McGoldrick (1980) and Nichols (1988).

Working with the subsystems of the family experiencing separation/divorce is beginning to be emphasized in the family therapy literature. This includes a focus on helping divorced persons to develop their relationship as parents (Isaacs, Montalvo, & Abelsohn, 1986; Keshet & Mirkin, 1985) instead of their spousal relationship. Therapeutic work with troubled adolescents in divorced and remarried family systems has been described by Keshet and Mirkin (1985). Sibling relationships (Eno, 1985) and treatment of the sibling subsystem (Nichols, 1986), previously neglected, have received attention recently.

## GENERAL APPROACH TO TREATMENT/INTERVENTION

Response to the Blakes' request for professional assistance in coping with their stress took essentially the following form: The marital partners were seen together initially. That was the beginning of a process of family systems assessment, pertinent individual diagnosis, and treatment/intervention based as appropriately as possible on the initial and continuing assessment. Intervention started with the first appointment, along with the assessment work. The children were seen together as a group later in the therapeutic process and the parents were seen once solely as parents. Individual sessions were held with one spouse after the other discontinued contact. At all stages the therapist attempted to keep the entire family system as well as the individual members in view. This included taking into account pertinent factors and systemic dynamics of the extended family system.

Responsibility for the therapy was shared in some ways. Initial questions such as "What brings you in?" and "What are you looking for?" were not simply queries for information from George and Joan Blake, for example. They also reflected a perception of the therapist's role and the bias that the clients' definition of their situation and expression of what they were seeking was an important guide for the therapeutic relationship and process. The therapist took the responsibility for the initial and ongoing assessment but shared the responsibility for the goals and the outcome.

The main purposes of assessment in the early stages are determining: (1) the most useful way of defining and describing the problem/s bringing clients to therapy; (2) what needs to be altered in order to deal effectively with the stress and restore the family to better and more satisfactory functioning; and (3) the most appropriate and useful techniques of intervention/treatment for effecting the desired change. Matchmaking (Weltner, 1985), or securing a fit between family style and therapeutic style/type of intervention, is considered here an important part of the treatment process.

Essentially, the assessment method used with the Blakes consisted of a combination of interactive inquiry and observation of the process of the interview that has been described elsewhere (Nichols & Everett, 1986; Nichols, 1988). While a variety of techniques such as sculpting, role playing, simulated situations, and psychological testing were available, they were not used because they did not appear to offer any significant additions to what could be obtained from interviewing, observing, and interacting with the clients.

## ASSESSMENT METHODS

A loosely articulated set of guiding concepts directed the assessment of the Blake family.

### Family Development

Attention was given to ways in which the family development was being affected or disrupted. What were the normal life-cycle developmental tasks that it should be fulfilling? For the marital partners? For the children?

What normative developmental transitions (e.g., career changes, shifts in stages of child development), systemic shifts (e.g., subtle changes in the internal balance of relationships within the system, from whatever sources), or systemic traumas (e.g., death of a child, loss of a career position) were occurring (Nichols & Everett, 1986)? Other important questions were: How cohesive is the family? How effective and adequate is the family's communication? How is the family's functioning being affected by the changes and the stress that are occurring?

Adjustment to a new situation precedes adaptation, according to McCubbin and Patterson (1983). Selye (1956) made a distinction between "two fundamentally different kinds of adaptation." Developmental adaptation is a simple, adaptive reaction without qualitative change. Redevelopmental adaptation is required when an entity organized for one type of action is forced to readjust itself completely to an entirely different kind of activity. Separation/divorce require both types of adaptation. For example, a different kind of parenting is required by separation/divorce. (Keshet & Mirkin, 1985).

### Family Functioning

How well was the family functioning before the stressful changes occurred? A brief period of exploration with Joan and George Blake provided the working hypothesis that, on a range of families' systems from optimal, adequate, midrange, borderline, to severely disturbed (Beavers, 1976, 1977), their family had been functioning in a midrange-mixed fashion. Patterns of both centripetal and centrifugal forces had prevailed. George Blake felt that the children had been pulled in and that he had been neglected and extruded at times. Joan Blake did not deny that this had been the case during some periods in the past.

Colon's (1980) model of family functioning, as freely adapted, provided some support for applying a midrange label to the family. The family organization included limited contact with the extended family on one side and extensive contact that provided some support and help in absorbing stress on the other. There were continuing problem areas that provided stress. George and Joan's spousal unit was not clearly separate from the sibling subsystem. There was some evidence of shifting cross-generational collusions, for example. Disagreements and inconsistency in parenting prevailed, resulting in a lack of clear but flexible rules for the children. Communication was partial and communicational difficulties remained unresolved. Rather strong limits on expressing negative affect existed, particularly on the part of George, who did not tolerate negative expressions well from either wife or children. There were denials of loss, frozen reactions, and limited acceptance of losses—especially the loss of a physically intact nuclear family—with a consequence of partial mourning by family members. Physically and economically, the Blakes had more than adequate amounts of food, shelter, and clothing, and rather open choice in occupational options and career development. Social contact was extensive and had been active until after the separation.

How did the family get off track? That question in a systemic approach generally is not considered nearly so important as the question of how it can get back on track. How can desired change be secured?

*Genogram*

Construction of a genogram (Guerin & Pendagast, 1976; McGoldrick & Gerson, 1985) covering three generations and part of the fourth provided a quick way to get information on the Blakes and their family relationships. Much of the information for the genogram was already available from simple background information forms (Nichols, 1988) completed by George and Joan prior to the first session. Constructing and using the genogram provided more than a rapid route to understanding the Blakes' intergenerational relationships and their potential connections with the presenting problems. Using the genogram also helped in comprehending the resources the couple and their children might have available for support and adjustment, restructuring, and consolidation in trying to cope with their stress and crises (McCubbin & Patterson, 1983).

## Motivation

Marital discord, especially when mixed with the presence or threat of separation, generally creates a difficult and ambiguous situation at the beginning of therapy. That is, any one or more of a variety of patterns of motivation for coming to treatment may be found. As noted elsewhere (Nichols & Everett, 1986), clarifying the motivational picture with regard both to why the partners have sought therapy and what they wish to do regarding the marriage is an early clinical task.

Are both partners there for the same reasons? Gardner (1976) pointed out, for example, that the spouse who wishes to get out of the marriage but feels guilty about doing so may attempt to assuage the guilt feelings in four ways. He or she may offer the mate money through a favorable financial settlement, attempt to send her or him back home to the support of parents, or try to find the rejected partner either a lover or a therapist.

## Systemic Issues

With the Blakes the early assessment had to be concerned with discovering the systemic issues reflected in the separation and in George's reluctance to come to therapy. Had the marital difficulties progressed to a stage of irreversibility? Was George going to be available for therapy? Could a mutually satisfying relationship be established between the partners? How were the children being affected? What kinds of changes could be effected in the parental subsystem, whether George and Joan continued as a spousal subsystem or became a former-spousal subsystem?

Part of the answers to these basic questions were sought through direct questioning and probing and observation of how the partners responded and related to each other in the interview situation. The ways in which they dealt with straightforward and commonsense suggestions for coping with some management tasks with their sons and to a simple homework assignment of separately writing down what they expected from their marriage and their spouse (Sager, 1976) also provided useful data. What did their answers reveal? What were their declared intentions? What kinds of attitudes were manifested in their verbal and nonverbal responses? To use Scheflen's (1974) felicitous phrase, one seeks to determine "how behavior means" as well as what it means.

*Assessment Summary*

At the end of two sessions with the Blakes the clinician constructed a summary based on the kind of family assessment described by Nichols and Everett (1986, pp. 205–215). Briefly, this involved the following elements:

1. *Demographic profile.* This was outlined in a genogram.

2. *Family developmental history.* This traced the highlights and transitions briefly from the spouses' families of origin through the partners' dating/courtship, mate selection, marriage, family formation, and the birth and rearing of their children. Significant changes, disappointments, and losses were noted.

3. *Presenting complaint.* This was a concise statement of the reasons the clients gave for seeking service, the source of their referral, a summary of their prior psychotherapeutic contacts, and pertinent medical information including present physical problems (none) and medication (none).

4. *Summary of early clinical assessment.* This was a four-level summary involving:

    a. Clinical impressions of both spouses as individuals, including their individual development, maturity, personal integration, capacity for intimacy and interdependency, and ability to handle anxiety and stress. Sufficient individual diagnostic work was done to allow for relevant differential diagnosis and use of DSM-III categories (American Psychiatric Association, 1980).

    b. Clinical impressions of interpersonal dynamics within the spousal subsystem. Similar evaluations of the parent-child and sibling subsystems were made in subsequent sessions. These included impressions regarding internal and external boundaries and patterns of enmeshment/disengagement, coalitions, triangles, and parentification.

      One interesting and highly relevant feature of the Blake situation was the fact that although there was considerable stress extant, the children did not appear to be manifesting malignant individual symptomatology. Early exploration with Joan and George elicited their impressions that their sons had been minimally affected by the marital tensions, although Joan voiced once again her concern that the youngsters not be "messed up by our problems." She emphasized the differences between her approach of trying to provide guidelines and principles and George's "inconsistencies." He contrasted her "rigidity" with his "spontaneity." Subsequent checking disclosed that the boys were not reflecting the family difficulties externally through delinquent behavior, school failure, or other common problems manifested in children and adolescents. Inside the family their reactions were taking predictable paths as they reacted to differences in parenting between their parents. Externally, their reactions took more subtle forms, such as overinvolvement in athletics and social life.

   c. Clinical impressions of broad family system and transgenerational coalitions, myths, and secrets. These included George's abuse of alcohol.
   d. Clinical impressions of the family system's social network patterns. These included various social contacts, the family's residential, educational, vocational/career, and religious environments.

*5. Etiology and characterization of problems.* This included a short statement of the probable level of family conflict and the clinician's assessment of the sources and nature of the problems leading to the current stress. A clear distinction often needs to be made between the presenting complaints of the clients and the significant problems and conflicts discovered by the clinician. With the Blakes there was agreement between clients and clinician that the spousal subsystem was the family subsystem in which the basic conflict was located and that the conflict was chronic, although with acute features in the present. Contemporary situational influences were intensifying longstanding conflict that had been exacerbated earlier by normative developmental transitions (e.g., childbearing) and systemic shifts (e.g., Joan's entry into graduate school). Lurking in the background was the movement of the oldest child toward departure from the nest within two years.

The summary of the assessment provided the basis for formulating the initial treatment goals and strategies and for making limited predictions about treatment outcome.

It should be noted that the kinds of assessment of individuals and developmental factors covered here are not part of the treatment orientation of many family systems therapists.

## DIAGNOSIS AND TREATMENT

What did the initial assessment phase disclose? What did the data mean when the pieces were all pulled together and interpreted? How were the questions of problem definition, needed changes in the system, and appropriate treatment methods and techniques answered?

Assessment, once again, is reserved here for describing the clinician's attempts to understand the family system and its constituent parts and their functioning. Diagnosis and differential diagnosis refer to individuals.

All three major family subsystems—marital/spousal, parental, and sibling—were undergoing stress and in a typical systemic fashion were mutually affecting each other. The more powerful subsystems—the marital/spousal and the parental—were both the more obvious sources of the family stress and the more overtly disturbed as a result of the malfunctioning. The children were essentially operating more as loosely related individuals than as a strongly interactive and supportive sibling subsystem.

### The Spousal Subsystem

With regard to the marital partners, George and Joan came in with a perennial inability to solve problems in certain key areas of marital and family interaction. Their complaints were that they had troubles with children, money, and sex, as well as with their different ways of looking at the world. The clinician's understanding of the marital relationship was that the "complementarity" between the partners had shifted after a few years of marriage. Originally George had felt steadied by Joan's conservatism and need for structure. She had found his venturesomeness and willingness to take chances attractive. Eventually, George had come to feel restricted by Joan's "let's wait, don't go so fast" attitudes and was rejecting when she did not accept his ideas or plans without question. He was both "turned off and rejected" by her reluctance to be spontaneous and innovative sexually. She was troubled by his refusal to "really talk" with her and his "desire just to get people to like him and agree with him." Neither partner was meeting the emotional and personal needs of the other very well, their changes over the years having led to a disruption of the original complementarity rather than toward an intensification.

The Blakes' elaborations on their current problems with sex, money, children, and different approaches to life indicated that both the parental subsystem and the spousal subsystem were significantly affected. This necessitated making clinical judgments regarding the most effective and promising routes for altering the functioning of those subsystems.

Where should the focus be placed—on the marital subsystem, the parental subsystem, both subsystems simultaneously, or on the family system as a whole? and who should be seen in interviews and in what patterns? Several factors argued for giving primary attention to working with the couple. These included the facts that the original request for help and the initial complaint focused on the marriage, that the difficulties in parental behaviors appeared to be strongly intertwined with the marital relationship, and that the relatively minor difficulties manifested by the children evidently were reactive to the parental actions and interactions.

Examining the marriage on the basis of several pragmatic criteria— commitment, caring, communication, and conflict/compromise (Nichols & Everett, 1986)—revealed its problematic future. The chronicity of the difficulties in conflict/compromise functioning, the severe problems in communication consisting both of an inability to convey meanings adequately and significant disagreements when they did understand what the partner meant, and an erosion of caring through the last few years preceding the current separation all contributed to a murky commitment picture. George had engaged in a few "one-night stands" during a separation several years earlier. This time he acknowledged that he indicated that he had seen "somebody on a casual basis, now and then, nothing serious, when I first moved out."

Given the tenuous commitment in the marriage, there were questions as to what the couple would do regarding therapy. Would they continue past the first couple of sessions? If they did, would the treatment contain marital therapy or divorce therapy?

*The Couple: Diagnostic Impressions*

The early diagnostic impressions of George were mixed. His impulsiveness and directly expressed desires for gratification and absence of restraint were marked. As he put it, he did not like to examine behaviors, to analyze things, and set up "a lot of rules," but preferred to "be natural and spontaneous." This cluster was not strong enough to put him into an antisocial category. Subsequently, it was learned that George was developing patterns of alcohol abuse and perhaps dependency. There were questions about his sexual development, including possible gender identity issues, that were never answered. The diagnosis of Atypical Personality Disorder was used because a personality disorder was clearly present but there was not enough information to make a more specific designation (American Psychiatric Association, 1980).

Joan, with her mixture of reactive depression and anxiety, fit rather clearly into the category of Adjustment Disorder with Mixed Emotional Features (American Psychiatric Association, 1980). Her occasional depressed mood with feelings of hopelessness and crying alternated with periods of worry and nervousness. There were understandable reactions to the situation of separation and uncertainty in which she found herself and her marriage.

## The Children

All three children, as noted, were giving some signs that the parental discord and separation were affecting them, but there was little that could be labeled pathological in their behaviors. Jimmy, 12, the youngest son, was found to be manifesting an Uncomplicated Bereavement reaction (American Psychiatric Association, 1980) associated with the loss of his father from the home and compounded by anxieties about the future. Sean, 16, and Bobby, 14, recently had distanced themselves from both parents, but were not exhibiting behaviors that were markedly different from the norms of their age groups.

## TREATMENT GOALS

A major goal for the therapist was to help the family members deal with the painful experience of disruption caused by separation—and divorce if that was the outcome—so that they could cope with the stress and adapt to the changes effectively. Successful personal adaptation has been described by Mechanic (1974) as involving the capacity and skill to deal with social and environmental demands, adequate motivation to face the demands without being overwhelmed by anxiety and discomfort, and the ability to maintain an adequate psychological equilibrium that permits facing the external demands rather than focusing totally on the internal pain. Members of a family facing separation/divorce may require a considerable amount of help in reducing their feelings of pain and distress so that they can use their skills in coping with the difficult external conditions.

Another goal was to prevent, if possible, the stressor of separation from sweeping the family into a crisis of major proportions. It has been noted

(Ahrons & Rodgers, 1987; McCubbin & Patterson, 1983) that if a family can make certain short-term adjustments adequately, using its existing resources and defining the situation so as to resist change inside the family system, it may prevent crisis from occurring. Changing some of the boundaries and patterns of interaction, as well as some values, was viewed by the clinician as contributing to the achievement of this goal. The larger part of this goal was the assistance of the family in making appropriate adaptation to the eventual outcome of the separation.

When traumatic stress occurs, three sets of factors—the catastrophic event, the victim's coping ability, and the situational context—determine how severe or intense the effect will be on the victim(s) (Figley, 1983). Although George saw himself as the victim because of feelings of being neglected earlier, Joan and the children were the reactors to the separation, because George had taken the action against their wishes. His departure had been a shock but not a total surprise because it had come after several months of conflict and overt buildup of tension and was the second time that he had left home.

## Coping

Joan had a long pattern of coping with difficult situations behind her in the marriage and, earlier, in her family of origin, where she had been responsible for the care of her younger sister. In the marriage she had taken the lion's share of the guidance and nurturance of the boys. Her efforts to get George to spend more time with them had been one of the continuing sources of marital friction. His departure actually had caused him to "spend more time with them than he usually did," according to a statement by Joan which George did not contest. Joan's version of the "fight or flight" coping pattern typically involved fighting, facing the situation as "reasonably and rationally" as she could. In this situation she was still reacting with certain amounts of denial while she struggled to maintain equilibrium. She was supported in her efforts, as were the children, by the fact that their situational context was solid. The family's affluence and the knowledge that George would provide gave the other family members some sense of economic safety and well-being.

George's ways of coping were quite different. A business "plunger" and "risk-taker," he typically tended to deny that there was a problem. If there was one that he could not ignore, he did not wish "to analyze, but to do something." Doing something often meant changing his business, changing the personnel, changing the environment.

*Other Issues*

The treatment approach begun in the early assessment phase focused, as noted, primarily on the needs and wishes of the spouses and secondarily on their children. A key issue for the clinician was the ascertainment of the availability of both partners and their spousal and parental subsystems for change. Another was the question of whether the parental subsystem could be altered so that the children received a higher degree of consistency and predictability from the parents, regardless of whether the parents remained married or were divorced.

## TREATMENT

The Blakes were not significantly different from a number of other families seen in clinical practice today, except that their level of affluence was well above that of the average client family. George, age 40, could be described in contemporary parlance as "undergoing a midlife crisis." Joan, age 39, had dealt with her personal "Who am I?" and "Is this all there is?" identity and meaning crisis of her early to middle-thirties a few years earlier.

*Session 1: Spousal Subsystem*

The first session began with typical questions concerning the spouses' complaints and expectations of therapy. Although some information had been given by Joan during the telephone contact, such an approach was deemed appropriate for establishing a beginning working relationship with the spousal subsystem.

During the ensuing part of the session, Joan said, concerning her husband, "I'm not certain what he wants. He doesn't allow expressions of anger" (by himself or anyone around him). George responded that he thought that people should follow a "naturalness" path, that he preferred to do that rather than to be "always dealing with things analytically." He made it explicit that he did not wish to examine what had happened in his marriage or in his life generally.

Following an exploration of their initial complaints, the clinician "wondered" if things had "always been this way" and asked the couple to tell him about their earlier relationship—how they met, what attracted them to the other, how things went in their dating, courtship, and early marriage, and how things had changed over the years. A sense of the nature and process of their interaction over the years and their changing needs and desires was thus obtained quickly.

After a time the clinician pointed out, "You think and move differently. You have different styles." The couple concurred. George nodded in agreement with Joan's confirming statement that "he's intuitive and a risk-taker; I'm conservative and move slowly. I don't move until I have all the facts, while George is a real risk-taker; he likes that." She proceeded to compliment his business acumen and success as an attorney and real estate investor and developer.

Such clinical efforts to "normalize" the differences helped to open the way for beginning to explore what the partners desired. With regard to expectations, George said, "I want somebody to share with. I feel like if I share with Joan there will be conflict." Her response was that he did not wish to deal with differences at all, that he wanted everything to run smoothly, his way, and that he would do anything to get people to like him and to agree with him. Joan added, "It's important for him to take care of the family economically," meaning that this was his only concern, rather than relating personally and emotionally to family members.

Definite differences between the partners emerged with regard to how they wished to rear the children and had tried to rear them. Joan indicated that she tried to follow principles with them and to be consistent. She added, "But he doesn't believe in principles, just in responding spontaneously to each situation. I feel that this causes inconsistency." George observed that he just wished to respond "naturally." They were able to laugh at the clinician's observation that "you went to different schools of child rearing," and then to consider calmly and with reasonable cooperativeness how they might jointly help their boys cope with the separation.

At the end of the first session the partners were given a homework assignment of thinking about and writing down their expectations for the marriage and for themselves and their spouse in the marriage.

*Session 2: The Spousal Subsystem*

Joan returned with a written list of expectations. George said that he had not written anything down, but that they had problems with sex and money as well as children. He indicated that he wanted Joan to be more titillating, more exciting, more playful, and more desirous of having sexual relations. He capsuled his view of the problem by saying, "She has a lower sex drive than I. It's as if she's just doing it."

Joan responded that she could not "simply throw switches" and become immediately active and responsive. "I need something [in terms of communication and exchange of affection] outside of the bedroom as well."

The therapy focused for a time on the changes that could be made in relating to each other. A portion of the second part of the session was devoted to the construction of a genogram and a brief look at the transitions that had affected their relationship.

## Session 3: The Spousal Subsystem

An "intimacy dance" ensued between the second and third sessions. Joan made some reconciliatory moves in George's direction. George withdrew and there was no contact between them for several days. Joan's explanation was that "I got too close, and he panicked."

George responded, "I'm afraid of settling for a less-than-satisfactory relationship. I haven't had a lover and a sex partner; I've had a friend and companion."

"He has me in a mold. I haven't been like that for a long time."

"She doesn't want or like sex."

"That's not true. When I try, he backs off. I don't know how to please him."

George came back with the statements, "I feel like things have to be done perfectly, like she wants them done. I have felt like sex was withheld when I wasn't good or we don't agree."

Exploration of how they felt they handled disagreements elicited Joan's claim, "He feels like you have to accept the other's position 100% or reject it [totally]."

"Well, it's become 100–0 over the last few years," retorted George.

At this point, as well as at others, the therapist redirected the conversation, suggesting that they speak directly to each other and make "I" statements about what they wanted changed. Explicit efforts initiated by the therapist to give them some experience in successful negotiation of differences succeeded in gaining some agreement on commonly held goals and values.

Following some successful work in clarification, Joan then made a decisive move, saying to George, "I don't feel you're committed to me. You may not be seeing her right now, but you've at least got your girlfriend on the back burner. You've lied to me about your relationship with her every step of the way. Unless you deal with me in good faith and end that relationship and give me a chance, and I mean work with me on our relationship, we don't have a chance. I'm trying as hard as I can, and I'll try to do even more, but I can't do it by myself."

George agreed after some discussion to sever any connections with a 25-year-old lawyer employed by his firm, although without admitting that a personal relationship existed with her.

*Session 4: The Spousal Subsystem*

George came back to the fourth appointment two weeks later to say that he had found the young woman a job with another law firm. He added, "Things have been going well. Joan could not be trying any more than she is, but I just don't want to be married any longer. It's not her fault." To his wife, he added, "I won't promise you that I won't see her anymore."

At that juncture George dropped out of treatment. He was amiable and friendly with the therapist and willing for Joan to continue. The indications were that he wanted her and the children to be safely attached to therapeutic support. Evidently, by providing them with generous financial support and a therapist, George was trying to make it easier for himself to make the separation permanent and get free to conduct both his personal affairs and his business as he wished.

*Session 5: The Parental Subsystem*

George was seen once more with Joan in connection with parenting issues. It was clearly emphasized that the joint session was concerned with their coparental tasks and relationship and not with their (broken) marital relationship (Ahrons, 1979). With help, they worked out some different patterns for visitation, handling holidays, and related matters. With respect to the discipline and guidance, they continued to disagree, George wishing to be "natural" and "spontaneous" and Joan desiring to rear the children by "sound principles." They also were given some assistance in accepting the idea that their sons could adapt to "different rules in different households," provided the parents were able to accept the fact that there were differences and not try to compel the children to make choices or take sides.

*Sessions 6 and 7: Individual*

Treatment focus then shifted to Joan and the children. She was seen individually both for her personal needs and as a representative of the parental subsystem. She was still finding it hard to accept George's decision and she verbalized feelings of guilt and failure. This began to change when twice, apparently by accident, she encountered George in public places in the company of the young lawyer with whom she had suspected he was having an affair. She then, because "I had to know for certain," drove over to George's apartment and found the woman's automobile there and witnessed the pair leaving the apartment together fairly early in the morning.

*Sessions 8–10: Individual*

Over the next three sessions Joan went through cycles of anger and ambivalence. Finally, she decided, "It looks as if George is in control and doing things the way he wants to do them and has no desire to change." She recapitulated what had transpired, including his actions prior to leaving home, and ended up with "the bottom line." "That was," she said, "when I finally said, 'Give up your girlfriend,' and he said, 'I don't want to be married anymore.' "

Joan decided to accept the fact that the marriage was over and filed for divorce. Part of the therapy during that stage was a psychoeducational approach that consisted of explaining the bereavement and loss process to Joan, the stages and reactions that persons typically go through when they lose someone. This was done with the overt recognition that "knowing what is happening and is about to happen doesn't necessarily lessen the pain or make it any easier to accept, but it can keep you from making the process worse, and it *may* make it easier to cope with the situation." Attention was also given to Joan's concerns about the children and their reactions.

*Sessions 11 and 12: The Sibling Subsystem*

The three boys were seen together on two occasions at this stage. Reiterating a point made to them in preparation for the session by their parents, the therapist indicated that their parents wished them to have the opportunity to talk about the separation and anything else that they wished to talk about with a professional person who was outside the family but who knew the family and was interested in being helpful.

Three outcomes of the sibling subsystem sessions were (1) exploration/clarification among the siblings of what they understood and felt regarding the marital breakup and how they were dealing with the situation, (2) the opening of more communication among the boys, and (3) the provision of some short-term support for the youngsters (Nichols, 1986).

This intervention was being conducted concurrently with efforts to help the available and custodial parent deal with the children's needs.

*Sessions 13–20: Individual*

The last eight sessions included one individual session each with two of the children who wished to deal with personal concerns and six meetings with Joan. Her coping attempts and efforts to move toward adaptation were disrupted on two occasions by actions of her husband that demonstrated again to her that he did not "care anything about anybody or anything except doing what he wants." Gradually, she settled down and resumed her graduate work after dropping out for a quarter during the roughest period. She began to secure a firm grasp of the fact that what she was going through was a process where things would continue to change over time. Some hope and lessening of discouragement were evidenced in Joan's periodic ability to point to how she was doing better and was feeling less stressed.

The siblings began to function much more as a mutually supportive family subsystem than they had previously. Of course, they still had their separate friends and pursuits outside of the home. Conflict between the middle boy and his mother decreased as he found that he could relate to both parents and did not have to make a choice or take sides between them. Adjustments in the time spent with his father, including the occasional opportunity to get some one-on-one time, lessened the youngest boy's feelings of loss. He did do some crying and received support from his brothers, who also acknowledged that they were troubled by the separation and forthcoming divorce but were accepting the changes.

Some attention was given to helping both the children and Joan adjust to the changes that had occurred in their interactions with the extended families. Joan was no longer included in holiday gatherings with the Blakes, the children going with their father. She began to work on new social relationships, retaining in a new form some friendships that she formerly had shared with George. He reportedly dropped all of their former social relationships except those that were directly connected with his law practice/real estate business.

Termination occurred with the understanding that there were some predictable stages of adjustment coming in the future for both the adults and the children (Kaslow, 1981; Kessler, 1975; Nichols, 1988; Wallerstein & Kelly, 1980). At the time of termination, the possibility of remarriage and the formation of a remarried family or families was not on the horizon.

## DISCUSSION

Several things contributed to the forms of interventions used with the Blakes. These included the nature of the family crisis, the strengths and difficulties manifested by the family system and the family members, and the motivations of the spouses, among others.

With respect to the nature of the crisis, the separation which eventually became solidified into divorce action came from inside the family, extended directly to all family members, came on gradually instead of cataclysmically and became long-term in duration, was of moderate intensity, and consisted of a stressor from human-made causes that could be reasonably well predicted so that the family came to believe that it could be controlled (Lipman-Blumen, 1975).

The midrange functioning and the strengths of the family were such that attention could be given to the establishment of appropriate boundaries between the subsystems by the methods chosen. Interventions, in Weltner's (1985) terms, included focusing on the problems of parent-child relations fairly directly, clarifying the "ideal" family structure in conformity with family expectations, and seeking generational clarity. Differentiation of family members and bridging of cutoffs (e.g., between the mother and the middle child) were sought (Weltner, 1985).

Motivation was not present to achieve a workable kind of commitment and intimacy between the spouses. The tenuous motivation of George regarding therapy especially made it essential that this factor be addressed without delay.

### Early Interventions

Family therapists were once described as tending to be either conductors or reactors in relation to the family system (Beels & Ferber, 1972). The distinction is essentially an artificial one for many family therapists, as the differentiation between assessment and intervention similarly is not sharp and definitive. The role taken by the therapist with the Blakes was a mixture, although tending to the reactive side and falling somewhere to the right of a pure consultive approach (Wynne, McDaniel, & Weber, 1986). At the same time that an effort was being made to elicit and delineate the presenting complaints/problems, the clinician was trying to establish a working therapeutic relationship with the Blakes.

The therapeutic approach was actively aimed at getting the Blakes involved in taking responsibility for their situation from the beginning. Redirection of communication and allowing the spouses to address each other rather than the therapist were used from the first session onward. Attempts were made to "normalize" the behaviors and difficulties that they were describing rather than casting them into a pathological framework.

The focus was put on delineating their situation as clearly as possible and trying to see what could be changed. Both the homework assignment of writing out their expectations and the construction of a genogram helped in this delineation. Efforts were made to get them involved in negotiating their differences, beginning with the comparatively less sensitive areas of their interaction and relationship.

Starting in such a manner has the advantages of either resulting in some positive change quickly or elucidating resistances quickly. This focus on change gave George what he said he wanted. It also precipitated another crisis. George could no longer blame his absence from home on Joan's indifference to him once she actively sought to relate to him in an intimate and committed fashion. Similarly, he could not maintain the fiction that nothing was really wrong, that things would be all right if his wife would only stop getting upset. The attempt to work with them therapeutically was abortive in part because it cracked the husband's facade of denial. When the wife demonstrated a willingness and ability to provide what he said he wanted, it made it impossible for the husband to continue drifting and avoiding a decision about getting out of a limbo situation in which he was "married but not married." The focus on change in family therapy stands in sharp contrast to the attainment of insight sought in psychoanalytic therapy. Looking for "why" things were the way they were instead of "what" could be done about the situation would have been counterproductive. For one thing, it had already been attempted by another therapist. Additionally, George's refusal to examine behaviors in depth, combined with his quick recitation of a litany of complaints about Joan's neglect, was too potent a resistive mixture to overcome. Joan also was faced with the need to demonstrate commitment to her mate as part of their reciprocal interaction.

Both George and Joan were given support and their personal privilege and responsibility for their decisions were underscored. For example, when Joan was pushing for a decision and commitment on George's part, attention was given to clarifying what each wanted, in an effort to reduce the feelings of coercion.

*Shifts in Intervention*

After it became apparent to both of the spouses that they were not going to work together on the marital relationship, it became possible to focus more explicitly on the parental and sibling subsystems and more necessary to deal with individual subsystems. The family life-cycle tasks of child rearing provided a guide for working with the partners once the transition was made to focusing on their coparental roles and relationship. Emphasis on the boundaries between generations was a significant part of this endeavor. As the family continued with its reorganization process, it appeared that George and Joan would be able to deal with their children reasonably well as "cooperative colleagues," rather than as "perfect pals," "angry associates," "fiery foes," or a "dissolved duo" (Ahrons & Rodgers, 1987).

Psychoeducational work was done not only with the couple as parents but also with individuals in the family system. As the permanence of the separation was affirmed, information on personal reactions to loss was used with both the wife-mother and with the children. Experience has indicated that comprehending what is happening and being able to predict what is coming help with the process of coping and adapting with change occasioned by separation/divorce (Nichols, 1977).

Sibling subsystem therapy in family systems reorganization has been described elsewhere (Nichols, 1986) as either adjunctive to the main family therapy or as the major therapeutic focus. Here it was adjunctive and brief. The family systems principle of maintaining the integrity of subsystems (i.e., seeing the children as a unit and not splitting one of them off to be seen with a parent) was followed with some success. Difficulties between the middle boy and his mother, for example, were picked up on as part of more general parent-child interaction when they were mentioned in a sibling session, rather than being marked out for separate treatment. The other boys helped their brother talk about and begin to deal with the difficulties, which were mainly fairly normative developmental issues. The solidification of the sibling subsystem that began in the sessions continued to help with the maintenance of appropriate subsystem boundaries after the conclusion of therapy.

Interventions in the last several sessions were aimed essentially at helping Joan to cope not only as a parent but also as an individual. There were brief crises when she was finally forced to face the fact that George had already emotionally divorced her and was continuing his relationship with the other woman. Otherwise, the emphasis was placed on helping her to obtain social support from available family members and friends, to form new social relationships as appropriate, and to get back on track with school. Relabeling, providing opportunity for some affective release and control, and coaching were among the other techniques used.

Always, the emphasis was on the fact that what was occurring was a process of family reorganization, that certain things would continue, and that others would come to an end and be replaced by new events and situations.

## CONCLUSION

One example of a family systems approach to a common family crisis — marital disruption leading to separation and divorce — has been described. This case was chosen because it permitted the illustration of intervention and clinical work with all subsystems of a nuclear family as it underwent transformation. It was also chosen because separation and divorce and the changes they bring are frequently encountered in clinical practice. Situations in which one partner has already emotionally divorced the other but does not wish to deal with the results of acknowledging that reality are also common.

The relative mildness of the tension between the partners and the containment of most of the difficulties between them so that the children were only moderately affected are much less common. A number of external factors that do not require mention here had contributed to the development of the current status of the marital relationship. The chronicity of the difficulties and the erosion of caring over several years had given the participants a considerable amount of opportunity to begin anticipating the possibility of an eventual end to the marriage. The intellect, sophistication, and abundance of economic resources of the spouses also assisted them in dealing with the situation in a "civilized" manner.

Had the family's adaptation been less effective and the level of pathology more severe, a family systems approach would have been used nevertheless. The intervention techniques might have been altered and a more authoritarian therapeutic stance employed. The principle of fitting the treatment techniques to the family, instead of fitting the family to the treatment techniques, would have been followed, however, as it was in this case.

The matchmaking schema of Weltner (1985) — in which different forms of intervention are considered appropriate for different levels of pathology or family organization and functioning — needs to be tested further in clinical practice.

Even more attention needs to be paid to family subsystems than was illustrated in this case, whether the source of stress is separation/divorce or some other disruptive force in the family system. Just as stepfamilies represent "a growing family therapy challenge" (Nichols, 1980), so the sibling subsystem (where one exists) represents a potentially positive resource that is underutilized in many therapy situations.

This case did not illustrate the kind of extensive supportive involvement of extended family members, including both the parents of the parents and the siblings of the parents, that frequently plays a significant role in family systems therapy. The absence of such members on Joan's side — only a stepmother was available, both parents being dead and the lone sibling overseas as a Protestant missionary — and George's departure from treatment limited extended family involvement.

A systems approach also can and often does involve working with other important systems that impinge on and interact with the family. School, work systems, church, and other parts of the community network may be addressed as important adjunctive systems that affect the way individuals live and function.

## REFERENCES

Ahrons, C. (1979). The binuclear family: Two households, one family. *Alternative Life-styles, 2,* 499–515.

Ahrons, C. (1983). Divorce: Before, during, and after. In H. I. McCubbin & C. R. Figley (Eds.), *Stress and the family, Volume 1: Coping with normative transitions* (pp. 102–115). New York: Brunner/Mazel.

Ahrons, C., & Rodgers, R. H. (1987). *Divorced families: A multidisciplinary developmental view.* New York: W. W. Norton.

American Association for Marriage and Family Therapy (1983). *Family therapy glossary.* Washington, DC: Author.

American Psychiatric Association (1980). *Diagnostic and statistical manual of mental disorders (3rd ed.).* Washington, DC: Author.

Anderson, C. M., Reiss, D. J., & Hogarty, G. E. (1986). *Schizophrenia and the family.* New York: Guilford.

Andolfi, M., Angelo, C., Menghi, P., & Nicolo-Corigliano, A. M. (1983). *Behind the family mask.* New York: Brunner/Mazel.

Aponte, H. (1976). Underorganization in the poor family. In P. J. Guerin (Ed.), *Family therapy: Theory and practice* (pp. 432–448). New York: Gardner Press.

Beal, E. W. (1980). Separation, divorce, and single-parent families. In E. A. Carter & M. McGoldrick (Eds.), *The family life cycle: A framework for family therapy* (pp. 241–264). New York: Gardner Press.

Beavers, W. R. (1976). A theoretical basis for family evaluation. In J. M. Lewis, W. R. Beavers, J. T. Gossett, & V. A. Phillips, *No single thread: Psychological health in family systems* (pp. 46–82). New York: Brunner/Mazel.

Beavers, W. R. (1977). *Psychotherapy and growth: A family systems perspective.* New York: Brunner/Mazel.

Beavers, W. R. (1985). *Successful marriage: A family systems approach to couples therapy.* New York: W. W. Norton.

Beels, C., & Ferber, A. (1972). What family therapists do. In A. Ferber, M. Mendelsohn, & A. Napier (Eds.), *The book of family therapy* (pp. 168–232). New York: Science House.
Berenson, D. (1976). Alcohol and the family system. In P. J. Guerin (Ed.), *Family therapy: Theory and practice* (pp. 284–297). New York: Gardner Press.
Bowen, M. (1978). *Family therapy in clinical practice.* New York: Jason Aronson.
Carter, E. A., & McGoldrick, M. (Eds.) (1980). *The family life cycle: A framework for family therapy.* New York: Gardner Press.
Colon, F. (1980). The family life cycle of the multiproblem poor family. In E. A. Carter & M. McGoldrick (Eds.), *The family life cycle: A framework for family therapy* (pp. 343–381). New York: Gardner Press.
Duvall, E. M. (1971). *Marriage and family development (4th ed.).* Philadelphia: J. B. Lippincott.
Eno, M. M. (1985). Sibling relationships in families of divorce. *Journal of Psychotherapy and the Family, 1* (3), 139–156.
Figley, C. R. (1983). Catastrophes: An overview of family reactions. In C. R. Figley & H. I. McCubbin (Eds.), *Stress and the family, Volume 2: Coping with catastrophe* (pp. 3–20). New York: Brunner/Mazel.
Gardner, R. A. (1976). *Psychotherapy with children of divorce.* New York: Jason Aronson.
Guerin, P. J., & Pendagast, E. G. (1976). Evaluation of family system and genogram. In P. J. Guerin (Ed.), *Family therapy: Theory and practice* (pp. 450–464). New York: Gardner Press.
Gurman, A. S., & Kniskern, D. P. (1981). Integrative family therapy: Toward the development of an interpersonal approach. In S. H. Budman (Ed.), *Forms of brief therapy* (pp. 415–457). New York: Guilford.
Howells, J. G. (1975). *Principles of family psychiatry.* New York: Brunner/Mazel.
Isaacs, M. B., Montalvo, B., & Abelsohn, D. (1986). *The difficult divorce: Therapy for children and families.* New York: Basic Books.
Jackman, L. S. (1976). Sexual dysfunction and the family system. In P. J. Guerin (Ed.), *Family therapy: theory and practice* (pp. 298–308). New York: Gardner Press.
Kaslow, F. W. (1981). Divorce and divorce therapy. In A. S. Gurman & D. P. Kniskern (Eds.), *Handbook of family therapy* (pp. 662–696). New York: Brunner/Mazel.
Keshet, J. K., & Mirkin, M. P. (1985). Troubled adolescents in divorced and remarried families. In M. P. Mirkin & S. L. Koman (Eds.), *Handbook of adolescents and family therapy* (pp. 273–293). New York: Gardner Press.
Kessler, S. (1975). *The American way of divorce.* Chicago: Nelson-Hall.
Liebman, R., Minuchin, S., Baker, L., & Rosman, B. L. (1976). The role of the family in the treatment of chronic asthma. In P. J. Guerin (Ed.). *Family therapy: Theory and practice* (pp. 309–324). New York: Gardner Press.
Lipman-Blumen, J. (1975). A crisis framework applied to macrosociological family changes: Marriage, divorce, and occupational trends associated with World War II. *Journal of Marriage and the Family, 3,* 889–902.
McCubbin, H. I., & Patterson, J. M. (1983). Family transitions: Adaptation to stress. In H. I. McCubbin & C. R. Figley (Eds.), *Stress and the family, Volume 1: Coping with normative transitions* (pp. 5–25). New York: Brunner/Mazel.
McGoldrick, M., & Gerson, R. (1985). *Genograms in family assessment.* New York: W. W. Norton.
Mechanic, D. (1974). Social structure and personal adaptation: Some neglected dimensions. In G. V. Cochlo, D. A. Hamburg, & J. E. Adams (Eds.), *Coping and adaptation* (pp. 32–44). New York: Basic Books.
Miller, J. G. (1969). Living systems: Basic concepts. In W. Gray, F. S. Duhl, & N. R. Rizzo (Eds.), *General systems theory and psychiatry* (pp. 51–133). Boston: Little, Brown.
Miller, J. G., & Miller, J. L. (1980). The family as a system. In C. K. Hofling & J. M. Lewis (Eds.), *The family: Evaluation and treatment* (pp. 141–184). New York: Brunner/Mazel.
Minuchin, S., Rosman, B. L., & Baker, L. (1978). *Psychosomatic families: Anorexia nervosa in context.* Cambridge, MA: Harvard University Press.

Mirkin, M. P., & Koman, S. L. (Eds.) (1985). *Handbook of adolescents and family therapy.* New York: Gardner Press.

Nichols, W. C. (1977). Divorce and remarriage education. *Journal of Divorce, 1,* 153–161.

Nichols, W. C. (1980). Stepfamilies: A growing family therapy challenge. In L. R. Wolberg & M. L. Aronson (Eds.), *Group and family therapy 1980* (pp. 335–344). New York: Brunner/Mazel.

Nichols, W. C. (1985). A differentiating couple: Some transgenerational issues in marital therapy. In A. S. Gurman (Ed.), *Casebook of marital therapy* (pp. 199–228). New York: Guilford.

Nichols, W. C. (1986). Sibling subsystem therapy in family system reorganization. *Journal of Divorce, 9* (3), 13–31.

Nichols, W. C. (1988). *Marital therapy: An integrative approach.* New York: Guilford.

Nichols, W. C., & Everett, C. A. (1986). *Systemic family therapy: An integrative approach.* New York: Guilford.

Sager, C. J. (1976). *Marriage contracts and couples therapy.* New York: Brunner/Mazel.

Schaefer, C. E., Briemeister, J. M., & Fitton, M. E. (1984). *Family therapy techniques for problem behavior of children and teenagers.* San Francisco: Jossey-Bass.

Scheflen, A. E. (1974). *How behavior means.* New York: Anchor/Doubleday.

Schultz, S. J. (1984). *Family systems: An integration.* New York: Jason Aronson.

Selye, H., (1956). *The stress of life.* New York: McGraw-Hill.

Sluzki, C. E. (1978). Marital therapy from a systems perspective. In T. J. Paolino & B. S. McCrady (Eds.), *Marriage and marital therapy* (pp. 366–394). New York: Brunner/Mazel.

Solomon, M. A. (1973). A developmental, conceptual premise for family therapy. *Family Process, 12,* 179–188.

Sprenkle, D. H., & Cyrus, C. L. (1983). Abandonment: The stress of sudden divorce. In C. R. Figley & H. I. McCubbin (Eds.), *Stress and the family, Volume 2: Coping with catastrophe* (pp. 53–75). New York: Brunner/Mazel.

Stanton, M. D., Todd, T. C., & Associates (1982). *The family therapy of drug abuse and addiction.* New York: Guilford.

Steinglass, P. (1978). The conceptualization of marriage from a systems perspective. In T. J. Paolino & B. S. McCrady (Eds.), *Marriage and marital therapy* (pp. 298–365). New York: Brunner/Mazel.

von Bertalanffy, L. (1968). *General system theory.* New York: Braziller.

von Bertalanffy, L. (1974). General system theory and psychiatry. In S. Arieti (Ed.), *American handbook of psychiatry, Vol. I (2nd ed.).* New York: Basic Books.

Wallerstein, J. S., & Kelly, J. B. (1980). *Surviving the breakup: How children and parents cope with divorce.* New York: Basic Books.

Watzlawick, P., Beavin, J., & Jackson, D. D. (1967). *Pragmatics of human communication.* New York: W. W. Norton.

Weltner, J. S. (1985). Matchmaking: Choosing the appropriate therapy for families at various levels of pathology. In M. P. Mirkin & S. L. Koman (Eds.), *Handbook of adolescents and family therapy* (pp. 39–50). New York: Gardner Press.

Wynne, L. C., McDaniel, S. H., & Weber, T. L. (1986). *Systems consultation: A new perspective for family therapy.* New York: Guilford.

# 4

# A Cognitive-Behavioral Approach

## ARTHUR FREEMAN and FLORA ZAKEN-GREENBERG

*The Williams family was self-referred by the mother, Mrs. Jane Williams. The reason given for the referral was the acting-out behavior of the 17-year-old son, Ian. Ian was reported to lose his temper easily and when he did, to be "uncontrollable." He had pulled a knife on his mother and 16-year-old sister, Dianne, ordered his sister around, demanded that she do things for him such as making him meals, and physically pushed her when she did not listen to him.*

*Mr. and Mrs. Williams had been separated for approximately three years but had not been able to negotiate a final termination of the marriage. Mr. Williams refused to have anything to do with his wife, and therefore had refused to become involved in the therapy. The relationship between the parents was vituperative. Mrs. Williams had taken Mr. Williams to court twice for failing to make his required child support payments. As a consequence, Mr. Williams was jailed on one occasion. The custody arrangement was that the children spend every second weekend with their father. The children both reported that they enjoyed these visits.*

*Mrs. Williams believed that parents "should be best friends with their children." She described her relationship with Dianne as good, but not her relationship with Ian. In spite of her report of a close relationship with Dianne, Mrs. Williams said that her children would not listen to her when she asked them to do something. Ian was worse than Dianne in this regard. The children appeared to listen to Mr. Williams out of fear. Mrs. Williams refused to "intimidate" the children in the same way.*

*She was reluctant to use punishment to force them to obey. She would like them to obey her because they loved her and cared for her. She stated, "Ian is like his father. He doesn't listen to me. He ignores me and is rude to me. He often mocks me. Everyone takes advantage of me because I'm such a nice person." She insisted that the problem was Ian's and that he needed individual therapy to solve his acting-out problem.*

Cognitive Therapy (CT), first developed for the treatment of depression (Beck, 1976; Beck, Rush, Shaw, & Emery, 1979), has over the past decade been applied to a broad range of clinical populations and clinical problems. CT has been utilized with great success in the treatment of stress and anxiety (Beck & Emery, 1985; Freeman & Simon, in press; Freeman & Ludgate, 1988); eating disorders (Edgette & Prout, in press; Fairburn, 1985; Garner & Bemis, 1985); personality disorders (Beck & Freeman, in press; Freeman, 1988; Freeman & Leaf, in press); substance abuse (Glantz, 1987; Glantz & McCourt, 1983); and suicidal behavior (Bedrosian, 1986; Freeman & White, in press; Freeman & Reinecke, in press). CT has further been applied to the treatment of couples (Abrams, 1983; Epstein, 1983; Epstein & Baucom, in press a, b); sexual enhancement of couples (Walen & Wolfe, 1983); the elderly (Glantz, in press; Hussian, 1987); families (Teichman, 1986, 1987, in press); children and adolescents (DiGiuseppe, 1987, in press; Grossman & Freet, 1987); and medical problems (Kinchla, 1987; Weinberg, 1987; Worden, 1987). Although CT is generally thought of as a short-term outpatient treatment modality, it has been applied to psychiatric inpatient groups (Bowers, in press; Freeman & Greenwood, 1987; Perris, Rodhe, Palm, et al., 1987; Schrodt & Wright, 1987). Given the demonstrated effectiveness of CT, its broad clinical usage, and its inherent good sense, it is an ideal model to utilize with the complex and often difficult stressors experienced in families.

The present chapter will attempt to outline the theory, conceptualizations, strategies, and techniques of a CT approach to treating stress in families. The foremost reason for the family as the focus of therapy is that the presented problem(s) may generally involve several members of a family and their interaction (e.g., physical or emotional abuse of elderly parents by children, abuse of children by parents, issues of child management, demonstrated needs for proper and appropriate parenting, general relationship issues). Often, when a family presents itself in the therapist's office it is because of legal remand, school referral, or referral by a pastoral counselor or clergyman. These referrals often come when problems have become severe or traumatic, rather than at the start of a crisis or conflict.

Because of the general crisis nature of the presenting problems, the therapist attempts to intervene in the family dynamics in a direct manner.

By involving the family members in the therapeutic process, the therapist can implement interventions more quickly, strengthen collaboration and mediate stigmatization. The cognitive therapist does not adhere to a classical *family systems* model, which implies that the issues that beset a family are generated within the family system and, therefore, can be best treated within the system. Frequently, certain members of a family need treatment or information. In other situations, an entire family requires treatment.

When a family is having difficulty coping with the stress associated with the next phase in the family life cycle, or when a family crisis has disrupted the normal progression through the family life cycle, it would be appropriate to engage the family in the therapeutic endeavor. The Williams family (fictitious name), referred to at the beginning of the chapter, is an example of a family that had not been able to cope with the stressors of normative transitions. They continued to experience conflict and ongoing adjustment difficulty, without the apparent resources to resolve or to mitigate the difficulties. Utilizing this family as a case example, we will demonstrate the applications of Cognitive Therapy to the treatment of a dysfunctional family.

## THE WILLIAMS FAMILY

Initially, Mrs. Williams tended to monopolize the family interview. When questions were directed to the children, she often responded. While very friendly, outgoing, and smiling at first, Mrs. Williams became visibly sad and depressed as the topic of the children's misbehavior was discussed. She was upset that the children "take advantage of my good nature" and stated, "They don't love me or care for me. If they did, they would prove it by being good." At several points in the interview, Mrs. Williams challenged the therapist to "fix these children." There was significant avoidance behavior in that Mrs. Williams refused to discuss any problems that she might have had other than managing the children.

Ian did very well in school. Mrs. Williams stated, "Ian is so intelligent that he can outsmart and manipulate anyone." Ian said that he thought that his mother asked too much of him and was unfair and unreasonable in her requests. Further, he felt that he was unfairly blamed for everything. When asked for an example, he offered the following: "My mother asked me to help with the spring cleaning on a Saturday. I had already made plans to go to the movies with my friends. Then she got real angry and started in about how I didn't care about her or my sister. The second thing has to do with my sister. She comes into my room and uses my stereo without my permission. She's broken it twice. I told her my room was off-limits and when she doesn't listen, I push her out. She (mother) defends her and yells at me for getting angry." Ian also said that Mrs. Williams complained about the father and said mean things about him: "She always questions us about what dad says, does, etc."

Initially, Ian was quiet and unresponsive while his mother spoke. When directly questioned, he was cooperative, willing, and eager to air his complaints. When questions were directed to his sister, he would answer for her or make comments about how spoiled he thought she was.

Diane appeared to be quiet and nervous. She spoke little during the session. She would respond to questions when asked, but did not elaborate. She would, however, respond with anger when Ian pushed her around. She reacted to Ian's statements by saying that she was angry with Ian because he bossed her around as if she were a slave: "When I'm watching television, he will tell me to get him something to eat, and he'll get furious if I don't get it for him." She agreed with her mother that Ian was the problem. She described Ian as being like their father: "I'm afraid of their anger." Given that she generally showed little emotion, she became quite angry when Ian described her as the villain, at which point Mrs. Williams came to Dianne's defense and Ian backed off and became quiet while his mother attacked him.

*Summary of Problems*

Ian's mood was a mixture of anger and frustration related to the injustices that he thought he was suffering. His general response was to feel attacked because of his perception (and the reality) that the women in the house were ganging up on him. He felt that he had to defend his position as the male of the house. Ian seemed to follow the discussion but from an observer role. He was generally reluctant to volunteer and participate in the discussion.

Mrs. Williams seemed to have very low self-esteem and was afraid that the therapist would blame her for the family problems. Her defense was to continually direct the attention to Ian's problems. Dianne was frightened and looked to Mrs. Williams for protection and help in dealing with Ian.

(It should be noted, that although there were ongoing conflicts between various family members, Mrs. Williams initially sought therapy for her son. She did not seek *family* therapy.)

THEORETICAL OVERVIEW

Cognitive Therapy (CT) is an ideal approach for the treatment of stress in the family. It is a short-term, active, directive, collaborative, psychoeducational, and dynamic model of psychotherapy. CT, developed by Aaron T. Beck (1966, 1976), is one of several therapies termed cognitive-behavioral models of therapy. These include the works of Ellis (1974a, 1974b, 1977, 1985), Lazarus (1971, 1976, 1981), and Meichenbaum (1977). The major therapeutic focus in the cognitive-behavioral models is to help the client examine the manner in which he or she understands and construes the world (cognitions) and to experiment with new ways of responding (behavioral). By learning to understand the idiosyncratic way in which he perceives himself, his world and experience, and the prospects for the future, the client can be helped both to alter negative affect and to behave more adaptively. The cognitive therapist mainly eschews the construct of the unconscious. A cognitive focus in therapy is not new (Adler, 1964; Bowlby, 1985; Frankl, 1985; Horney, 1939; Sullivan, 1953).

Cognitive Therapy (CT), which is a psychoeducational or coping model as opposed to a mastery model, states that a major goal of therapy is to increase the client's skills so that he or she can more effectively deal with the stressors of life, and thereby have a greater sense of control and self-efficacy in his or her life. The directive focus of the model involves the therapist being actively involved with the client or client family in the therapeutic collaboration. The therapist can offer hypotheses for consideration, act as a resource person, or directly point out areas of difficulty.

The CT model posits three issues in the formation and maintenance of the common psychological disorders: the cognitive triad, the cognitive distortions, and the schemata. The triad involves the individual's view of self, world and experience, and the future. Virtually all client problems can be subsumed under one of these three areas. By beginning to focus and structure an understanding of the client problems, the therapist can develop hypotheses about the client's life issues and thereby develop a conceptualization of the client problems within the cognitive-behavioral framework.

An individual can view life experience in a variety of ways. These distortions may be unrealistically positive where the individual may ignore severe chest pain because the client believes that he is "too young to have a heart attack." Other life perceptions may be overwhelmingly negative. It is this latter group of distortions that often become the initial focus of the therapy. The CT therapist works to make the client's idiosyncratic perceptions manifest, both in content and style. By doing so, the therapist can develop an understanding of the individual and family distortions. The personal and/or family distortions become the thematic directional signs that point to the underlying schemata. The types of distortions include:

1. *All or Nothing Thinking*
   "I'm either a success or a failure."
2. *Mind Reading*
   "They probably think that I'm incompetent."
3. *Emotional Reasoning*
   "Because I feel inadequate, I am inadequate."
4. *Personalization*
   "That comment must have been directed toward me."
5. *Global Labeling*
   "Everything I do turns out wrong."
6. *Catastrophizing*
   "If I go to the party, there will be terrible consequences."
7. *Should Statements*
   "I should visit my family every time they want me to."
8. *Overgeneralization*
   "Everything always goes wrong for me."
9. *Control Fallacies*
   "If I'm not in complete control all the time, I will go out of control."
10. *Comparing*
    "I am not as competent as my coworkers or supervisors."
11. *Heaven's Reward Fallacy*
    "If I do everything perfectly here, I will be rewarded later."
12. *Disqualifying the Positive*
    "This success experience was only a fluke. The compliment was false."

13. *Perfectionism*
    "I must do this perfectly or I will be criticized and a failure."
14. *Time Tripping*
    "I screwed up my past and now I must be vigilant to secure my future."
15. *Objectifying the Subjective*
    "I must have this belief that I must be funny to be liked, so it is fact."
16. *Selective Abstraction*
    "All of the good men are taken or gay."
17. *Externalization of Self-worth*
    "My worth is dependent upon what others think of me."
18. *Fallacy of Change*
    "You should change your behavior because I want you to."
19. *Fallacy of Worrying*
    "If I worry about it enough, it will be resolved."
20. *Fallacy of Ignoring*
    "If I ignore it, maybe it will go away."
21. *Fallacy of Fairness*
    "Life should be fair."
22. *Unrealistic Expectations*
    "I must be the best all the time."
23. *Filtering*
    "I must focus on the negative details while I ignore and filter out all the positive aspects of a situation."
24. *Being Right*
    "I must prove that I am right, as being wrong is unthinkable."
25. *Fallacy of Attachment*
    "I can't live without a man." "If I was in a relationship, all of my problems would be solved."

Although all of the above distortions are stated in the first person; they can also apply to family groups.

A major focus of family-centered therapy is on understanding and explicating the underlying rules/beliefs/schemata held by families and family members. Beck (1966, 1976, 1978) and Freeman (1986) have suggested that schemata generate the various cognitive distortions seen in patients. These schematas or basic life rules begin to be established as a force in cognition and behavior from the earliest points in life and are well fixed by the middle childhood years. They are the accumulation of the individual's learning and experience within the family group, religious group, gender group, ethnic or regional subgroups, and the broader society. The particular extent or effect that a schema has on an individual's life depends on: (1) how strongly held that schema is; (2) how essential the individual sees that schema to his or her safety, well-being, or existence; (3) the individual's previous learning vis-à-vis the importance and essential nature of a particular schema; (4) how early a particular schema was internalized; and (5) the lack of disputation that the individual engages in when a particular schema is activated.

The schemata are very rarely isolated and separate but, rather, occur in various combinations and permutations which are quite complex. The schemata become, in effect, how one defines oneself, both individually and as part of the family group. The schemata can be active or dormant, with the more active schemata being the rules that govern day-to-day behavior. The dormant schemata are called into play to control behavior in times of stress. The schemata may be either compelling or noncompelling. Noncompelling schemata can be rather easily modified. Compelling schemata are those that the individual or family cannot deny and respond to frequently and powerfully.

The CT approach to family therapy, therefore, promotes self-disclosure of individual cognitions in order to increase mutual understanding through enhanced knowledge and understanding of the thoughts, beliefs, and attitudes of the different family members. Since early schemata develop and are modified within the family group, cognitive therapy with families provides a context for observing these schemata in operation, for testing and modifying family members' distorted perceptions and cognitions.

Schemata are in a constant state of change and evolution. From the child's earliest years there is a need to alter old schemata and develop new ones to meet the different and increasingly complex demands of the world. The infant's conception of reality is governed by his limited interaction with the world, so the infant may initially perceive the world as his crib and the few caretakers who care for and comfort him. As the infant develops additional skills of mobility and interaction, he then perceives his world as significantly larger. During the exploratory period, the child develops mobility to begin to examine his world close up. One way of conceptualizing the change process is to utilize the Piagetian concept of adaptation with its two interrelated processes of assimilation and accommodation. Environmental data and experience are only taken in by the individual as the individual can utilize these data in terms of his or her own subjective experiences. The self-schemata then become self-selective as the individual may ignore environmental stimuli that he or she was unable to integrate or synthesize. The assimilative and accommodative processes are interactive and stand in opposition, one with the other. There is an active and evolutionary process where all perceptions and cognitive structures are applied to new functions (assimilation), while new cognitive structures are developed to serve old functions in new situations (accommodation). Some individuals may persist in utilizing old structures without fitting them to the new circumstances in which they are involved. They may further fail to accommodate or build new structures.

Family schemata are often difficult to alter because they are generally reinforced by the other family members. If, for example, a particular family schema is "Family secrets should/must not be shared with outsiders," the therapist can expect that any family member who speaks up will be censured, either overtly or covertly, by the other family members.

Some schemata may engender a great deal of emotion and be emotionally bound by the individual's past experience, by the sheer weight of the time in which those schemata have been held, or by the relative importance and meaning of the individuals from whom the schemata were acquired. There is a cognitive element to the schemata which pervades the individual's thoughts and images. The schemata are cognitive in that we can often, with the proper training, describe schemata in great detail; we can also deduce them from behavior or automatic thoughts. Finally, there is a behavioral component which involves the way the belief system governs the individual's responses to a particular stimulus or set of stimuli. In seeking to alter a particular schema that has endured for a long period of time, it is necessary to help the family or individuals within the family to deal with the belief from as many different sides as possible. A purely cognitive strategy would leave the behavioral and affective aspects untouched. The affective strategy is similarly limited and, of course, the strict behavioral approach is limited by its disregard for cognitive-affective elements.

In many cases we find that the individual's particular schemata are consensually validated. Significant others help not only to form the schemata, but also to maintain the particular schemata, be they negative or positive. McGoldrick, Pearce, and Giordino (1982) stress that families view the world through their own cultural filters so that the particular belief systems may be familial or more broadly cultural. Family systems theorists have described the phenomenon of the entire "system" working toward maintaining a balance. If an individual within a family system attempts to change that system or alter his or her strength of belief in the system, the system may be mobilized into action to close ranks against the "heretic" or to work toward keeping the individual within the system. This is a situation often seen in working with adolescents. As the adolescent begins to make changes toward a more functional style of behaving, which may involve an alteration in his or her belief system, it is not unusual for the family to be unhappy or even disgruntled about the results of therapy. They may even threaten to or actually remove the adolescent from therapy, claiming that he or she is now "worse." By "worse" these families often mean that the adolescent is at greater variance with the family schemata. While the adolescent's pretherapy behavior was undesirable and destructive to both self and others, it appears that in developing a new belief system or modifying a belief system, the individual may run afoul of the family schemata and be seen as destructive.

An example of family schemata based on the culture in which the family is immersed might be basic rules regarding sexual behavior, reaction to other racial, ethnic, or religious groups, or particular religious beliefs. Related, and very much a part of the family or cultural belief system, are those belief systems that may be rooted in a religion's theology or its tradition. A family belief about heaven and hell may be part of the dogma of a religion; however, much of the "religious" response that individuals have is to the tradition of the religion that has been developed over a number of years within small cultural groups. One would find, then, for example, that Jews from an eastern European tradition (Ashkenazic) hold different traditional beliefs from those raised in the Mediterranean area (Sephardic).

A client will often describe him/herself as displaying particular characteristics "as far back as I can remember." Objective observation may support the client's view that he or she has behaved a certain way since early childhood. What, then, differentiates the child who develops a schema that is held with moderate strength and amenable to change later on and the individual who develops a core belief that is powerful and apparently immutable? We may posit several possibilities: (1) In addition to the core belief, the child maintains a powerful associated belief that he/she cannot change; (2) the belief system is powerfully reinforced by parents or significant others; (3) while the dysfunctional belief system may not be especially reinforced, any attempt to believe the contrary may not be reinforced or may even be punished (i.e., a child may be told, "You're no good"); a second possibility would be that the child is not told he or she lacks worth, but any attempt to assert worth would be ignored; (4) the parents or significant others may offer direct instruction contrary to developing a positive image (i.e., "It's not nice to brag" or "It's not nice to toot your own horn because people will think less of you").

## GENERAL TREATMENT APPROACH

At the beginning of the therapy, a problem list is established. Each of the presenting problems is investigated with the family as a group to get an overview of the problem(s). Subsequent to that initial interview, each participating member is interviewed. We have found that there are often issues that will not come up within the family interview but that need to be stated and understood by the therapist. Further, certain issues that may impact on the family difficulty are not, we think, appropriate for family discussion (i.e., sexual performance difficulties of mother or father). Although the therapist may learn of family secrets, we have found the possible keeping of secrets a worthwhile risk in exchange for the additional information and insight into the dynamic workings of the family. Once the problem list is developed, it can then be prioritized within a family session. Issues of greatest dysfunction or possible threats to health and well-being would be placed higher in the hierarchy.

A full developmental, family, social, occupational/educational, medical, and psychiatric history is taken for each family member. These data are essential in helping to develop the treatment conceptualization. This conceptualization will, of necessity, be based on family and developmental histories, test data, interview material, and reports of previous therapists or other professionals. This conceptualization must meet several criteria. It must (1) be useful, (2) be simple, (3) be coherent, (4) explain past behavior, and (5) be able to predict future behavior. Part of the conceptualization process is the compilation of a problem list, referred to above. The reason for choosing one problem as opposed to another as the primary, secondary, or tertiary foci of the therapy depends on many factors. A particular problem may be the primary focus of therapy because of its debilitating effect on the family. In another case, there may be no debilitating problem and the focus may be on the simplest issue, thereby giving the family practice in problem solving and some measure of success. In a third case, the choice of a primary focus might be on a "keystone" problem, that is, a problem whose solution will cause a ripple effect in solving other problems. Having set out the treatment goals with the family, the therapist can begin to develop strategies and the interventions that will help effect the strategies.

The therapist is not limited to meeting with the family as a group. There are many different treatment configurations that can be used. In working with the Williams family, the therapist could meet with the mother alone, each of the children individually, the children together, or the entire family. It might be possible to meet with Mr. Williams alone, given that he will not meet with Mrs. Williams. The frequency of the meetings is also negotiable.

Having established and agreed upon a problem list and focus, the individual sessions are then structured through agenda setting and homework. Rather than having the therapy session meander like the mighty Mississippi, the therapist can, by setting an agenda, help to focus the therapy work and to make better use of time, energy, and available skills. Agenda setting at the beginning of the session allows each family member to put issues of concern on the agenda for the day. We would make the point that families often become client-families because they have lost their ability to organize and problem solve. By setting an agenda, a problem-solving focus is modeled for the family by the therapist. A typical agenda might include:

1. A brief overview of the week's interactions/problems.
2. Review of individual or family homework.
3. Problem focus, i.e., specific areas of discussion.
4. Wrap-up and review of the session.


ASSESSMENT METHODS

There is a plethora of assessment instruments utilized in clinical settings representative of a diversity of theoretical orientations. Most assessment instruments were originally designed to be used in the assessment of individuals. However, when they are combined with clinical judgment and creativity, they may be adapted for use with families. When depression is a primary problem, the Beck Depression Inventory (BDI) can be used.

The Beck Depression Inventory (Beck, 1978) is a self-report measure which consists of 21 items designed to reflect the overall level of depression. In terms of family dynamics, the depressed family member may be hopeless about positive changes, may attribute family problems to his or her perceived shortcomings, and frequently compares him- or herself negatively to the other family members. This is often validated by the family. Weekly administration of the BDI to family members may serve to provide objective data regarding therapeutic progress in coping with depression, as well as an aid in helping family members check out and validate (or invalidate) their assumptions about each other by opening up channels of communication.

When anxiety is a target symptom, the Beck Anxiety Inventory (BAI), a 21-item self-report symptom checklist, may be used. The BAI was designed to measure the severity of anxiety-related symptoms (Beck, Epstein, Brown,

& Steer, in press) and to complement the BDI. As with the BDI, the BAI may be a useful weekly, objective measure of each family member's overall level of anxiety, may be used as an aid in communication skill training, and helps to take the focus off the identified patient (IP) and onto all of the family members.

The Hopelessness Scale (HS) was developed as a measure of the nega-tive view of the future, and the intensity of that view (Beck, Weissman, Lester, & Trexler, 1974). Although the HS is frequently used in conjunction with the BDI as a measure of potential suicidal behavior, it may also be used as an indicator of each family member's perception of possible change in the family. This measure may also be used as an index of change. As family members experience and perceive change, the level of hopeless-ness decreases.

The BDI, BAI, and HS are basically measures of dysfunctional thoughts and symptomatology that are generated by underlying assumptions and core beliefs. The Dysfunctional Attitude Scale (DAS) is a quantitative measure of the maladaptive underlying assumptions (Weissman & Beck, 1979). This scale provides measures of vulnerability, attraction/rejection, perfectionism, imperatives, approval, dependence, autonomous attitudes, and cognitive philosophy, allowing the therapist to determine what are the individual maladaptive assumptions, how they overlap or discriminate, and what are the shared maladaptive family assumptions. These assump-tions can then be challenged in the family system, upsetting the homeosta-sis of the system and opening it up for interventions leading to change.

Another scale, based on the cognitive model, that may be adapted for use with families is the Sociotropy-Autonomy Scale (SAS), which was originally developed as a measure of relatively stable individual differences in motivational patterns in two major areas. These two areas refer to affiliation, labeled sociotropy, and achievement, labeled autonomy. It is hypothesized that these two personality styles may mediate a vulnerabil-ity to depression. An individual scoring high in sociotropy is one who is invested in maintaining warm interpersonal relationships in order to satisfy strivings for "intimacy, sharing, empathy, understanding, approval, affection, protection, guidance and help" (Beck, Epstein, & Harrison, 1983, pp. 1–2). Such an individual may be particularly vulnerable to interpersonal losses, separation, or rejection. Conversely, the individual scoring high in autonomy may be more invested in him- or herself, in acquisition of power, and in control over their environment. A high autonomous individual is particularly vulnerable to failure in achieving desired outcomes, and to situations in which freedom of action is thwarted or constrained. When given to family members, the SAS provides information about the sociotropy and/or autonomy of family members and the overlap in personality style between family members. The SAS can also help to provide hypotheses about family communication problems. The Williams family provides an excellent example of the structure and communication problems between autonomous and sociotropic members. The relatively more autonomous style of Ian and Mr. Williams combined with the relatively more sociotropic style of Mrs. Williams and Dianne serve to fix the roles within the family. The fact that these sociotropic or autonomous roles are often part of cultural or gender-related schemata must be taken into account.

## THERAPEUTIC INTERVENTIONS

As we listen to the automatic thoughts, we must, as therapists, question what allows the maintenance of dysfunctional behavior. The major factor would appear to be the self-consonance of the belief system. If a particular belief is only partially believed by family members, it is much easier for them to give it up because they are giving up a small piece of a belief system rather than giving up what they see and regard as "self." The more chronic client or family, including those with chronic "neurotic" behaviors and character disorders often see their symptoms as "me/us." They will readily verbalize "This is who I/we are and this is the way I/we have always been." Often the family perpetuates and shares in this belief. By asking them to challenge or directly dispute their dysfunctional beliefs, we are then asking them to directly challenge their very being. When the challenge to self is perceived, the family most usually responds with anxiety. They are then placed in a conflict situation about whether they would prefer to maintain their particular dysfunctional symptoms or to experience anxiety. As they see themselves defined by the problem, they hesitate to give up the problem because it would leave them nothing but an empty shell. We can then see that any challenge to the self can be the result of a careful, guided discovery based on collaboration as opposed to a direct, confrontational, and disputational stance.

Several techniques can be taught to the family members to help them question both the distortions and the schemata that underlie them, as well as to help them respond in more functional ways.

### 1. Idiosyncratic Meaning

The therapist cannot assume that a term or statement used by a client is completely understood by the therapist or family members until the client is asked for meaning and clarification. The present volume is a case in point. The term *family therapy* might have very different meanings for different authors. Therefore, it is essential to question the client directly on the meanings of their verbalizations. While this may appear to be intrusive, it can be structured by the therapist as a way of making sure that the therapist is not merely in the right ballpark in understanding, but is on target. This also models for the family active-listening skills, increased communication, and a means for checking out assumptions.

## 2. Questioning the Evidence

People use certain evidence to maintain ideas and beliefs. It is essential to teach family members to question the evidence that they are using to maintain and strengthen an idea or belief. Questioning the evidence also requires examining the source of data. The client who is depressed often gives equal weight to all sources. A parent who appears to frown at his/her child may be used by that child as evidence that he or she is unloved and thus may as well kill him/herself. Many clients have the ability to ignore major pieces of data and focus on the few that support their dysfunctional view. By having the client question the evidence with family members, the therapist can achieve a fuller accounting. If the evidence is strong and accepted by several family members, the therapist can help to structure alternative ways of either perceiving the data or changing behaviors so that the evidence no longer exists.

## 3. Reattribution

A common statement made by clients is, "It's all my fault." This is commonly heard in situations of relationship difficulty, separation, or divorce. Although one cannot dismiss this out of hand, it is unlikely that a single person is totally responsible for everything going wrong within a family. Depressed clients often take responsibility for events and situations that are only minimally attributable to them, while the family may reinforce this view. The therapist can help the client distribute responsibility among all relevant parties. If the therapist takes a position of total support (e.g., "It wasn't your fault," "She isn't worth it," "You're better off without her," or "There are other fish in the ocean"), he or she ends up sounding like friends and family that the client has already dismissed as being an undiscriminating cheering squad, and not understanding his or her position. The therapist can, by taking a middle ground, help the family member to reattribute responsibility and not take all of the blame, nor unrealistically shift all blame to others.

## 4. Examining Options and Alternatives

Many individuals and families see themselves as having lost all options. Perhaps the prime example of this lack of options appears in suicidal clients. They see their options and alternatives as so limited that among their few choices, death might be the easiest or simplest one. This cognitive strategy involves working with the client to generate additional options.

## 5. Decatastrophizing

This is also called the "What if?" technique. This involves helping the family to see if they are overestimating the catastrophic nature of a situation. Questions that might be asked of the family member include, "So what?" "What is the worst thing that can happen?" of "And if it does occur, what would be so terrible?" This technique has the therapist working against a "Chicken Little" style of thinking. If the family sees an experience (or life itself) as a series of catastrophes and problems, the therapist can work toward reality testing. The family members can be helped to see the consequence of their life actions as not all-or-nothing and therefore less catastrophic. It is important that this technique be used with great gentleness and care so that the family members do not feel ridiculed or made fun of by the therapist.

## 6. Fantasized Consequences

In this technique family members are asked to fantasize a situation and to describe their images and the attendant concerns. Often clients describe their concerns and, in the direct verbalization, they, as well as their family, can see the irrationality of their ideas. If the fantasized consequences are realistic, the therapist can work with the family to realistically assess the danger and develop coping strategies. This technique allows the clients to bring into the consulting room imaged events, situations, or interactions that have happened previously or that they see as happening in the future. By having the client move the fantasy to the "reality" of being spoken, the images can become grist for the therapeutic mill. The fantasy, being colored by the same dysfunctional thinking that alters many of the client perceptions, may be overly negative. The explication and investigation of the style, format, and content of the fantasy can yield very good material for the therapy work, especially involving feedback from the other family members.

## 7. Advantages and Disadvantages of Maintaining a Particular Belief or Behavior

This technique can help a client/family to gain a balance and perspective. This may be seen as one of the scaling techniques, having the family move away from an all-or-nothing position to one that explores the possibility of an experience, feeling, or behavior having both negative and positive possibilities. By focusing on the advantages and disadvantages of a particular behavior or way of thinking, the family can achieve a perspective on the problem. This technique can be used to examine the advantages and disadvantages of acting a certain way (e.g., dressing in a particular way), thinking a certain way (e.g., thinking of what others will think of you), feeling a particular way (e.g., sad). While the family will often claim that they cannot control their feelings, actions, and thoughts, it is precisely the development of this control that is the strength of cognitive therapy.

## 8. Turning Adversity to Advantage

There are times that a seeming disaster can be used to advantage. Losing one's job can be tremendously stressful, but may, in some cases, be the entry point to a new job or even a new career. Having a stressor imposed on us may be seen as oppressive and unfair, but may be used as a motivator. This CT technique appears to ask the client to look for the silver lining in the cloud. Given that distressed individuals and their families have taken a view that often results in their finding the darkened lining to every silver cloud, looking for the kernel of positive in a highly stressful situation can be very difficult for many clients. Family members will sometimes respond to the therapist pointing out any positive aspects with greater negativity. They may accuse the therapist of being unrealistic or a Pollyanna. The therapist can point out that the positive view that he (the therapist) offers is no less real than the family's unrealistically negative view.

## 9. Guided Association/Discovery

Through simple questions such as, "Then what?" "What would that mean?" and "What would happen then?" the therapist can help the family explore the significance they see in events. This collaborative, therapist-guided technique stands in opposition to the technique of free association, which is basic to the psychoanalytic process. The use of what we call the chained or guided association technique involves the therapist working with the family members to connect ideas, thoughts, and images. The therapist provides the connections to the clients' verbalizations. The use of statements such as, "And then what?" and "What evidence do we have that that is true?" allow the therapist to guide the clients along various therapeutic paths, depending on the conceptualization of the problem(s) and the therapeutic goals.

## 10. Use of Exaggeration

By taking an idea to its extreme, the therapist can often help to move the family to a more central position vis-à-vis a particular belief. Care must be taken to not insult, ridicule, or embarrass family members. Given a hypersensitivity to criticism and ridicule, some clients may experience the therapist who uses paradoxical strategies as making light of their problems. The client may see things in their most extreme form. When the therapist takes a more extreme stance (i.e., focusing on the absolutes "never," "always," "no one," "everyone"), the family will often be forced to move from their extreme view to a position closer to center. There is the risk, however, that family members may take the therapist's statement as reinforcement of their position of abject hopelessness, or family members may see the therapist as aligning with one member against the family. The therapist who chooses to use the paradoxical or exaggeration techniques must have (1) a strong working relationship with all family members, (2) good timing, and (3) the good sense to know when to back away from the technique.

## 11. Scaling

For those family members who sees things as "all or nothing," the technique of scaling or seeing things as existing on a continuum can be very helpful. The scaling of a feeling can force clients to utilize the strategy of gaining distance and perspective. Since family members or the entire family may be at a point of extreme thoughts and extreme behaviors, any movement toward a midpoint is helpful.

## 12. Self-instruction

We all talk to ourselves. We give ourselves orders, directions, instructions, or information necessary to problem solve. Meichenbaum (1977) has developed an extensive model for understanding self-instruction. According to Meichenbaum's model, the child moves from overt verbalization of instructions to subvocalization to nonverbalization. This same process can be developed in the adult. The different family members can start with direct verbalization which, with practice, will become part of the behavioral repertoire. They can be taught to offer direct self-instructions or, in some cases, counterinstructions. In this technique, the therapist is not introducing anything new. Rather, the clients are being helped to utilize and strengthen a technique that we all use at various times.

## 13. Thought stopping

Dysfunctional thoughts often have a snowball effect for the individual. What may start as a small and insignificant problem can, if left to roll along, gather weight, speed, and momentum. Once on the roll, the thoughts have a force of their own and are very hard to stop. Thought stopping is best used when the thoughts start, not in the middle of the process. The client can picture a stop sign, hear a bell, or envisage a wall. Any of these can be helped to stop the progression and growth of the thoughts. A therapist hitting the desk sharply or ringing a small bell can serve to help the client to stop the thoughts. The memory of that intervention can be used by the client to assist their thought stopping. There is both a distractive and aversive quality to the technique.

## 14. Distraction

It is difficult to think about several things simultaneously. Distraction can be used to provide interference with dysfunctional thoughts. It involves teaching the client to focus on external or internal distractors to effectively deal with dysfunctional thinking on a short-term basis. It might involve counting, or focusing on calming and pleasant images, or competing behaviors. While this technique is a short-term one, it is very useful to allow family members the time to establish some degree of control over their thinking. This time can then be used to utilize other cognitive techniques.

## 15. Direct Disputation

Although we do not advocate arguing with a client or a family, there are times when direct disputation is necessary. A major guideline for necessity is the imminence of a suicide attempt. When it seems clear to the clinician that a family member is going to make an attempt, the therapist must directly and quickly work to challenge the hopelessness. While it might appear to be the treatment technique of choice, the therapist risks becoming embroiled in a power struggle or argument with the client. Disputation coming from outside the client may, in fact, engender passive resistance or a passive-aggressive response that might include suicide. Disputation, argument, or debate are potentially dangerous tools. They must be used carefully, judiciously, and with skill. If the therapist becomes one more harping contact, the individual family members may turn the therapist off completely.

## BEHAVIORAL TECHNIQUES

The goals in using behavioral techniques within the context of cognitive therapy are manifold. The first goal is to utilize direct behavioral strategies and techniques to test dysfunctional thoughts and behaviors. By having the individuals or entire family try feared or avoided behaviors, old ideas can be directly challenged. A second use of behavioral techniques is to practice new behaviors as homework. Certain behaviors can be practiced in the office, and then practiced at home. The family can have homework ranging from acting differently toward one another, practicing active listening, being verbally or physically affectionate, or doing things in a new way.

## DIAGNOSIS AND TREATMENT PLAN
## FOR THE WILLIAMS FAMILY

Based on the test data and the family history gathered in the clinical interview, it was clear that the family dynamic involves reciprocal interactions between all of the family members. Although Mr. and Mrs. Williams no longer met or spoke (except through their respective lawyers), they were still very much involved emotionally. Their inability to write *finis* to their marriage had to be noted.

The initial problem list generated with the Williams family included:

*For Ian:*
1. Increasing Ian's compliance with house rules.
2. Decreasing the physical interaction between Ian and Dianne.
3. Allowing Ian greater privacy at home.
4. Increasing problem solving skills.

*For Mrs. Williams:*
5. Having Mr. and Mrs. Williams deal with their ongoing relationship in a more adaptive manner.
6. Improving the interaction at home between Mrs. Williams and the children.
7. Assertiveness training for Mrs. Williams.

*For Dianne:*
8. Assertiveness training for Dianne.
9. Improving ability to deal with the anger expressed by Ian and Mr. Williams.

The family chose to work on reducing the conflict at home. The goal for all of the members was to have greater peace without a perceived surrender of individual autonomy. Inasmuch as effective problem solving was not a skill in the Williams family repertoire, the therapist had to teach the members effective negotiation, the differences between assertion and aggression, and techniques for being assertive. Once the family members were able to start effective problem solving on small points, the therapist was able to extend the skills to larger areas of life. An example was arranging Dianne's use of Ian's stereo—responsibility for proper usage and consequences for any damage that she might cause.

In a more abstract area, the family theme of competition had to be modified to a more collaborative interaction.

## TREATMENT APPROACH

The general approach to treating this family was broken down into three segments. First, the assessment phase stressed not only gathering test data, but also identifying and making explicit the individual and family cognitive distortions (e.g., Mrs. W: "Everyone takes advantage of me"; Ian: "Everyone gangs up on me"; and Dianne: "Ian's anger scares me"). The central theme of all these thoughts were ideas stemming from the second leg of the cognitive triad: negative thoughts about the world and experience. These thoughts reflect certain underlying personal and family schemata. For example, "Children should respect their parents," "Nice people get good things," "The world should be fair," "Parents should be friends with their children," and (conversely) "Children and parents should be friends."

The third phase of the treatment was divided into two subphases: the skill-building phase (the behavioral focus) and the disputation-of-distortion phase (the cognitive focus). During this stage of therapy, the focus shifted between challenging the dysfunctional thoughts and behavioral skill building to testing out the thoughts.

The Williams family, both individually, and as a group, were encouraged to voice their perceptions and distortions about the intentions and behavior of others. They were helped to evaluate their distortions and to reality test their thoughts. Reality testing was a new focus for the family. Tentatively, at first, Ian, Dianne, and Mrs. Williams all tried to test out previously strongly held ideas. A favorite (and functional) question that was modeled by the therapist was "What do you mean by that?" When any family member made a statement that was not clear, other members began to ask for meaning and clarity, rather than responding to idiosyncratic distortions of what was said or meant.

Ian and Dianne were encouraged to negotiate solutions to problems on their own, without Mrs. Williams serving as arbitrator. Mrs. Williams felt neglected because the children were problem solving without her. The therapist worked with her on issues of separation, independence, and autonomy for her and for the children. This led into the issue of her dependence on her husband and her reluctance to effect a final break through a divorce. She was helped to assess the advantages and disadvantages of a divorce. The issue of being legally and emotionally apart from Mr. Williams reflected several gender-related schemata about being a single woman, the proper place for a woman in a relationship, and general ability and right to assert herself. Her thoughts that the children would be hurt and would be against the divorce were tested out in the family sessions. Both Ian and Dianne voiced their support for Mrs. Williams. Mrs. Williams sought out an attorney and pursued a divorce.

Assertiveness training was used as a basic problem-solving model. The differences between the passive, aggressive, and assertive approach to problem solving were discussed and taught. Family homework involved utilizing assertive behaviors with each other.

Finally, Mr. Williams appeared to become quite upset when his previously unchallenged words and behaviors were less powerful with the children.

The family was seen over a seven-month period. Family sessions were held on the average of every other week. The alternate week's sessions were mixtures of individual sessions with each of the family members. Three factors contributed to the termination of the therapy. The primary factor was a loss of insurance benefits to pay for the sessions. Other factors were Ian's getting a job and a loss of motivation for treatment.

When family work was terminated, the negative and hostile interactive style of the family had changed. Family conflict was lessened though not totally ameliorated. Periodic phone calls to the therapist were used as a way of dealing with issues as they began to heat up, but before anyone got burned.

The Williams family left therapy with increased coping strategies, more open communication, and a willingness and interest in testing out perceptions. The net result was that the Williams family had made significant progress in relating.

## REFERENCES

Abrams, J. (1983). Marital therapy. In A. Freeman (Ed.), *Cognitive therapy with couples and groups.* New York: Plenum.

Adler, A. (1964). *Social interest: A challenge to mankind.* New York: Capricorn Books.

Beck, A. T. (1963). Thinking and depression: 1. Idiosyncratic content and cognitive distortions. *Archives of General Psychiatry, 9,* 324–333.

Beck, A. T. (1966). *Depression: Causes and treatment.* Philadelphia: University of Pennsylvania Press.

Beck, A. T. (1976). *Cognitive therapy and the emotional disorders.* New York: International Universities Press.

Beck, A. T. (1978). *Depression Inventory.* Philadelphia: Center for Cognitive Therapy.

Beck, A. T., & Emery, G. (1985). *Anxiety disorders and phobias.* New York: Basic Books.

Beck, A. T., Epstein, N., Brown, G., & Steer, R. A. (in press). An inventory for measuring clinical anxiety; Psychometric properties. *Journal of Consulting and Clinical Psychology.*

Beck, A. T., Epstein, N., & Harrison, R. (1983). Cognitions, attitudes, and personality dimensions in depression. *British Journal of Cognitive Psychotherapy, 1,* (1), 1–16.

Beck, A. T., & Freeman, A. (in press). *Cognitive therapy of personality disorders.* New York: Guilford Press.

Beck, A. T., Rush, A. J., Shaw, B. F., & Emery, G. (1979). *Cognitive therapy of depression.* New York: Guilford Press.

Beck, A. T., Weissman, A., Lester, D., & Trexler, L. (1974). The measurement of pessimism: The Hopelessness Scale. *Journal of Consulting & Clinical Psychology, 42,* 861–865.

Bedrosian, R. C. (1986). Cognitive and family interventions for suicidal patients. In A. Freeman, N. Epstein, & K. M. Simon (Eds.), *Depression in the family.* New York: Haworth Press.

Bowlby, J. (1985). The role of childhood experience in cognitive disturbance. In M. J. Mahoney & A. Freeman (Eds.), *Cognition and psychotherapy.* New York: Plenum.

Bowers, W. (in press). Inpatient treatment with Cognitive Therapy. In A. Freeman, K. M. Simon, H. Arkowitz, & L. Beutler (Eds.), *Comprehensive handbook of cognitive therapy.* New York: Plenum.

DiGiuseppe, R. (1987). Cognitive therapy for childhood depression. In A. Freeman, N. Epstein, & K. M. Simon (Eds.), *Depression in the family.* New York: Haworth Press.

DiGiuseppe, R. (in press). Cognitive therapy with children. In A. Freeman, K. M. Simon, H. Arkowitz, & L. Beutler (Eds.), *Comprehensive handbook of cognitive therapy.* New York: Plenum.

Edgette, S. & Prout, M. (in press). Cognitive therapy for eating disorders. In A. Freeman, K. M. Simon, H. Arkowitz, & L. Beutler (Eds.), *Comprehensive handook of cognitive therapy.* New York: Plenum.

Ellis, A. (1974a). *Growing through reason.* North Hollywood, CA: Wilshire.

Ellis, A. (1974b). *Humanistic psychotherapy: The rational-emotive approach.* New York: McGraw-Hill.

Ellis, A. (1977). *Reason and emotion in psychotherapy.* Secaucus, NJ: Citadel Press.
Ellis, A. (1985). Expanding the ABC's of rational emotive therapy. In M. J. Mahoney & A. Freeman (Eds.), *Cognition and psychotherapy.* New York: Plenum.
Epstein, N. (1983) Cognitive marital therapy. In A. Freeman (Ed.), *Cognitive therapy with couples and groups.* New York: Plenum.
Epstein, N., & Baucom, D. (in press, a). *Cognitive marital therapy.* In A. Freeman, K. M. Simon, H. Arkowitz, & L. Beutler (Eds.), *Comprehensive handbook of cognitive therapy.* New York: Plenum.
Epstein, N., & Baucom, D. (in press, b). *Cognitive marital therapy.* New York: Brunner/ Mazel.
Fairburn, C. (1985). Cognitive-behavioral treatment for bulimia. In D. M. Garner & P. E. Garfinkel (Eds.), *Handbook for psychotherapy for anorexia nervosa and bulimia.* New York: Guilford Press.
Frankl, V. (1985). Logos, paradox and the search for meaning. In M. J. Mahoney & A. Freeman (Eds.), *Cognition and psychotherapy.* New York: Plenum.
Freeman, A. (Ed.) (1983). *Cognitive therapy with couples and groups.* New York: Plenum.
Freeman, A. (1986). Understanding personal, cultural, and family schema in psychotherapy. In A. Freeman, N. Epstein, & K. M. Simon (Eds.), *Depression in the family.* New York: Haworth Press.
Freeman, A. (1988). Cognitive therapy of personality disorders. In C. Perris, H. Perris, & I. Blackburn, *Theory and practice of cognitive therapy.* Heidelberg: Springer Verlag.
Freeman, A., & Greenwood, V. (1987). *Cognitive therapy: Applications in psychiatric and medical settings.* New York: Human Sciences Press.
Freeman, A., & Leaf, R. (in press). Cognitive therapy of personality disorders. In A. Freeman, K. M. Simon, H. Arkowitz, & L. Beutler (Eds.), *Comprehensive handbook of cognitive therapy.* New York: Plenum.
Freeman, A., & Ludgate, J. (1988). Cognitive therapy of anxiety. In P. Keller & L. Ritt, *Innovations in clinical practice.* Mansfield, PA: Professional Resource Exchange.
Freeman, A., & Reinecke, M. (in press). *Cognitive therapy for suicidal behavior.* New York: Springer.
Freeman, A., & Simon, K. M. (in press). Cognitive therapy of anxiety. In A. Freeman, K. M. Simon, H. Arkowitz, & L. Beutler (Eds.), *Comprehensive handbook of cognitive therapy.* New York: Plenum.
Freeman, A., & White, D. (in press). *Cognitive therapy for suicidal behavior.* In A. Freeman, K. M. Simon, H. Arkowitz, & L. Beutler (Eds.), *Comprehensive handbook of cognitive therapy.* New York: Plenum.
Garner, D. M., & Bemis, K. (1985). *Cognitive therapy of anorexia nervosa.* In D. M. Garner & P. E. Garfinkel (Eds.), *Handbook for psychotherapy for anorexia nervosa and bulimia.* New York: Guilford Press.
Glantz, M. (1987). Day hospital treatment of alcoholics. In A. Freeman & V. Greenwood (Eds.), *Cognitive therapy: Applications in psychiatric and medical settings.* New York: Human Sciences Press.
Glantz, M. (in press). Treatment of the elderly. In A. Freeman, K. M. Simon, H. Arkowitz, & L. Beutler (Eds.), *Comprehensive handbook of cognitive therapy.* New York: Plenum.
Glantz, M., & McCourt, W. (1983). Cognitive therapy in groups with alcoholics. In A. Freeman (Ed.), *Cognitive therapy with couples and groups.* New York: Plenum.
Greenwood, V. (1983). Cognitive therapy with the young adult chronic patient. In A. Freeman (Ed.), *Cognitive therapy with couples and groups.* New York: Plenum.
Grossman, R., & Freet, B. (1987). A cognitive approach in group therapy with hospitalized adolescents. In A. Freeman & V. Greenwood (Eds.), *Cognitive therapy: Applications in psychiatric and medical settings.* New York: Human Sciences Press.
Horney, K. (1939). *New ways in psychoanalysis.* New York: W. W. Norton.
Hussian, R. (1987). Problem solving training and institutionalized elderly patients. In A. Freeman & V. Greenwood (Eds.), *Cognitive therapy: Applications in psychiatric and medical settings.* New York: Human Sciences Press.

Kinchla, J. (1987). Cognitive approaches to management of the type A behavior pattern. In A. Freeman & V. Greenwood (Eds.), *Cognitive therapy: Applications in psychiatric and medical settings.* New York: Human Sciences Press.

Lazarus, A. A. (1971). *Behavior therapy and beyond.* New York: McGraw-Hill.

Lazarus, A. A. (1976). *Multimodal behavior therapy.* New York: Springer.

Lazarus, A. A. (1981). *The practice of multimodal therapy.* New York: McGraw-Hill.

McCarthy, B. (in press). *Cognitive therapy applied to sex therapy.* In A. Freeman, K. M. Simon, H. Arkowitz, & L. Beutler (Eds.), *Comprehensive handbook of cognitive therapy.* New York: Plenum.

McGoldrick, M., Pearce, J. K., & Giordino, J. (Eds.) (1982). *Ethnicity and family therapy.* New York: Guilford Press.

Meichenbaum, D. (1977). *Cognitive behavior modification.* New York: Plenum.

Minuchin, S., & Fishman, H. C. (1981). *Family therapy techniques.* Cambridge, MA: Harvard University Press.

Perris, C., Rodhe, K., Palm, A., Abelson, M., Hellgren, S., Lilja, C., & Soderman, H. (1987). Fully integrated in and out-patient services in a psychiatric sector: Implementation of a new model for the care of psychiatric patients favoring continuity of care. In A. Freeman & V. Greenwood (Eds.), *Cognitive therapy: Applications in psychiatric and medical settings.* New York: Human Sciences Press.

Schrodt, R., & Wright, J. (1987). Cognitive therapy and medication as combined treatment. In A. Freeman & V. Greenwood (Eds.), *Cognitive therapy: Applications in psychiatric and medical settings.* New York: Human Sciences Press.

Sullivan, H. S. (1953). *The interpersonal theory of psychiatry.* New York: W. W. Norton.

Teichman, Y. (1986). Cognitive family therapy. *British Journal of Cognitive Psychotherapy,* 2, 1–10.

Teichman, Y. (1987). Family therapy of depression. In A. Freeman, N. Epstein, & K. M. Simon (Eds.), *Depression in the family.* New York: Haworth Press.

Teichman, Y. (in press). Cognitive family therapy. In A. Freeman, K. M. Simon, H. Arkowitz, & L. Beutler (Eds.), *Comprehensive handbook of cognitive therapy.* New York: Plenum.

Walen, S. R., & Wolfe, J. L. (1983). Sexual enhancement groups for women. In A. Freeman (Ed.), *Cognitive therapy with couples and groups.* New York: Plenum.

Weinberg, J. (1987). Group cognitive behavior therapy for sexual rehabilitation of spinal cord injured clients. In A. Freeman & V. Greenwood (Eds.), *Cognitive therapy: Applications in psychiatric and medical settings.* New York: Human Sciences Press.

Weissman, A., & Beck, A. T. (1979). Development and validation of the Dysfunctional Attitude Scale. Paper presented at the meeting of the Association for the Advancement of Behavior Therapy, Chicago, 1979.

Worden, J. W. (1987). Cognitive therapy with cancer patients. In A. Freeman & V. Greenwood (Eds.), *Cognitive therapy: Applications in psychiatric and medical settings.* New York: Human Sciences Press.

Wright, J., & Schrodt, R. (in press). Cognitive therapy and pharmacotherapy as combined treatments. In A. Freeman, K. M. Simon, H. Arkowitz, & L. Beutler (Eds.), *Comprehensive handbook of cognitive therapy.* New York: Plenum.

# 5

# The Strategic
# Rapid Intervention
# Approach

## J. SCOTT FRASER

*The Taylor family had been traumatized two weeks before they contacted the crisis/brief therapy team. Late one night the Taylors awoke to find a shadowy figure in their bedroom going through their drawers. When Mr. Taylor asked who it was, the man showed his gun. Demanding that the couple lie on their stomachs, the intruder asked where their money and jewelry were. He told them not to cry out if they didn't want their son in the next room to be hurt. They both heard the phone being yanked out of the wall, and the phone cords being pulled off, apparently to be used to tie them up. Mrs. Taylor was unaware of the intruder's gun until it went off. Not knowing that the shot had been an accident, and sure that her husband had just been killed, a strange, detached sense of calm overtook her as she thought, "So this is how it ends . . . executive style . . . first him and now me." This thought was broken by the reassuring movement of her husband, and then by the sinking realization that their 17-year-old son, Dan, awakened by the shot, had entered the room. When the burglar demanded that their son lie face down between them, the couple's terror peaked again. Then, suddenly, the voice again told them not to call for help. They heard footsteps on the stairs and the front door slam. He was gone.*

*When Mrs. Taylor called us two weeks later, she hadn't been able to sleep more than a few hours a night since the break-in. She was constantly fearful, especially of the dark, and she was unable to concentrate at*

122

*work. Her husband had been taking care of both police reports and insurance details while he stayed up most nights with her. He was throwing himself into home and work projects, yet he was becoming scattered and diffused in his attention as his exhaustion increased. Their son, aggravated by his parents' response, and frustrated by newly locked doors and windows and by a new burglar alarm, was engaging in escalating arguments with his parents.*

## THEORETICAL OVERVIEW

This event marks a crisis point, or a dangerous opportunity, in the lives of the Taylors. It is dangerous in that the members of this family and the patterns of interaction among them may deteriorate as a result. Mrs. Taylor may begin a cycle of self-doubt and fear, which might lead to chronic insomnia, phobias, family alienation, social isolation, job loss, among other possibilities. Other family members may come to see and treat her as somehow altered, sick, or bad, and thus further reinforce a cycle of problem generation. Mr. Taylor may gradually build resentment over his wife's fears and begin to alienate himself from her through either withdrawal or gradually escalating arguments over the irrationality of her fears. He also may succumb to exhaustion, physical illness, or job loss. Their son's increasing frustration and arguments might not only lead to a reinforcement of his mother's sick role or his father's stress cycle, but also increase his alienation from his parents and contribute to generalized disputes in other areas of family life or social interaction. The crisis may, on the other hand, create the opportunity for increased marital or family cohesion, enhanced self-respect or respect for the strengths of others, or the alteration of prior problematic family patterns and the initiation of new and more flexibly adaptive ones.

### Process Based Systems

A systemic view of crises is at the heart of the Strategic Rapid Intervention model. The approach is based upon the idea that families and other social systems evolve and elaborate through their responses to a series of internal and external variations or changes. Through an interaction of the system members' unique and/or normative ideas about themselves, about their own or others' roles, or about a given event, and their actions upon those ideas, a patterned interaction evolves. This interaction both confirms and alters the members' ideas and transactions in a cyclical manner.

System members' constructs shape the process of their transactions, and this process reciprocally shapes their constructs as a general family pattern evolves. As a relatively open social system, the family is subject to both internal and external, large and small, rapid and gradual variations. The response of the system and its members to these variations is generally an attempt at either an assimilation of the change into the ongoing system patterns, or an accommodation of those patterns in response to the change. No matter what the nature of the variation, the system's response to it either gradually or rapidly helps the system and its members to define or redefine themselves and thus to evolve. This has been termed a process/constructive view of systems (cf. Fraser, 1984, 1986b).

*Crises*

Appropriately, the Chinese characters which symbolize crisis are "wei-chi," combining the characters for danger and opportunity (Dai, 1970). Dictionary definitions of crisis focus upon it as the turning point for better or worse; as an emotionally significant event or radical change of status in a person's life; or as the point in time when it is decided whether an affair or course of action shall proceed, be modified, or terminate. Caplan (1964) has described crises as sharply time-limited points of disruption of the usual stability of a system wherein usual direct problem-solving mechanisms do not work, and where alternate methods are either limited, unavailable, or not chosen.

Developmental life transitions such as marriage, birth of a first child, children leaving for school, adolescence, and children leaving home, among others, can be critical incidents. These can be described as *internal* variations or *developmental life crises* because they are inherent to the normal development of most family systems (cf. McCubbin & Figley, 1983). Similarly, other incidents like a rape, a mugging, a job loss, a critical illness, a premature family member death, or a break-in can be equally critical. These are *external* variations or *incidental life crises* in that they are both unpredictable events introduced from interaction with the external environment, and they do not occur in all family systems (cf. Aquilera & Messick, 1978; Jacobson, Strickley, & Morley, 1968; Morrice, 1976; Silverman, 1977). There is another unique set of crises which are represented by the repetitive and escalating violence of wife battering or child abuse. These may be termed *endogenous life crises* in that they represent discrete events inherent to a unique yet characteristic set of internal family patterns that produce them (cf. Fraser, 1988; Pagelow, 1984; Walker, 1979).

*Rapid Change*

Crises can represent major turning points in the life of a system. Across the history of sciences, and certainly in the social sciences, there has been a bias toward gradualism, or the assumption that all change is slow, rational, and orderly (Gould, 1982). In recent years, across a broad range of scientific areas, there has been a growing realization that rapid, all-or-nothing change is much more the norm than once thought. Without going into detail, the concepts of catastrophe theory in math, bifurcations in chemistry, flow patterns in physics, and punctuated equilibrium in anthropology, all indicate that major system changes are capable of occurring in rapid, discontinuous jumps. These phenomena are exemplified by such things as the major shift in the flow of a stream following the slight shift of a reed or a rock; the rapid, discontinuous jumps in the development of crystals; the growth of entirely new chemical combinations rather than a return to former chemical states following the agitation of high heat; the appearance of major new evolutionary animal life forms in relatively short periods of time without expected Darwinian evolutionary links; or the decision point phenomenon for a threatened dog where only slight variations will determine whether it will attack or turn and flee. Thus, rather significant changes in system patterns are not only possible, but highly probable at crisis points.

Gerald Caplan (1964), one of the founding fathers of crisis theory, suggests that times of crisis generally last from four-to-six weeks from initial crisis point to ultimate resolution. During this time, there is an initial interruption of relatively stable patterns, followed by the marshaling and application of the range of usually effective coping patterns. If these are effective in assimilating the change, the system will then move on with only minor variation. If, on the other hand, initial attempts at dealing with the crisis are not successful, new rounds of coping attempts are employed, generally using variations of the original coping patterns only with greater intensity or duration of application. Such a redoubling of efforts and agitation in the system may then result in some major shifts to what can be described as either a system breakdown or a move to a new, more adaptive set of patterns. Therefore, *it is the nature of the system's response patterns surrounding a crisis point which become a critical focus in determining the future course of the system.* The four-to-six week life cycle of a crisis response represents a critical window of opportunity during which the system's response patterns can either assimilate the change, produce system deterioration, or move the system to an entirely new and potentially more flexible and adaptive set of patterns.

*Negotiating Change*

The major focus of attention for crisis intervention is, therefore, the facilitation of the way in which social systems like the family negotiate change. In pursuing this focus, the main concepts employed by the Strategic Rapid Intervention (SRI) approach are derived from the highly relevant work of the Mental Research Institute (MRI) in Palo Alto, California (Fisch, Weakland, & Segal, 1982; Watzlawick, Weakland, & Fisch, 1974; Weakland, Fisch, Watzlawick, & Bodin, 1974). In their study of the process in which systems negotiate change, the MRI group has generated the important concepts of *first and second order change* and *first and second order reality*.

Briefly stated, this view suggests a response to change quite similar to that described by Caplan (1964). As a response to system variations or difficulties, the system's repeated employment of its usual patterns with escalating adjustments in intensity, frequency, and duration, are termed *first order changes*. These are changes within the rules or normal patterns of the system which nevertheless maintain or do not fundamentally alter those patterns. Their employment may help the system assimilate the change, or their repeated use may not only be fruitless, but actually serve to further *escalate* the problem, while they narrow or reduce the probability that other, possibly more effective options will be tried. This may be seen as a positive feedback cycle wherein the more the first order solution is employed, the worse the problem gets. In contrast, a *second order change* is a change *of* the particular rules, premises, or patterns of a given system.

The following example may be helpful in understanding these concepts. I once observed a bird to be caught in a large, two-story vestibule. There were open double doors below and a very large plate glass window above them. The bird, after having flown in the doors and up and finding itself trapped, had apparently turned, looked through the plate glass window, and, assuming that "that way is out," flew toward the window. When confronted with the inability to negotiate the window, the bird then engaged in a variety of first order changes or solutions to get out. It flew hard and soft. It flew at the top, the middle, and the bottom of the window. It flew into the window with its head, its sides, and its breast, all to no avail and with increasing panic and exacerbation of its crisis. Interestingly, the solution to the bird's dilemma, which was easy to see from my vantage point, was a second order change, and characteristically represented the exact opposite of what the bird was doing. It represented an *alteration in premise, pattern, or rule*. Instead of flying forward and up, it needed to fly back and down. Yet, also characteristically, such a second order change would have appeared *contradictory or paradoxical* from within the premises and patterns of the bird's solution-generated dilemma. The danger of the bird's escalating first order solution pattern is that it may severely injure or even kill itself against the window. In actual fact, such a stunning blow became an opportunity for the bird, in that it finally "knocked itself silly" against the window, thus jamming its former solution pattern, fluttered down to the ground, and upon gaining composure, flew out the open door.

Such solution-generated dilemmas can be commonly seen in such clinical situations as insomniacs whose conscious attempts to will themselves to sleep are the very things that inhibit sleep, which is itself a spontaneous loss of consciousness. Men or women with the sexual problems of not being able to attain an erection or an orgasm, respectively, often engage in such deliberate and focused solution attempts that their attention is directed away from the sensuality of the sexual interaction, which itself tends to lead to excitement and release. Those with panic attacks who then become anxious over when they will next become anxious do more to increase the probability and intensity of future attacks than they do to inhibit them. In each case, doing less of the same, or often even doing somewhat the opposite of what they have done in the past, provides the solution. This sometimes happens serendipitously, or as the result of accidental disruptions of ongoing patterns, but it is also often the focus of what we in the helping disciplines find ourselves doing in therapy. This is *the interruption of vicious cycles* which often evolve around the negotiation of crisis points.

The concepts of first and second order reality relate generally and simply to the ideas, concepts, or descriptions used by members of a given system in describing the way things are. Simply stated, *first order reality* may be described as an agreed-upon and useful description of the way things are in a given context. A *second order reality* may then be described as an alternate and equally or even more useful description of the way things are within the same context. These descriptions are often referred to as premises, frames, or reframes of reference. Within a given system, there is a multiplicity of unique and shared premises or frames in relationship to what constitute appropriate roles, behaviors, or definitions of situations, for example. In the case of the bird in the vestibule, the assumption that the way out was through the plate glass window illustrates a premise or frame of reference of the nature of the situation. The implicit assumption that more of the same solution will be helpful (i.e., "If at first you don't succeed, try, try again") is another assumption or frame on the nature of change. Similarly, the assumption that I can will myself to sleep, or to spontaneous sexual excitement, or to the absence of any future anxiety are also frames on the nature of the way things are.

The compelling logic of these frames of reality is generally based upon the success of these ideas in past interaction within the system, and/or from the teaching and experiences gained from within the family, subculture, or cultural context. Some of these constructs or frames are broadly shared within and across families within a culture, such as general definitions of the appropriate role of a good mother, father, or child. Others emerge uniquely from the specific history of interaction patterns within a given system, such as always approaching strangers with caution rather than trust, or being uniquely suspicious or reactive to authority for example. No matter what the framework on reality, the frame influences choice of action, as do actions confirm or alter frames in a reciprocal way.

*The major goal* of much of SRI is the interruption of vicious problem cycles, the initiation of second order change, and the instigation of new virtuous cycles. The creation of a second order reality or a reframing of a role, action, or situation is quite often an integral element to facilitating second order change.

*A final core concept* of the SRI model is the assumption that all change, though inevitable, creates varying degrees of unpredictability, and is therefore anxiety provoking. Thus, when variations are introduced, be they developmental transitions, incidental intrusions, or endogenous crisis events, the system and its members react in attempts to preserve or recapture their perceived sense of former predictable stability. A corollary to this point, however, is that these same attempts at maintaining a predictable constancy are often the very actions that amplify the variation and increase the probability of change. There is an inherent ambivalence which grows around a crisis point. The system members become increasingly uncomfortable around their ineffective attempts to change the situation, and they become increasingly aware of the need to change their solution patterns, yet they are understandably reluctant to try new untried options and introduce even more unpredictability into their lives. Nevertheless, this is probably the most promising time for the system to incorporate such new patterns, given the apparent ineffectiveness of the old ones. If an intervenor can respect this reluctance and utilize the ambivalence toward change, they may enhance the probability that the system will move to some truly new and creative patterns.

The term *rapid intervention* rather than *crisis intervention* has been chosen deliberately. The definition of a crisis varies from one therapist to the next and from one system to the next. What one therapist or family member may see as a crisis, another may define as a mere inconvenience. What is important is to intervene rapidly at the point of difficulty to take advantage of the inherent flux in patterns, to prevent deterioration, and enhance the probability of initiating new and more positive patterns in the system in the future.

## GENERAL APPROACH TO TREATMENT/INTERVENTION

As stated in the section above, the main focus of SRI, true to that of traditional crisis theory, is upon the *response patterns* which surround crisis points. As with most other generic crisis intervention approaches (cf. Aquilera & Messick, 1978; Burgess & Baldwin, 1981), there is a deemphasis upon the analysis of past history as a predeterminant or a curative factor, and instead the analysis and alteration of current interaction is the goal. While it is acknowledged that historically generated family patterns and constructs contribute to the nature of the crisis response pattern, it is assumed that altering current response patterns will have more effect upon varying historical patterns and ideas than vice versa.

A major assumption made is that the course of these patterns will be critical to the future functioning of the family system, and that slight alterations in pattern at these times can have great reverberating future effects within the system to its great benefit or detriment. A second assumption is that it is highly desirable to intervene at times of crisis because the system is probably the most receptive to new patterns at these times, and that such slight pattern shifts can not only avoid future problem generation, but also initiate possible positive future patterns. A final emphasis is the reminder that rapid, all-or-nothing pattern changes are not only possible, but also to be expected around crisis points, and that the limits of a therapist's influence are somewhat expanded at this time to be able to help shape the nature of these shifts which may have far-reaching influence on the future of the system patterns.

What is unique about SRI as compared to more traditional approaches is that it adds a systemic element to the analysis and intervention into these crisis response patterns. The actions of the therapist can be seen to be very deliberate and planful, based upon an analysis of the nature of the crisis, and the system members' unique constructs and solution patterns; hence the term "strategic." Furthermore, because the system's solution-generated crisis response cycle is usually based upon conventional wisdom, or at least upon logical attempts at solution, and the intervening therapist is often trying to alter or reverse these patterns, the therapist employing this approach often engages in prescriptions, interactions, and positions that may look contradictory to the common logic or appear to be "paradoxical." Finally, because intervenors using this approach deliberately attempt to analyze, understand, utilize, and/or alter system members' assumptions or frames of reference to help initiate crisis response pattern change, they are often perceived to be overly calculating, manipulative, or ingenuine. An attempt will be made to make each of these points more understandable and consonant to the role of a crisis intervenor in the following sections. The reader should be aware, however, that these are common perceptions of a strategic view of problems and treatment from the position of other observers.

In the succeeding analysis and intervention into the Taylors' case presented at the beginning of the chapter, the reader should note a number of these factors. While precursing patterns and ideas are noted as they contribute to the current crisis response, focus is put upon analyzing and altering the current problem patterns. As will be discussed in the next section, decisions are made about the nature of the crisis and the probability of any commonly expected generic response patterns to this type of crisis. Any specific or unique response patterns or frames of reference characteristic to this family and contributing to the crisis response cycle will be noted. The existence of any possible vicious cycles will be assessed, and minimal yet significant goals will be set. Some of these specific goals of pattern or concept alteration may initially appear paradoxical to the family members or the therapist, and they will need to be analyzed to assure a logical fit within the constructs of the therapist and the frameworks of the family members. Finally, an intervention strategy will be designed and implemented, taking into account both generic and specific response patterns and constructs of the family members, as well as their ongoing response to our intervention.

## ASSESSMENT METHODS

Before proceeding into assessment methods in the SRI approach, a brief but important note should be made about its position on traditional assessment methods and diagnostic categorization. While it is acknowledged that major psychological tests of intelligence or "personality," and major diagnostic constructs of psychosis, depression, anxiety disorders, and so on, can be of varied use in many situations, their use may be impractical at least, and not useful or overly biasing at the worst, in crisis situations. Diagnostic testing not only is impractical in a rapid response situation, but also tends to lend an individual focus to the assessment and attribution of pathology, and thus loses the interactional context of the system's response patterns which often make problematic behaviors both more understandable and alterable. The use of traditional psychiatric diagnostic categories not only further serves to locate and attribute pathology to individuals, but also frequently has little to say about what should be done to alter the pathology, once attributed. This position is, of course, inherent to the family systems and general system theory schools of thought from which the SRI approach is derived.

Instead, the assessment process in this approach is involved with the assessment of the *nature* of the particular crisis, the nature of any expected *generic response* patterns, the nature of the system's unique or *specific response* patterns and constructs, and the way these factors combine to generate the system's specific response to the crisis, and any subsequent *solution-generated problem cycles* that exist or have begun. All of this information is gathered through the interview process.

What is meant by assessing the nature of the crisis is that a determination is made of whether it is developmental, incidental, or endogenous in nature. There is some important information available in even this preliminary judgment. A *developmental* life crisis is somewhat predictable and normative, and the system members, though struggling with it, may have expected it, may have gone through it themselves, or watched others move through it. They may have received advice from family and friends on how to deal with it, or there may be some particular family or subcultural traditions on how to negotiate it. There may also be a body of information available to the therapist from the child or family development literature which may aid the therapist and the family members in understanding the range of normal actions and helpful responses at these transitions. The traditional role of guiding and protecting a child may need minor alterations when the child shows panic or tantrum at the first day of kindergarten. Protective patterns may only reinforce the child's sense that there is something to fear. A supportive yet firm limit needs to be set by the parent, instilling confidence in the child by the parent's willingness to leave him or her on their own. Failure to make this transition may help to initiate what may soon come to look like school phobia.

An *incidental* life crisis is by nature unexpected. Because of this inability to prepare, and the assumption that an event such as this would never happen in the safe and predictable patterns of a system member's life, trauma is often greater. Given that there are usually no established family norms of how to respond to these crises, response patterns are more often influenced more strongly by cultural assumptions on the nature of the crisis and the specific patterns unique to the given family or social network in question. This does not mean, however, that there is not a body of literature available to the therapist regarding how family systems commonly respond to the specific incidental crisis, as will be noted below in a discussion of generic response patterns. The generic response patterns to rape, sudden or impending death, or disaster, among others, can be usefully shared and employed in dealing with such incidental crises.

*Endogenous* crises such as incidents of battering or child abuse or neglect, come to be periodic, escalating, yet also somewhat predictable crises within some family systems. If the therapist is aware of the literature on the commonly seen cycles and assumptions within these systems, this knowledge can be used to predict future incidents, interrupt current patterns, or even to utilize these patterns in the process of both resolving the crisis and initiating new processes. For example, the honeymoon, or loving respite, phase of the battering cycle may actually be used to engage the man in allowing the woman more freedom or access to resources (cf. Fraser, 1988).

*General Response Patterns*

Implied in the above determinations of the nature of the crisis is a consequent assessment of both *generic and specific response patterns.* *Generic* response patterns are those which, through reference to the developmental, clinical, or research literature, we may come to expect as normative within our culture or given subcultures. These are patterns such as those surrounding a child's transition to adolescence, or their leaving home; or the commonly expected phases of response to grief, or the often-seen phases through which rape victims may pass; or the typical cyclical patterns of tension building, violence, and honeymoon seen in battering relationships. As implied above, knowledge of these patterns can provide greater prediction and control for both the therapist and the family members in crisis. It may also help system members to normalize their reactions and avoid labeling themselves or others as somehow deviant, or to avoid trying to change something which is part of a normal process, such as adolescent rebellion or initial fears of situations resembling a traumatic event. *Specific* response patterns are those constructs and patterns unique to the specific system in crisis. These include how the members describe the event or behavior in question, what they typically do to resolve such perceived difficulties, and their commonly or uniquely taken positions on how change occurs, how outsiders are treated, and so on. These are the elements and patterns that set each system apart from others and that contribute to the unique characteristics of the particular crisis response of each separate network. It is these constructs and interaction patterns, in combination with any generic response patterns, that are crucial to an accurate assessment of the crisis-engendered problem and the ultimate design of the intervention.

*Questions*

In gathering this information, a set of typical questions are asked following an MRI model of assessment (Fisch, Weakland, & Segal, 1982; Watzlawick, Weakland, & Fisch, 1974; Weakland et al., 1974). These are such questions as "What is the problem?" as defined similarly or differently by each system member. How or in what ways is it a problem for them? What have the system members done about it? How has this worked? Is this what they usually do about such problems? Have they done all that they would usually do, or used all of their typically available resources in this situation? If not, why not? Have they shared their situation with others? What have others told them to do about the problem, if anything, and if they have tried this, how has it worked? What is their best guess about the reasons for the problem? Is anyone being assigned blame, or is anyone being labeled sick or deviant? What do they feel needs to change? What would a small beginning of this change look like? Who is most motivated for change and for what reasons? Who are the relevant members of this problem-generated system? Are there other key elements involved such as schools, courts, doctors, or others, and if so, in what way and with what influence? What is the typical language, values, and world view of the major involved parties?

*Session Model*

All of this information is gathered through the initial three phases of a six-phase general interview model which is highlighted in Figure 1 and further sketched out through a set of brief memory points for each phase in Table 1. This interview process has been described in greater detail elsewhere (Fraser, 1986a), so a briefer description will be offered here. This interview model offers a set of structured phases through which any initial contact may proceed, whether over the telephone, in a home, in an emergency room, or in an office. The above noted information is collected in a cyclical process of moving from joining with the system, to informa-

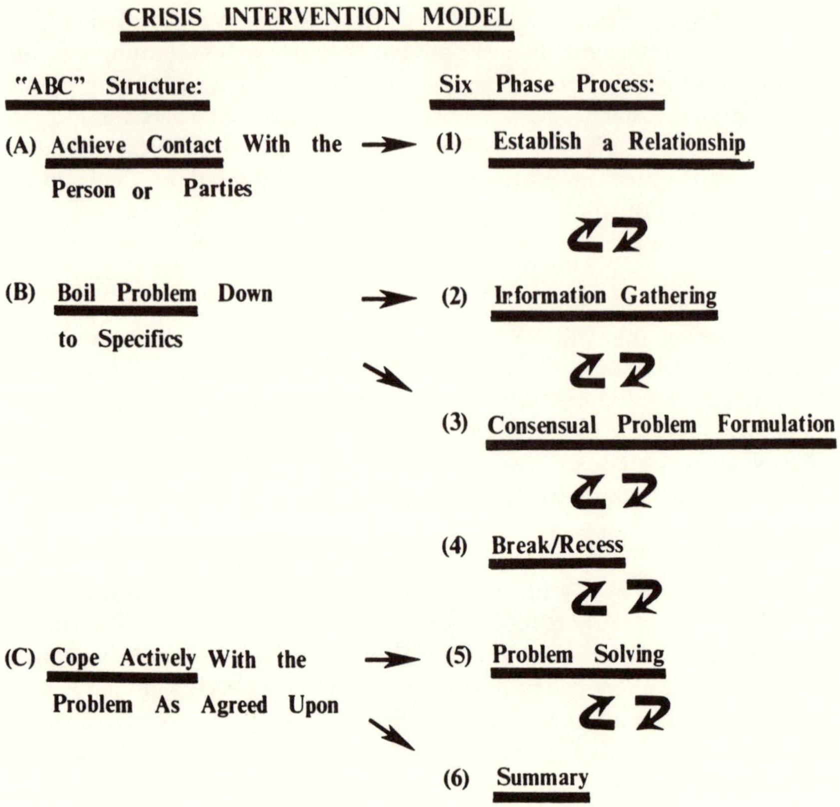

## CRISIS INTERVENTION MODEL

| "ABC" Structure: | Six Phase Process: |
|---|---|
| (A) Achieve Contact With the → Person or Parties | (1) Establish a Relationship |

ↄⱬ

| (B) Boil Problem Down to Specifics → | (2) Information Gathering |

ↄⱬ

(3) Consensual Problem Formulation

ↄⱬ

(4) Break/Recess

ↄⱬ

| (C) Cope Actively With the → Problem As Agreed Upon | (5) Problem Solving |

ↄ ⱬ

(6) Summary

*Figure 1.* Crisis intervention model.

tion gathering, to a consensual formulation of the problem. At this point, a brief break is taken to regain perspective on the problem, the system, and the interview process, during which the case is briefly reviewed with another therapist external to the case. Preliminary ideas are developed on the nature of the problem, the initial goals, and the design of a possible intervention. In the problem-solving and summary phases, the therapist's ideas are woven with the system members' interactions to evolve an intervention, a therapeutic contract, and a plan of action and some possible homework, or outside tasks for the system members. In the summary phase, any progress or movement shown by the clients from the beginning to the end of the interview is noted, the process of what has happened and of what has been concluded in the interview is reviewed,

## TABLE 1
### Crisis Intervention Model

1. *Relationship Establishment*
   a. Explicit empathy.
   b. Focus on emotions.
   c. Therapist's calm confidence.
   d. Therapist's warmth and genuineness.
   e. Therapist's intrusiveness and directiveness.

2. *Information Gathering*
   a. Focus on why today.
   b. Focus on current problem.
   c. Focus on coping mechanisms tried already.
   d. Focus on nature of support system—as either a resource or as a "cause."
   e. Emphasis on behavior change to more productive actions.
   f. Deemphasis on "insight"—emphasis on mobilization to change situation.
   g. Focus on "normalizing" or accepting distress as OK given the situation.
   h. Therapist is presented as an emphathic, calm, warm, hopeful, intrusive leader.
   i. Therapist moves from trust-inducing "parent" to an initiative-encouraging peer—fosters maturity.
   j. Unsatisfied needs are assessed—wants, goals, why they aren't met.

3. *Consensual Problem Formulation*
   a. Problem agreed upon as the client sees it.
   b. Problem statement must make sense to client.
   c. Purpose is to clarify the range and limit of the problem.
   d. Problem stated clearly enough so as to imply action to be taken.

4. *Break Taken to Distance, Process, Problem Solve*
   a. Purpose is for *both* client and therapist to gain perspective on the problem and the session so far.
   b. Problem solving starts here—each party looks for alternatives.
   c. Therapist processes with another therapist outside system.
   d. Used also to test client motivation for problem solving.

5. *Problem Solving*
   a. Both client and therapist examine alternative courses of action.
   b. Aimed at the goal of at least a return to last previous best level of functioning.
   c. Not looking for "character restructuring."
   d. Aims to achieve small behavioral alterations.
   e. Structured planning conducted.
   f. Initiative and responsibiity gradually shifted to the client along with confidence in his ability to change.
   g. Actions planned in line with client's goals, values, unmet needs.
   h. Symptomatic relief sought.
   i. Support system included.
   j. Plans for further help in change are laid down—other therapy, referrals, etc.

*(continued)*

## TABLE 1 (continued)

6. *Summary*
   a. Steps used in interview are reviewed.
   b. Client's progress in interview is made clear.
   c. Plans arrived at are reviewed.
   d. How plans are to be implemented is reviewed.
   e. Future stress points are reviewed and predicted.
   f. Sources of further help are reviewed.
   g. Assessment made of client's level of hopefulness, trust, expectations of change to meet needs, spontaneous expressions of relief and appreciativeness.

and the clients are reminded of any therapeutic contracts or homework tasks that have been agreed upon or assigned.

*Case Example*

The Taylors' case may help to enlighten this process. The Taylors were a white, middle-class couple in their mid-forties, both working in professional business positions, living in an urban neighborhood, with two children — a son (17), and a daughter (20). At the first telephone contact, it became apparent that the nature of the current crisis was *an incidental one*. The break-in had been an unexpected traumatic event with the potential of loss of life, and the clear invasion of privacy, loss of property, and loss of the sense of perceived safety. This judgment led the therapists to expect some variations of *a post-traumatic stress reaction* among the family members as a generic response pattern, even before the family was seen in the initial interview. Common elements of such response cycles include initial shock, denial, panic, and numbness or depersonalization, followed by varying patterned attempts to reconstruct and consolidate the experience into the ongoing patterns of the system members' lives. Initial responses within this early consolidation period may vary from generalized fear and rumination, to heroic attempts to make things right and safe again for others, to flat denial. There is a characteristic repeated reviewing of the event, and similar voices or situations may trigger flashbacks of the incident, often when this is least expected or most inconvenient. Guilt or feelings of powerlessness over not having been able to prevent or stop the incident are common, as is a frequent sense of shame that others might find out that this has happened to them. Ultimately, the way in which the system members move through this initial response phase will influence their eventual success at constructing, understanding, consolidating, and integrating the traumatic event into the patterns of their future lives. Flashbacks or generalized or specific fears, for example, may become an ongoing yet disruptive pattern; or the system members may simply become more realistically cautious about their safety in given situations; or the incident might actually serve to initiate a positive new path for one or another of the system members or for the system as a whole.

Because all three of the family members living at home had gone through the traumatic event and all of them were in some way dealing with its aftermath, the three of them were invited to the initial interview together. The 20-year-old daughter who was not living at home was not included. As it happened, the 17-year-old son was not brought to the initial interview because the mother didn't want to disrupt his life further by having him miss a play-off game in which his baseball team was involved.

## System Selection

It should be noted that just because this approach is based upon system-oriented constructs, this does not mean that all members of a given system are required to be seen or involved. Who is seen in therapy is more a product of who is judged to be important to the problem cycle than who might be judged to be a member of a formal system or family network. In this case, all members who had been involved in the break-in were chosen for several reasons. The main reason was that when several people are involved in the same traumatic event, this can be both confirming and frustrating. It can be confirming in that they can all affirm their experience as real and shared. It can be frustrating in that each system member may respond very differently in style and pace in resolving the crisis. One's style of response may frustrate another, or one member's apparent speed in recovery may cause others to wonder what is wrong with them that they have not yet adjusted. Second, in adjusting to such an unexpected, traumatic event, retelling it in the presence of others becomes an important process in consolidating it into the system members' experiences and reestablishing a sense of predictable safety. We wanted to both gain information on each member's style of response and offer the experience of jointly retelling the event in our selection of members for the initial interview.

## Recent History

In the initial interview we learned a number of things. The couple reiterated that the major problem was Mrs. Taylor's sleeplessness, distractibility, and general fearfulness in adjusting to the recent break-in. After each had recounted for us the events of the night of the break-in, they went on to say that the past two years, and particularly the last six months, had been stressful times for them all. What we learned was that two years ago they had discovered that their daughter had been abusing alcohol, and the entire family was engaged in first an inpatient and then an outpatient alcohol rehabilitation program. This was successful in that she had shown no signs of relapse since. However, six months ago, two weeks before a planned family reunion at Christmas, their daughter and her boyfriend had stolen the family van and run away. Eight days before Christmas, the police found the van, and the couple picked it up from the police and went right to the airport to greet their arriving family. Within a month, they found that their daughter was on the west coast, was pregnant, and had married the disapproved-of boyfriend. Then, just six weeks ago, at the end of school, their son, an excellent student, had called his mother up to his room in the morning and showed her that he had just cut his wrists. Shortly following the couple's discussions with their son, which revealed his distress over a friend moving away and the loss of a girl friend, he seemed to turn around and immerse himself in a summer job and a softball team which he enjoyed. Then the break-in happened.

*General Patterns*

The Taylors had always been close and supportive as a couple. Their daughter had always been very social yet rebellious. Their son had always been a good student, yet somewhat of a "loner." He had always been close to his mother and had been very supportive of her during his sister's runaway. Mr. Taylor was a very flexible and amiable man, who was successful in business. Mrs. Taylor had always been a high energy, "take charge" kind of person at home and at work, where she was an aid to a chief executive. Although she would periodically collapse with exhaustion, she liked having things go right and helping other people to look good.

The most relevant factors here, however, concerned how the family members were relating to the problem as they defined it—and that was Mrs. Taylor's reactions to the break-in. In short, their solution patterns were as follows. Realizing that the burglar had not yet been caught, they had a burglar alarm system installed. They hid their valuables, nailed shut their windows, and double-locked their doors and screen doors. Most of the lights in the house were being left on at night, and Mr. Taylor went through a nightly ritual of checking all closets and behind all doors before he turned off the downstairs lights, turned on the alarm, and came upstairs. The Taylors were sleeping with the bedroom light on. Mrs. Taylor had been staying awake most of the nights, and her husband had been staying up as long as he could to comfort her. When she did drift off to sleep, she would awaken and sit straight up at the sound of their son going to the bathroom, or getting up early to go to his summer job. She was nervous and distractible at work, and even though she tried to go on as usual, she would jump at someone's voice or touch and break down in tears. Mr. Taylor had been trying to help by taking over the tasks of dealing with the police, the courts, insurance, and so on. He seemed to immerse himself in a number of projects at home and at work, yet he was finding himself more and more tired and distractible. Their son, frustrated by his parents' reactions, and especially by his mother's fears, had engaged in a series of arguments over the irrationality of their responses.

## DIAGNOSIS AND TREATMENT PLAN

In the Taylor case, much information was offered. However, the data most relevant to the SRI model were those relating to *the problem defined*, the *relevant solution patterns surrounding it*, and the *related frames of reference* of those system members dealing with it. In this case, there is a family network responding to the *incidental life crisis* of a robbery, and evolvng through the *generic response patterns* of a post-traumatic stress response. The other recent crises of alcoholism treatment, runaway, and suicide gesture are considered relevant to the family's stress level, indicative of some prior problematic interaction patterns, relevant to the assessment of prior coping patterns, and probably contributive to the current extent of the family members' reactions. They are not, however, considered to be the main focus of intervention.

### Specific Response Patterns

The *specific solution-generated problem patterns* in this family are several. First of all, each of the Taylors appears to be *attempting to master the traumatic event by avoiding it*, and each is doing so in his or her own way. Mrs. Taylor maintains a state of agitated fearfulness and rumination while she attempts to forget about it and move on with things. However, the more she attempts not to think about it and to be brave, the more the event and its fear overtake her at the least opportune times. Mr. Taylor is making heroic efforts to protect the others and move things back to normal, and in doing so he is not only not acknowledging his own stress, but is in fact increasing it. Their son, in essentially denying the impact of the event on himself and others, is not only alienating himself from the support and comfort of others, but he is also escalating the very reaction in his mother over which he is so aggravated, namely her "irrational fears." Each of these solution patterns is a well-meaning attempt to adjust to the traumatic event, yet each tends not only to exacerbate their own distress, but also to feed and escalate the problem patterns of the others.

*Major Goals*

Therefore, the overall goal of the intervention from the therapists' view is to help the family to evolve through the post-traumatic stress cycle as rapidly as possible and with the best possible results through minor adjustments in current interactions and ideas. The focused goal of the family at the least was for Mrs. Taylor to be able to sleep again at night. The specific goals of the treatment were to interrupt Mrs. Taylor's "uncontrollable" ruminations, compulsions, and ritualistic checking, and her sense of being out of control and "crazy." Relatedly, Mr. Taylor's denial of his own stress and his attempts to help the others also needed interruption. The family needed to stop their attributions of deviance and vulnerability and, instead, begin to see themselves and their responses as normal, strong, and in control. Finally, interruption of their son's escalating arguments was critical.

In starkly interactional terms, we would want Mrs. Taylor to attempt to bring on, rather than to avoid, her anxiety and fear; Mr. Taylor to acknowledge his stress and ask for help from his wife; the family to see their individual and collective reactions as a demonstration of strength and sure movement toward control; and the son to help his mother with her irrational fears by suggesting that she experience them, or at least not give them up too soon. Each of these goals represents not just a stopping of a vicious cycle, but the actual reversal of former solution patterns. Each may be seen as a second order change in some form. As such, each may seem contradictory or paradoxical when viewed from the frameworks of the family members, the therapists, or possibly even the reader. It is crucial, therefore, for each of these changes to make sense to the family members and to the therapist if compliance with directives and interventions is to be gained. (For a more complete discussion of this issue of paradox, the contradiction of common wisdom, and the need for clear frameworks of understanding for the therapist, please refer to Fraser, 1984.) In this case, a logical reframing was designed for each member, as well as for the family collectively. This will be discussed further in the next section. The framework that made sense to the therapists in this case was the reversal of vicious cycles in each instance and the empowerment of each family member through an acknowledgment and utilization of their own strengths and resources.

In each of these instances and in others, the goal of SRI is to design interventions that introduce dissonance into the problem patterns surrounding the crisis response. This may not only disrupt deteriorating response patterns and prevent future difficulties, but may also open the opportunity for new and more productive interactions to initiate. In so doing, the current constructs and interaction patterns of the system are identified, respected, and used as much as possible to help to instigate a new pattern. The following section on the treatment approach may help to further bring this process to life.

## TREATMENT APPROACH

The Taylor case took a total of seven sessions spaced over about eight weeks to be resolved, with the addition of a one-month and a six-month follow-up. Within these sessions, the couple was seen twice, Mrs. Taylor was seen alone three times, the son was seen alone once, and the father and son were seen together once. Following the initial telephone call, an emergency room visit was arranged during which Mrs. Taylor was prescribed a mild sleeping medication. The following will outline the major steps of the interventions designed and implemented as concisely as possible.

### Normalizing

As noted earlier, one objective in the resolution of traumatic stress is to allow the parties to share, reconstruct, and consolidate the experience with others. This was designed and achieved in the initial session as the intervention assessed the traumatic event by asking each partner to share their version of the break–in. A second major objective was also initiated in the first session. This was the normalization of the family's responses as distressing yet common variations in responding to such a traumatic stressor. Instead of implicitly taking a position of reassurance that everything would be all right now, we agreed with their apprehensions and precautions, given that the intruder had not yet been caught. We also agreed that they might not want to let down their guard too quickly under the circumstances. These messages were designed both to be empathic and to counter the common statements offered by clients and others around them that their distress is not normal and must be quickly gotten over. If the clients protest that their reactions are too strong or need to change more quickly, they must convince us of this rather than vice versa. This reverses some typical patterns with helpful others, and offers the clients the chance to observe themselves making a case for change rather than having others do so for them. Furthermore, following the recounting of the series of crises through which the family had been in the recent past, their strength was deliberately emphasized through our expressions of amazement that the family was holding up as well as they were, given their level of prior stress. The impact of this position was confirmed during the next session when the couple both commented how much better they felt since realizing the real impact of the extended series of stresses which they had been under.

*Symptom Reframing*

Another major objective was initiated toward the end of the first session as we discussed with Mrs. Taylor our observation that she had not allowed herself to acknowledge the full impact of all of the crises preceding and including the break–in. We wondered whether one reason that many of her apprehensions would come on so intensely and unexpectedly was because she was not allowing herself to truly experience them and understand their meaning. After gaining some agreement with this, we asked Mrs. Taylor if she would be willing to allow herself to experience some of these apprehensions in small doses and whether Mr. Taylor would be willing to help her remember to consistently set aside some convenient time daily to do so. We allowed that this was a very difficult task which might be asking too much of them, yet we hoped that they could understand how it might help. The couple agreed to do so.

*Symptom Prescription*

This intervention, which some might describe as a "symptom prescription," was designed to reverse the process of Mrs. Taylor trying not to think about the incident, and yet ending up in agitated rumination when it was least convenient, at work or at bedtime. If she was able to do the task, she would be demonstrating some control over it and learning more about the content and process of her distress. If, on the other hand, she was unable to regularly bring up her concerns on a planned basis (and this is a very likely possibility, given that it essentially asks her to deliberately plan to get out of control, and to observe and learn from this), she may come to the realization with great relief that her fears are not ready to just leap out at her if she doesn't keep them under tight control. It furthermore served to reverse the subtle position of her husband from one of trying to calm her down in numerous and varied ways, to one of reminding her to be worried, so to speak. Our discussion of why we thought that it would be good for her to do this is an example of a frame that we constructed to make the prescription understandable. The couple found it understandable, yet, if they hadn't, there may have been a number of alternative ways of helping it to be meaningful. The couple did comply with the homework and Mrs. Taylor found it increasingly harder to do. We were somewhat disappointed and puzzled over why this might be so. Her response was that she didn't know, but she thought that maybe she was beginning to get through this.

## An Intervention-Generated Problem

Regarding Mrs. Taylor's increasing sleep deprivation and the associated sleep loss of her husband, a decision was made immediately to use a mild sleeping medication to interrupt the cycle of growing exhaustion and confusion. This, in fact, did work by increasing quite quickly the Taylors' sleep to around five to seven hours per night, and consequently increasing their cognitive and emotional resources. However, it also produced the common and unfortunate side effect of a perceived dependence upon the pills for sleep, a question of whether sleep would come normally again, and a fear of what would happen if the pills were unavailable. Thus, one of our initial and temporary solution attempts had initiated its own solution-generated problem cycle.

Our response to this was a simple alteration in the physician's prescription cycle. After the first 10-day prescription was used, we had the physician prescribe the same 10-day prescription, but for a 30-day period before refill and to be taken as needed. We empathized with Mrs. Taylor over this distressing yet typical course of sleeping medication application and emphasized that she use them on only those nights when she felt most likely to be unable to sleep—remembering always to put some aside for some future nights that might actually be worse.

Her response to this change was rather quick. Realizing that she needed to cut back on the medication so that she would have it as a buffer when she "really needed it," she went four of the next seven nights without its use and slept just as well. After this, she never used another pill. Our stance on this was one of "pleasant surprise," puzzlement, and caution.

We asked her if she wasn't demanding too much of herself or trying to move too quickly, and reminded her to be sure to feel free to take a pill when she felt she really needed it. She responded that while she appreciated our support, she really didn't want to take the pills forever, that she was finding that she could sleep now rather well without them, but that it was reassuring to know that they were available if she really needed them. This simple shift reversed several patterns. It required her to interrupt her pill taking in service of being cautious about being able to depend upon it when she most needed it. Furthermore, our puzzled and cautious stance (as opposed to one of talking her out of pill dependence and congratulations over her success) gave her a chance to demonstrate, explain, and convince us of her reasons, resources, and strength in refusing to depend upon the medication. This position not only interrupted the cycle, but also empowered Mrs. Taylor and gave her a new sense of control over her situation.

## The Argument Cycle

Turning now to the cycle of escalating arguments and growing distance between mother and son, we sought to reverse this pattern as well. The more the son pointed out the irrationality of his mother's fears and demanded that she explain herself or stop, the more the mother felt the need to defend her fears and felt a growing loss of control and concern over her state of deviance as she realized that she couldn't just stop her anxiety and her ritual attempts to reduce it. This, of course, only increased her anxiety, while it built resentment toward her son. Similarly, the more the mother acted on her anxieties, the more the son was reminded and confronted by the sense of loss of control and threat around the event which he was trying to put aside and move himself on. This inflated his attempts to have her stop.

## Intervention with the Son

We achieved much of this in a single session with the son. Without explicitly describing his recent depression and suicide gesture, the son told of a recent time when he felt overwhelmed. He said that he had then gotten through this when he realized that he was in charge of his own life, and that if he didn't act to change things, nobody else was going to be able to do much for him. As a result of this, he had started reaching out more to friends, and things were really going much better for him. He wished that someone had told him about this before, and that is why he had been trying to convince his mother of this fact. In response to this, we empathized with him and commended him on his insight and strength, and for his values in attempting to help his mother with her similar situation.

We continued then by pointing out that *his only error seemed to be in the way he had approached his task.* He agreed with us that until he had really bottomed out in his own life, he probably wouldn't have taken this valuable advice as particularly relevant, and even if he had he might not have owned it and pursued it so strongly as his own. So we began to discuss some alternative approaches to helping his mother come to her own conclusions. Rather than trying to talk his mother out of her distress, *he could help her to experience it enough so that she herself might bottom out as he had and thus be more ready to take charge of her own life again.* After telling him of a time when I had become so frustrated at my teenaged sister-in-law, only to later realize that her actions were the same as those I had struggled with at her age, I (as the intervenor) agreed with him that this situation might be very hard because it was like looking in a mirror and not liking what you saw.

We then talked about some new stances which he might consider, including sharing his own experience with her and encouraging her to feel the full extent of her distress if she was to ever be able to come to her own decision to change it. This included specific actions like reminding his mother to turn lights on, to be sure to check thoroughly behind doors and in closets, apologizing for trying to talk her out of her fears, and instead, reminding her that they were probably still very real for her, and asking her if she was really ready to give up any of her distressing behavior which he might notice her beginning to stop doing. He was not to do any of this, however, unless he truly felt that it would be helpful for his mother and if he could offer his stance sincerely and without cynicism. As a bright young man (and yet to our pleasant surprise), he commented that he realized that this would offer her choices of whether to engage in the old problem behavior or not, while offering her a better sense of control and power. We also felt, of course, that it would give her a better feeling of support, while ending the cycle of alienation from, and reestablish some closeness with, her son. This is an example of understanding, respecting, and using the particular framework and values of a client, and then building new, different, and more productive solution patterns based upon existing premises or ideas (cf. Fraser, 1983).

The outcome of this reversal in the son's stance was also quite positive. To his surprise, when he shared his experience with his mother and suggested that she probably needed to get worse before she could get better, her response was to tell him that she didn't want to get worse, and she shared with him the ways in which she saw herself getting over this. Initially, there were some times when his mother did turn on or leave on a light, or lock a screen door. Quite soon, however, he began to notice more lights being left off, screen doors left open, and closets going unchecked. When he asked if his mother was sure she wanted to do these things, she noted there was no need anymore.

### Altering the Helping Cycle

The final target objective was with Mr. Taylor. In his heroic attempts to help the others, he was overlooking his own stress responses, wearing himself down, and beginning to be more frustrated and alienated from his wife. The initial directive for him to remind his wife to attend to her distress made the first step in altering the pattern. The second step was *for him to share his distress with his wife.* We encouraged this by reminding him of how strong his wife had always been, and by pointing out how his sheltering of her from the reality and extent of his own stress had been denying her the opportunity to reassert her skills in helping. As he began to do so, he was pleased to see the old, familiar reactions of his wife as she offered some needed comfort and perspective for him.

### Results

By the end of the fourth week of treatment, the Taylors were sleeping through the night unassisted. Mr. Taylor had taken a long weekend to go fishing at his wife's insistence. Their son had stopped his arguments with his parents and was engaged once more with his friends. Mrs. Taylor subsequently went on a business trip to the West Coast for four days on her own during the sixth week. By week seven, the whole family agreed that things were back to normal.

We agreed to meet again in four weeks, during which time they were each to allow themselves some time to return to their earlier feelings and actions at the time of the trauma. At the four-week follow-up, each of them had found this hard to do given that their situation seemed to have consolidated. At the six-month follow-up, there had been several crisis events for their daughter, including a fire which necessitated she and her husband moving briefly into the Taylor home, and a motorcycle accident with their daughter's husband. Furthermore, the burglar had been caught. There had been no recurrences of the former sleeplessness and agitation, and the family reported actually feeling more comfortable and stronger than before despite this new series of events. Noting how impressed we were with all of them, and reminding them that they were free to contact us at any time, we closed the case.

## TREATMENT PROCESS

In contrast to those of many other family therapy and system-based approaches, the goals of SRI are not major alterations in family structure. Instead, through a focus upon altering system member's constructs and interaction patterns surrounding a crisis point, the goals are to resolve current problems, avert further ones, and possibly initiate some new and more viable processes within the system. In achieving these ends, there are a number of major tactics or interventions that may be noted.

Three major categories of interventions were illustrated in the Taylor case. These options are to: (a) *reframe, or alter premises;* (b) *accept current frames or premises, and build new action based upon them;* or (c) *prescribe the current interaction patterns with some alteration in the reason for performing them or in the way in which they are performed.* An example of *pure reframing* or altering premises was the redefinition of the Taylors' stress response from one of pathology, lack of control, and vulnerability, to one that was a common response to such traumatic stress and that demonstrated that they were well on their way to regaining control.

An example of *accepting current premises and building new action* was when the son's motive of having his mother pull things together and direct her own life again was used to have him accept and prescribe her distress rather than trying to argue her out of it. Another example was when Mrs. Taylor's motive to have the sleeping pills in case she couldn't sleep without them was used to have her stop using them so she would have some if she really needed them. Similarly, Mr. Taylor's motive to help his wife to regain her ability to take charge was used to have him share his own distress with her and ask for help, rather than treating her as an invalid while he sheltered her from his own stress.

The main variations around the theme of *prescribing current solution patterns* involved the therapists, the husband, and the son all prescribing rather than forbidding Mrs. Taylor from fully experiencing her distress and acting upon it. As noted earlier, in each variation, the prescription placed Mrs. Taylor in a therapeutic double bind wherein any response would represent a positive change. If she experienced her distress as prescribed, this indicated a new control over her feelings and actions. Taking mental notes on the particulars of her distress while she was experiencing it would, in itself, interrupt the spontaneity of it. Finally, attempting to lose control in a planned and deliberate way, for a positive set of reasons, is itself contradictory and makes it less likely that she will be able to feel out of control and distressed. Any problem in becoming distressed is likely to be a pleasant surprise for anyone who has felt that they would become so when they would least expect it if they weren't on perpetual guard. Of course, if Mrs. Taylor experiences any reaction against so many others attempting to direct her actions and feelings, she is more likely to resist these efforts by interrupting her pattern and doing something different.

In general, as noted in detail above, the treatment process proceeds from initial contact, through problem definition; identification of the problem-generated system involved; identification of any generic and specific solution patterns; designation of goals; design and implementation of a treatment strategy; analysis of responses and adjustment of interventions; analysis of outcome; termination; and follow-up. The number of sessions is not always strictly limited, yet usually ranges from one to 10, spaced flexibly over from five weeks to a year. Given the limited goals of intervention, and the theoretical stance that minor shifts in concept or process can have increasingly positive and major effects, the treatment process is most often brief, deliberate, and intense by design.

With most crisis encountered by therapists defined as vicious cycle, solution-generated problem patterns, the process of intervention moves toward identifying the concepts and processes that feed these patterns and turning them toward new and more productive ends. In the process of this endeavor, there are a range of intervention stances that have been identified, named, and usually referred to as therapeutic tactics. A number of these have been referred to above, yet it might be helpful to review them, note some others more explicitly here, and have them related more broadly to a wider range of crises. In reviewing these tactics, it must be remembered that they are merely variants of interventions that follow from the basic concepts underlying the SRI model. Furthermore, they are applied sensitively and are uniquely dependent upon the particular nature of the crisis, the involved system, and the solution-generated problem cycles in focus. Whereas some are employed in most crisis contacts, others are used only selectively, based upon an analysis of the particular system and problem pattern.

## SRI SELECTED TACTICS

*Normalizing*

Normalizing is the term used for the placing of the person or family's responses in the context of normal response patterns, given the nature of the stressor. It is broadly applicable across crisis situations. People in crisis, whether developmental or incidental, have usually not encountered this type of situation before and are thus often unaware of the range of response patterns and emotions which are usually involved. Many feel shame at not being able to handle it themselves or have been trying to deny or change emotions which can be expected given the crisis, and which will change on their own as the crisis is resolved. Normalizing system members' responses may, in some instances, be the only intervention needed. In most situations it generally helps in reducing shame, in increasing clients' perceived control, and in undercutting pathogenic labels. Broadly speaking, without minimizing the felt pain of the situation, normalizing is usually received as a "welcome to the club" message.

*Predicting*

Predicting is a variation of normalizing. It most often involves providing generic response-pattern information on the particular developmental or incidental crisis. It tends to increase clients' perceived control by anticipating future phases and inoculates them against overreaction. This occurs with grieving clients when common phases of denial, anger, guilt, and bargaining, among others, are discussed. Another example is with rape victims when the common patterns of rape trauma or post-traumatic stress cycles are reviewed. This therapeutic intervention is also helpful with battered women who, after learning of the cyclic phases of tension building, explosion, and honeymoon, may be able to more clearly identify their situations and possibly act upon them differently in the future. Similar help is received when other normal aspects of a particular developmental life crisis are reviewed or when anticipation of the next expected transition is discussed.

A final note on predicting is that it is frequently used upon successful termination to inoculate the clients against catastrophizing over the next minor life difficulty encountered. After having made rapid and successful changes, clients generally feel that their new success is fragile and must be cautiously protected. Such overly rigid or cautious stances may actually undercut clients' flexibility to deal with new difficulties, or cause them to see a new difficulty as proof that they haven't changed after all. The therapist's prediction that, for instance, "life is a roller coaster" and thus new dips can be expected, or that new life difficulties should be expected as just part of the human condition and should be looked forward to as the next growing edge for the family, are thus helpful predictions upon successful termination.

## *"Go Slow" Messages*

Despite the perceived urgency of most crisis situations, and often because of this urgency, it is most often useful for the therapist to offer a message for the clients to "go slow" or to proceed with some caution about change. This may be either an implicit or explicit message, the reason being that most people, when confronted with the necessity for change, will view this with no small degree of anxiety. Sometimes the nature of the change is actually already known to the clients or others are already urging it; yet often the greater the realization or the stronger the urging, the greater will be the client's apprehension and reluctance to move. In the face of such urgency, gentle therapeutic cautions are most often welcomed. Such cautions tend to offer clients a chance to discuss their need to make possible risky shifts, and to discuss possible pitfalls without the pressure to actually act. If the clients then do elect the change, it is thus done much more of their own volition, to their own credit, and with "their eyes wide open." Furthermore, if the clients reconsider and decide not to move yet, they experience much less shame in the face of the therapist's cautious stance than if strong advocacy had been employed.

Although little is lost by adopting this stance across the range of crises encountered, it becomes especially important in those crisis situations that normally pull for strong advocacy from concerned others. Although this is not always the case, in situations such as wife battering, helpful others are often moved in their compassion and revulsion to strongly advocate that the woman leave. Whereas on one level this makes complete sense, on another it may actually be defeating the foundations of its purposes. Given the nature of the endogenous patterns of battering relationships (cf. Pagelow, 1984; Walker, 1979), a number of factors may make it very difficult for the woman to leave. Simply telling her to do so may not only yield shame and alienation from the intervenor if she does not do so, but also may confront her with a sense of powerlessness in her situation. Direct advocacy does not always empower. If the therapist finds that helpful others have urged a woman to leave and she still has not done so, then empathic and supportive "go slow" messages along with a discussion of the common dilemmas and patterns of a battering relationship may go much further toward eventual change than more of the same urging. (For a more complete discussion of strategic interventions in battering relationships, please refer to Fraser, 1988.)

*Restraints from Change*

Although seemingly contradictory to the traditional role of a therapist, therapeutic restraints are often helpful in amplifying client motivation for change, and in keeping the responsibility and credit for that change in the clients' hands. Soft restraints are an amplification of the "go slow" message and tend to take the form of explicit cautions, often using examples that the clients themselves may have brought up earlier. These are used to give clients the chance to respond to real or perceived hurdles with the therapist. They enable the clients through their counterarguments to not only solidify their commitment to the new action, but also anticipate their reactions to its possible pitfalls.

Thus, for parents who wish to stop nagging their teenager about being responsible, and instead to start allowing the teenager to meet the consequences and responsibilities of his or her own actions, several mild restraints might be offered. One caution is that this might look like a lack of caring on the parents' part. Another might be that they might not be able to withstand the pain of their child's mistakes. Still another might be that they may give in when their child severely tests the limits of their new stance. If the parents are dissuaded by any of these or other restraints, then it is reasonable that they not take this stance yet. On the other hand, if they argue successfully in each instance, they will be more prepared and committed to the action once taken. Furthermore, when they do encounter problems with their new stance, there is no shame to it. This just provides more information to use in refining their transition with the therapist. Soft restraints in some form are useful across a variety of crisis situations when a new position is about to be adopted by the clients.

Hard restraints, on the other hand, are used selectively and usually in instances where the system patterns are best described as reactive to outside influence or authority. There are some instances where clients' major motives are reaction against authority, or the taking on of challenges, or where they are unwilling to take new action unless it is clearly done of their own volition, and so on. In these unique systems, clients may elect to take new stances if they are seen as being prohibited, or at least cautioned against by the therapist or another outside authority. In most cases, the tactic of splitting described next is often most useful.

## Splitting

Splitting is a method of delivering a hard restraint without the therapist having to either own or defend the message as their own. Usually, a prediction of failure, inability to change, or refusal to change is attributed to the opinion of an authoritative colleague or an alternative theory. The therapist presents this as a point of information which he or she does not fully agree with, yet which should probably be shared. The objective of this stance is to enlist the clients' reaction to the position in service of new actions that might prove it wrong, while maintaining a supportive therapist–client relationship. This stance, as with the hard restraint, is used only occasionally, in accordance with consultation, and as judged uniquely appropriate to the particular patterns of a specific client system such as an oppositional abusing family, a reactive teenager, or a reluctant abusing spouse. In essence, these stances attempt to elicit new and positive actions based upon existing motives which are most often seen as malevolent or resistive (cf. Fraser, 1988).

## Positioning

In positioning, the therapist deliberately adopts a stance toward the clients or their problem which is often nearly the opposite of that taken by most helpful others within or relating to the problem system. This often takes the form of a general statement such as, "Given your situation, and all that you've been through, I'm amazed that you are doing as well as you are." Far from being discouraging, this stance tends to be a welcome relief to people in crisis who typically feel out of control and overwhelmed. It is also a very different message than that usually received from most others, who tend to offer encouragement that things are not that bad, as well as suggestions for how to make things better. Such a positioning stance was taken in the Taylor case, when we showed amazement over their strength in the face of multiple crises. This pulls for people to explain their strengths rather than describe their perceived failings. It furthermore tends to be undeniably empathic.

This is a broadly useful stance with depressed and suicidal clients. These clients are often involved in a cycle of having others attempting in some way to "cheer them up" and offer helpful new options. Too frequently these interactions lead only to more depression, alienation, and anger. Either the others have not been able to understand the depressing situation, or if they have, then the person may feel even more despondent because they are unable to do what others find to be so logical and simple. Such patterns generally lead to both emotional and physical isolation, as well as frustration on the part of everyone involved. Furthermore, suicidal statements frequently draw denial from others that things can really be that bad, or attempts to forbid the person from feeling the depth of their depression or from taking any action on it. Again, the person is often left feeling denied, misunderstood, and even more hopeless. The simple therapeutic stance of acknowledging and confirming the person's depressing circumstance, and wondering over how they have been able to tolerate it as well as they have, is the cornerstone of most effective intervention in suicidal crises. This position tends to be empathic and to acknowledge the person's strength, and establishes a groundwork for collaboration toward some new possible options.

## Reframing

Reframing can occur on its own or in conjunction with another message or directive. It can be an intervention in itself or aid in the understanding and acceptance of another message. It is essentially the offering of an alternate description of a current action, situation, person, or role that fits the facts as well or better than old frameworks. It is used to initiate new patterns or block old ones. Reframing is a pervasive intervention that cuts across virtually all strategic interventions in crisis and otherwise. It is especially useful at crisis points in that these situations usually produce what amounts to a "premature hardening of the constructs" within the given system. Familiar perspectives and premises are clung to more tightly at such times of distress and impasse, thus prepetuating rigid definitions and repetitive solutions. Altering such frames is often the watershed point from which the shift to new patterns flows. The Taylor case described earlier is full of examples of reframings that are typical of SRI model interventions across the wide range of crises.

## Prescribing

Prescribing refers to directing clients to engage in new or current behavior patterns with some alteration in purpose, deliberateness, or manner of performance. Prescriptions are usually accompanied by some form of frame to increase understanding and compliance. They are most frequently used in instances where the clients are attempting to master a problem by avoiding it, as was Ms. Taylor, or where repetitive cycles of thoughts or interactions are perceived to be out of control by the clients. As described in the Taylor case, such prescriptions tend to place the clients in a therapeutic "double bind" wherein, once engaged, the problem cycle becomes changed no matter what happens. For Ms. Taylor, if she was able to bring on her fears, she not only had the opportunity to learn more about them, but she was also demonstrating that they were under her own control. If she was unable to bring on these fears despite deliberate trying (and this is likely, because she was attempting to will something which formerly occurred spontaneously), then she had the chance to see that they might not be so pervasive and strong after all. This is an exact parallel to the prescription of panic attacks in clients experiencing recurring cycles of severe anxiety. Other prescriptions such as those given to Mr. Taylor or to his son are designed to reverse interaction patterns and thus free new options.

As noted above, a listing of intervention variations such as this can hardly avoid looking like a laundry list of techniques to be tried at will. It bears repeating that these interventions derive from both an understanding of systemic assumptions and from a clear assessment of the problem-generated system and the solution-generated problem in question. Their creative application in helping a system interdict a crisis-engendered problem cycle is what evolves in the process of a strategic rapid intervention.

## CONCLUSION

Crisis points are inherent in the life cycle of social systems like the family. Whether they are developmental, incidental, or endogenous, they have unmistakable impact on the evolution of the system. Although crisis usually has a negative connotation, the ultimate effect may actually be very positive. System response patterns, as they attempt to assimilate or accommodate to a crisis point, have the greatest impact upon eventual outcome, and they are thus the prime target of intervention.

When a system confronts a crisis, its usual coping patterns, assumptions, and ideas are called upon to aid in resolution. Often they are adequate and assimilate the change. Frequently, they themselves change to accommodate the shift created by the crisis. Equally as often, they are reemployed with redoubled intensity in the face of initial lack of success. These are the cases in which solution-engendered, vicious problem cycles evolve and require some intervention. It is in these cases that the concepts of first and second order change and reality which underlie the SRI approach are most appropriately applied.

One of the strengths of the SRI approach is that it provides a useful and flexible model for integrating the literature on crises with that of system-based intervention into a practical model of intensive and brief intervention. It focuses upon the characteristic crisis response patterns classically described by Caplan (1964) as the locus of change. It furthermore uses his described four-to-six week crisis life cycle as a window of opportunity for rapid intervention, and the initiation of small yet significant changes which might have been impossible to achieve at other times. It looks toward turning vicious cycles into virtuous ones by understanding, respecting, and using the strength of system patterns themselves toward positive ends.

In preparing this chapter, an attempt has been made to be as explicit as possible about theory, but more particularly about the details of practice. This has been done through case presentation, analysis, and detailed delineation of models and tactics. The only drawback is that it presents a narrowed problem focus and an artificial sense of detached application of technique. All that can be said to balance this is that the SRI model has been effectively applied within the Crisis/Brief Therapy Center for over 10 years across the broad range of crises. Unfortunately, only a mono-graph with subchapters relating to varying crisis applications would do this justice.

Second, it should be remembered that the interventions generated from the SRI model flow from a creative application of its underlying concepts to the specific crisis pattern of each unique system encountered. Interventions are designed and tailored with respect for the specific goals, concepts, and patterns of each system. They are not *done to* the system in some detached, rote, or mechanical way. Because it is painful and deliberate, the SRI model may generate the illusion of calloused detachment from the human suffering in which it intervenes. Instead, as will all effective therapy, it is only as effective as it is practiced with sensitivity, empathy, respect, and compassion for the people involved. In many ways, because the model asks that the therapist be informed about crisis patterns, attentive to the specific ideas and interactions of the system, and aware of a range of effective interventions and general goals, it may enable a more empathic and effective stance than intervention without such an explicit model.

Finally, the overall goals of the SRI model are much similar to both the usual requests of clients and the evolving context of mental health care today. The general goal of SRI is to enable a system in crisis to disengage from, and thus move positively beyond, escalating problem cycles in dealing with an intrusion or transition. Whereas there may be numerous systemic or historical factors that could be defined as problems or targets for change, the focus of change is upon the patterns surrounding the crisis. It is often hoped that alterations in these focused concepts and patterns may have positive ripples in altering other system interactions, but this is not necessary for success.

Most system members themselves do not ask for major "character restructuring" or system change. Instead, their requests are usually for help in negotiating the crisis and reducing their distress with the greatest respect and the least disruption of their comfortable ideas and prior patterns as possible. The SRI stance assumes that life is not trouble free; that there are many useful variations for living it; and that successful resolution of this crisis may, if nothing else, better prepare the clients for handling the next one. Successful clients often do come back at other distress points, and not necessarily to tap the therapist's strength, but instead because they remember how the therapist understood, respected, and helped the system tap its own strength in the past.

Such a stance as this is most in keeping with the growing movement in the mental health care field today of "brief therapy throughout the life cycle." This was, in fact, the topic of one of the best attended symposia at the most recent meeting of the American Psychological Association (Canter, Budman, Cummings, & Beckman, 1987). The fundamental concept here is that mental health services need to organize themselves to deliver time-limited services at periodic times of incidental crisis or life transition throughout a system's life cycle, rather than long-term treatment designed to ease all major problems. The strength of the system is respected in addressing its current problem patterns around each distress point and providing new skills and resources only as needed. This is similar to the model of the family doctor who attends periodically to the physical health and needs of family members as they move through their lives, supporting the body system's defenses against each new assault or intrusion and inoculating against others. In response to this endeavor, the field will need a set of flexible new models with which to organize its response. With its focus upon the nature of life crises and transitions, its respect for and utilization of system principles of intervention, and its adaptable range of application and ability to incorporate multiple approaches, the SRI model may prove extremely useful.

# REFERENCES

Aquilera, D., & Messick, J. (1978). *Crisis intervention: Theory and methodology* (3rd ed.). St. Louis, MO: C. V. Mosby Company.

Burgess, A. W., & Baldwin, B. A. (1981). *Crisis intervention theory and practice: A clinical handbook*. Englewood Cliffs, NJ: Prentice Hall.

Canter, A. H., Budman, S. H., Cummings, N. A., & Berkman, A. S. (1987). *Brief psychotherapy—Variations on a theme*. Paper presented at the 95th Annual Convention of the American Psychological Association, New York.

Caplan, G. (1964). *Principles of preventive psychiatry*. New York: Basic Books.

Dai, B. (1970). Etymology of Chinese word for "crisis." *Voices*, 70–71.

Fisch, R., Weakland, J. H., & Segal, L. (1982). *The tactics of change: Doing therapy briefly*. San Francisco: Jossey-Bass.

Fraser, J. S. (1983). Paranoia: Interactional views on evolution and intervention. *Journal of Marital and Family Therapy, 9*, 383–391.

Fraser, J. S. (1984). Paradox and orthodox: Folie à deux? *Journal of Marital and Family Therapy, 10*, 361–372.

Fraser, J. S. (1986a). The crisis interview: Strategic rapid intervention. *Journal of Strategic and Systemic Therapies, 5*(1 & 2), 71–87.

Fraser, J. S. (1986b). Integrating system based therapies: Similarities, differences, and some critical questions. In D. E. Efron (Ed.), *Journeys: Expansion of the strategic-systemic therapies*. New York: Brunner/Mazel.

Fraser, J. S. (1988, in press). Strategic rapid intervention in wife beating. In C. Chilman, F. Cox, & E. Nunnally (Eds.), *Families in trouble* (Vol. 3). Newbury Park, CA: Sage Publications.

Gould, S. J. (1982). *The panda's thumb*. New York: W. W. Norton.

Jacobson, G. M., Strickley, M., & Morley, M. (1968). Generic and individual approaches to crisis intervention. *American Journal of Public Health, 58*, 338–343.

McCubbin, H. I., & Figley, C. R. (1983). *Stress and the family, Volume 1: Coping with normative transitions*. New York: Brunner/Mazel.

Morrice, J. K. W. (1976). *Crisis intervention: Studies in community care*. New York: Pergamon Press.

Pagelow, M. D. (1984). *Family violence*. New York: Praeger.

Silverman, W. H. (1977). Planning for crisis intervention with community mental health concepts. *Psychotherapy: Theory, Research and Practice, 14*, 293–297.

Walker, L. E. (1979). *The battered woman*. New York: Harper Colophon.

Watzlawick, P., Weakland, J. H., & Fisch, R. (1974). *Change: Principles of p0 mation and problem resolution*. New York: W. W. Norton.

Weakland, J. H. Fisch, R., Watzlawick, P., & Bodin, A. M. (1974). *Brief therapy: Focused problem resolution*. Family Process, 13, 141–168.

# 6

# A Psychoeducational Approach

## GARY HARDLEY and BERNARD G. GUERNEY, JR.

*The J. family was referred by a crisis center which had also referred Mrs. J. to a Safe House. The extreme stresses the family members reported included: stress between Mrs. J. and her family of origin; a continuing pattern of spouse abuse by the husband; a hyperactive child who was violent with other children at school and his brother at home; a recent, very traumatic, spontaneous miscarriage; intergenerational conflict of the husband with the wife's family of origin; the wife's psychological abuse of her husband; the wife's aligning with the children against him; and the husband's extreme frustration with his wife's premenstrual behaviors. Mrs. J. had spent the preceding weekend at a Safe House to escape physical abuse from her husband. The crisis worker reported that Mr. J. was extremely angry at her for taking the children with her, but that both husband and wife wanted marital reconciliation.*

*Mr. J., an instructor at a local high school, was 38 years old and Mrs. J., a housewife, was 33. The J.'s, who had moved into the community two years earlier from the mid-west, had two boys: L., age eight, and O., age five. L. had been diagnosed as hyperactive and was on Ritalin for his hyperactivity. O. was having nightmares apparently related to his older brother's violent and hostile treatment toward him and the violence of his father toward his mother. Mrs. J. reported that her father, now deceased, had been an alcoholic and had been psychologically abusive to her. There was great conflict between Mr. J. and Mrs. J.'s family of origin. These problems had greatly increased since Mrs. J.'s mother had refused to come and assist her during her recovery from a miscarriage. Both she and her husband were very hurt and disappointed*

*about that. Mr. and Mrs. J. also reported that Mrs. J.'s mother was highly*
*rejecting of Mr. J. and that this had significantly increased since Mrs. J.*
*told her mother about the physical abuse. In fact, at the time of entering*
*therapy, Mr. J. was quite alienated from Mrs. J.'s whole family, including*
*her brothers and a sister. This stood in contrast to the couple's relation-*
*ships with Mr. J.'s family of origin, which both Mr. and Mrs. J. agreed*
*were positive.*

The goals of a psychoeducational approach can include all of the goals
of other family therapies. Such goals may include: symptom removal; the
resolution of presenting problems; the overcoming of other relevant problems that may be discovered in the course of working with the family; and
equipping the family to make better use of whatever resources the community may provide. Unlike other approaches, psychoeducation should
have, as we see it, an additional goal of enrichment: that is, it should seek
to add to the family's repertoire a set of attitudes and skills that will enable
them to provide one another with psychosocial support, to resolve difficulties
that arise in future stages of family life, and to relate more effectively to
their social and vocational environments far into the future.

The difference between the psychoeducational and other approaches
does not lie in an allegiance to or a rejection of any particular psychotherapeutic theory. It is broad enough to cover therapies based on almost any
theoretical position. To be sure, as an educational approach, whatever else
it draws upon it always must draw on a theory of learning. But there can
be a psychoanalytic, a humanistic, an interpersonal, a behavioral, or a
systems-oriented approach that follows a strictly psychoeducational model.
Conversely, there can be a therapy based entirely on learning theory that
does *not* follow the psychoeducational model at all; indeed, it may be
true that most learning-theory-based therapies are not psychoeducational
in nature.

The psychoeducational model may be illuminated by considering the
two other major models of psychotherapeutic intervention. The first, in
historical order, is the spirit model. This model is based on the view that
psychological/interpersonal problems are caused by evil spirits and that
remediation is accomplished by an exorcism or religious conversion. This
model is perhaps the most prevalent model worldwide in the minds of
ordinary people and is a model that is by no means absent in the United
States today. However, it is virtually defunct among those reading this
book. Hence, we need not discuss it further except to point out that a
cognitive model never just dies. It continues until some other model that
fulfills the same need for understanding and action arises to replace it.

Such a replacement occurred for the educated classes at about the turn of the century.

At that time, the spirit model was replaced by the medical model. We believe that the psychoeducational model is now similarly replacing the medical model of psychotherapy/family therapy. Contrasting the medical model with the psychoeducational model will help to clarify the nature of the psychoeducational model. We have dealt elsewhere with the many differences in attitudes and procedures that distinguish the two models (B. G. Guerney, 1977a, 1985; B. G. Guerney, L. F. Guerney, & Stollack, 1971/72; B. G. Guerney, Stollack, & L. F. Guerney, 1970, 1971). So here we will touch only briefly on the topic. The medical model paradigm is: illness (or maladjustment) → diagnosis → prescription → therapy → cure. In contrast, the psychoeducational paradigm is: motivation (or ambition) → value/goal choices → instructional-program selection → attitude change/skill acquisition → goal achievement (satisfaction). As indicated earlier, the elimination of negative experiences (i.e., "symptom," in the language of the medical model) can be chosen as a goal within the psychoeducational model. However, within the latter model, one would usually discuss the issues in terms of acquisition of positives rather than removal of negatives. For example, rather than talking about eliminating a phobia, one would think in terms of acquiring courage. Rather than eliminating anxiety, one would think in terms of achieving an optimal level of tensions. Rather than eliminating "frigidity," one would think in terms of achieving sexual enjoyment and orgasm. This represents much more than a mere change in terminology—it reflects a whole way of approaching problems and influences all of the behaviors of the therapists and the whole orientation and reaction of the client to the therapeutic (i.e., learning) process.

It is also important to recognize that the psychoeducational approach can, and in our view should, take into full account the psychodynamics of the client and the psychodynamics involved in the therapeutic process. The need to take into account feelings, defense mechanisms, and the like is no less important to the psychoeducational therapist than it is to any other therapist.

Likewise, in family therapy, the therapist works to change the system as well as the individuals within the system. It is also important to recognize that the psychoeducational approach is appropriate for all of the same types of psychological problems as other psychotherapeutic approaches. And it is as useful as other psychotherapeutic approaches in serving as an adjunctive treatment for problems which, in our view, are primarily biochemical illnesses (e.g., bipolar depression and schizophrenia).

The key difference between the medical model and the psychoeducational model is that psychoeducational model practitioners do not typically *use* their psychotherapeutic skills to effect changes in their clients. Rather, typically, they *transfer* or teach pertinent portions of their psychotherapeutic skill to their clients so that the clients may use those skills to help themselves. It is based on the concept of *empowering* clients. In the case of families, such skills are used not only to help the identified client him- or herself, but also by family members to help one another resolve their problems. The goal is to transform a family system that had been pathogenic to one that is therapeutic and that will be permanently supportive and growth-enhancing. It is not an eliminative or subtractive process, seeking only to eliminate a problem and thereby restore one to a state of normalcy. Rather, it is an additive process, one in which the objective is to give knowledge and skills to the client that he or she had not previously had and that usually are also lacking in the population at large.

An historical perspective on the development of the psychoeducational approach to therapy in general has been provided elsewhere (Authier, Gustafson, B. G. Guerney, & Kasdorf, 1975). The growth of this approach in the last 15 years has been rapid and diverse (see L'Abate & Milan 1985; Larson, 1984; Levant, 1986; Marshall & Kurtz, 1982). With respect to family therapies following a psychoeducational model, examples are provided by Anderson (1983); B. G. Guerney (1964); Patterson, Reid, Jones, & Conger (1975); and Robin (1979).

Relationship Enhancement (RE) therapy (B. G. Guerney, 1977b) will be used here to illustrate the psychoeducational approach. Of the three major mediums in psychoeducational therapies—didactic, experimental, and skill training—RE emphasizes skill training.

Research has shown skill training to be highly effective in producing positive changes (e.g., Giblin, Sprenkle, & Sheehan, 1985; Ginsberg, 1977; B. G. Guerney, Coufal, & Vogelsong, 1981; B. G. Guerney, Vogelsong, & Coufal, 1983; Jessee, & B. G. Guerney, 1981; Ross, Baker, & B. G. Guerney, 1985). When careful attention is paid to generalization and transfer-of-training in a therapy, the client carries the skills learned into the world outside the therapy hour. We believe this process provides an uncommon advantage. For example, through generalization/transfer, RE is designed to create a family system that offers therapeutic help and always-available social-emotional support to each member of the family. Families who have completed RE therapy are unlike other families—unlike average families and unlike families who have undergone non-skill-training types of therapy. They differ in that they have undergone extensive training with the goal of assuring that their attitudes and interpersonal behaviors will be therapeutic and supportive in times of need. They also differ from other families because, in the course of the therapeutic process, they have practiced and refined the capacity to support one another over and over again both in the therapist's office and on their own at home.

## THEORETICAL OVERVIEW
## OF RE FAMILY THERAPY

In working with families, the view is taken that the most efficient route to change lies in changing the system—that is, changing the *patterns of interaction* among family members, the family's dynamics. Both intrapsychic and interpersonal changes are sought in an integrated way to accomplish system change. The following three assumptions are made: (1) creating significant change in any part of the system—that is, in an individual—results in the system changing; (2) conversely, creating significant changes in the rules governing the interaction among individuals in the family—that is, changing the system—produces changes in the individuals within the family; (3) accomplishing both types of changes in an *integrated* way produces the fastest and longest-lasting changes.

The theoretical structure underlying the procedures used in RE therapy draws in a selective, integrative manner from all of the major schools of psychotherapy: psychodynamic, humanistic, behavioral, and interpersonal. From the psychodynamic, or Freudian school of thought, RE draws the view that it is very important to take into account psychological defense mechanisms, to allow emotional catharsis, and to bring unconscious motives, thoughts, and feelings to awareness, that is to facilitate insight. Within our theoretical system, all such concepts are reconciled with learning theory as explicated by Dollard and Miller (1950). We reject the modes of therapeutic behavior that are *distinctively* psychoanalytic and psychodynamic in nature, regarding them as generally inefficient and sometimes counterproductive because they frequently create resistance which, in turn, retards appropriate emotional catharsis and insight. We also reject from the Freudian psychodynamic school the notion that early trauma, sexual fantasies, and rivalries lie at the root of most emotional or interpersonal difficulties and are the most important factors stimulating defense mechanisms.

Rather, we believe that defense mechanisms are stimulated mainly in the cause of defending the self-concept and preserving self-esteem. This view of a self-concept as a paramount consideration in achieving constructive change comes, of course, from the Rogerian humanistic theoretical framework. Also drawn from the Rogerian theoretical framework is the importance of creating a warm, accepting interpersonal climate as the major mechanism for reducing psychological defenses, permitting catharsis, and bringing about insight and an increased capacity for constructive, attitudinal, and behavioral change. However, unlike Rogers, we believe that in addition to creating these conditions, it is necessary, in order to expedite and to maximize lasting change, to teach clients particular intrapsychic and interpersonal skills which will allow them to resolve personal and interpersonal problems, resolve internal and interpersonal conflicts, and achieve mastery and growth.

From learning theory, we accept the view that social reinforcement and modeling are powerful tools for effecting change. However, we reject the notion that analyzing stimulus-response relationships and reinforcement contingencies should be the sole basis for expediting or understanding therapeutic change. Rather, in addition to accepting the psychodynamic and Rogerian principles mentioned earlier, we draw from Adler and others the view that the understanding and changing behavior can be greatly facilitated by viewing people primarily as mastery-striving, future-anticipating, and feeling-driven beings.

Perhaps the most important of all the theoretical foundations upon which RE family therapy rests is that of interpersonal theory, particularly the views of Harry Stack Sullivan as these have been elaborated by Leary (1957). We accept the notion that personality is best understood and changed by understanding and changing interpersonal patterns of interaction. We also view the family as the most potent factor for good or bad in the development of personality and in the changing of personality. We accept the notion of "interpersonal reflexes" and the notion that individuals "train" others around them to respond to them in ways that allow them to use their favored interpersonal responses. We believe that most pathology results from inflexibility in patterns of interpersonal responses and from an inability to perceive that one's interpersonal reflexes often serve ends that are counterproductive to achieving conscious goals. A major way in which RE therapy may be viewed as creating change in personality and in family patterns is that previously unconscious, reflexive, conditioned, interpersonal reactions are brought into awareness and brought under the individual's conscious control and can be used to fulfill the individual's personal and interpersonal goals. In RE, the therapist seeks to bring people who perceived no way out of misery-breeding personality and interaction patterns to the recognition that they, indeed, can control their interpersonal responses and, therefore, create positive patterns of relationships and reshape their personality in accord with their own goals.


## GENERAL APPROACH TO TREATMENT

RE family therapy may be used with a wide variety of cases; hence, there is no "typical" case. The case illustration presented at the beginning of the chapter was chosen because of the high level of stress involved; because it shows the ways in which the two types of RE family therapy (child, or filial, or CRE, and RE therapy) may be combined and because it shows the way separate meetings with individual family members may be intermingled with family-group meetings.

The two types of RE family therapy have been described in chapters (e.g., L. F. Guerney, 1983) and a book (B. G. Guerney, 1977b), and illustrated in videotapes for professionals (Figley, & B. G. Guerney, 1976; Vogelsong & B. G. Guerney, 1977; Vogelsong & B. G. Guerney, 1978). There are manuals for clients and therapists (B. G. Guerney, 1986a, 1986b; L. F. Guerney, 1978) and sets of audiotapes to facilitate skill-learning by clients (B. G. Guerney & Vogelsong, 1981). Child Relationship Enhancement (CRE) Family Therapy or Filial Therapy (L. F. Guerney, 1987) is designed for children ages 12 or under. The other type of RE therapy is designed for children over 12 years of age (but may sometimes be appropriate with those as young as seven or eight). In CRE family therapy, parents of children are taught the theory and methods of client-centered play therapy. They then conduct therapeutic play sessions with their children to help the children express themselves emotionally and to overcome traumas and intrapsychic and interpersonal conflicts. In RE family therapy, clients are taught nine skills, the purposes of which may be briefly described as follows:

1. *Expressive* skill enables clients: (a) to better understand their own emotional/psychological/interpersonal needs; (b) to express those needs to others in ways least likely to engender unnecessary defensiveness, anxiety, conflict, and hostility, and most likely to engender sympathetic understanding and cooperation; and (c) to face up to conflicts and problems with others more promptly and more positively in terms of their own goals and needs and to do so with less anxiety.

2. *Empathic* skill enables clients: (a) to better understand the emotional/psychological/interpersonal needs of others and (b) to elicit more relevant, prompt, frequent, open, honest, trusting, and intimate behaviors from others.

3. *Discussion/Negotiation* skill enables clients to preserve a positive emotional climate in working through problems and conflicts, to avoid unnecessary or deleterious digressions, and to bring discussions expeditiously to the root issues.

4. *Problem/Conflict Resolution* skill enables clients to devise, and to help their intimates to devise, creative solutions to problems — solutions that maximize mutual need-satisfaction and are likely to prove both workable and durable.

5. *Self-change* skill enables clients to accomplish changes in their attitudes/feelings/behaviors in order to implement interpersonal agreements and objectives.

6. *Helping-Others-Change* skill enables clients to help others to change their attitudes/feelings/behaviors in order to implement interpersonal agreements and objectives.

7. *Generalization* skill enables clients to use relationship-enhancing skills in their daily life.

8. *Teaching* ("facilitative") skill enables clients to train others to use relationship-enhancing skills in daily life, i.e., to train others to treat them in ways most likely to enhance their own self-image, psychological well-being, and interpersonal relations.

9. *Maintenance* skill enables clients to maintain usage of such skills over time.

The first step in RE family therapy is to discuss in detail with the family the problems and stressors they face. The family members are helped to see how the therapeutic methods and the skills they will acquire will allow them to resolve their problems and to accomplish their individual and collective goals. If there is a crisis that must be resolved immediately, the therapist may partially suspend the teaching process in the earliest session(s) in order to resolve that problem quickly. That is, the therapist may *use* his or her RE skills to directly help the family resolve the crisis rather than concentrating on *teaching* the skills to the family. (Often, even this process partially takes the form of teaching, in that the family is made aware in a brief and general way of the nature of the skills the therapist is using, and the family is helped to put them into immediate use, albeit without full comprehension of why they are doing what they are asked to do.)

Next the clients are taught the skills. The paradigm followed in teaching each skill is: to explain its purpose; to clarify the attitudes that must be adapted to employ the skills successfully; to present the specific behavioral guidelines and steps necessary to perform the skill; to demonstrate wherever feasible exactly how the skill would look when it is put into practice; to coach the participants word-by-word and act-by-act in their practice of the skills; to see to it that the skills generalize/transfer to the daily behaviors of the family members at such times as they may be helpful.

Home assignments are given for each skill. They may read about the skills and/or listen to demonstration tapes that contrast skilled versus unskilled discussions of common conflicts. They practice using the skills together at home. Initially, these home practice sessions are taped and brought in for supervision. They complete various questionnaires and performance logs. The readings and forms are contained in a client manual (B. G. Guerney, 1986a). (Reading and writing skills are desirable to speed the process, but illiterates can be taught skills without difficulty.)

The topics to be discussed are decided upon jointly by the therapists and the clients. In consultation with the clients, the therapist tightly controls the issues and problems discussed. Except when crises must be handled immediately, the topics initially chosen are designed to keep the anxieties of the participants at a low level so they can concentrate effectively on skill mastery. The emotional intensity and depth of the problems discussed are then increased in accordance with the skill levels attained by the family members. Once the skills are mastered, it is an unusual feature of RE family therapy that the therapist does not allow saliency of problems to be a major factor in determining what is discussed. Rather, the therapist controls the problems selected so that what is discussed are only the deepest, most fundamental family problems—the ones that seem at the root of many other problems—as these are perceived by the family and/or the therapist.

The paradigm generally followed after the first or second session is as follows: home assignments are reviewed and supervised; follow-up evaluations are conducted of problem solutions reached in previous sessions; positive observations, attitudes, and feelings about the behaviors of other family members are shared; a topic is chosen for resolution based on depth and significance; the use of the clients' skills in working on that topic is closely supervised; each such problem is followed through to its solution either within the sessions or at home, unless the discussion of a deeper and more fundamental one has replaced it; finally, the home assignments are negotiated and explained.

For RE therapy, a method for establishing length of treatment was designed which is believed to optimize the advantages and minimize the disadvantages of a time-limited format and the more usual open-ended format. This method has been labeled a "time-designated" format (B. G. Guerney, 1977a). At intake, some agreement is reached as to either (a) the probable time of completion, or (b) the time for which the least-willing member of the family will agree to a trial period. When that time is reached, an evaluation is made as to whether the goals of the family members have been successfully met and whether termination should take place. If the therapist and clients agree that more time is desirable, then a new specific number of further hours is designated and a time is set for the next evaluation.

We have found it desirable to conduct family therapy in double sessions, that is, the typical family RE session lasts one and one-half hours. Generally, families with serious problems require 15 to 25 office sessions for successful completion. Usually, clients have also put in about that many additional hours working at home to resolve their problems. The criteria involved in evaluating sessions include such things as whether all of the significant presenting problems of the family—and all these that the therapist sees as significant—have been successfully resolved and whether the family members have successfully generalized the skills to daily use within and outside the family.

## DIAGNOSIS, ASSESSMENT METHODS, AND TREATMENT PLAN

All of the methods of individual diagnosis, from interview through objective to projective testing, might be used for individual diagnosis. The purpose of such testing would be to determine whether—instead of, or in addition to, family therapy—medication, hospitalization, individual therapy, or referrals to sources of financial aid or to support groups of various kinds might be helpful. Formal assessment of family dynamics is not considered an effective use of time in RE therapy. The procedures and types of family interactions that would facilitate this type of diagnosis are seen as counterproductive in terms of establishing the appropriate client attitudes for the RE approach. Unlike the medical model, the psycho-educational model does not require that the therapist know exactly why things are going wrong. Rather, it concentrates on teaching the family skills that will make things go *right*. It concentrates on developing attitudes and behaviors that embody satisfying and goal-fulfilling family structure and function.

As Tolstoy observed, every family is unhappy in its own fashion, while all happy families resemble one another. In RE therapy, the therapist tries to teach the families what they need to know and to do to fall into the latter category. In our view, it dissipates energy and creates resistance for the therapist to spend time trying to elicit and understand the unique patterns that may be creating unhappiness in each separate family. Such a fault-finding task, if it is to be done at all, is best left to the family itself once the skills they need to do it have been acquired. Moreover, when families bring the attitudes and behaviors they will be taught into play, family dynamics change, and to spend time mapping what one expects shortly to be only of historical interest does not seem to be an efficient use of therapeutic time.

Assessment of progress generally is done by observation and by interview. However, for research purposes, there are certain measures that we have found particularly useful in assessing progress among the families with whom we work. These are: Bienvenu's (1968) Marital Communication Inventory; the marital adjustment tests by Locke and Wallace (1959), or Spanier (1976); the Family Life Questionnaire; the Interpersonal Relationship Scale; the Handling Problems Change Scale; the Satisfaction Change Scale; the Relationship Change Scale; the Verbal Interaction Task; the Acceptance of Others Scale; the Self-Feeling Awareness Scale, and a modified version of Beaubien's Parent/Adolescent Communication Checklist (Guerney, Vogelsong, & Coufal, 1983). Those measures not referenced independently may be found in the Appendix to the book, *Relationship Enhancement: Skill-Training Programs for Therapy, Problem Prevention and Enrichment* (B. G. Guerney, 1977b).

One level of diagnostic decision making applies to whether or not an RE approach was an appropriate intervention for this particular client or family and, if so, whether additional referrals were required. A second level of decision making has to do with whether or not the clients are willing to undertake the therapy. As we believe should be the case with any type of therapy, the diagnostic process at this level is ongoing throughout the therapeutic endeavor. The major questions are whether special methods, interventions, or referrals are necessary for potential suicide, potential homicide, substance abuse, present or incipient psychosis, sexual or physical abuse, criminal behavior, or medical problems. The therapist is also concerned with deciding what combinations of individual, dyad, or family-group sessions will be the most effective. Timing is sometimes the critical variable in this regard. For instance, in the case being discussed, the eight-year-old boy jumped up on the couch and screamed that he would never come into play therapy with his father or with his father watching. Later on in therapy, he not only accepted his father's involvement but valued it.

For the J. family, appropriate medical care was already in place. The RE approach was deemed the treatment of choice. No additional or adjunctive therapies or support groups were deemed desirable. Mr. and Mrs. J. were entirely willing to undergo the therapy, and the therapist was confident that the children would be involved when necessary. The session formats chosen at various times will be discussed in the section on treatment.


## THE TREATMENT PROCESS

### Treatment Length and Pattern

Mr. and Mrs. J. were seen together for 19 weekly sessions and then for a subsequent six sessions at monthly intervals. Mrs. J. was seen for five individual sessions. Mr. J. was offered individual sessions at any time he wanted them, but he did not wish any. He was extremely supportive of his wife's requests for private sessions. The focus of the individual session was to help Mrs. J. think through her own perceptions and feelings and then to develop a skilled way to communicate those to her husband, her family of origin, and her friends using RE skills.

The older child, L., was seen in CRE therapy starting two weeks after the marital therapy began. Until the family conflict subsided significantly, L. was seen in CRE by the therapist with his mother observing.

### Core Skills Phase

In the intake session, the clients already have seen the skills modeled as they discussed the issue of importance to them. In the early core skill sessions, the therapist used the RE response category of "Troubleshooting" to share his own values about abuse with the couple as follows:

I want both of you to know . . . what I believe personally and professionally about abuse so that there is no misunderstanding between either of you and myself. I believe that everyone has a choice in how we respond to any situation and that no one ever makes us act in certain ways. I believe that you, Mr. J., had a number of options when you believed that your wife was being provocative.

You could have done what you are doing now (i.e., coming for help), and I want to commend both of you for seeking professional help. I also believe that you, Mr. J., also could have left the situation until you were calm enough to deal with it appropriately. Or, I believe you could have expressed yourself with honesty and compassion so that a more constructive outcome resulted from the conflict between you. I will teach you the skills to do that if you choose to stay in treatment with me.

The therapist then explained the underlying rationale of RE: that they would be trained in skills that would greatly increase their ability to understand themselves and others, to resolve the issues and problems they had described earlier, and to develop new ways of interacting which would better fulfill their positive goals for their relationships—relationships with others in their own and each others' families of origin, with their children, and with others in general, such as coworkers and superiors at work. The therapist further explained that it would be desirable to delay the more serious and upsetting problems until they had achieved a fairly good level of mastery of the core skills. In the meantime, it would be desirable to refrain from trying to change one another; instead, they should try their best to exercise restraint in their dealing with one another.

As is customary, the therapist saw to it that both parties were fully involved in the discussion and had ample opportunity to raise questions and objections. As is usually the case, this couple's questions were directed toward gaining a better understanding of the principles, procedures, and skills, and how they might work, rather than raising serious objections to the ideas or practices described.

Toward the close of the first session, the therapist indicated that if they chose to study and practice under indirect supervision at home, as well as under direct supervision at his office, they could progress more rapidly. Both Mr. and Mrs. J. agreed to do work at home before the second session. One of the assignments negotiated was that they read the first two chapters in the *Relationship Enhancement Manual* ( B. G. Guerney, 1986a)—Empathic and Expressive skills. They also agreed to listen to one of the audiotaped examples wherein an unskilled discussion of a conflict between a married couple is followed by their skilled discussion of the same topic. (Their assignment here is to attend to the *process* rather than the topic and to note the differential effects of skilled versus unskilled behaviors on the progress the couple made.) This couple also agreed to spend a brief amount of practice time in which one person would talk about nonrelationship topics while the other responded empathically.

Then, they were to reverse their roles in discussing a second similar topic. As usual, to increase the probability that the homework actually would be done, the therapist had the couple agree to a specific time for doing these assignments.

In RE therapy, when the clients have agreed to do home assignments, the therapist begins the next session by asking what they have done, reinforcing them for what was done, getting their reactions to the experience, and providing teaching and supervisory comments. Mr. and Mrs. J. had no questions after their first home assignment and said that it went well.

Because of the inherent high level of stress and urgency, the therapist made use in the earliest sessions of one type of RE response called "laundering," in which person A responds to the therapist as if the therapist were person B. The therapist then repeats the response to person B, but "cleans" it by following the guidelines of Expressive skill. (This includes not only bringing to the surface and deepening the emotions involved, but most important, bringing to the surface the positive feelings that underlie the negative feelings.) Person A always is asked to confirm the therapist's version or to modify it if it does not reflect A's true beliefs or feelings. Then, the same process takes place in the other direction (B to A). In the course of the dialogue, each person also is always responded to empathically by the therapist while the therapist is in the role of his or her partner. In this manner, each person is receiving empathic understanding as if from his or her partner.

Mainly, because of the inclusion of the positive feelings underlying the negatives, this type of intervention usually has a very salutary effect in increasing mutual understanding and reducing stress. An example of positives underlying negatives probably would be helpful here. If, say, the wife angrily accuses the husband of ignoring her, neglecting her, and not caring about her, the underlying positives are that she sees him as a desirable companion and that she cares a great deal about him and how he treats her because he is very important to her (and, eventually in the interchange, when she is ready to think about it, because she *loves* him). The turning point, the great stress reducer, the great impetus to really work out the problem, usually occurs when the underlying positives, especially love, are brought to the surface and are stated in such a way as to be believable to the initially "attacked" party. This couple was quite willing and able to uncover positive feelings about one another (specifics to be mentioned later), and this did help to reduce stress and raise the couple's hopes.

The therapist continued in the early sessions to demonstrate and coach Empathic skills. In RE therapy (with the exception of Troubleshooting) the couples talk to one another rather than to the therapist, and they do so only in skilled ways. It is the therapist's job to see that they acquire the skills and use them consistently and to achieve the deepest levels of emotional exchange.

Ascending the difficulty scale to nonthreatening but now relationship-pertinent issues, the couple next discussed positive feelings. The positive attitudes and feelings that Mr. J. expressed to his wife, for example, were that she was pretty, affectionate, caring, a good cook, and a good manager of the home. Mrs. J. said that her husband was a good provider, had high ethical standards, was loving, and was generous. In addition to being the next logical rung on the difficulty ladder, the sharing of positives generally has a very salutary, stress-reducing effect on relationships. It reminds each person of the positive things they probably were not thinking about under present stressful conditions, thereby restoring, at least briefly, a slightly better balance to their views about each other. It also serves to strengthen the idea that the relationship is worth saving and increases optimism that the relationship may again become a satisfying one.

The next phase in progressing up the ladder of difficulty is discussion of enhancement issues. An enhancement issue is one in which one person asks for a change in the usual pattern of doing things which he or she desires and believes would help to make the relationship more enjoyable, and about which the other person is not likely to have any serious objections. The therapist ascertains before beginning the discussion that the other party does not perceive the general nature of the request to be threatening, or anxiety-producing, or distasteful; albeit, he or she may have views about how the idea might be implemented that would differ from the partner's. Examples of frequently chosen requests are to regularly spend more time together, go somewhere pleasurable together, or work together on household tasks. This kind of discussion provides the appropriate opportunity to first practice Expressive, Discussion/Negotiation, and Problem/Conflict Resolution skills. The problems and conflicts *will* involve conflicts such as when to do it, how often to do it, and how much money to spend doing it. But these conflicts are embedded in a positive context and, hence, strong emotions are not likely to interfere with skill learning. The success in working out these conflicts and agreeing on a new positive step serves to "walk them through" the same problem-resolution skills that they later will be applying to difficult conflicts. Also, implementing the agreement strengthens the relationship directly by increasing positive interactions. Finally, it increases their *faith* that they can, indeed, work through differences to a mutually satisfactory conclusion. In their first run-through, the J.'s successfully agreed on specific times and ways to gain "quality time" together. The J.'s learned and generalized the basic skills quickly. They reported that they were extremely helpful in their daily interactions (such generalization does not usually happen so early in therapy). The core skills phase lasted for three or four sessions.

*Resolving Minor Problems Phase*

The next step on the ladder of difficulty is using the skills to resolve *relatively* minor (yet chronic or frustrating) issues. At this phase, rather severe difficulty was encountered with this couple. Mr. J. had great difficulty following Expressive guidelines or even waiting for his wife to finish her empathic statements when he felt she was off-target. While good at being empathic, Mrs. J. sometimes broke into tears. Hence, the therapist frequently had to troubleshoot. One type of occasion for Troubleshooting occurs when the therapist believes it is necessary for him to report his own feelings or values (as in the earlier example with respect to abuse). Another occasion for Troubleshooting is when the client breaks down emotionally or the usual RE routine must be altered for some other reason. When that happens, the client talks directly to the therapist, rather than to the spouse, and receives empathic responses from the therapist instead of the spouse. This continues until the therapist feels the usual process can resume. The therapist uses Expressive skills and Structuring responses (explanatory statements) to facilitate such a return to the usual procedures. A key problem hindering the usual process at this point, and requiring the Troubleshooting, was that Mrs. J. believed that if her husband became upset with her in the sessions, he later would physically abuse her. The Troubleshooting sequence of empathy, followed by Structuring, is exemplified by the exchange which took place about this issue:

| | |
|---|---|
| *Mrs. J.:* | I am afraid that N. will get angry about what I say in here and will express that anger in an aggressive way when we leave here. |
| *Therapist:* | You are afraid that N. will not like what you say in here and will hurt you after you leave the session, and that makes it very difficult for you to express your thoughts and feelings. |
| *Mrs. J.:* | Yes. |
| *Therapist:* | (to Mr. J.) I'm wondering what you think and feel about your wife's feelings and concerns. |
| *Mr. J.:* | I can appreciate her concerns, but if she would not provoke me, I would never lose control! |
| *Therapist:* | It would help you stay in control if your wife would not do or say things that really upset you; but you also appreciate her fear. |
| *Mr. J.:* | Yes. |

*Therapist:*     I want to enter into an agreement with both of you so that we can continue to make progress and avoid any further violence between you. I want you both to know that for the time being, because of the nature of the problem, you can call me at any time and come into the office and discuss the situation immediately, or you can call me and talk to me on the phone. [The therapist believes such an understanding is essential in providing structure and security in abuse situations.] You may even do that in the night time if necessary. [He gives them his home telephone number.] I want you to agree that you will avoid serious discussions about your problems until you are skilled and can discuss the situation in a skillful manner, or else wait until you are in my office to discuss them.

Both agreed that this would be helpful, and they appreciated the offer to be helpful at the time of a crisis. If the calling privilege is misused or abused, it becomes a Troubleshooting issue that must be resolved in therapy. (But not at the time of the phone call.) The calling privilege was not abused in this case. They called only once. At that time, they came into the office to discuss the issue immediately. (The therapist rescheduled someone else's appointment to accomplish this.)

In the course of this and other discussions, Mrs. J., for the first time, described to Mr. J. in depth her feelings about her husband's abuse. She felt understood about this for the first time in their marriage. By the close of the discussions, he had acknowledged his abusive behavior and accepted responsibility for avoiding it in the future regardless of how Mrs. J. behaved. This recognition began a healing process and opened the way for further discussions of deep issues.

An example of the type of problem solved in this phase of RE therapy involves a problem that eluded the J.'s solution for over a year. A major cause of friction was created by Mrs. J.'s need to allow the children some freedom to play while Mr. J. was very often in conflicting need for quiet so that he could study toward an advanced degree. By using the RE Problem/Conflict Resolution skills, in a short time they were able to come up with a complex of creative ideas related to their problem. Mrs. J. would change the way she spent her time in a way that would be more enjoyable for her because it allowed her to get away from the house and housework. At the same time, it would allow the children to play and her husband to have quiet time. The way in which this was to be accomplished was by Mrs. J. taking the children on a regular trip to a public park or to the library. Additional creative changes in the utilization of various rooms in the house also allowed the children to play in the house in a way significantly less disturbing to Mr. J. when he needed to study. These changes were then implemented and worked very well.

## Resolving Major Problems Phase

Once clients have the skills to do so, they are assisted in choosing the most important, most fundamental conflicts in family relationships. Rather than the usual procedure of allowing clients to discuss topics most salient to them at the moment, in RE therapy clients are channeled into discussing only fundamentally important topics (unless, of course, they can persuade the therapist that a genuine emergency exists requiring alteration of this plan). During this phase of therapy, all the topics mentioned as stressful in the beginning of this chapter were discussed — for example, the wife's psychological abuse of Mr. J. and its relation to PMS, the intergenerational alienation, how to assure that the abuse problem would not arise again. By using the skills under the supervision of the therapist, and with the therapist using Troubleshooting and other special RE techniques as necessary, the clients were able to reach deeper levels of mutual understanding in these areas. They were able to decide to make appropriate changes in their behavioral interactions and to successfully implement these behaviors. The changes resulted in progressively lower levels of stress and higher levels of marital satisfaction. The following example of such changes concerns their relationship to their children.

Discipline and general ways of relating to the children were a major problem in the family. Through applying Discussion/Negotiation skills, they came to realize that much of the family's difficulties stemmed from the fact that Mr. J. expected Mrs. J. to control the children for him. Through applying Problem/Conflict Resolution, Self-Change, and Helping-Others Change skills, they decided upon, and brought to reality, the solution that Mr. J. himself — using his RE skills when he did so — should communicate his feelings and desires about the children directly to them and take corresponding responsibilities for enforcing related limits.

Probably more important than the specific relations worked out was that the J.'s learned that each truly did have the other's best interest at heart. As this recognition grew, trust grew. As trust grew, it became easier and easier to use the skills and to build further trust and understanding.

*Generalization skills* also are emphasized during this advanced phase of RE therapy. Generalization skill training, among other things, involves the identification of the triggers that set off unskilled behavior, which in turns leads to strong negative emotion, dissatisfaction, and discord. Learning the skill of generalization is learning how to transform the emotion-arousing stimuli that set off unskilled behavior into cues for RE skill usage. Sometimes, when working toward deeper understanding of issues, or toward catharsis, or toward generalization, it is desirable to suspend the Expressive skill guideline that calls for discussions of the past to be tied to present feelings. Under certain circumstances, it is desirable to allow clients to get in touch with feelings from their childhood and to express them cathartically without *immediately* relating them to current feelings or ideas. Physically or psychologically abusive relationships experienced by clients in their family of origin are examples of the types of background experiences that often make suspension of that guideline desirable. This was the case with the J's. Through such sharing of their experiences relating to their families of origin, especially Mrs. J.'s cathartic recollections and expressions about her father, compassion and understanding between the J.'s were increased. This opened the way to a highly significant change in their current relationship.

The emotionally expressive sharing of their family backgrounds set the stage for RE skill generalization in an area of major conflict. Habitually, whenever Mrs. J. criticized members of her own family of origin for any reason, Mr. J. joined the attack with his own criticism. This led to anger and defensiveness as Mrs. J. felt the conflicting need to *defend* her parents against such an attack. Mr. J., as part of generalization training, learned to change the trigger involved into a cue for RE skill usage. And, next, he learned to change the response to that cue. It was changed from "join the attack" to "use RE skills." That is, he learned to respond empathically to Mrs. J's frustration and anger instead of joining the attack. The change here served multiple helpful functions: (a) it helped Mrs. J. to deal with the negative feelings toward her parents, and to develop solutions to the problems that aroused these feelings; (b) it expanded the couple's ability to generalize/transfer skill usage by allowing them to see that generalizations to situations outside the therapy hour could be very valuable.

*Individual sessions* are unusual in RE therapy. However, Mrs. J. felt strongly that she wanted time alone with the therapist to work through her thoughts and feelings in certain areas before sharing them with her husband. She wanted to be able to share her thoughts and desires with her husband, not with confusion and tentatively, but clearly and with conviction after having worked through her feelings and wishes independently with the therapist. And, as indicated earlier, Mr. J. was entirely in favor of this. Early experience showed that Mrs. J. made good use of the sessions and used them for the stated purpose (rather than, say, simply to complain or emote about her husband in his absence). Examples of the kinds of issues for which individual sessions were granted and successfully resolved were Mrs. J.'s complete puzzlement over why certain things her husband did upset her so much, the ways she wanted to be treated by her husband and her mother, and deciding what sorts of things she should and should not feel duty bound to do with and for her children and her husband.

*CRE sessions* were conducted in order to help the children work through their problems directly and to help train the parents to relate better to the children, and, among other things, to learn to set appropriate limits. Both children expressed their extreme anger in the sessions. L., the eight-year-old, spent the *entirety* of many of the early 45-minute sessions violently throwing and beating up the bop-bag. The younger boy usually played the part of a mean dragon in his early sessions and often talked and worked on themes of mastering fear. After several months of such cathartic and mastering sessions, the older boy came to his parents and said, "O. can sleep in my room tonight, and we will just be friends." It turned out that this was his way of announcing the end of his war with his brother. From then on, he no longer abused him. His teachers also reported the end of his aggressive behavior at school. And O.'s nightmares gradually ceased. When therapy ceased, as is usual in CRE, "special times" replaced the therapy session. (Special times, usually half-an-hour to an hour each week, are reserved for joint pleasurable activities with a single child, with the parent's responding empathically to the child.) These continue to this day with the J. family.

*Self-Change, Helping-Others-Change, and Maintenance skills* are also taught during the stage of discussing significant problems. Training in Self-Change skill was initiated when Mrs. J. wondered how she could change her defensive response to her husband's concern about her PMS difficulties. She recognized that she was very difficult to get along with during her period, and she did not want to take out her frustrations on her husband and children. Medication was helping, but she was still having difficulty emotionally. Problem/Conflict Resolution skills were used to develop a clear and specific agreement between Mr. and Mrs. J. Then, Self-Change and Helping-Others-Change skills were applied: Mrs. J. chose how she wanted to be reminded to consider whether her screaming and verbal abuse toward Mr. J. during her periods might be due to PMS rather than to his behavior [her choice: his asking that question]. He agreed to that. She decided how she would express appreciation to Mr. J. for his reminders. ["Thanks for asking me."] Mr. J. agreed to "catch her being good" when she was not verbally abusive to him during her periods or when she ceased upon being reminded. Self-Change and Other-Change skills were, of course, practiced in a number of sessions whenever changes were agreed upon for oneself or the other person.

Maintenance skill is emphasized in the ending phase of treatment. Mr. and Mrs. J. were taught how to request skillful interactions *whenever* one of them felt the need to do so. For instance: "It would be very helpful to me if you would say that skillfully" would remind the other person to use the skills to discuss touchy relationship issues. The couple was also encouraged to use the skills *whenever* they were helpful to either partner, even when the problem was a personal or job-issue, not a relationship issue, and to set aside some time for skill-usage, even when there was no special conflict or urgency to do so. The couple agreed that they would continue to use the skills and used all of the skills in the final session to plan an extended visit with Mr. J.'s family. They skillfully made plans for time to be separate, for together time, for family time, and for intergenerational family time. They agreed upon the method for dealing with problems, in private, that might arise during the trip.

The case was closed on this successful and happy note. All the presenting problems had been eliminated or significantly improved. The relationship has remained essentially stress-free up to the present time, approximately eight months after termination.

## CONCLUSION AND FUTURE DIRECTION

The psychoeducational approach is one that concentrates on building family strengths. When the psychoeducational process is a complete and effective one, these patterns of strengths replace a pathogenic system with a therapeutic system. The skills and the functions and processes they have created prevent future serious problems from developing when transitions to new stages of family development and change are required. The particular psychoeducational approach we have described here accomplishes this strength building by systematic psychosocial skill training with careful attention paid to the transfer/generalization of these skills into daily life. It changes functional and structural aspects of the family and changes family processes and "rules" so that members of the family not only can resolve the inevitable conflicts that arise in family life, but also will offer effective guidance and psychological support to one another.

In the case presented, it seemed advisable to use a mixture of both child RE family therapy and RE family therapy. The change process also involved a combination of some individual and some conjoint sessions. Whatever the format, appropriate catharsis was always encouraged, and the central focus always remained on family processes. The individual was permitted the kind of intrapsychic self-exploration that would facilitate system change. This intrapsychic exploration and change was always coordinated with the necessary changes in the family system—the two types of change were coordinated in a synergistic fashion. As a result, the family was not only able to successfully resolve all the presenting problems, but at follow-up gave every indication that the new changes would endure and would be sufficient to successfully handle transitions to future stages of the family life cycle.

The efficacy of the psychoeducational approach to therapy in general has been established in many research projects with a wide range of populations (L'Abate & Milan 1985; Larson, 1984; Levant, 1986; Marshall & Kurtz, 1982). But much research remains to be done with special populations. With RE, for example, there is empirical research supporting the efficacy of RE with university clinic populations and community mental health populations (L. F. Guerney & B. G. Guerney, 1985), as well as with special populations such as delinquents (B. G. Guerney, Vogelsong, & Glynn, 1977), alcoholics (Matter, McAllister, & B. G. Guerney, 1984; Waldo & B. G. Guerney, 1983), and wife batterers (B. G. Guerney, Waldo, & Firestone, 1987; Waldo, 1986; Waldo, 1987). But some of these special-population studies were not sophisticated in design. There are also many additional special populations (e.g., families where there is incest or depression) in which there is only clinical evidence of efficacy. For still other populations (e.g., eating disorders of adolescents), even clinical evidence is sparse or nonexistent. While different RE formats—group and individual, spaced and massed (i.e., marathon) sessions—have been shown to be effective (L. F. Guerney & B. G. Guerney, 1985), there are no RE studies, and we are not aware of any with other psychoeducational approaches, that compare these formats with one another, or the appropriateness of different formats for different populations. Likewise, although RE studies cut across a variety of socioeconomic classes, the relative efficacy of different formats for different socioeconomic or cultural groups has not been compared. The same is true for other psychoeducational approaches. Thus, a great deal of clinical, empirical, and experimental research remains to be done.

## REFERENCES

Anderson, C. (1983). A psychoeducational program for families of patients with schizophrenia. In W. R. McFarlane (Ed.), *Family therapy in schizophrenia.* New York: Guilford Press.

Authier, J., Gustafson, K., Guerney, B. G., Jr., & Kasdorf, J. A. (1975). The psychological practitioner as a teacher: A theoretical-historical practical review. *The Counseling Psychologist, 5*(2), 31–50.

Bienvenu, M. J. (1968). *Counselor's guide to accompany a marital communications inventory.* Durham, NC: Family Life Publications.

Dollard, J., & Miller, N. E. (1950). *Personality and psychotherapy.* New York: McGraw-Hill.

Figley, C., & Guerney, B. G., Jr. (1976). *The conjugal Relationship Enhancement program* [thirty-four minutes, 16 mm film, or ¾- or ½-inch video]. University Park, PA: Individual and Family Consultation Center.

Giblin, P., Sprenkle, D. H., & Sheehan, R. (1985). Enrichment outcome research: A meta-analysis of premarital, marital and family interventions. *Journal of Marital and Family Therapy, 11*(3), 257–271.

Ginsberg, B. G. (1977). Parent-adolescent Relationship Enhancement development program. In B. G. Guerney, Jr. (Ed.), *Relationship Enhancement: Skill-training programs for therapy, problem prevention, and enrichment.* San Francisco: Jossey-Bass.

Guerney, B. G., Jr. (1964). Filial therapy: Description and rationale. *Journal of Counseling Psychology, 28*(4), 303–310.

Guerney, B. G., Jr. (1977a). Should teachers treat illiteracy, hypocalligraphy, and dysmathematica? *Canadian Counsellor, 12*(1), 9–14.

Guerney, B. G., Jr. (1977b). *Relationship Enhancement: Skill-training programs for therapy, problem prevention, and enrichment.* San Francisco: Jossey-Bass.

Guerney, B. G., Jr. (1985). The medical vs. the educational model as a base for family therapy research. In L. F. Andreozzi & R. F. Levant (Eds.), *Integrating research and clinical practice.* (pp. 71–79). Rockville, MD: Aspen Systems Corporation.

Guerney, B. G., Jr. (1986a). *Relationship Enhancement manual (Participant's manual).* P. O. Box 391, State College, PA 16804: IDEALS.

Guerney, B. G., Jr. (1986b). *Relationship Enhancement: Marital/family therapist's manual.* P. O. Box 391, State College, PA 16804: IDEALS.

Guerney, B. G., Jr., Coufal, J., & Vogelsong, E. (1981). Relationship Enhancement versus a traditional approach to therapeutic/preventative/enrichment parent-adolescent programs. *Journal of Consulting and Clinical Psychology, 49,* 927–939.

Guerney, B. G., Jr., Guerney, L. F., & Stollak, G. (1971/72). The potential advantages of changing from a medical to an educational model in practicing psychology. *Interpersonal Development, 2*(4), 238–245.

Guerney, B. G., Jr., Stollak, G. E., & Guerney, L. F. (1970). A format for a new mode of psychological practice: Or, how to escape a zombie. *The Counseling Psychologist, 2*(2), 97–104.

Guerney, B. G., Jr., Stollak, G., & Guerney, L. F. (1971). The practicing psychologist as educator—An alternative to the medical practitioner model. *Professional Psychology, 2*(3), 276–282.

Guerney, B. G., Jr., & Vogelsong, E. (1981). *Relationship Enhancement demonstration tapes* [audio cassette recordings]. University Park, PA: Individual and Family Consultation Center.

Guerney, B. G., Jr., Vogelsong, E., & Coufal, J. (1983). Relationship Enhancement versus a traditional treatment: Follow-up and booster effects. In D. Olson & B. Miller (Eds.), *Family studies review yearbook* (Vol. 1, pp. 738–756). Beverly Hills: Sage Publications.

Guerney, B. G., Jr., Vogelsong, E., & Glynn, S. (1977). *Evaluation of the Family Counseling Unit of the Cambria County Probation Bureau.* P.O. Box 391, State College, PA 16804: IDEALS.

Guerney, B. G., Jr., Waldo, M., & Firestone, L. (1987). Wife battering: A theoretical construct and case report. *The American Journal of Family Therapy, 15*(1), 34–43.

Guerney, L. F. (1978). *Parenting: A skills training manual* (2nd ed.). P.O. Box 391, State College, PA 16804: IDEALS.

Guerney, L. F. (1983). Introduction to filial therapy. In P. Keller & L. Ritt (Eds.), *Innovations in clinical practice: A sourcebook* (pp. 26–39, Vol. II). Sarasota, FL: Professional Resource Exchange.

Guerney, L. F. (1987). The parenting skills program: A manual for parent educators. P.O. Box 391, State College, PA 16804: IDEALS.

Guerney, L. F., & Guerney, B. G., Jr. (1985). The Relationship Enhancement family of family therapies. In L. L'Abate & M. A. Milan (Eds.), *Handbook of social skills training and research* (pp. 506–524). Somerset, NY: John Wiley & Sons.

Jessee, R., & Guerney, B. G., Jr. (1981). A comparison of Gestalt and Relationship Enhancement treatments with married couples. *The American Journal of Family Therapy, 9*, 31–41.

L'Abate, L., & Milan, M. (1985). *Handbook of social skills training and research*. Somerset, NY: John Wiley & Sons.

Larson, D. (1984). *Teaching psychological skills: Model for giving psychology away*. Monterey, CA: Brooks/Cole.

Leary, T. (1957). *Interpersonal diagnosis of personality*. New York: The Ronald Press.

Levant, R. F. (1986). *Psychoeducational approaches to family therapy and counseling*. New York: Springer.

Locke, H. J. & Wallace, K. M. (1959). Short marital adjustment and prediction tests: Their reliability and validity. *Marriage and Family Living, 21*, 251–255.

Marshall, E. K., & P. D. Kurtz (1982). *Interpersonal helping skills*. San Francisco: Jossey-Bass.

Matter, M., McAllister, W., & (unlisted) Guerney, B. G., Jr. (1984). Relationship Enhancement for the recovering couple: Working with the intangible. *Focus on Family and Chemical Dependency, 7*(5), 21–23.

Patterson, G. R., Reid, J. B., Jones, R. R., & Conger, R. E. (1975). *A social learning approach to family intervention: Families with aggressive children*. (Vol. I.) Eugene, OR: Castalia Publishing.

Robin, A. L. (1979). Problem solving communication training: A behavioral approach to the treatment of parent-adolescent conflict. *The American Journal of Family Therapy, 7*, 69–82.

Ross, E. R., Baker, S. B., & Guerney, B. G., Jr. (1985). Effectiveness of Relationship Enhancement therapy versus therapist's preferred therapy. *The American Journal of Family Therapy, 13*(1), 11–21.

Spanier, G. B. (1976). Measuring dyadic adjustment: New scales for assessing the quality of marriage and similar dyads. *Journal of Marriage and the Family, 38*, 15–28.

Vogelsong, E., & Guerney, B. G., Jr. (1977). *The Relationship Enhancement program for family therapy and enrichment* [45 minutes, 16 mm film, sound, ¾- or ½-inch video]. University Park, PA: Individual and Family Consultation Center.

Vogelsong, E., & Guerney, B. G., Jr. (1978). *Filial therapy* [34 minutes, 16 mm film and ½- or ¾-inch videotape]. University Park, PA: Individual and Family Consultation Center.

Waldo, M. (1986). Group counseling for military personnel who battered their wives. *Journal for Specialists in Group Work, 11* (3), 132–138.

Waldo, M. (1987). Understanding and treating men arrested for spouse abuse. *Journal of Counseling and Development, 65*, 385–388.

Waldo, M., & B. G. Guerney, Jr. (1983). Marital Relationship Enhancement in the treatment of alcoholism. *Journal of Marital and Family Therapy, 9*(3), 321–323.

# SECTION III

# Treating Specific Family Stressors

# 7

# Intrafamily Child Sexual Abuse

## TERRY S. TREPPER

> The Frederick family was in ruin. Mother had recently discovered
> that her husband of 13 years had molested their 11-year-old daughter,
> Amy. Their other child, a boy of nine named Paul, announced in the car
> that he had caught Father and Amy naked in her bedroom one night
> while Mother was at work. When confronted later that night, Father did
> not deny the facts, but said it wasn't that big a deal, he had only fondled
> her and kissed her a few times, and while it was wrong, he did not feel
> that it did any real damage. Amy stated that what had happened was
> her fault, because she asked her dad a question about sex (which he
> ended up "answering" through demonstration). Mother was confused,
> shocked, angry, and frightened, and insisted that the family seek help.
> She had heard the director of a sex abuse treatment program on the
> radio recently and called him to find out what to do.

Given the growing magnitude of the problem of intrafamily child sexual
abuse* in our society, along with its enigmatic nature, it is not surprising
that therapists have been looking for knowledge to help them sort out
often-confusing and contradictory information. For a problem that received

The program described herein is based on research conducted through the Family Studies
Center, Purdue University Calumet, and at Midwest Family Resource, Chicago, IL. The
author wishes to thank Mary Jo Barrett, M.S.W., director of Midwest Family Resource, for
her important contributions to this chapter.
    *The terms "intrafamily child sexual abuse" and "incest" will be used interchangeably
here, although technically "incest" can refer to nonabusive and/or adult-adult sex between
relatives.

so little attention until a few years ago, there has been an increasing number of books, articles, and training workshops for clinicians working with incest families.

There are a number of reasons why therapists are becoming more concerned with intrafamily child sexual abuse. First, most therapists will encounter incest as either a primary presenting problem in family therapy or as an adjunctive issue in individual counseling. There may not actually be more families engaging in incestuous activities than in the past, but more cases are coming to therapists' attention, partly because of increased societal sensitivity to the problem and partly because of more stringent reporting laws (Bullough, 1985).

Second, a number of municipalities across the country are experimenting with providing intensive therapy services to some incest families who previously would have been disunited. There are a number of reasons for this, not the least of which is the lower cost, to the state, of therapy rather than foster placement. Also, if successful, this option is clearly less stressful for the family. This increase in therapy as an alternative to foster placement and/or incarceration means more therapists will need to be trained specifically in incest therapy.

A third reason for increased clinician concern is that therapists working with incest families have discovered the cases to be the most challenging and complex, requiring a variety of skills and sensitivities rarely required in other cases (Trepper & Traicoff, 1983), and yet most clinicians feel inadequately trained for these difficult cases (Dietz & Craft, 1980).

*Impact on Individuals and Families*

No matter how upsetting the problem of intrafamily child sexual abuse seems to therapists, the major impact of the problem is felt by the family and its members. And although there is much debate about the ultimate effect of incest on individuals (cf. Scott & Stone, 1986; also, Constantine, 1981; Henderson, 1983; Herman, Russell, & Trocki, 1986), families presenting for treatment are usually under catastrophic stress for two obvious but important reasons.

First, the abuse itself may have been a nightmare for all involved. This is especially true for the victim, where the stress and responsibility that the sexual abuse places on her* can be overwhelming (Hartman & Burgess, 1986). The profound guilt and confusion many of the offending parents

---

*The female pronoun is used simply for facility. It is not uncommon for boys, as well as girls, to be victims of intrafamily child sexual abuse.

feel can also lead to pervasive stress. And upon the disclosure of the incest, many nonoffending parents are overcome by feelings of inadequacy and guilt for not being cognizant of the abuse occurring in their homes.

Second, even when the abuse itself does not have the profound impact it might, all identified abusing families experience the cataclysmic intrusion into their lives by social service agencies. Some have suggested that the way in which incest families are "managed" may lead to much of the long-term negative consequences previously attributed to the incest itself (Tyler & Brassard, 1984).

*Theoretical and Philosophical Orientation*

At our treatment center, orientation to assessment and treatment of intrafamily child sexual abuse is predicated on a desire to reduce the overwhelming psychosocial stress that emerges from the abuse. We view sexual abuse as *both* cause and effect of family problems. Most important, we view intrafamily child sexual abuse as stemming from and being maintained by a multitude of factors that need to be assessed and ultimately reduced. Although we typically employ family therapy as a primary intervention mode, the needs of individuals are addressed with equal fervor.

Our treatment model is most akin to structural family therapy because we find it most aligned with our theoretical orientation of restructuring the family to reduce its vulnerability to incest. However, we utilize intervention techniques from a variety of available sources. And in doing all of this, we never lose track of the primary concern, which is to protect the child from further abuse, both during treatment and for the rest of her life. To accomplish both of these goals requires providing the child not only with "protection" but giving her the tools to protect herself.

## INTRAFAMILY CHILD SEXUAL ABUSE
## AS A STRESSOR

Obtaining accurate information concerning the incidence and prevalence of intrafamily child sexual abuse has been difficult. We have seen estimates climb from one child in one million in the 1950s (Weinberg, 1955) to 16% in the 1980s (Russell, 1983). There are few consistent findings in the empirical literature; instead we find wide variations among studies. There are a number of reasons why obtaining accurate data on the extent of the problem is so difficult. These include problems of utilizing consistent operational definitions of "intrafamilial" and "sexual" and "abuse"; a concern that *incidence* studies are limited to cases that come to the attention of the authorities, thus missing perhaps a majority of instances; and the problem that *prevalence* studies are usually limited to retrospective responses from clinical populations.

Some researchers are attempting to improve the methodology for obtaining accurate data on the incidence and prevalence (e.g., Russell, 1983); however, even with improved methods of data collection, we have still not satisfactorily discovered if one-third or one-tenth families are involved with incest. What we can discern from the available statistics is the following: (1) Although sibling incest is likely the most common, father-daughter and stepfather-stepdaughter abuse accounts for three-quarters of all *reported* cases (Kempe & Kempe, 1984, p. 47); (2) sexual abuse is five times more likely in reconstituted families (Finkelhor, 1980); and (3) although it is less common, father-son, mother-son, and mother-daughter abuse is being reported in increasing numbers (Chasnoff et al., 1986; Dixon, Arnold, & Calestro, 1978). We can with a sad confidence state that sexual abuse in the family is not the uncommon occurrence once thought in the 1950s; it is, instead, a large part of a great many families' life experiences.

*Definitions*

It has been somewhat difficult to define intrafamily child sexual abuse in a way that satisfies everyone working in the field. One of the main controversies is whether there is really a distinction between intrafamilial and extrafamilial child sexual abuse. Some writers (e.g., Conte, 1986; Finkelhor, 1984; Frude, 1982) have argued that intrafamilial and extrafamilial sexual abuse are more similar than not, and that the issue is the perpetrator rather than the system in which he or she operates. Others (e.g., deChasnay, 1985; Trepper & Traicoff, 1983) suggest that although there are similarities between intrafamilial and extrafamilial abusers, there is something inherently different when sexual abuse occurs within a family context, and that in terms of treatment a family systems view offers the best chance for ameliorating the problem for this and future generations.

Our program uses Russell's (1984) definition of intrafamily child sexual abuse, which includes any kind of exploitive sexual contact that occurs between relatives before the victim turns 18. If the contact was desired *and* was with a peer (with the age difference less than five years), then it is not considered abusive. Obviously, most cases of father-daughter or stepfather-stepdaughter incest would be included using this definition.

## PHYSICAL AND SEXUAL ABUSE

It is unclear what role violence plays in intrafamily child sexual abuse. Although our stereotype of the sex abuser includes images of violence and rape, it is not obvious at all from empirical data whether this is the case. In one retrospective study of adult incest victims, almost 50% reported their fathers had been violent along with the sexual abuse (Herman & Hirschman, 1981). However, others (e.g., Julian & Mohr, 1980; Larson & Maddock, 1984; Vander Mey & Neff, 1986) have found violence to be rare or used only as a last resort, and that incest perpetrators seem unlikely to be violent in nature (Panton, 1979).

### Effects of Incest on the Family

Most clinicians operate from the underlying assumption that incestuous activities are extremely harmful for the child victim and family. While there is empirical support for the contention that incest is harmful, the evidence is certainly not as overwhelming as one might imagine given our complete and automatic acceptance of the assumption (Constantine, 1981; Henderson, 1983). Since we base most of our legislative, casework, and clinical decisions on the assumption that there are serious negative effects on victims, it is unfortunate that only a few studies have attempted to examine the consequences of incest (cf. Scott & Stone, 1986).

From the few empirical studies completed on the long-term effects of incest on the victims (e.g., Becker et al., 1984; Herman, Russell, & Trocki, 1986; Meiselman, 1978; Tsai, Summers & Edgar, 1979; Scott & Stone, 1986), one can draw the following conclusions:

1. Most victims are not severely psychologically impaired in adulthood. Studies using clinical samples are more likely to find more seriously disturbed subjects than studies using nonclinical samples.
2. Most adult "survivors," even if not seriously psychologically impaired, were subjectively upset by the experience (Herman, Russell, & Trocki, 1986).
3. The most common long-term negative consequence of incestuous abuse is the presence of a response-inhibiting sexual dysfunction (Becker et al., 1984).
4. Whether or not victims will have long-term negative effects may be mediated by their emotional and cognitive responses at the time of the incident (Tsai, Summers, & Edgar, 1979) or by the

presence or absence of parental support in childhood (Fromuth, 1986).

5. There is an increased likelihood of severe long-term negative consequences with an increase in the amount of physical abuse or coercion used at the time (Herman, Russell, & Trocki, 1986).

6. Other than sexual dysfunction, the most common psychological problems found include low self-esteem, tendency toward denial as a defense mechanism, and difficulty in developing close interpersonal relationships (Owens, 1984).

Although little has been written about the negative effects of incestuous abuse on nonabused family members, most clinicians working with such families will attest to the incredible pain and suffering felt by all. Besides the obvious pain resulting from the discovery and the intrusion of outsiders into their lives, the mother may harbor guilt, anger, and mistrust feelings; the nonabuse siblings may feel shame, anger, fear of the offending parent, and even jealousy over the "special" relationship between offending parent and victim.

*Although the incest had only occurred for a little more than a year, the effects were clearly felt by other family members, even before the discovery. Paul, the younger brother, was feeling a keener competition with his sister than he had before, and he reported feeling jealous of the special attention his sister was getting from his father. Father and Mother's relationship was strained, for no apparent reason as far as Mother was concerned. And Amy's grades in school had deteriorated to the point that parent-teacher's conferences were held; no clear reason was ever discovered. All of these problems now began to make more sense to Mother.*

## HOW FAMILIES COPE WITH INCEST

### Functional Strategies

Part of the enigma of incest is that it is both culturally taboo and yet a component of a great many people's fantasy structure. Few, for example, would describe an incest *fantasy* as pathological in and of itself. Therefore, what is clearly forbidden is the *behavior*, and the question, therefore, must be: "What strategies can individuals and families use to prevent a fantasy from becoming a behavior?" Some have even viewed incest as a "coping strategy" in and of itself, whose purpose it is to solve other psychological and family related problems (Alexander, 1985; Henderson, 1983; Machotka, Pittman, & Flomencraft, 1967). This conceptualization, as one would imagine, has been highly criticized by nonsystems-oriented theorists (Brickman, 1984).

Whether or not intrafamily child sexual abuse occurs in families that are already vulnerable to it depends upon the presence of a number of individual and family coping mechanisms (Trepper & Barrett, 1986b). These include the following:

*Appropriate family communication.* Family therapists working with intrafamily child sexual abuse have long known that these families usually demonstrate extremely impaired communication patterns. Some essential skills for effective family communication, according to Olson and Killorin (1985) include:(a) tracking each other's communication; (b) giving clear and congruent statements to each other; (c) respecting each other's feelings and messages; and (d) encouraging frequent discussions of feelings and relationships. Families who consistently demonstrate these effective communication skills would be very unlikely to be *able* to engage in long-term incestuous activities.

*Knowledge about incest.* With increased interest and understanding of the incest problem, more and more people are becoming cognizant of what to be aware of with regard to possible sexual abuse in their own family. Families whose members are knowledgeable about the causes, effects, signs, and symptoms of sexual abuse are also less likely to be incestuous.

*Assertiveness.* Intrafamily child sexual abuse can be thought of, in part, as a function of *over*assertiveness on the part of the offending parent. However, it is clear that assertiveness on the part of the rest of the family, especially the child victim, is an important preventative mechanism. An assertive individual is not only able to say no to unwanted sexual advances, or to tell someone when abuse is occurring, but also able to trust her own feelings and to do so without guilt or shame.

*Outside resources.* One characteristic of many abusing families is a tendency to distrust those outside the family, to be socially isolated. Families who trust and utilize outside-the-family people or organizations during periods of stress and crisis are less likely to abuse, and once in-volved with abuse have somewhere to turn to "nip it in the bud." These outside resources can include formal therapy, a church, and self-help groups.

*Dysfunctional Strategies*

Unfortunately, many families vulnerable to incest do not or cannot utilize effective coping mechanisms and become incestuous. These fami-lies develop patterns of behavior surrounding the incest that not only does not solve the problem, but also creates a whole new set of problems. Many of these actually *increase* the likelihood for further abuse, increase the dysfunctional relationships, and can lead to the eventual disuniting of the family. These can include:

*Secretiveness.* Incest, because of its powerful social unacceptability, must operate in secrecy. The blurring of generational boundaries, already a problem when an adult has sex with a child, becomes greater when the offending parent encourages or forces the child to keep it secret from the other parent. A secret of this magnitude, upon whose keeping may decide the fate of the family, would be a tremendous burden for anyone to bear. For a child, it can be disastrous.

*Denial.* Tied to secretiveness, this defense mechanism is often used not only by the offending parent, but also by the rest of the family. The purpose of denial, of course, is to protect against the overwhelming negative reality of committing the "worst" taboo. Denial may take a variety of forms: denial of facts, denial of awareness, denial of impact, and denial of responsibility.

*Family withdrawing into itself.* A family engaging in secretive and denying behavior is ultimately going to have to withdraw socially and emotionally into itself to maintain these other defenses. And although the incestuous family may have its own serious communication and struc-tural problems, the risk of disclosure is too great to allow members to openly become involved in intimate outside-the-family relationships. This, of course, exacerbates the dysfunctional patterns already present by increasing the number and intensity of the family interactions. The fear that outside relationships will lead to disclosure is a real one; most discoveries are precipitated by the child victim confiding in a friend or sweetheart, who then alerts those who take action.

*Increased coercion.* Although most incestuous families are not physically abusing, most offending parents do use a varying degree of coercion to maintain and keep secret the sexual relationship with the child. This coercion may be anywhere on a continuum from subtle seduction and increasing privileges, to inferred threats of family ruin, to actual physical abuse. As previously discussed, the increased use of coercion has been associated with an increased likelihood of long-term psychological problems for the victim.

*Substance abuse.* Whether or not substance abuse is a cause or effect of intrafamily child sexual abuse is unclear. What is known is that most offending parents engage in alcohol or substance abuse before and during incestuous episodes (Cavallin, 1986; Maisch, 1973; Virkkunen, 1974). Substances can be used by offending parents as an excuse for the abuse, and as a dysfunctional coping strategy for the guilt and anxiety associated with the abuse.

*Victim behavior.* One way child victims "cope" with prolonged abuse, particularly when their attempts to stop the abuse are continually unsuccessful, is to engage in extreme "victimlike" behavior. The "acting out" can take the form of behavior disorders, running away, becoming sexually promiscuous, and a plethora of other personally dysfunctional behavior. This pattern may become long-term and affect the child victims' future psychological and social health.

*Mother becoming incompetent.* In abusing families where the mother knows about the abuse but is unable to prevent it, she may develop symptoms of depression and generally retreat into a psychological "incompetence." It is not clear whether this is a cause or an effect of the incest, but certainly her withdrawal exacerbates the problem as time goes on, which again makes her less able to prevent further abuse. Particularly lost are her abilities to parent effectively.

*Nonabused siblings developing symptoms.* The nonabused siblings in a family can develop dysfunctional coping strategies such as developing psychological symptoms and behavior disorders. This may be their attempt at either gaining attention lost to the child who is engaged in the "special" relationship with the adult, or stopping the sexual abuse by forcing the parents to focus on them.

*The Frederick family resorted to many of the classic dysfunctional strategies in response to the incestuous relationship between Father and Amy. Father made Amy promise to keep it a secret because Mother would surely leave him if she ever knew. And besides, this was definitely the* last *time this would ever happen. While it was occurring, Father denied the* facts *of the incest ("It won't happen again"), along with denying the* impact *("It really isn't hurting her"); Amy denied the appropriate* responsibility *("It was really my fault for asking him the sexual question"); and Mother denied* awareness *all along, although there were many signs that later she agreed were obvious. Paul also began to steal from Mother's wallet during this time, perhaps as a means of gaining attention, or perhaps as a means of distracting the family from the more subtle but painful changes occurring along with the incest.*

## ASSESSMENT OF INTRAFAMILY
## CHILD SEXUAL ABUSE

Various treatment strategies have been reported for the victim, offender, and family. In general, treatment approaches that include family therapy have been viewed as the most effective, particularly when combined with other modes (Dixon & Jenkins, 1981). Descriptions in the literature of programs using a multicomponent treatment package include Anderson and Shafer (1979), Justice and Justice (1979), Giaretto (1982), and Barrett, Sykes, and Byrnes (1986).

The treatment approach described here is based on Trepper and Barrett's (1986a) multiple systems model for the treatment of intrafamily child sexual abuse. It is a family-therapy-based, multicomponent program that has been used successfully for over 10 years in a number of treatment centers in the United States.

The program is based philosophically on the vulnerability-to-incest model of causation. This model states that all families are endowed with a degree of vulnerability to incest and that the presence of specified factors increase a family's vulnerability. These factors, to be described specifically in the next section, include socioenvironmental, family system, individual, and family-of-origin factors. A vulnerable family may still not manifest incestuous episodes, however; also needed is the presence of a precipitating event, and a lack of or impairment in coping mechanisms. Interventions are designed to reduce the family's vulnerability to incest, decrease the likelihood of precipitating events, and increase their coping strategies.

The specific therapeutic goals are to: (1) protect the child from further abuse; (2) change the family structure so as to make further abuse unlikely; (3) decrease the family's vulnerability to incest along a variety of dimensions; (4) increase their coping strategies; and (5) encourage the victim to become assertive and competent, so that she does not remain victimlike for the rest of her life. The program attempts to maintain the delicate balance between protecting the child and minimizing the trauma of intervention for the entire family.

The assessment of families is an ongoing process, but is formally initiated during Stage One of treatment (to be discussed later). It is accomplished through a combination of standardized tests and structured interviews of the family system and individuals within the family.

In our program, the vulnerability-to-incest model is used as an assessment schema. This model was described in detail previously (Trepper & Barrett, 1986b), but will be briefly explained here in terms of assessment procedures. The therapist assesses the presence and magnitude of factors shown to contribute to a family's vulnerability to incest. Also assessed is the presence and significance of precipitants to incestuous episodes, and the degree to which normal coping mechanisms operate.

*Socioenvironmental Factors*

The environment in which a family operates has a profound impact on that family and its members. Our society, while formally stating its horror and dismay over intrafamily child sexual abuse, unfortunately also gives tacit approval to physical and sexual violence against children and women. A number of researchers have identified socioenvironmental factors that seem to be linked to intrafamily child sexual abuse (Finkelhor, 1978; Gaudin & Pollane, 1983; Vander Mey & Neff, 1986). Based on this body of work, the therapist assesses the family and individual member's on the following:

1. How positively do family members view films and books with physical and sexual violence against men and women? What type of erotic or pornographic material does the offending parent enjoy? Are incest themes common?
2. Is a family theme revering privacy for the family present (e.g., "Its no one's business what we do in this family")?
3. Do family members, particularly the offending parent, ascribe an inferior status to women and children?

4. Is the family socially (and perhaps physically) isolated from others?
5. Has the family experienced an inordinate amount of stress during the past year?

The presence and magnitude of these factors can best be assessed through structured interviews with the family and individual members, although questionnaires could be developed which would ascertain similar information.

*Family System Factors*

The family system structure as a whole has been increasingly focused upon as contributing to the development and maintenance of intrafamily child sexual abuse (deChasnay, 1985). Although this area has only recently begun to receive empirical attention, based upon consistent clinical descriptions certain major areas of the family system seem particularly linked to the development of incest.

Certain family structures seem to operate most frequently in incest families (Trepper & Barrett, 1986b). For incest to occur it has been theorized that the offending parent or the child victim must cross the theoretical generational boundary line and virtually end up on the same side. This can take a variety of forms, but the therapist must assess how and under what circumstances this happens.

What is the family sexual style? Larson and Maddock (1984) have identified four major motivations for sexual abuse: (1) *affection seeking*, where the sexual needs are linked to emotional and affectional needs on the part of the offending parent; (2) *pansexual*, where the family is highly "sexualized" in all areas of their life, and sex with the child is an extension of this "lifestyle"; (3) *hostile*, where the intent is aggressive, the family is highly conflictual, and the sexual abuse is often punitive; and (4) *violent rape*, where the intent is the infliction of pain or humiliation and is often associated with such severe psychopathology as psychosis. These categories do overlap for some families, but one style usually predominates at a time and is easy to assess through thorough family interviewing.

The therapist can also assess the family structure using the Circumplex model of family functioning. A test called FACES III (Olson, Portner, & Lavee, 1985) is used to measure the family's adaptability to change and its level of cohesion, both extremely important areas to understand in developing treatment plans. The marital relationship, particularly the sexual aspect, is assessed using a structured interview form, The Purdue Sexuality Questionnaire.*

In remarried families extra assessment information is gathered concerning the amount of time the family has been together, the emotional bondedness felt by the family (especially the offending parent and the child), the cognitive structure of the offender regarding incest (i.e., does he consider abusing his *step*daughter incestuous?), and the presence of preincestuous hostility and conflicts among reconstituted members.

## Individual Factors

Ideally, all of the individual family members will be formally assessed to determine their contribution to the abuse and to assess how the abuse (or living in an abusing family) has affected them. Although the empirical literature does not offer a definitive set of characteristics for individuals, the following are often cited as contributing to a family's vulnerability:

### Offending father.

1. The degree of pedophilia present, although incest fathers tend to be less pedophile-oriented than extrafamilial abusers (see Quinsey, Chaplin, & Carrigan, 1979).
2. The degree of hypersexuality or sexual addiction present. Also, some men respond to sexual dysfunction by sexually abusing a child, who is seen as less threatening. A number of sexual inventories are available; the Purdue Sexuality Questionnaire is used as a structured interview guide.
3. How involved with the child care and nurturance of the children as babies was the father? This factor has been empirically shown to be one of the most important (Parker & Parker, 1986).
4. The level of impulse control present in the father. This can be measured using standard objective personality inventories such as the MMPI.
5. The father's cognitive view of his "rights" as a father. Does he see himself as "in charge" and in control of everything in the family? Again, standard-type personality tests can measure this factor.
6. Other types of abusive behavior. There is some controversy in the field about whether the incest father is also physically abusing. If

---

*Available from the author.

he is, the degree, under what condition, and the cognitive structures underlying its occurrence need to be assessed.

7. The degree of sociopathy present. Does he have the ability to
   empathize with others (particularly the child victim), and to
   what degree does he experience guilt? Personality testing is usually successful in assessing this trait.

8. The type and extent of denial present. For incest to occur, some
   form of denial is usually present, either of facts, awareness,
   responsibility, or impact. This can easily be assessed through
   direct questioning by the therapist.

9. The presence of severe psychopathology, such as psychosis. This
   is very rare, but must be assessed. Standardized tests and, of
   course, clinical information received from the individual and
   other family members should elucidate the presence of psychosis.

*Nonoffending mother.* Although the nonoffending mother can in no
way be held *responsible* for the abuse, there have been characteristics
commonly attributed to the mother that can be viewed as partially
contributing. These include:

1. The degree of passivity and/or dependency present. Many incest
   mothers appear to be extremely passive and dependent, even in
   the face of accusations by their daughters that they are being
   sexually abused. This is more difficult to assess directly, but can
   often be observed in family sessions.

2. Mother being absent or incapacitated. This can be emotional
   absence as well. Again, observation in family sessions and interviews with the other family members often provides useful information on this dimension.

3. The presence of a sexual dysfunction or lack of interest in sex. The
   Purdue Sexuality Questionnaire or another similar structured
   sex history form can help provide this information.

4. A reversal of roles with her daughter. That is, does she allow her
   daughter to act as surrogate mother to the other children, or even
   to act as surrogate wife (not in sexual ways) to her husband? This
   can only be assessed observationally by the therapist.

5. If applicable, the reasons she did not inform others when she
   discovered the abuse, or denied the abuse when she was confronted
   with it. Common reasons include fear of negative consequences
   from her husband; shame; a fear that family problems would
   worsen if her husband were jailed, particularly economic prob-

lems; and finally, a fear of severe disruption for her other children should the family be disunited.

*Daughter.* Similar to our view of the incest mother, the child victim can in no way be held *responsible* for her own abuse. There are, however, characteristics commonly attributed to the incest daughter that should be assessed. These include:

1. The degree to which the victim seeks attention and affection. Although all children need attention and affection, it is important to assess how this need may interact with the father's needs for affection and result in inappropriate sexual behavior.
2. The presence of a seductive manner as a way to gain love and attention. This stance may have been taught through the years by the sexualized relationship with her father.
3. The presence of a self-esteem problem. Self-esteem is measurable through standardized personality inventories.
4. The degree to which she plays the role of "rescuer" in the family. Does she explain her role in the incest in terms of protecting father or mother?

*Family of origin.* Were either of the parents abused, sexually or physically? What was the nature of their relationship with their parents? Was love withheld or conditional? How did the parents view their own abuse, and what are their theories around the relationship between their being abused and their abusing their own children? These questions are essential during individual or couple sessions with the parents.

*Precipitating Events*

What are the precipitants to incestuous episodes? Specifically to be assessed is the presence of alcohol or substance abuse, situational acute stress, and changes in the family's life. These can be assessed both through structured interviews and with the aid of standardized tests such as the Life Changes Inventory (Olson et al., 1982), and with any of the many alcohol and substance abuse indexes available.

*Coping Strategies Available*

What coping mechanisms do the family have available to them? The Family Coping Skills Inventory (Olson et al., 1982) is quite useful in providing initial information and hypotheses, which can then be expanded upon in structured interviews.

*After entering the program, the Frederick's were assessed both as a family and individually. Socioenvironmental factors contributing to the problem included: (1) an acceptance in this family of stereotypic male-female sex roles, with fathers being the dominant member, with others to do what he says; (2) the family experiencing unusual financial stress during the year prior to the abuse, and Mother "having" to go back to work to "help out." This also provided an opportunity for the abuse to occur. The family system factors included: (1) The family being assessed as an "affection-seeking" type, with the abuse seen as occurring within a loving rather than a violent context; (2) the family structure appeared to be most like the "Father Executive" type, where the "in-charge" Father coerced the affection-seeking daughter to take the role of wife. A long-standing alliance between Father and Amy against Mother made this more tenable. The family was also viewed as rigid with regard to flexibility to change and enmeshed with regard to family cohesion. The individual factors noted included: (1) Father's need for affection, the fact that he was not typically involved with the "parenting" of the children, problems with impulse control, and a strong tendency toward denial (no other serious psychopathology was noted, nor was a pedophile orientation present); (2) Mother's general dependency upon her husband, leading to a tendency to deny the potential devastating reality of incest in the family, along with an inclination to defer her wife and mother role to her more assertive daughter. The family-of-origin factors assessed include: (1) the information that Father was emotionally neglected by his parents, and in fact was raised for most of his childhood by a series of relatives; and (2) the surprising information that Mother was sexually abused by her live-in maternal grandfather for a number of years when she was about Amy's age. The precipitating events included Father's drinking (although not heavily) prior to each episode, along with the incest occurring only when mother was at work at night.*

## TREATMENT OF INTRAFAMILY CHILD SEXUAL ABUSE

Our treatment program is called Multiple Systems Therapy, reflecting our ongoing assessment and intervention upon the many systems (social, legal, family, individual, etc.) that contribute to and maintain incestuous abuse. In our program, each family's treatment is individualized. In each case, however, therapy is designed to reduce the family's vulnerability factors, decrease precipitating events, and increase coping skills. The treatment program itself is conceptualized in three stages: (1) Creating a Context for Change; (2) Challenging Patterns and Expanding Alternatives; and (3) Consolidation.

*Stage I: Creating a Context for Change*

Families entering therapy for incest are usually there under duress and in a high state of confusion, crisis, and hopelessness. They are as often more concerned with the maintenance of the family unit as reducing the sexual abuse, and are thus almost invariably highly resistant to therapy. This is viewed as a normal reaction to a severe crisis and not necessarily a sign of pathology. However, this inherent resistance must be dealt with or therapeutic intervention will not be possible. Stage I is conceptualized as the initial period of therapy during which the family's natural resistance to intensive intervention is reduced and rechanneled. This stage usually lasts between three and six months, but it is not uncommon for an unusually entrenched family system to stay in Stage I for a year or more. The formal assessment described in the previous section occurs during the first few sessions of therapy.

*Using other systems therapeutically.* Incest families referred for therapy almost always have a number of other systems affecting their lives, and not always in a functional or compassionate way. State social and pro-tective services, the court, the district or city attorney, and the police all may have a say in the family's future. Sometimes the advice or counsel provided by one agency is contradictory from that of another agency. In any event, the therapist must realize that these outside agencies are very much a part of the therapeutic (or antitherapeutic) process, and must act accordingly.

In our program, representatives of these other agencies are immediately made part of the treatment team. We do this by initiating contact with them even prior to treatment, then scheduling a pretreatment conference with everyone. Another meeting is scheduled with the entire family and these representatives to clarify issues specific to the case, such as visitation if a father or child is removed from the home. The purpose of this careful coordination of services is to isomorphically present to the family a structure consistent with that which is being prescribed in therapy. In other words, the "other systems" in their lives should not appear more disorganized and have more dysfunctional boundaries than the family itself.

*Joining the family.* The process of joining in therapy has been well described (e.g., Minuchin, 1974). The therapist communicates to the family an understanding of the complexities of incest, that everyone has a role in making the situation better, and that change is possible (Barrett, Sykes, & Byrnes, 1986). Although the sexual abuse itself is not condoned, the family's style and structure are initially accommodated by the therapist. Although difficult, particularly when the family's style is significantly different from the therapist's, it is essential to successfully join to reduce the potential for continued resistance.

*Reframing/positive connoting.* Another important Stage I intervention involves the reframing and positive connoting of family actions. Although the sexual abuse should never be positively connoted, family members' motives, feelings, and nonsexual actions can be, as can other problematic aspects of the family's interactions. Positive connoting and reframing also permits therapy to be less heavy-handed and to help the therapist create more positive workable realities. Incest families presenting for treatment typically see themselves as helpless and hopeless, and reframing and positive connoting help promote a sense of hope and a sense that change is possible. Some examples might include the therapist connoting: (a) the *intent* behind the incest as affection-seeking rather than abusive; (b) the mother's anger at her daughter as her attempt to firmly take control of the family and make things right because she loves them all so much; (c) the chaos present in the family as reflecting high energy and independence among family members; and (d) the daughter's withdrawal during therapy sessions as demonstrating her thoughtful, observational, and analytical style.

*Family structural session.* This session, first described by Barrett, Sykes, & Byrnes (1986), is an insight-oriented, educational experience in which the therapist presents examples of different family structures vulnerable to incest (e.g., the "Father Executive," where the father is the autocratic ruler of the family and sex with his daughter is a "right" of his accepted by himself and perhaps even his daughter). The family is asked to discuss these structures and to speculate which ones are applicable to them. They are then asked to describe and draw a structure that they feel would not lead to sexual abuse. That model becomes the benchmark for successful therapy, with the therapist returning to that picture often during the course of treatment to ask questions, such as, "Is what you did today something your ideal family structure would do?"

This is a powerful intervention for a number of reasons: First, it provides a common language for the therapist and family. Second, it partially answers the gnawing question, "How did this happen to us; how are we different from other families?" Third, it provides a visual goal for therapy (i.e., the family can "see" what it is they should look like when they are not abusing). Fourth, it expands the solution to the problem to include the entire family, giving all a sense of involvement.

*Negative consequences of change.* A fairly common intervention among family therapists for reducing resistance, this involves asking members to ponder all of the reasons they should *not* change their family's characteristics that make them vulnerable to incest. Most people initially insist that there are *only* positive consequences to change. However, with prodding, family members can become extremely insightful, seeing some very important maintainers of their problem. After a list of the negative consequences is compiled, the therapist then encourages the family to proceed slowly through therapy, in effect paradoxically suggesting that change may in fact be too difficult. This usually leads to the family's insistence upon more rapid change, and thus greater cooperation in therapy.

*Apology session.* The final major intervention in Stage I is the Apology session, described in detail elsewhere (Trepper, 1986). This session is a family ritual in which the parents both formally and publicly apologize to their children for what has happened in the family, and then each takes responsibility for the piece which is theirs. The offending father, for example, apologizes and takes responsibility for the sexual abuse itself, for any subsequent encouragement of the children to lie, and for any denial he may have expressed. The parents and children are prepared for the Apology for a number of sessions prior to this intervention. The parents are worked with, for example, to make certain that they understand the task and can execute the apology in a sincere fashion. This session serves as a new beginning for most families, as it signals the movement from Stage I to Stage II, from being resistant and mistrusting of therapy to accepting responsibility for their actions and being truly committed to change.

*Stage II: Challenging Patterns and Expanding Alternatives*

Stage II represents the period of therapy where most of the actual structural family changes occur. Whereas during Stage I the family is "joined" and the family structure is assessed, now the family is confronted and challenged to change the factors that make them vulnerable to incest. This is done through a variety of individual and family interventions which are designed for each family based on their assessment. Because incestuous family systems are usually quite resilient, this stage often lasts approximately one year.

*Individual sessions.* Individual sessions are provided most often to the offending parent to explore family-of-origin contributions to his vulnerability. Another individually oriented offender intervention involves the meta-phor that different "parts" of the same person are operating at the same time, so that, for example, the selfish sexually abusing "part" operates along with the loving and supportive father "part." Through a series of Gestalt-like exercises during individual sessions, these "parts" do battle and are eventually reconciled. Individual sessions are also provided for the victim, as needed, to provide support in resisting inappropriate advances by adults, to become more assertive, and to help reconcile her ambivalent feelings toward her father and sometimes mother.

*Family sessions.* Family therapy is the cornerstone of our Multiple Systems Therapy, and the entire family is seen at least for half of all total sessions. The only exception to this is that if the offending parent is denying the *facts* (i.e., insisting he or she did not abuse the child), we would not have the child and parent together in therapy. A combination of structural/strategic, behavioral, and insight-oriented interventions are used to change the family sexual style, structure, and communication patterns. For example, if a family is assessed to be rigid and enmeshed, then interventions are designed to increase flexibility to change and to decrease their overinvolvement with one another.

*Group sessions.* Group therapy for offending parents and for victims are an integral part of therapy. The purpose of group therapy is to: (1) reduce the denial of facts, awareness, responsibility, and impact through the social influence of the group; (2) improve strategies for reducing likeli-hood of either abusing or being abused; and (3) provide a support system for expressing commonly held feelings. Group therapy, like the individual therapy, is coordinated with the family sessions, and the group leader is continually cognizant that the ultimate goal for most is a reintegration of the family unit. Special care is taken to focus the group on personal change (i.e., "What can *I* do to make myself and the family better?") rather than on blame.

Throughout Stage II, the family is constantly being assessed for reduction of vulnerability factors. Is the family learning to handle stress? Is the family adhering less to sexual stereotypes? Is the family structure now showing appropriate boundaries between offending parent and child victim? Has the communication between spouses opened up? Has the offending father's rigid thinking become more flexible, and has the mother's passivity changed and has she become more assertive? Have the parents understood the contribution of their family-of-origin patterns on this family's current difficulties? When most or all of these can be answered yes, then the family is ready to enter the final stage of therapy, Consolidation.

## Stage III: Consolidation

Up until this point, the family has been challenged fairly assertively by the therapist to try new patterns of behavior and styles of thinking. This final stage is characterized by the therapist pulling back and encouraging the family to act on their own volition. This is done at first by asking family members to plan activities for the session and to make their own homework assignments. Sessions are then held every other week and then once a month. Finally, the family has a final "formal" session to review the entire course of therapy, what they have learned, how they have changed. Therapy is now complete, except for follow-up phone calls and sessions every six months. The therapist has now become an additional "coping strategy" for the family, and they are encouraged to call if ever any need arises, no matter how small.

*The Frederick family was in therapy for almost two years. The treatment specific goals were the following: Stage I: (1) reduce the family's resistance to outside intervention; (2) reduce the member's denial; (3) have Father rather than Amy take responsibility for the incest; and (4) increase their awareness of the role their dysfunctional family structure has in the abuse. Stage II: (1) encourage alternative ways to handle stress; (2) confront the family's acceptance of sex-role behaviors, particularly those that subjugate women; (3) encourage increased flexibility to change; (4) encourage the family to develop friends and activities outside the family; (5) improve the relationship between Father and Mother, in terms of communication, affection and sexuality, and support for each other's emotional needs; (6) break the alliance between Father and Amy, improve the relationship between Mother and Amy, and help Father and Paul begin to develop a relationship with each other; and (7) allow the parents to sort out their feelings about their own childhood relation-ships with their families. Stage III: (1) allow the family to accommodate all of these changes into their own family style; and (2) monitor that Amy does not slip into "victimlike" behavior and continues to be able to protect herself from any type of abuse in the future.*

## CONCLUSION

The treatment of intrafamily child sexual abuse is a relatively new area, and the utilization of multidimensional integrated treatment programs, such as our Multiple Systems Model, is even newer. Although it was urgent that such programs be developed to manage the enormous influx of recently referred cases to mental health systems, it is equally urgent that now empirical research be conducted to test the efficacy of such programs. Studies comparing family, individual, group, and multifaceted programs are needed to help elucidate what treatment is best for what family under what conditions. Until that time, we can only rely on our best clinical judgment and hope that the result is doing more good than harm.

## REFERENCES

Alexander, P. C. (1985). A systems theory conceptualization of incest. *Family Process, 24*, 79–88.

Anderson, L. M., & Shafer, G. (1979). The character-disordered family: A community treatment model for family sexual abuse. *American Journal of Orthopsychiatry, 49*, 436–445.

Barrett, M. J., Sykes, C., & Byrnes, W. (1986). A systemic model for the treatment of intrafamily child sexual abuse. In T. S. Trepper & M. J. Barrett (Eds.), *Treating incest: A multiple systems perspective.* New York: Haworth Press.

Becker, J. V., Skinner, L. J., Abel, G. G., Axelrod, R., & Cichon, J. (1984). Sexual problems of sexual assault survivors. *Women and Health, 9*, 5–20.

Brickman, J. (1984). Feminist, nonsexist, and traditional models of therapy: Implications for working with incest. *Women and Therapy, 3*, 49–67.

Bullough, V. L. (1985). Child abuse: Myth or reality? *Council for Democratic and Secular Humanism, 5*, 51–52.

Cavallin, H. (1966). Incestuous fathers: A clinical report. *American Journal of Psychiatry, 122*, 1132.

Chasnoff, I. J., Burns, W. J., Schnoll, S. H., Burns, K., Chisum, G., & Kyle-Spove, L. (1986). Maternal-neonatal incest. *American Journal of Orthopsychiatry, 56*, 577–580.

Constantine, L. (1981). Child-adult sexual experiences: New studies report some positive outcomes. *Sexuality Today, 4*(50), 1–2.

Conte, J. R. (1986). Sexual abuse and the family: A critical analysis. In T. S. Trepper & M. J. Barrett (Eds.), *Treating incest: A multiple systems perspective.* New York: Haworth Press.

deChasnay, M. (1985). Father-daughter incest: An overview. *Behavioral Sciences and the Law, 3*, 391–402.

Dietz, C. A., & Craft, J. L. (1980). Family dynamics of incest: A new perspective. *Social Casework, 61*, 602–609.

Dixon, J., & Jenkins, J. O. (1981). Incestuous child sexual abuse. A review of treatment strategies. *Clinical Psychology Review, 1*, 211–222.

Dixon, K. N., Arnold, L. E., & Calestro, K. (1978) Father-son incest: Underreported psychiatric problem? *American Journal of Psychiatry, 135* (7), 835–838.

Finkelhor, D. (1978). Psychological, cultural, and structural factors in incest and family sexual abuse. *Journal of Marriage and Family Counseling, 4*, 45–50.

Finkelhor, D. (1980). Risk factors in the sexual victimization of children. *Child Abuse and Neglect, 4*, 265–273.

Finkelhor, D. (1984). *Child sexual abuse: New theory and research.* New York: The Free Press.

Fromuth, M. E. (1986). The relationship of childhood sexual abuse with later psychological and sexual adjustment in a sample of college women. *Child Abuse and Neglect, 10*, 5–15.

Frude, N. (1982). The sexual nature of sexual abuse: A review of the literature. *Child Sexual Abuse and Neglect, 6*, 211–223.

Gaudin, J., & Pollane, L. (1983). Social networks, stress, and child abuse. *Children and Youth Services Review, 5*, 91–102.

Giaretto, H. (1982). A comprehensive child sexual abuse treatment program. *Child Abuse and Neglect, 6*, 263–278.

Hartman, C. R., & Burgess, A. W. (1986). Child sexual abuse: Generic roots of the victim experience. In T. S. Trepper & M. J. Barrett (Eds.), *Treating incest: A multiple systems perspective.* New York: Haworth Press.

Henderson, J. (1983). Is incest harmful? *Canadian Journal of Psychiatry, 28*, 34–40.

Herman, J. (1981). *Father-daughter incest.* Cambridge, MA: Harvard University Press.

Herman, J., & Hirschman, L. (1981). Families at risk of father-daughter incest. *American Journal of Psychiatry, 138*, 967–970.

Herman, J., Russell, D., & Trocki, K. (1986). Long-term effects of incestuous abuse in childhood. *American Journal of Psychiatry, 143*, 1293–1296.

Julian, V., & Mohr, C. (1980). Father-daughter incest: Profile of the offender. *Victimology, 4*, 348–360.

Justice, B., & Justice, R. (1979). *The broken taboo: Sex in the Family.* New York: Human Sciences Press.

Kempe, R. S., & Kempe, C. H. (1984). *The Common Secret: Sexual Abuse of Children and Adolescents.* New York: W. H. Freeman.

Larson, N., & Maddock, J. (1984). Incest management and treatment: Family systems vs. victim advocacy approaches. Paper presented at the 42nd Annual Convention of the American Association for Marriage and Family Therapy, San Francisco.

Machotka, P., Pittman, F. S., & Flomenhaft, K. (1967). Incest as a family affair. *Family Process, 6*, 98–116.

Maisch, H. (1973). *Incest.* London: Andre Deutsch.

Meiselman, K. (1978). *Incest: A psychological study of causes and effects with treatment recommendations.* San Francisco: Jossey-Bass.

Minuchin, S. (1974). *Families and family therapy.* Cambridge, MA: Harvard University Press.

Olson, D. H., & Killorin, E. (1985). *Clinical rating scale for the Circumplex model of marital and family systems.* Family Social Science, University of Minnesota, St. Paul, MN.

Olson, D. H., McCubbin, H. I., Barnes, H., Larsen, A., Muxen, M., & Wilson, M. (1982). *Family inventories.* Family Social Science, University of Minnesota, St. Paul, MN.

Olson, D. H., Portner, J., & Lavee, Y. (1985). *FACES III.* Family Social Science, University of Minnesota, St. Paul, MN.

Owens, L. H. (1984). Personality traits of female psychotherapy patients with a history of incest: A research note. *Journal of Personality Assessment, 48,* 606–608.

Panton, J. H. (1979). MMPI profile configurations associated with incestuous and non-incestuous child molesting. *Psychological Reports, 45,* 335–338.

Parker, H., & Parker, S. (1986). Father-daughter sexual abuse: An emerging perspective. *American Journal of Orthopsychiatry, 56,* 531–549.

Quinsey, V. L., Chaplin, T. C., & Carrigan, W. F. (1979). Sexual preference among incestuous and nonincestuous child molestors. *Behavior Therapy, 10,* 562–565.

Russell, D. E. H. (1983). The incidence and prevalence of intrafamilial and extrafamilial sexual abuse of female children. *Child Abuse and Neglect, 7,* 133–146.

Russell, D. E. H. (1984). The prevalence and seriousness of incestuous abuse: Stepfathers vs. biological fathers. *Child Abuse and Neglect, 8,* 15–22.

Scott, R. L., & Stone, D. A. (1986). MMPI measures of psychological disturbance in adolescent and adult victims of father-daughter incest. *Journal of Clinical Psychology, 42,* 251–259.

Trepper, T. S. (1986). The apology session. In T. S. Trepper and M. J. Barrett (Eds.), *Treating incest: A multiple systems perspective.* New York: Haworth Press.

Trepper, T. S., & Barrett, M. J. (1986a). Introduction to the multiple systems model for the treatment of intrafamily child sexual abuse. In T. S. Trepper & M. J. Barrett (Eds.), *Treating incest: A multiple systems perspective.* New York: Haworth Press.

Trepper, T. S., & Barrett, M. J. (1986b). Vulnerability to incest: A framework for assessment. In T. S. Trepper & M. J. Barrett (Eds.), *Treating incest: A multiple systems perspective.* New York: Haworth Press.

Trepper, T. S., & Traicoff, E. M. (1983). Treatment of intrafamily sexuality: Issues in therapy and research. *Journal of Sex Education and Therapy, 9,* 14–18.

Tsai, M., Summers, S. F., & Edgar, M. (1979). Childhood molestation: Variables related to differential impact of psychosexual functioning in adult women. *Journal of Abnormal Psychology, 88,* 407–417.

Tyler, A. H., & Brassard, M. R. (1984). Abuse in the investigation and treatment of intrafamilial child sexual abuse. *Child Abuse and Neglect, 8,* 47–53.

Vander Mey, B. J., & Neff, R. L. (1982). Adult-child incest: A review of research and treatment. *Adolescence, 17,* 717–735.

Vander Mey, B. J., & Neff, R. L. (1984). Adult-child incest: A sample of substantiated cases. *Family Relations, 33,* 549–557.

Vander Mey, B. J., & Neff, R. L. (1986). *Incest as child abuse: Research and applications.* New York: Praeger.

Virkkunen, M. (1974). Incest offense and alcoholism. *Medical and Scientific Law, 14,* 124.

Weinberg, S. K. (1955). *Incest behavior.* New York: Citadel.

# 8

# Adolescent Substance Abuse

## FRED P. PIERCY and THORANA S. NELSON

*Kevin Murphy was a manipulative but likeable 17-year-old in trouble. He had recently totaled the family car while driving drunk. A search of his school locker turned up marijuana and barbiturates. Kevin was already on probation for shoplifting. His parents initiated family therapy because they were informed that, if they refused, Kevin would be expelled from school. Also, therapy was mandated by the court as a condition of probation.*

*Still, Kevin made light of his misconduct and involvement with alcohol and drugs, and blamed others for his troubles. He usually had several beers with his father in the evening. He resented his mother "trying to run" his life and attempted to undercut her. Kevin had a 12-year-old brother, David, who did well in school. It was Kevin who seemed to drain his parents of their energy and resolve. However, as we shall see, Kevin's family played a role in inadvertently maintaining his substance abuse and misbehavior. With professional help, Kevin's family was able to learn to provide the context for positive change to occur.*

In this chapter, we discuss one family therapy model that appears to have promise for adolescents like Kevin. This model was developed as part of a large, multiyear research grant, and employs what we believe are theoretically compatible, operationalizable, and teachable skills from structural, strategic, functional, and behavioral family therapies (Piercy & Frankel, 1985).

### INCIDENCE

Kevin is not alone. The average youth tries marijuana and alcohol at about age 13 (IFCDFY, 1985). In a recent survey of Indiana junior high school students, by the age of 12, 85% had tried alcohol and 69% had tried marijuana (IFCDFY, 1985).

Teenage abuse of illicit drugs (except for cocaine) has declined in recent years (Johnston, O'Malley, & Bachman, 1986). Of approximately 16,000 high school seniors surveyed in 1985, 5% had used marijuana at least 20 times in the previous month compared to 11% in 1978. Despite this apparent decline, adolescent use and abuse of drugs and alcohol continue to be a problem. Alcohol use is particularly prevalent: 66% of the high school seniors surveyed in 1985 reported having used alcohol the previous month (Johnston, O'Malley, & Bachman, 1986).

Drunk driving is the leading cause of death for young people between the ages of 16 and 24. Approximately 14 teenagers die and 360 are injured each day in alcohol-related traffic accidents. Annually, teenager alcohol-impaired driving accidents are costing society approximately six billion dollars in damages, hospital costs, and related losses (DARE, 1986). Beyond the costs related to traffic accidents are the financial and emotional burdens that families, schools, court systems, and employers pay as a result of adolescent alcohol and drug use.

## EFFECTS ON TEEN AND FAMILY

Substance use and abuse impact a wide range of systems: the person using the drug, his or her family and peer group, schools, health systems, and society in general. For the individual, the chemical itself can produce dangerous effects, such as brain and liver damage. Cross-tolerance and dependence or addiction may become problems.

Long-term substance abuse usually is accompanied by behaviors that prevent normal development (Rosenthal, Nelson, & Drake, 1986). Youngsters who are busy getting and using drugs are not developing social and career skills. Substance abuse also impairs judgment, which can lead to unsafe behaviors such as driving while drunk. Teenagers are notorious for thinking they can "handle it."

There is much family stress in attempting to find ways to deal with the medical, emotional, and societal effects of the substance use once it is discovered. In Kevin's family, his mother obtained tranquilizers from her physician to help her deal with her feeling of anxiety; Kevin's father's work performance suffered; his parents' arguing increased; and Kevin's younger brother became withdrawn and appeared sad in school.

Society also pays a high price for teenage substance abuse in the form of traffic deaths and injuries, accidental (or not-so-accidental) overdoses, and the costs related to the arrest and treatment of adolescent substance abusers (DARE, 1986). Also, a teen's potential benefit to society often goes unrealized as a result of drug-related activities.

## SOURCES OF STRESS

Conditions that influence teenage substance abuse are many and varied, and include personality characteristics, possible genetic factors, coping mechanisms, family dynamics, parenting styles, and peer and social pressures. Some teenage substance abusers are described as aggressive, impulsive, depressed, and having low self-esteem (Hawthorne & Menzel, 1983). These youth are often less religious, come from broken homes, and have close relatives who use or abuse chemicals (Kite, 1980).

Kandel, Treiman, Faust, and Single (1975) identify three categories of adolescent drug use, each with accompanying behaviors related to etiology, evidence, and response. The first is considered related to experimentation and peer involvement with legal drugs such as alcohol and diet pills. The second is also peer-related, but involves the use of marijuana or other illicit drugs. The third, most serious, involves the use of addictive drugs such as cocaine or heroin. Teenagers in the first category may not be involved in dysfunctional family dynamics, and their families may respond effectively when the substance use is discovered (Rosenthal, Nelson, & Drake, 1986). Teenagers in the second group may or may not be involved in dysfunctional family dynamics. Discovery of substance use may be stressful for families in both these groups, but effective coping skills can alleviate the stress effect. Parental behaviors and communication seem to have little relation to hard-core substance abuse by teenagers in the third group (Fors & Rojek, 1983), and coping responses are less effective.

Families' responses to substance abuse can also be stressful. Parents may exaggerate their usual problem-solving behaviors. When these fail, the family must also cope with feelings of inadequacy. Parents may also respond by attempting to "fix" the problem with inconsistent or ineffective discipline. Often, as in Kevin's family, the signs of substance abuse are not noticed until a pattern of abuse is established and an outside source, such as the police, call it to the parents' attention. In such cases, embarrassment may also affect the parents' ability to respond effectively.

## FUNCTIONAL FAMILY COPING

Adolescent substance use is frightening for families. They often need to enlist professional assistance, something that is difficult for many families.

Families who cope well are those who communicate well and who encourage independence of members while remaining supportive and caring. Also, they deal with problems directly rather than blaming or involving others unnecessarily. They may be temporarily stuck and need the advice of professionals, but they are able to use suggestions and advice well, and to integrate new skills. These families typically have parents or guardians who are clearly in charge, allow appropriate adolescent responsibility and decision making, admit mistakes, and can negotiate rules and consequences. Rules are generally clear and consequences are straightforward, fair, and consistently applied. Children in such families have developing senses of themselves as autonomous individuals, feel safe and secure, understand rules and consequences, and are able to assert themselves in age-appropriate ways.

When faced with unusual stress, functional families are able to work together and support each other, to assess the situation objectively, and to generate alternatives from both past and present experience. They are able to effectively use the expertise of a physician, counselor, or other professional.


## DYSFUNCTIONAL FAMILY COPING

Many of the responses to the discovery of teenage substance abuse are similar to the family's typical responses in other crises. For example, the sequence of events in Kevin's family was similar to that when he was in other kinds of trouble. His mother and father initially confronted him about his drug use and, when he denied it, his father acted helpless, argued with his wife, and then withdrew. Kevin's mother, angry with his father for abdicating responsibility, angrily confronted Kevin. Kevin became belligerent and his mother gave up. Sometime later, Kevin's father attempted to reason with Kevin with little success. He eventually offered Kevin a beer and told him about some of his own problems. The whole family was upset and, about this time, Kevin's grandfather needed hospitalization for a reaction to his cancer chemotherapy.

What appears as a stressor in the family, the discovery of Kevin's substance abuse, can also be seen as part of a larger picture of interactions and attempted solutions. Family members can get mired in well-meaning behaviors (like yelling and reasoning) that are simultaneous attempted solutions and problems. This is not to say that families cause teenagers to use drugs, but that they are caught in a game in which the rules prevent other kinds of solutions. The resulting responses are part of the patterns of behavior that maintain the drug abuse. (For those interested in further discussion of the dynamics of adolescent substance abuse in a family context, see Kaufman, 1985; Rosenthal, Nelson, & Drake, 1986; and Stanton, Todd, & Associates, 1982.)

Frequent dysfunctional family dynamics that may include adolescent substance abuse are united fronts (Minuchin, 1974), dysfunctional hierarchies, and triangling or detouring (Stanton et al., 1982). Parents who are disagreeing but are unable to resolve their differences may turn their united energies on their teenager, blaming the family's problems on him or her. The teenager may then use or abuse drugs as either a way of coping (Fisch, Weakland, & Segal, 1983) or as an attempt to distract the parents from their disagreement (Friedman, 1974). Parents may then double their ineffective attempts to control their child, and in this way may inadvertently increase the troublesome behavior.

Teenagers whose parents are functionally immature may also use drugs as a solution to the family's dysfunctional dynamics (Stanton et al., 1982). The teenager may have difficulty in becoming more mature than he or she perceives his or her parents to be. In such cases, drug use may be an attempt to separate from the family. The teenage drug user may appear independent, but be heavily dependent upon his or her family for money, food, support, and a place to occasionally recuperate. This "pseudoindividuation" results in the parents' feeling simultaneously helpful and not in control of their child.

Other parents, unable to effectively cope with previous stresses in the family, may not have the internal resources necessary to cope with their adolescent's acting out. What began as youthful experimentation may become dangerously worse because of parental frustration or helplessness. Parents with unresolved disagreements may use their child as a scapegoat or as a way to "get at" each other. For example, they may attempt to enlist the child as an ally in one of their arguments.

Kevin's family did this very thing. His father (Jerome) and mother (Carol) were stressed by the recent illness and death of Jerome's mother and the current terminal illness of Jerome's father. Kevin tried to help his parents by staying out of their way when his mother was unhappy. He would often act as a companion to his father, joining him for a beer and "grown-up" chat. As his attempts to please them failed, he quit trying at school and spent more time with his friends. With few resources for earning money, he began to sell pot and uppers. Each family member played a special part in the drama: Kevin's mother by attempting to pull the family together, Kevin's father by trying to be a buddy to Kevin, Kevin's brother by doing things for his parents to be proud of, and Kevin by distracting his parents from some of their other troubles.

Kevin and his family are stuck; they don't know how to deal effectively with the problems they face and the consequences of those problems.


## GENERAL APPROACH TO TREATMENT

As stated previously, the family therapy model we are presenting was developed as part of a large, multiyear grant from the National Institute on Drug Abuse. This model was culled from existing models that have been effective with juvenile delinquents (Barton & Alexander, 1981; Patterson, 1983) and adult heroin addicts (Stanton et al., 1982). The model employs compatible skills from structural, strategic, functional, and behavioral family therapies. All of these family therapies are similar in that they: (a) monitor behavior and interpersonal interactions; (b) conceptualize problems interactionally rather than in terms of individual pathology; (c) appreciate the function of problem behaviors in families; (d) conceptualize the family process as maintaining problems; (e) emphasize the present over the past; (f) attempt to change behaviors and/or behavioral sequences; (g) employ instruction and coaching in therapy; (h) assign homework to generalize and solidify change; and (i) see their goal as restructuring interactions by way of behavioral or cognitive change in order to change the presenting problem. Each of the six major goals of our integrated treatment model are identified and briefly discussed below. (For a more detailed presentation of this model, see Piercy & Frankel, 1985.)

*1. Decrease the family's resistance to treatment.* The therapist's first job is to reduce the family's defensiveness and thus to strengthen the therapist's potential influence. To this end, we emphasize the importance of the therapist's use of *relationship skills* and *positive connotation.*

Alexander and his associates (Alexander, 1973; Alexander, Barton, Schiavo, & Parsons, 1976; Barton & Alexander, 1977, 1981; Parsons & Alexander, 1973) have found that the therapist's ability to establish a relationship with a family through the demonstration of such skills as humor, warmth, and empathy is positively related to low family dropout rates and positive outcome. The importance of such *relationship skills* are emphasized throughout the therapy process.

*Positive connotation*, the positive labeling of what was previously considered negative behavior, is particularly useful in helping the therapist gain entrance and influence in some families. Even when the behaviors are self-destructive (like drug use) or particularly obnoxious, the *intent* behind them can be understood and appreciated, yet not necessarily condoned. For example, the therapist might say to a parent, "You shout at your daughter because you really want her to know how important this whole thing is to you." Or a therapist might tell a drug-abusing teenager, "You've picked a dangerous way to get this family together, but they *are* together now. I sense a lot of caring. They clearly want something better."

2. *Restrain immediate change.* In order to increase maneuverability, the therapist initially presents him- or herself as cautious about pushing for changes that may have unknown and potentially uncomfortable or dangerous consequences. This involves discussing the *consequences of change* with a family and emphasizing the need to *go slow* (Fisch, Weakland, & Segal, 1983).

Families may be subtly and unconsciously invested in maintaining a teenager's drug abuse. For example, the drug abuse might be taking attention away from the parents' marital or other problems. (In Kevin's family their inability to cope effectively with loss and grief may have been a factor in Kevin's behavior.) To explore such possibilities, the therapist may wish to ask the family about any conceivable negative *consequences of change*. The family may either acknowledge and seriously discuss the existence of negative consequences (e.g., that they would have to face their own marital problems), or deny negative consequences and attempt to prove the therapist wrong by demonstrating that they do indeed want to change.

The *go slow* message is usually given early in therapy to convey the idea that change is difficult, requires considerable adjustment, and may not always result in the desired behaviors. In suggesting that a family "go slow," the therapist resists a "cheerleader" role, forcing the family to provide the motivation for change and pacing the family's ability to change and adjust. A "go slow" message normalizes setbacks ("So you didn't change everything this week. So what? It's taken you years to develop this problem" or "Maybe we went too fast. Maybe David's not ready for Kevin to change"). A "go slow" message also makes it less likely for a family to do poorly as a way of proving the therapist impotent or incompetent. After all, the motivation for change is squarely on the family's shoulders—they have to convince the therapist that they are indeed ready to change.

3. *Establish appropriate parental influence.* Families with a drug-abusing adolescent often have confused or blurred hierarchical boundaries. In many cases, the teenagers appear to be in charge of the parents. A cornerstone of this approach to family therapy is to return parents to their

rightful place as executives and authorities within the family. This may be accomplished either directly or indirectly. Direct interventions include supporting the parents in setting and carrying out family rules related to issues such as appropriate curfews and chores. When direct approaches fail, the therapist may employ more indirect or paradoxical procedures (e.g., "I think it may be too hard or scary for you two to agree on rules to set for your son. Or maybe the problem just hasn't gotten bad enough yet to get your attention . . . ").

For a more detailed discussion of both direct and indirect ways of supporting parental influence, see Piercy and Frankel (1986).

4. *Gather systemic information about the presenting problem.* The therapist should, in the context of the clinical interview, assess drug use in terms of *behavioral sequence* and *function*.

The *behavioral sequence* is assessed by determining how family members' behaviors are linked to the drug use. What happens interactionally before, during, and after a drug abuse episode? If a behavioral sequence can be identified, the therapist can proceed to look for ways to alter it.

The interpersonal *function* (Alexander & Parsons, 1982) of the drug use may be assessed at the same time as the behavioral sequence. Does the drug abuse result in the adolescent becoming more involved with his parents (i.e., a "closeness" function) or less involved with his parents (i.e., a "distance" function)? If, for example, a drug abuse incident resulted in parents giving long lectures to their teenager, a closeness function would be surmised. If, on the other hand, drug use was followed by long periods of isolation from parents, a distancing function would be assessed. The assessment of such functions is often helpful in fitting an intervention to a particular family style, as discussed below.

5. *Interrupt dysfunctional sequences of behavior.* Behavioral cycles around drug use may be broken in a variety of ways consistent with structural family therapy (e.g., empowering the parents by supporting mutual rule setting), strategic family therapy (e.g., predicting and/or prescribing who will do what during the next family argument), or behavioral family therapy (e.g., behavioral contracting).

Whenever possible, the therapist's intervention should be consistent with the family's interpersonal style and the hypothesized interpersonal function of the drug use. For example, if the family typically comes together after a drug abuse incident (through long lectures to the teenager—a closeness function), the therapist would attempt to devise an intervention to break the behavioral cycle in ways that would still allow the family to rally together yet decrease the drug use. A home token economy is one example of a possible intervention that would allow the family to be close while monitoring positive instead of negative behavior.

Likewise, an intervention consistent with a distancing function would respect the fact that the teenager and his or her parents may generally have minimal involvement with one another, or at the least that drug use decreases involvement. One possible intervention would be to help the teenager contract with his/her parents for increased freedom from parental interference in return for responsible, drug-free behavior. For example, if the teenager would abide by certain curfew times and house rules, his or her parents could agree to consider increasing the curfew after a period of time and lay off any "third-degree" interrogations.

The range of interventions is limitless. The challenge for the therapist is to devise an intervention that the family will "buy," that is consistent with the family's style, and that is potent enough to change the context and structure of the family so that the predictable behavioral sequence around drug abuse can be broken.

*6. Provide assertion skill training to the drug-abusing adolescent and his or her siblings in the context of the family which will strengthen their ability to actively resist pressures to engage in drug use.* Assertion training has been used successfully to decrease anxiety (Wolpe, 1973), to increase the ability to speak for one's self (Salter, 1949), to increase self-direction and personal choice, lessen dependence on the evaluations and manipulations of others (Alberti & Emmons, 1974), and to decrease aggressive and explosive behaviors (Eisler, Hersen, & Miller, 1974; Frederiksen, Jenkins, Foy, & Eisler, 1976).

Through assertion training conducted with the teenager both alone and in the context of the family, the youth may learn how to say no to peer pressure related to drug use and other manipulative behaviors. Assertion training is also meant to help the teenager learn to communicate with both peers and parents more clearly, directly, and respectfully, rather than using aggressive or passive responses that may have sparked arguments in the past. Also, assertion-training procedures can help teenagers learn social skills that were stifled because of their drug-related behavior (Spoth & Rosenthal, 1980). In addition, parents can learn negotiating skills with teenagers that work better than authoritarian styles that may be more useful with younger children.

The steps in assertion training include: (a) assessment of interpersonal deficiencies, (b) specification of situations that cause problems; (c) therapist's modeling of more appropriate responses; (d) review, discussion, and feedback; (e) covert rehearsal of new behavior; (f) overt rehearsal of new behavior; (g) feedback from therapist; and (h) in-vivo application of new assertive behavior within therapy sessions and through structured homework assignments.


## ASSESSMENT METHODS

Two types of assessment may be employed. The first type involves a battery of tests that may be given to each client family. Therapists also may actively employ a second, more informal type of assessment to chart the course of treatment. The battery of instruments we use to determine treatment effectiveness (which are given by independent researchers immediately before treatment, after treatment, and at six-month, one-year, and two-year follow-ups) are identified and briefly discussed below. Although we used these assessment instruments primarily for research purposes, they also could be used for clinical assessment and planning.

*Assessment Instruments*

*Polydrug Use History Questionnaire.* This one-page checklist was adopted for our study from an earlier questionnaire developed by Lewis and his colleagues (1979) for adult heroin addicts and their spouses. This questionnaire assesses the extent to which a person has used any of 15 classes of drugs during the previous year, previous six months, previous month, and previous week.

*Dyadic Formation Inventory (DFI).* This inventory includes 25 items which assess several dimensions of marital relationships. The DFI includes the following subscales: (a) dyadic interaction; (b) dyadic inclusiveness; (c) dyadic exclusiveness; (d) pair commitment; (e) couple identity; and (f) identification as a pair (Lewis, 1972, 1973a, 1973b, 1973c; Lewis, Filsinger, Conger, & McAvoy, 1980).

*Family Adaptability and Cohesion Evaluation Scales (FACES III).* FACES III includes measures of family cohesion (the degree to which family members are separated from or connected to their family), family adaptability (the extent to which a family system is flexible and able to change), and family communication. These theoretical concepts are based on the Circumplex model of Olson, Russell, and Sprenkle (1979).

*Family Problem Assessment Scale (FPAS).* Feldman's (1982) Family Problem Assessment Scale is a family goal attainment scale that elicits quantifiable self-report data from each family member regarding presenting problems. We have adapted Feldman's (1982) scale by asking families to arrive at a *consensus* regarding the perceived severity of presenting problems.

*Parent-Adolescent Communication Inventory (PACI).* This inventory assesses the views of both adolescents and their parents regarding their communications with each other (Barnes & Olson, 1982). The two subscales in this inventory are Open Family Communication and Problems in Family Communication.

*Kvebaek Family Sculpture Test (KFST).* This is an innovative family diagnostic and research tool (Cromwell, Kvebaek, & Fournier, 1980) that involves family members, both individually and collectively, placing objects representing family members on squares within a 1 × 1 meter game board. Each family member's "real" and "ideal" profiles are indicated on a recording form representing a duplication of the sculpture grid reduced in size.

*Social Interaction Scoring System (SISS).* This observational coding system involves the use of a Datamyte Event Recorder, a portable microcomputer, to record behavioral code categories of verbal and physical responses, emotional affect, commands, and complies (Conger, 1976; Conger & McLeod, 1977).

*Urinalysis.* A full spectrum urinalysis is conducted at pretest, posttest, and each follow-up for both the drug-abusing adolescent and his or her siblings. In addition, urinalyses are conducted on a random basis throughout therapy.

### Informal Assessment Procedures

A second set of assessment procedures that the therapist may actively employ as part of treatment may be thought of as fitting into three categories, those that *determine the nature and extent of the teenager's drug use*, those that *assess the family's functioning*, and those that *assess larger systems issues.*

The therapist may *determine the nature and extent of the teenager's drug use* by employing physiological measures such as urinalysis and blood testing and by carefully questioning the teenager and his or her parents. Assessment should go beyond a "dipstick" determination of the presence or absence of substances in the teenager's system (Marlatt, 1983). Instruments such as the Drug Use Index (Douglas & Khavari, 1978) or the Michigan Alcoholism Screening Test (Selzer, 1971) can assist the professional in assessing the extent of drug use. Physiological, paper-and-pencil, and interviewing assessment techniques should all be employed, as none is completely reliable on its own (Bernhardt, Mumford, Taylor, Smith, & Murray, 1982).

Family members often disagree about the nature of the drug use and the sequences of behaviors around it. It is useful in such cases to ask the family to gather baseline data about the troublesome behaviors. Asking the parents to gather information about their teenager's behavior, about related behaviors in the family, and about substance abuse in general can be part of the assessment of the adolescent's drug use and behaviors, of the family's ability to cooperate in therapy, and of the family's ability to benefit from direct rather than indirect therapeutic techniques.

Second, the therapist may *assess the family's functioning* by examining issues such as hierarchy, boundaries, and coalitions. What rules have the parents implemented? How have they carried them out? How do the parents cooperate? Does the teenager side with one against the other? Who seems to have the most power in the family? Is the family organized or disorganized, close or distant? In addition, as discussed in the above section, the therapist attempts to assess typical sequences of family behavior around drug abuse and other misbehavior, and examines the interpersonal function (closeness or distance) of the drug use. Communication patterns are also informally noticed to determine if the teenager or his or her parents might benefit from assertion skill training.

The family's functioning may also be assessed through more formal instruments such as FACES-III (mentioned above) and the Family Assessment Device (Epstein, Baldwin, & Bishop, 1983). Recent events in the family can be adding to both the substance abuse problems and the family's ability to cope with it. The Family Inventory of Life Events (McCubbin & Patterson, 1983) can be useful to the therapist in obtaining a clear picture of the family's recent history. Knowing the family's typical style of functioning and problem solving can help the therapist determine a treatment plan. Functional but "stuck" families require different kinds of help (usually more direct) than long-term dysfunctional or severely disorganized families (who may require more indirect methods of help).

Third, the therapist may *assess larger systems issues* by inquiring into the peer relations of the teenager, school and work environments of family members, and involvement of other systems such as child protective services and the police. This will help the professional assess the numbers and kinds of systems involved with the family and the extent of their involvement. Questions should also be asked regarding the involvement of other medical and mental health professionals so that treatment efforts can be coordinated. (For a more detailed discussion of assessment issues and procedures related to adolescent substance abuse and families, see Nelson, Rosenthal, Harrington, & Mitchelson, 1987; Rosenthal, Nelson & Drake, 1986).

## DIAGNOSIS AND TREATMENT PLAN

The case of Kevin and his family will be used to briefly illustrate the role of informal assessment within the treatment protocol. Before the therapist ever met Kevin, he had a flexible integrative treatment plan in mind that emphasized present behavior, family structure, and interpersonal process. (See General Approach to Treatment above.) The specifics of how the treatment plan would be implemented depended on initial test data, as well as information that would unfold during the course of treatment — information such as the presenting problem and the family's previous attempts to change it, the family's present structure and rules, predictable sequences of behavior, the hypothesized function of the drug use, and the communication skills of the family members.

During the initial assessment session the family underwent our extensive test battery, and certain diagnostic information was obtained to determine Kevin's appropriateness for treatment. For example, it was determined that although Kevin had experimented with marijuana and barbiturates, he was *not* physically addicted to or dependent upon drugs and therefore did not require detoxification. It was also determined that Kevin was not an imminent threat to himself or others. The therapist also understood the conditions of therapy as they related to the court order, the probation officer, and Kevin's school. With these major issues attended to, informal assessment and treatment progressed in concert.

## TREATMENT APPROACH

Our family therapy model for teenage drug abuse is geared to last about 12 sessions. Generally, the treatment falls into four phases, with various skills associated with the goals previously mentioned, as shown in Table 1.

TABLE 1
Skills Emphasized at Each Phase of Treatment

| Phase 1 (Joining) | Phase 2 (Implementation) | Phase 3 (Facilitating/ Monitoring) | Phase 4 (Termination) |
|---|---|---|---|
| Weeks 1–2 | Weeks 2–5 | Weeks 6–11 | Week 12 |
| Join through relationship skills | Give directives to break up dysfunctional sequences of behavior | Monitor and facilitate progress regarding directives, change strategies, and assertion training | Assess progress |
| Positively connote certain problem behaviors | Set up change strategies consistent with interpersonal function | If little progress has been made, discuss again the possible consequences of change | Emphasize positive changes |
| Redefine drug abuse as a family problem | | | Develop with the family a plan for the continuation and generalization of positive changes as well as a plan for working on unresolved problems/ issues |
| Discuss consequences of change/"go slow" | Continue support of parental authority | | |
| Support parental authority | | | |
| Investigate behavioral sequences | | | |
| Assess interpersonal function of drug abuse | | | |

To illustrate the course of therapy for Kevin and his family, the application of the skills related to each of the six major goals of our integrated treatment model (see p. 214) will be described briefly below.

*Decreasing the Family's Resistance to Treatment*

In the first session, the therapist made personal contact with each family member around his or her job, hobby, or schoolwork. It was found that Kevin and his father enjoyed watching baseball games, that David was on a community basketball team, and that Kevin's mother enjoyed cooking and belonged to several community organizations. Each family member also was given the opportunity to give his or her view of what the family problems were, and what changes were needed or desired. Even in the first session, the therapist noticed that Father and Kevin did a lot together, as did David and Mother. Mother was clearly the disciplinarian, yet did not seem to have Kevin's attention, much less respect. It was also noted that discussion related to grandparents was avoided.

Throughout therapy, the therapist attempted to decrease the family's resistance by using humor and demonstrating respect to each family member. He genuinely liked the family and showed it.

The therapist labeled Kevin's angry outbursts as "energy," Mother's nagging as "caring enough to set limits," Father's softness as "wanting to protect Kevin," and David's withdrawal as "knowing how to look good." Such positive connotations were well accepted by the family and gave the therapist considerable maneuverability. The therapist increased his "money in the bank" with the family as therapy progressed. Withdrawals on this goodwill came later when the therapist began restructuring and directly intervening.

*Restraining Immediate Change*

Early in therapy the therapist discussed possible negative consequences of Kevin's "cleaning up his act." The therapist, for example, asked David, "If Kevin quit getting into trouble, would Mother and Father spend more time with Kevin or less time?" David responded, "Less time," which prompted the therapist to suggest that the family might have nothing to talk about or rally around if Kevin quit his drug use and brushes with the law. The parents denied this, but the therapist remained skeptical.

The therapist also mentioned that many families that give up one problem to worry about find an even bigger problem that they have been ignoring. Again, the therapist turned to young David and asked, "What would your parents worry about if they didn't have to worry about Kevin?" After a pause, David said, "Granddad, I guess." The parents explained that Granddad was Jerry's father, Otis Murphy, who had chronic emphysema, and had recently been diagnosed as having inoperable cancer. His wife of 30 years had recently died after a long struggle with leukemia. Otis lived a block from the Murphy's but "didn't want to be a burden." Otis was invited by the parents to attend the therapy sessions, but decided not to because of his difficulty getting around. In discussing Otis, it became clear that the entire family, and especially Kevin, wanted to make Otis's last days happy, but had a hard time talking about his illness.

The family agreed that a possible consequence of Kevin's improvement would be having to face head-on Otis's impending death. The therapist cautioned the family to "go slow" in considering possible changes. The parents, however, emphasized that they were indeed ready to do whatever was necessary to help Kevin.

The knowledge of Otis and his condition gave the therapist an immediate, non-drug-related, positive task for the family to tackle later in therapy— that of supporting Otis and coming to grips with his illness. (The reader should be aware that a large proportion of drug abusers appear to have unresolved issues related to death or terminal illness in their immediate families. See Coleman, 1981).

*Establish Appropriate Parental Influence*

The therapist attempted in a variety of ways to put the parents in a cooperative, executive role; together they were to set limits for Kevin and monitor his behavior. However, Kevin acted like a martyr who was being unfairly treated, Father's resolve weakened, and Mother verbally attacked Father. As a result, no limits were set, and for the first few weeks of therapy Kevin appeared clearly in charge. These exchanges helped the therapist understand the family's typical way of functioning around problems.

To prevent Kevin from distracting his parents and to set a boundary between the parents and children, the therapist eventually asked Kevin and David to leave the room while the parents agreed upon rules they could both live with and enforce. The therapist also discussed with the parents what could go wrong and how Kevin might attempt to undercut them and test their resolve. In addition, the therapist helped the parents learn how to set limits and follow through with consequences through role playing certain situations. The following week the parents came to therapy without their children and practiced some more. The therapist coached the parents and provided feedback. The therapist predicted difficulty and cautioned against going too fast.

When the whole family came to the next session, the parents presented to Kevin, as a team, a curfew time and what they would do if he came home late (which was to *not* let him go out the following evening). Kevin tried to appeal to his father as before, but the parents stood their ground. Hereafter, a regular part of therapy sessions involved discussing limits and consequences and supporting the parents in maintaining them. (The reader will note that the therapist employed assertion-training procedures to help the parents work together to set limits. While assertion training was originally included in this model as a skill to help the drug abuser and sibling learn to say no to drugs, we have found it particularly useful for helping parents reestablish their parental influence.)

*Gather Systemic Information About the Presenting Problem*

As stated above, a cycle was noticed that involved Father's colluding with Kevin against Mother and Mother's attempting to engage Father through Kevin. The therapist investigated this cycle in more detail and found that a predictable sequence included Kevin's misbehaving and Mother's attempting to exert consequences. Although Father initially agreed with the consequences, he usually softened and reduced them. This infuriated Mother, who then attacked Father, withdrew, and sulked. Father would begin to drink and eventually offer a beer to Kevin. When this sequence was in progress, David would be on his own and looking good (or siding with Mother), and Otis would momentarily be forgotten. The next day, Father would have forgotten most of what had gone on and would try to convince Mother that he "meant well" and that it would be "different next time."

The therapist hypothesized that Kevin's misbehavior and drug abuse served a closeness function, as did Father's drinking and Mother's nagging. Clearly, the parents seemed to increase their involvement with Kevin and each other around his acting out.

## Interrupt Dysfunctional Sequences of Behavior

The dysfunctional cycle mentioned above was interrupted in several ways, not the least of which involved getting the parents to set limits as a cooperative team and follow through with these limits. Discouragement was forestalled through the "go slow" messages.

Related to this, an intervention that interrupted this cycle, supported the influence of Mother and Father, and was consistent with the interpersonal function of closeness will be described. (Unfortunately, there is insufficient space to adequately do justice to the effort and artistry that went into this intervention. Suffice it to say that it is not as easy as we make it sound!)

The first part of the intervention involved the therapist's facilitating a contract between Kevin and his parents around Kevin's friends and whereabouts. The outcome was the agreement that Kevin would (a) stay away from Bill, a known drug dealer, (b) stay off of drugs and alcohol, (c) let his parents know where he was in the evenings, and (d) be home by 10:00 p.m. on weeknights and 11:00 p.m. on weekends. In return, his parents would be willing to (a) let him borrow the car on one weekend evening and (b) consider contracting for a later curfew in two weeks. Appropriate consequences for infractions were also specified. In order to challenge Kevin's competitive spirit and allow him to prove the therapist rather than his parents wrong, the therapist bet Kevin a dollar that he could *not* live up to his end of the agreement. Kevin grinned and accepted the bet.

After the contract was agreed upon and written down, the therapist said:

I am concerned, in one way, about this agreement. If it is followed, you'll (to the parents) see less and less of Kevin. You are a close family. I hate to think that the only way you can see each other is if Kevin gets into trouble again. What I suggest is that you take a few minutes right now and discuss what you all can do this week as a family to help Otis, since he's so sick.

With some prompting from the therapist, the family decided to have Otis over for dinner on two evenings when their favorite professional baseball team would be on television. Mother offered to teach Kevin how to bake lasagna, which would be a special surprise to Otis.

The evenings with Otis were useful in that they were something the whole family could do together that were *not* related to Kevin's misbehavior or drug use. In fact, Kevin's responsible behavior (baking the lasagna) could be praised. Through such assignments used in tandem with behavioral contracts, the parents learned how to redirect Kevin and, at the same time, to find ways to remain close that didn't involve Kevin's drug use or misbehavior.

*Provide Assertion Skill Training to the Drug-Abusing Adolescent and His or Her Siblings in the Context of the Family which will Strengthen Their Ability to Actively Resist Pressures to Engage in Drug Use*

As Kevin began to show more cooperation around the house and have "clean" urinalysis results, the therapist began to use him as a consultant, as illustrated below.

*Therapist:*   Kevin, I know you are saying no to drugs now, which is great, but David will probably have to face some of the same challenges you have. Why don't you show him how you say no to drugs? Let's pretend I just offered you some downers, what would you say?

*Kevin:*       No way. I don't want that stuff.

*Therapist:*   And what if I kept pushing you?

*Kevin:*       I'd probably say "stuff it" and walk away.

*Therapist:*   Great! You don't have to put up with that — and you don't have to feel like a creep either.

*Kevin:*       It's my life. No one can make me take drugs.

The therapist then involved David in learning to say no.

| | |
|---|---|
| *Therapist:* | David, do you think you could do what Kevin just did? Could you say no to drugs? |
| *David:* | I guess so. |
| *Therapist:* | We'll see. Kevin, pretend to be a 12-year-old whom David knows, and offer him some marijuana. |
| *Kevin:* | David, I've got some grass here. Let's go smoke it. |
| *David* (softly): | No, no way. |
| *Therapist:* | Good, David. You said no right off the bat and looked him directly in the eye. Now say no again, but louder, and don't smile. |
| *David* (louder): | No! |
| *Therapist:* | Great! I believe you. (to Kevin) Do you believe him? |
| *Kevin:* | I sure do. |
| *Therapist:* | This time, Kevin is going to keep after you, David. After you tell him no once and he keeps on, just get up and walk away, OK? . . . |

With the use of such assertion-training procedures, David began to learn the important skill of saying no to drugs. And just as importantly, Kevin began to view himself as competent and responsible.


## SIGNS OF TREATMENT COMPLETION/EFFECTIVENESS

In our particular research project, we examine change through multiple levels of inference (e.g., self-report, behavioral coding) and multiple units of analysis (e.g., individual, couple, family). However, we believe that the sine qua non of effective treatment is change in the presenting problem. In Kevin's case, treatment would be successful if his drug use stopped and if his behavior (e.g., school attendance, acts of misconduct) improved. Our marker, then, for completion of therapy is significant improvement in the presenting problem, with the family demonstrating the skills to maintain this change. By these criteria, Kevin's treatment was successful. Time will tell if Kevin and his family are able to maintain the changes begun in therapy.


## CONCLUSION

Adolescent drug abuse is at an epidemic level and represents a powerful stressor to the entire family. In this chapter, we have discussed adolescent drug abuse and have presented one therapy model that tackles this problem in the context of the family. Our preliminary findings have been encouraging. However, some cautions are warranted.

First, the model presented here is not a panacea. Adolescent drug use is too multidimensional and pervasive for one approach to be *the* answer. Also, there are times that other systems (e.g., organized crime, peers) and the power of the drugs themselves may dwarf the family's resources to change (Piercy & Frankel, 1986). The family may not be able to organize functionally even with therapy; other treatment, such as inpatient hospitalization or group home placement, may be necessary.

Finally, the model presented here is not a cookbook approach. While it provides a useful map for the therapist, the therapist's creativity is critical, as is collaboration with other systems. Together, much can be accomplished in our journey toward effective treatment of adolescent drug abuse. The model mentioned in this chapter represents an important initial step in this journey.

## REFERENCES

Alberti, R. E., & Emmons, M. L. (1974). *Your perfect right.* San Luis Obispo, CA: Impact.

Alexander, J. F. (1973). Defensive and supportive communication in normal and deviant families. *Journal of Consulting and Clinical Psychology, 40,* 223–231.

Alexander, J. F., Barton, C., Schiavo, R. S., & Parsons, B. V. (1976). Systems-behavioral intervention with families of delinquents: Therapist characteristics, family behavior, and outcome. *Journal of Consulting and Clinical Psychology, 44,* 656–664.

Alexander, J. & Parsons, B. V. (1982). *Functional family therapy.* Monterey, CA: Brooks/Cole.

Barnes, H., & Olson, R. H. (1982). Parent-adolescent communication. In D. H. Olson, H. I. McCubbin, H. Barnes, A. Larsen, M. Muxen, & M. Wilson, *Family Inventories.* St. Paul, MN: University of Minnesota.

Barton, C., & Alexander, J. (1977). Therapist skills as determinants of effective systems-behavioral family therapy. *International Journal of Family Counseling, 5,* 11–20.

Barton, C., & Alexander, J. F. (1981). Functional family therapy. In A. S. Gurman & D.P. Kniskern (Eds.), *Handbook of family therapy.* New York: Brunner/Mazel.

Bernhardt, M. W., Mumford, S., Taylor, C., Smith, B., & Murray, R. M. (1982). Comparison of questionnaire and laboratory tests in the detection of excessive drinking and alcoholism. *Lancet, 1,* 325–328.

Coleman, S. B. (1981). Incomplete mourning in substance-abusing families: Theory, research and practice. In L. R. Wolberg & M. L. Aronson (Eds.), *Group and family therapy.* New York: Brunner/Mazel.

Conger, R. D. (1976). *A comparative study of interaction patterns between deviant and non-deviant families.* Unpublished Ph.D. dissertation, University of Washington, Seattle.

Conger, R. D., & McLeod, D. (1977). Describing behavior in small groups with the datamyte recorder. *Behavior Research Methods and Instrumentation, 9,* 418–424.

Cromwell, R., Kvebaek, D., & Fournier, D. (1980). *The Kvebaek family technique: A diagnostic and research tool in family therapy.* Jonesboro, TN: Pilgrimage.

DARE (1986). Some figures about kids and substance abuse. *DARE Newsletter, 1* (1), 1.

Douglas, F. M., & Khavari, K. A. (1978). The Drug Use Index: A measure of the extent of polydrug usage. *International Journal of the Addictions, 13,* 981–993.

Eisler, R. M., Hersen, M., & Miller, P. M. (1974). Shaping components of assertive behavior with instructions and feedback. *American Journal of Psychiatry, 131,* 1344–1347.

Epstein, N. B., Baldwin, L. M., & Bishop, D. S. (1983). The McMaster Family Assessment Device. *Journal of Marital and Family Therapy, 9,* 171–180.

Feldman, L. (1982). *Family problems assessment/family strengths assessment.* Mimeographed paper, Chicago Family Institute.

Fisch, R., Weakland, J. H., & Segal, L. (1983). *Tactics of change.* San Francisco, CA: Jossey-Bass.

Fors, S. W., & Rojek, D. G. (1983). The social and demographic correlates of adolescent drug-use patterns. *Journal of Drug Education, 13,* 205–222.

Frederiksen, L. W., Jenkins, J. O., Foy, D. W., & Eisler, R. M. (1976). Social-skill training to modify abusive verbal outbursts in adults. *Journal of Applied Behavior Analysis, 9,* 117–126.

Friedman, P. H. (1974). Family system and ecological approach to youthful drug abuse. *Family therapy, 1,* 63–78.

Hawthorne, W., & Menzel, N. (1983). Youth treatment should be a programming priority. *Alcohol Health and Research World, 8,* 46–50.

IFCDFY (1985). The 1980 Indiana school drug study survey of junior high drug users. (Reprinted in *DARE Newsletter* (1986), *1*(2), 4).

Johnston, L. D., O'Malley, P. M., & Bachman, J. G. (1986). *Drug use among high school students, college students, and other young adults: National trends through 1985.* Rockville, MD: National Institute on Drug Abuse.

Kandel, D. B., Treiman, D., Faust, R., & Single, E. (1975). Adolescent involvement in legal and illegal drug use: A multiple classification analysis. *Social Forces, 55,* 438–458.

Kaufman, E. (1985). *Substance abuse and family therapy.* New York: Grune & Stratton.

Kite, W. R. (1980). *Presenting problems of adolescents in treatment: A survey of comprehensive-care adolescent programs. Executive summary.* St. Louis, MO: Comprehensive Care Corp.

Lewis, R. A. (1972). A developmental framework for the analysis of premarital dyadic formation. *Family Process, 11,* 17–48.

Lewis, R. A. (1973a). A longitudinal test of a developmental framework for premarital dyadic formation. *Journal of Marriage and the Family, 35,* 16–25.

Lewis, R. A. (1973b). Social reaction and the formation of dyads: An interactionist approach to mate selection. *Sociometry, 36,* 409–418.

Lewis, R. A. (1973c). The Dyadic Formation Inventory: An instrument for measuring heterosexual couple development. *The International Journal of Sociology of the Family, 3,* 207–216.

Lewis, R. A., Conger, R. D., McAvoy, P., & Filsinger, E. E. (1979). Opiate-involved life styles and couple relationships. A grant from NIDA, 1 R01 DA–02286–01.

Lewis, R. A., Filsinger, E. E., Conger, R. D., & McAvoy, P. (1980). *The assessment of quality of opiate-involved relationships.* A paper presented at the Family Observation, Behavioral Assessment & Intervention Conference, Arizona State University.

Marlatt, G. A. (1983). Controlled drinking controversy: A commentary. *American Psychologist,* 1097–1110.

McCubbin, H. I., & Patterson, J. M. (1983). Stress: The Family Inventory of Life Events and Changes. In E. E. Filsinger (Ed.), *Marriage and family assessment* (pp. 275–297). Beverly Hills, CA: Sage.

Minuchin, S. (1974). *Families and family therapy.* Cambridge, MA: Harvard University Press.

Nelson, T., Rosenthal, D., Harrington, R. G., & Mitchelson, D. (1987). Assessment of adolescent substance abuse. In R. G. Harrington (Ed.), *Testing Adolescents* (pp. 178–199). Kansas City, MO: Test Corporation of America.

Olson, D. H., Russell, C. S., & Sprenkle, D. H. (1979). Circumplex model of marital and family systems II: Empirical studies and clinical intervention. In J. Vincent (Ed.), *Advances in family intervention, assessment and theory.* Greenwich, CT: JAI Press.

Parsons, B. V., & Alexander, J. F. (1973). Short-term family intervention: A therapy outcome study. *Journal of Consulting and Clinical Psychology, 41,* 195–201.

Patterson, G. (1983). *Coercive family process.* Eugene, OR: Castalia.

Piercy, F., & Frankel, B. (1985). *Training manual: Purdue Brief Family Therapy.* Center for Instructional Services, Purdue University, West Lafayette, IN 47906.

Piercy, F. P., & Frankel, B. (1986). Establishing appropriate parental influence in families with a drug abusing adolescent: Direct and indirect methods. *Journal of Strategic and Systemic Therapies, 5* (3), 30–39.

Rosenthal, D., Nelson, T., & Drake, N. (1986). Adolescent substance use and abuse: A family context. In G. Leigh & G. Peterson (Eds.), *Adolescents in families* (pp. 337–357). Cincinnati, OH: South-Western.

Salter, A. (1949). *Conditioned reflex therapy.* New York: Farrer, Straus, & Giroux.

Selzer, M. L. (1971). The Michigan Alcohol Screening Test: The quest for a new diagnostic instrument. *American Journal of Psychiatry, 127,* 1653–1659.

Spoth, R., & Rosenthal, D. (1980). Wanted: A developmentally oriented alcohol prevention program. *Personnel and Guidance Journal, 59,* 212–216.

Stanton, M. D., Todd, T., & Associates (1982). *The family therapy of drug abuse and addiction.* New York: Guilford.

Wolpe, J. (1973). *The practice of behavior therapy.* New York: Pergamon Press.

# 9

# Parent-Adolescent Conflict

## JUDITH L. FISCHER and
## MARCIA D. BROWN-STANDRIDGE

The parents, in their mid-thirties, appeared bright, articulate, motivated, conscientious, and at a loss as to what to do with 14-year-old
Donald. The father, Donald Sr., worked as an engineer and described
himself as a self-made man educated in the Navy. His wife, Nikki, had
been working as an accounts manager but was between jobs, having
been laid off. While the boy went by the nickname "Don," his father
asked to be addressed as "Jim," a shortened version of his middle name.

The parents had been quite content with Don's "average" performance in school until a few months back when he stopped studying and
began to spend most of his time either sleeping or playing computer
games. Most recently, he was getting up late for school, failing his
subjects, and "throwing temper fits" whenever his irresponsible conduct was confronted. Jim and Nikki brought Don to therapy following a
referral from their son's school principal. There was no previous history
of any family member necessitating mental health services. During the
first session it was mentioned in passing that Don's older sister, Alexa,
had died at the age of 12 in a freak accident when he was only six. A
neighbor child had swung a golf club wildly while they were playing
and accidentally hit her in the head. Don was the only witness.

---

The case example introduced in this chapter is chosen for its ramifications for the whole
family, beyond the original parent-child conflicts that first prompted treatment. Client
names have been changed to protect confidentiality, and consent for use of their case in
teaching and research was obtained from the family.

231

When parents present their child for treatment as *the problem*, family therapists typically wonder if the parent-child dilemma has simply become the easiest "ticket" for the family to enter the clinical arena. For many parents, the agenda of "fixing" the child problem becomes so paramount that other relevant aspects of their own life stressors fade to the background. While parental focus zeroes in on the troubled child, the therapist probes other areas of vulnerability to see if the child's behavior is a logical response to a much larger and deeper family context.

As illustrated throughout this chapter, the family story depicted during the first therapy session may only be the "tip of the iceberg." The extent to which parents will benefit from therapy exclusively designed to relieve a child's difficulty is contingent upon how embedded the child's "symptom" is in the family's historical legacy. If the parents can be guided to link the child's problem to an understanding of the child's developmental hurdles, and can begin to remember their own experiences at that age, the family practitioner may be able to assist not only the child but also the parents in getting past unresolved issues that may have previously impeded growth for the whole family.

The developmental tasks of children and adolescents, as well as those of adults and parents, specify differing life scripts, with inherent possibilities for varying parent-child conflicts due to family-member agendas that are at variance with each other. Such altercations do not arise solely from the child or solely from the parent, but as part of a multidirectional socialization process. Not only do parents influence children, but so do children influence their parents (Peterson & Rollins, 1987).

> *In the case of the nuclear family presented above, family coping resources were sufficient early on in the parents' marriage. Once their first child reached adolescence, however, this new stage strained to the limit everything they had learned from the preceding generation. The adolescence of the elder child called into question all the unresolved issues from Jim and Nikki's own adolescence, and everything that was left without closure in raising Alexa was then carried by her younger brother, Don. All the various puzzle pieces were recursive, but the therapist was often proceeding without the "big picture." Issues emerged only as quickly as family members were ready to face them.*

The period of adolescence, when the child is aged 10 to 15, is almost unanimously represented as the time of greatest conflict and stress in families (Mattessich & Hill, 1987; Montemayor, 1983, 1986; Richardson, Galambos, Schulenberg & Petersen, 1984; Silverberg & Steinberg, 1987).

The potential for such a crisis portends that the clinician must have a thorough grasp of the issues likely to be raised at the time of this difficult transition.

For the purpose of assessing and treating parent-child conflicts similar to those exhibited in the case study, this chapter combines theoretical underpinnings from the human development and family socialization literature (Ackerman, 1980; Kidwell, Fischer, Dunham, & Baranowski, 1983; Mattessich & Hill, 1987; Peterson & Rollins, 1987) and integrates these with contextual family therapy (Boszormenyi-Nagy & Spark, 1984; Boszormenyi-Nagy & Ulrich, 1981; Frank, 1984a,b). Assumptions are drawn from a systemic framework, from the anticipated developmental tasks of both parents and their early-adolescent children, from the type of family response that may be expected following catastrophic events, and from a review of functional versus dysfunctional coping mechanisms. The family case will be woven into the fabric of this schema a little at a time, much as the therapist discovered crucial pieces of information only gradually. The latter part of the chapter will describe the treatment process in more detail and draw conclusions based on an integration of theory, research, and practice (Olson, 1976).

## Systemic and Contextual Assumptions

Peterson and Rollins (1987) have reviewed several approaches to examining socialization, including systemic and contextual perspectives. Adapting their assumptions to a holistic view of parent-child conflicts, nested within the family agenda of achieving broader socialization tasks, leads to the following: (1) the family and its context and/or surrounding networks are involved in parent-child conflict; (2) conflict is multidirectional in that all members of a social network or family can influence each other simultaneously; (3) not only do individuals influence individuals, but dyads (e.g., husband-wife subsystems) influence individuals (e.g., a child) and also other dyads or triads (such as sibling subsystems); and (4) the larger social community (as represented by schools, church, employers, and neighbors) influences parent-child conflicts, as well as the latter spilling over to the functioning of the former.

A parent's difficulties with a child may show up in a parent's drop in work performance, in estrangement and isolation from friends, and in strained relationships with members of the social network. For the child's part, his or her difficulties with a parent may become channeled toward troubles at school, with the law, with peers as well as other family members, and in somatic and other complaints.

*Don became unmanageable with his schoolwork after his mother*
*had to spend more time at home due to her recent unemployment. The*
*more she was home to supervise things Don had typically done on his*
*own, the more helpless and resentful he became. The more needy he*
*came across, the more Nikki tried to be the kind of mother who would*
*"be there" to care for him. Naturally, if she needed to stay at home to get*
*him up for school and oversee his studies, this full-time job left little*
*time for her to pursue her career. In turn, pressure to stay home to solve*
*the problem created tension between Nikki and Jim. As long as Nikki*
*was neither bringing in income nor solving the problem with Don, she*
*was vulnerable to criticism. Jim's role as the aloof breadwinner began*
*to seem awfully convenient to her, but her focus shifted to Don's*
*problems at school from Jim's problems with her. Marital issues were*
*buried to meet the immediacy of being needed as a parent.*

In the contextual family therapy literature (Boszormenyi-Nagy & Spark,
1984; Boszormenyi-Nagy & Ulrich, 1981; Frank, 1984a, 1984b), Boszormenyi-Nagy echoes many of the above transactional assumptions and
introduces unique concepts, such as families' "invisible loyalties." The
term "invisible loyalties" has to do with the relational accountability
between family members which inevitably becomes entangled in parent-
child conflicts. Parents are prone toward judging their children based on
what *they* were taught was owed the family legacy. Children are more
likely to try to get out from under such a burden and struggle to individu-
ate their own identity, yet they get caught in the realization that without
their parents they would never have had sustenance.

Each generation attempts to balance the ledger with respect to the
parents' expectations but, in fact, never quite measures up. Parents, via
their children, are trying to appease *their* parents' hopes for them. The
more that "accounts" have been left unsettled across the generations, the
more "indebted" the succeeding generation's children will be. Indebted
children seek to relieve indebted parents of their burden, but inevitably
retaliate when on some level they grasp that they are being unrealistically
encumbered with their parents' accumulated debts. Instead of such rebellion readjusting the parent-child reciprocity, the child can end up even
more indebted for daring to be so disloyal as to question the system.

As Boszormenyi-Nagy and Ulrich (1981) relate, "No family member
can alone judge whether the ledger is in balance" (p. 164). Children look to
their parents for direction in growing up. Their parents, in turn, look to
them as confirmation that adult tasks in parenting have been mastered
properly. When parents have had a hard time breaking away from their

families of origin in terms of establishing their own identities, similar efforts on the part of the offspring will become a rehash of old family themes. Parents then will not be reassured enough of their own maturity to provide a secure foundation for launching the independence of their sons and daughters.

> *Nikki's unemployment coincided with Don's entry into early adolescence. At 14, he was a reminder of the unfinished business Nikki and Jim left behind with their folks when they married at 14 and 15 respectively. Nikki felt obliged to stay at home and be a good parent to spare Don some of the pain she had endured in leaving home at that age* (Haley, 1980). *Already one child had been lost, and the idea of another one leaving home, even emotionally, was unbearable. In a sense, Don "owed" Nikki and Jim the chance to "get it right" this time in terms of raising an adolescent—with no premature departures due to early marriage or sudden death. To ensure such an arrangement, special protection was needed. And Nikki unwittingly volunteered to stand guard.*

## DESCRIPTION OF THE STRESSOR

The onset of a child's puberty signals the beginning of the end of that person "needing" parents. For parents who need to be needed, the child's bid toward independence may be stressful in and of itself. Add to that dilemma any other catastrophic life events that detract from a healthy resolution of the transition, and the family may get "stuck" due to overload (Minuchin, 1974).

### Developmental Tasks of Parents and Early Adolescents

While much of the parent/early-adolescent conflict literature focuses on the developmental tasks of early adolescents, less attention has been given to the developmental hurdles of their parents facing midlife. Early adolescents unavoidably confront the challenge of gaining emotional separation from parents (Fleming & Adolph, 1986; Silverberg & Steinberg, 1987; Youniss, 1983). By way of contrast, middle adolescents (14–17) are concerned more with competency and mastery, and later adolescents (17–21) zero in more on intimacy issues and begin to test the waters for establishing a life partnership with another human being (Fleming & Adolph, 1986). Emotional separation from parents is not limited to breaking away from parental mindsets, but involves a transformation in the relationship between the adolescent and the parents (Youniss, 1983). Youniss (1983) characterizes the transformation as:

> . . . a dialectic between rank individuality at one extreme and stulti-fying enmeshment in the parent-child relationship at the other. The resolution is made through individuation, which allows the adolescent both to declare separateness from parents and distinctiveness from their ascriptions and to accept connectedness with parents. (p. 96)

Unfortunately, both parents and children may make unnecessary attributions about the process of growing up. That is, family members may believe that to grow up, to become mature, is to cut themselves off from parents. If the parents who make such an attribution have reason to believe that this "breaking away" will be traumatic, they may engage in behaviors and manipulations to hold tight to that child without ever discovering that their original attribution is built on a faulty premise.

In one of the few studies to examine parental well-being and parent-adolescent conflict, Silverberg and Steinberg (1987) outline adult problems at midlife as well as stressors parents experience in their parental role:

> . . . while middle adulthood is not a period of psychological upheaval and dramatic crisis for most individuals . . . , these years may be a time of stress, diminished marital satisfaction, life reappraisal, and increased introspection about the physical and psychological self for many adults. . . . Some writers have even suggested that it is, in part, *because* children, and the family system, are moving into the adolescent years that parents engage in self-examination and experience psychological strain or change . . . . (p. 294)

Silverberg and Steinberg (1987) further report several possible outcomes for parents of teenagers. Transformations in the parent/early-adolescent relationship, centering about the child's strivings for autonomy, may result in some parents feeling less competent in the parental role. Stress may mount when the child pushes for more autonomy than the parent is capable of allowing. Furthermore, the authors note that mothers tend to be more symptomatic than fathers, and they link this greater propensity to mothers' roles being more central in child rearing. In their study, mothers were more likely to base some sense of self and psychological well-being on the quality of the relationship with their children. Hence, when children seem to withdraw or test that relationship, mothers may be particularly susceptible to questioning their abilities as parents and themselves as competent individuals.

At least some parent-adolescent conflicts appear to come about when the transition periods for adults and children coincide or collide (Kidwell et al., 1983). In addition, parental discord may be related to children's problems (Jacob & Seilhamer, 1985). Developmental tasks facing each generation, as well as the attributions about these developmental tasks, may set the stage for conflict.

## Normal Conflicts

In a series of reviews, Montemayor (1983, 1986) has delineated the normal conflicts of parents and adolescents. He estimates that four-to-five million families in the United States run into conflict that is sufficiently stressful that some families will seek help (Montemayor, 1983). The amount of conflict typically experienced is at a high level, occurring daily. Only distressed married couples report greater levels of conflict (Montemayor, 1986).

Typical conflicts concern everyday, mundane matters: school work, social life, and household chores (Smith & Forehand, 1986). Richardson et al. (1984) indicate that early adolescents are generally satisfied with their family life, although conflict with parents occurs most often over issues of freedom and responsibility. Teenagers are likely to test limits surrounding household chores, family rules, privileges, and academic activities. Interpersonal issues make up most of the conflicts between early adolescents and their parents and siblings (Montemayor & Hanson, 1985). When there are conflicts over rules, these occur more often with parents than with siblings.

Harris and Howard (1984) relate that while more than 50% of young students said parents criticize them for being disobedient, lazy or messy, girls were more vulnerable to charges of not getting along with others and boys were more often accused of not being goal- and achievement-oriented. In addition, "Goal oriented themselves, fathers tend to be impatient with offspring who do not have their feet firmly on the ground" (Harris & Howard, 1984, p. 120). Without making distinctions between boys and girls, Weiner (1980) estimates that some 25% of children will unexpectedly perform poorly in school. Between a third and a half of referrals of children to psychologists or psychiatrists are because of school-learning problems (Weiner, 1980).

*Don was acutely aware that he was never going to be a stellar student, no matter how hard he tried. He was also cognizant of the fact that Jim wanted him to work hard while he was still young to save him the aggravation his father had encountered on the job, Jim being the only employee at his level without a college education. Finding it difficult enough to find something to be good at in school, Don was also saddled with the responsibility of preparing for a better life than that remarkably attained by the self-made man who sired him.*

## Catastrophic Life Events

Although connections have not been firmly established between life events (which place children and adolescents at risk for adjustment problems) and subsequent parent-child conflicts, the evidence is suggestive that such an association may be present. According to Johnson (1986), stress experienced by children and adolescents as a result of life events may play an important role in various types of ensuing health and adjustment problems. Carranza (1972) conjoins life stress with lowered academic performance (as noted above, a frequent source of parent-child conflict). On the other hand, while Sterling, Cowen, Weissberg, Lotyczewski and Boike, (1985) agree with Johnson (1986) that life changes are associated with child/adolescent adjustment, they counter with the following:

> . . . that life changes may be related to adjustment problems of some children but not others, strongly suggests the importance of considering such (moderator) variables in child life stress research. (p. 91)

Any unexpected life stresses which convolute an already strained parent-child accountability system can be expected to up the ante of obligation of the child who aspires to then be "the family healer" (Boszormenyi-Nagy & Spark, 1984, p. 188). The child can take the parents' minds off of their own unsettledness by providing the immediacy of a symptom. There is a tendency under crisis for family members to want to rally together. Such rallying together is ill-timed and out of synchrony with the adolescent who is just beginning to test his or her own wings.

## PRIMARY SOURCE OF STRESS
## FOR THE FAMILY

*Jim, Nikki, and Don were hit with a triple whammy just as Don was beginning to embark on becoming his own person. Not only was he at a crucial age in the family legacy, but he was just coming to understand that he was now being granted the privilege to live longer than Alexa. The family did not seek help, however, until yet another wedge was thrown into the situation—Nikki's unexpected unemployment. The crisis potential occurring historically with the onset of adolescence in this family was confounded by sustained grief over the loss of a family member, and ultimately the loss of an economic role for the mother. Nikki's unemployment became the precipitating event for the family to no longer feel capable of handling matters on their own. But because Alexa's death was so far removed from the current agenda of assisting Don in school, the presenting problem for treatment was confined to his difficulties.*

## Unemployment as a Family Stressor

Past research reveals that professionals derive considerably more ego satisfaction from their work than do other work groups (Gurin, Veroff & Feld, 1960). Studies (Friedlander, 1966; Orzack, 1959; White, 1977) note that professionals view work as more central in their lives than leisure, and consequently problems with self-concept, identity, and family disruption are more associated with job loss for them than for their nonprofessional counterparts. The unemployed person has a propensity to either feel "sick" or develop diagnosable symptoms (Brenner, 1971; Cobb, 1974; Cook, Cummins, Bartley, & Shoper, 1982; Gore, 1978; Hill, Harrison, Sargeant, & Talbot, 1973; Kasl, Gore, & Cobb, 1975; Leventman, 1981; O'Brien & Kabanoff, 1979). Leventman (1981), in particular, underscores the fact that in many cases there is a "delayed reaction to unbearable strain" (p. 152).

As early as 1942, Ginsburg emphasized that psychological consequences to unemployment were similar to ". . . the loss of love the child suffers from a rejecting parent, especially a child who has not done anything to deserve it" (p. 442). More recently, Bebbington, Harry, Tennant, Strut, and Wing (1981) found that unemployed samples in their study developed more psychiatric-type symptoms than those comparably employed. The more common reactions to unemployment include depression (Donovan & Oddy, 1982; Feather, 1982; Feather & Barber, 1983; Feather & Davenport, 1981; Kasl & Cobb, 1982), increase in suicide (Boor, 1980; Humphrey, 1977; Sainsbury, 1955; Tuckman & Lavell, 1958; Windshuttle, 1980), purposelessness (Jahoda & Rush, 1980), and apathy (Windshuttle, 1980). A sequence of shock, relief, and relaxation (Kaufman, 1982) characterizes the most immediate stage which lasts from one to two months.

May and Brown-Standridge (in press), on the basis of Voydanoff's (1983) and Lehman, Williams, and Wortman's (1987) conclusions, liken sudden unemployment to the sudden, unexpected loss of a spouse or child, resulting in significantly more and long-lasting distress. Both catastrophic events share similarities in that whatever "facade of togetherness" the family has tried to maintain prior to the crisis will be pressed to the limit under such duress (May & Brown-Standridge, in press).

## Death of a Family Member as a Family Stressor

One of the more serious life events to confront a family is the death of a child. According to Johnson's (1986) review, the only factors more stressful for children than the death of a sibling include a pregnancy of an unmarried adolescent; the death, separation, or divorce of parents; and a negative visible deformity. In modern times, the death of a sibling is a relatively rare event. For children born in 1950, only 35 per 1,000 suffered the death of a sibling before the living child reached age 15. On the other hand, as many as 295 per 1,000 children born in 1870 witnessed the death of a sibling (Uhlenberg, 1978).

Accidents are the leading cause of death among youth, with 49 per 100,000 deaths caused accidentally. Overall, death took 191 per 100,000 youth in 1984. At the turn of the century this figure was 590 per 100,000 young people (Wetzel, 1987). Thus, the death of a young person is a rare event today, with most families left untouched by this calamity. Besides death of a family member, other family events may lead to similar ramifications in terms of trauma, stress, and dysfunction in the family. For example, the unwanted pregnancy of a child or the "loss" of a child to substance abuse, delinquency, or unacceptable lifestyle may evoke similar dynamics and result in similar consequences for family members.

Fleming and Adolph (1986) imply that families who tend to bury traumatic events through the creation of family secrets will have the toughest time negotiating a viable adjustment period:

> A family is traumatized by the death of one of its members . . . and, as a result of their collective and individual pain, survivors are often confronted with a sense of loneliness and isolation as communication with other family members dwindles. It is not surprising that . . . adjustment to a sibling's death (is) a function of family coherence, with adolescents from a family that encouraged closeness and communication experiencing fewer grief complications. (p. 111)

The death of a sibling complicates the achievement of the developmental tasks of adolescence. The early adolescent working on emotional separation from parents may have to contend with his or her fears about leaving the security and predictability of the family (Fleming & Adolph,

1986). But more often, the adolescent is bound too close to the family by the parents. Persistent adolescent rebelliousness may result from frustrations in attaining autonomy in a nonsupportive environment (McNeil, 1986). The parental "holding on" can result not only in recalcitrant behavior, but also in an increase in negative interactions throughout the family.

> *Discussion of Alexa's death was handled matter-of-factly during the first therapy session. Answers to questions were crisp and succinct. Questions regarding Don's difficulties in school, by comparison, were given long, flowing responses. Each family member, prior to Nikki's unemployment, had settled into a routine of going about his or her business with all the resiliency of tin soldiers. The family managed. When Nikki began to stay home due to lack of work, the family balance that held in the symmetry of each individual's "tunnel vision" regarding work or school was thrown off kilter. Her worries concerning Don not only functioned to prevent a repeat of the last generation's excursion into "instant adulthood," but also offered her a lifeline to Jim. Don's productive bids for autonomy were virtually blocked by the attention of a full-time parent. By developing problems at school, Don got his father active in family concerns, although the vicious cycle of parental attention/limited child autonomy became even more entrenched. Each family member had become polarized, and the family pattern of estrangement served to calcify any move to stretch beyond what the family had been before Alexa's death. It became Nikki's role to worry about Don, Jim's role to worry about Nikki's handling of Don, and Don's role to worry that he would never alone be an adequate substitute for the daughter his parents were never allowed to raise to adulthood.*

## FUNCTIONAL FAMILY COPING

Moderator variables that ameliorate or potentiate parent-child conflict have been suggested by Sterling et al. (1985) and others to include such factors as social supports, parental attachment, Type A (rigid)/Type B (adaptable) personality styles, family routines, locus of control, perceived competence, and gender. Garbarino, Sebes, and Schellenbach (1984) indicate that low-risk families have more protectors and more buffers while high-risk families have more potentiating factors, that is, greater vulnerability to developmental challenges. Flexibility, rather than calcification, is a key variable necessary in family life as the child becomes an adolescent (Schulman, 1985).

A parental style characterized as authoritative, with parents in charge and attentive to children's needs, is associated with fewer disagreements than either a permissive or an authoritarian parental style (Hill & Holmbeck, 1987). The importance of parenting as a key factor in child development has been underscored by Hauser, Vieyra, Jacobson, and Wertlieb (1985) who report that although the majority of children exposed to adversity grow up to enjoy productive, normal lives, the parents' ability to allow the child autonomy is a key factor in this favorable outcome. Further, parents of "invulnerable" children are less possessive and anxious and are more likely to sanction positively the child's own path to individuation. In addition, healthier communication between parents and children distinguish families of "invulnerable" children.

By comparison, parents of disturbed adolescents interfere with the child's autonomy and differential functioning (Hauser et al., 1985). Such parents engage in more binding interactions with their children. Fischer (1980), comparing families with disturbed adolescents, found that although parents of disturbed adolescents recognize and identify the needs of their adolescents, they are less involved in meeting those needs than are parents of nondisturbed adolescents. In addition, less open communication profiles families with a disturbed adolescent, as compared with families with nondisturbed adolescents.

The importance of open communication is stressed by a number of authors. Open communication can influence a child's understanding and provide emotional support (Weber & Fournier, 1985). Furthermore, a family rule which permits emotional expression is a factor in minimizing or preventing the appearance of exacerbating health and behavioral problems (Koch, 1985). McNeil (1986) underscores the importance of aboveboard, helpful discussion of death concerns in the family context. Unfortunately, as desirable as open communication may be, it is not often practiced. Thirty percent of adolescents in McNeil's study wished they could talk more about death with their parents. Parents also wished for greater communication in this area but felt inadequate to broach the subject.

> *Nikki and Jim took special pains to ease six-year-old Don through the transition after Alexa died. He was assisted during both the wake and the funeral. His parents were very open with him in terms of discussing how much they were likely to be more "overprotective" with him now that she was gone. Although it sometimes sent them "into a panic" when he failed to come home on time, he was granted the usual adventures away from home such as playing with friends and riding his bicycle.*

## DYSFUNCTIONAL FAMILY COPING

Unfortunately, apart from identifying child, adolescent, and parent symptomatology as a consequence of parent-child conflict, the literature is less forthcoming in identifying processes by which dysfunctional conflict arises in the first place. Montemayor (1986) suggests that conflict is expressed by children as oppositionalism. Conflicts are most frequently resolved by withdrawal (Montemayor & Hanson, 1985). Thus, conflicts often are not really settled or worked out, as indicated in Montemayor's (1986) remarks: " . . . poor communication and problem solving techniques may lead to persistent and repetitive conflict which is rarely, if ever, resolved" (p. 22). And McCubbin, Needle, and Wilson (1985) have noted the

> potentially dysfunctional nature of even constructive and wellness-promoting coping strategies. . . . Adolescents may adopt coping behaviors which propel them into other stressful circumstances which may in turn add to their burdens of responsibility and difficulties (pp. 59, 54).

Dysfunctional conflicts are rarely resolved but are dealt with instead by withdrawal and silence. In a catastrophic life event, such as the death of a sibling, open communication in the family is preferable but not typical. Moreover, parents may overcompensate by trying to realize all their dreams in the surviving child.

Factors that seem to diminish open communication about death are comprised of family norms about okay and not-okay topics, the wish on the part of parents to protect children from the discomfort accompanying loss, and the feelings of inadequacy and failure surrounding death. For example, children aged five and six, display fantasy reasoning in reaction to death. Their cognitions are egocentric, are imbued with magical thought, and exhibit varying degrees of symbolism related to their own limited experience (Weber & Fournier, 1985). However, children this young can be influenced by open communication and will follow the lead of their parents and others in emulating both positive and negative ways of handling crises (Weber & Fournier, 1985).

Implicated in truncating the exchange of open communications about death are feelings that society expects one to get on with one's life in a comparatively short amount of time. Research supports that grieving must go on for years, not months. "This failure to plumb the depths of one's own anguish may cause serious problems later when unresolved grief erupts" (Fleming & Adolph, 1986, p. 113). By necessity, survivors need to address unacceptable feelings to recover, as recorded by Fleming and Adolph (1986): " . . . they need to encounter their own ambivalence and to remember their anger and resentment toward the deceased" (p. 102).

> By the time Jim, Nikki, and Don entered treatment, the subject of Alexa's death was a closed issue. There were strong indications via body language and abrupt changes in the subject that the family was avoiding this emotionally charged topic with distance maneuvers.

## GENERAL APPROACH TO TREATMENT/INTERVENTION

Contextual family therapy (Boszormenyi-Nagy & Spark, 1984; Boszormenyi-Nagy & Ulrich, 1981) takes into account various layers of patterns in families, from systemic to intrapsychic functions. Of the more prominent systemic approaches to treatment, Boszormenyi-Nagy's lens offers considerably more depth (in terms of family members' unconscious processes) and breadth (in terms of family system processes across generations) than popular brief-therapy orientations (such as structural [Minuchin, 1974] or strategic [Haley, 1976, 1980] family therapy).

A wider scope was necessary with Jim, Nikki, and Don because they were obviously sitting on a family secret that encouraged "defensive collusion" between them (Boszormenyi-Nagy & Spark, 1984, p. 170). Alexa was presented as no more than closed-book history when in fact the impact of her death was a grievous, present-day reality. Had the clinician proceeded only with Don's presenting problem, a more penetrating therapeutic experience could have eluded the whole family.

## ASSESSMENT METHODS

The only formal procedure for assessment, beyond the clinical appraisal of individual, family, and cross-generational patterns, involved a urinalysis for Don. This test was conducted after the intake interview to rule out possible substance abuse, in light of Don's sudden disinterest in responsibility. Test results were negative.

## DIAGNOSIS AND TREATMENT PLAN

Systemic diagnosis and treatment were recursive. The family was understandably not ready to tackle the depth and breadth of their difficulties all at once. Assessment occurred piecemeal as various stumbling blocks were removed.

The family arrived in crisis because school authorities were sounding an alarm. The end of the school year was approaching and Don would have to make up "incompletes" or run the risk of having to repeat a grade. While Don had never been an outstanding student, this was the first time he was in trouble for not following directives.

The first session revealed that Nikki was immersing herself in Don, apparently to compensate for her recent unemployment: "We're failing everything and we're not figuring out why." Don's failures automatically became intertwined with her own. Don appeared quietly angry with his parents but could be quite appropriate to someone outside the family inquiring about his situation. Jim was as characteristically tuned out of the family as Nikki was tuned in. Nikki assumed the role of primary spokesperson and Jim would get drawn into conversation only as Don began to open up about his disappointment in being just an average student, without the advantage of popularity among his peers.

Jim openly identified with such feelings of inferiority, recounting his own adolescence: "I don't think that Donald is doing anything different than I did . . . I know that my doing that affected me drastically." The first piece of the family legacy emerged: Jim worked extra hard *without* much education so that Don would benefit from working hard *with* education. Don was breaking a cross-generational rule by not valuing education or hard work, and in the process began to look like an ingrate. This was all the more irritating to Jim since he likewise procrastinated during his younger years and felt he had had to pay for it later on.

Because of the crisis nature of the school referral, it was important to disrupt destructive patterns rather quickly. Don appeared to be burdened with the "super glue" function he was providing for his parents. All conversation between Nikki and Jim was routed through him. His response was sullen and passive-aggressive. The initial plan was to get the family back to preunemployment functioning as soon as possible. This would require Nikki to get reactivated in her career and both parents invested in allowing Don to either face his responsibilities or face the consequences. In addition, the natural identification between father and son would be rechanneled to a more positive alliance. The family's walls surrounding discussion of Alexa were left as a back burner issue for the time being.

## TREATMENT APPROACH

The first four sessions focused on Don's *under*responsibility being related to Nikki's *over*responsibility for him, and to Jim's high expectations of Don. The objective was to increase closeness between father and son as a buffer to increasing distance between mother and son. Following the pacing set by the family system, marital issues were not forced (Haley, 1980).

Task assignments did not begin until the second session, after substance abuse had been eliminated as a possible confounding factor. Nikki complained that she was spending her mornings pleading with Don to get up for school. Don reportedly would wait until the very last minute to get out of bed and then would make a mad dash for the school bus. The aftermath would be that Nikki would ruminate that she was failing as a mother. Both parents were united by the therapist around the task of getting Don an alarm clock, and by the next week he was awakening on his own. This new context exploded the myth that Don needed help to be responsible.

When Don tested the new system by missing the school bus one day the following week, Nikki refused to drive him so he would avoid being late. She alerted him and the school personnel that she would not be covering for him anymore. This event served to elicit congratulations from the therapist and from Jim. During session five, Don began to ask responsibly for assistance himself. He was still behind in school but requested help in figuring out what to do. With minimal direction, he was prompted to check out his situation with his teachers. The best he was able to work out was to make up some of the incompletes, but summer school was the only option for a couple of his courses. Don conceded that he had been treated fairly.

After six weeks, the school year was ending and the parents expressed pleasure with Don's progress. Father and son were engaging in more productive activities and Nikki was freer to pursue her former interests. At this point, to continue treatment would have meant that the spotlight would have shifted away from Don. Jim and Nikki dropped clues that they felt confident to conduct matters on their own. Indeed, they were normalizing whatever parent-adolescent conflicts occasionally occurred.

The therapist opted to agree that the problem they originally came in to solve was, in fact, under control. Their changes that contributed to the improvement were underscored in a termination session. The family was left with one caveat, however. The practitioner related that at some point they would probably recognize that their difficulty in talking about Alexa would need to be addressed. The comment was not disputed and therapy was terminated amiably.

A whole year transpired before Nikki again initiated contact. This time she wanted to come in alone. She stated that there were no taxing problems with Don. Rather, she presented *herself* as "the problem." By this time, she was back to work but was spending money compulsively. The family was overextended by $9,000 in credit because of expenditures for things that were not needed. Nikki was ready to discuss her own history, and the therapist capitalized on issues bubbling to the surface by connecting them to the loss of Alexa. In this way, past and present began to take on new meaning:

| | |
|---|---|
| *Nikki:* | My dad always gave me everything I asked for. He never said no. Then I married Jim and we didn't have much money. Our first 17 years I accounted for every penny. I resented being quizzed, being treated like a child. I was bad with money; he was good with money. The way he expressed himself was with money. I associated love with gifts and money. |
| *Therapist:* | What sends you out spending? |
| *Nikki:* | Depression would, loneliness would. The last year I can't say if it was depression—my self-esteem went real low. I didn't like myself at all—still don't. I just didn't feel right. I don't know why; it's like I'm on a time bomb. . . . Jim's such a strong man I'm not sure he understands how much I depend on him. I avoid arguments, but when I'm at work on a professional level I'll argue till hell freezes over. |
| *Therapist:* | How did it change after your daughter died? |
| *Nikki:* | The first year I think I was in shock . . . I worried about Donald. I . . . he'd get on a bike and I'd just almost panic. I just . . . and I'd sit Donald down and I'd explain to him, "Donald, I'm going to overreact because of this fear I have of something happening to you that I cannot prevent." Donald dealt with that fairly well. I think Jim had the same fears but he was able to cope with it. . . . She's been gone seven years. . . . |
| *Therapist:* | But what I wonder is . . . how that affected the shopping, the spending money? |
| *Nikki:* | It got worse. |
| *Therapist:* | A lot worse. |
| *Nikki:* | Mmm-hmm. You're out of control till it runs itself out. |
| *Therapist:* | What stops you? |
| *Nikki:* | It's as though somebody flips a switch off. Then that's where I talk about fear coming in. What if Jim finds out about this? . . . I can't stand it when someone I love is disappointed in me because then I feel like I should have tried a lot harder. |

*Therapist:*    From the time you were little, things represented goodness and
                love on someone else's part. . . . You have an extraordinary
                need to be the perfect wife and mother. As accountant, you
                knew when things were right and wrong. . . . You have taken it
                (Alexa's death) on as your fault. . . . .
*Nikki:*        I was late that day. . . . (tears)
*Therapist:*    You wanted to be perfect with Donald and that didn't work.
                "He'll know I love him by giving him all these things." You're
                doing it (spending) for all the ways you didn't know how to do
                it, trying to make up for it (Alexa's death). What sets you off is
                "not being good enough."

   Nikki was behaving like the ultimate personification of the "indebtedness" metaphor. She left home before she was really old enough to
establish her own identity. Her sense of personal boundaries blurred into
what her dad, her husband, her son, and even what her deceased daughter
thought of her. Overspending was a graphic way of calling attention to the
fact that her emotional debts were beyond her ability to pay. She was
unable to square what she owed her father because he spoiled her. She had
let down her family by not being there the day Alexa was fatally injured.
   Nikki agreed to bring Jim and Don to the next session. There were no
spending binges in the interim. The therapist enlisted her supervisor (the
second author) and a treatment team to serve behind a one-way mirror.
The following sequence was prompted by a phone-in from the supervisor
which encouraged Nikki to share what the spending was supposed to
replace.

*Therapist:*    You need to try to tell people what's missing.
*Nikki:*        I can't do it. I feel lonely, real empty and I don't know why.
                It's . . . I'm 35 years old. I ought to be able to deal with anything.
                I don't feel like I'm appreciated for anything I do. I'm just . . . I
                get the feeling I'm the maid and the hooker down the street. I
                just have these bad feelings. I don't know. I can't talk to him
                about it because it sounds stupid. It sounds like, "Well, kid,
                grow up." I don't want him to be my daddy. . . . My dad was
                never home. He worked all the time. When my parents did
                fight it was over money. . . . When we were first married we
                fought all the time. The first seven years we were too young.
*Therapist:*    Was there ever a time when there wasn't an empty feeling?
*Nikki:*        Before Alexa was killed—the two years before, there was not
                that empty feeling.

| | |
|---|---|
| *Jim:* | Just about the time her and Alexa were startin' to get close . . . I've often wondered if that didn't feel bad. (tears) I kinda had my time, but she didn't have hers. |
| *Nikki:* | We buried it, because it hurts. (tears) |
| *Jim:* | Donald and I have talked more about Alexa than Nikki and I. . . . |
| *Therapist:* | It (the spending) was a way of filling a void, dealing with a loss. |
| *Jim:* | I never really thought about Nikki's position. She had the worst position. I spent the first five years watching every penny. |
| *Nikki:* | And I would tell Jim, "You're not my dad." When he wouldn't let me buy things, I'd go ask my dad. |

From this sequence, it becomes clearer that there was no boundary around the marital subsystem from the outset. The story gradually unfolded that, after marriage, Jim joined the Navy and Nikki was sent to live with his parents. When she gave birth to Alexa, she was told to go to school while they attempted to raise their granddaughter as their daughter. The mother-daughter bonding was disrupted during those early years, and the weight of guilt in never being able to get those years back was already overwhelming, even before the accident. But being away from home when the incident occurred and having no closure, no good-byes, no way to make things right with Alexa, were devastating.

| | |
|---|---|
| *Nikki:* | It's as though I'm living in hell over it. Alexa and I argued the night before she was killed . . . Christmas . . . it was November. She wanted a sewing machine, a real expensive one, and I said, "Alexa, we can't afford it." We just moved here and it was a big argument with her, and she'd been sick a week, and I had worked all week. The day she was killed I was late and I just keep thinking if I had been on time that it wouldn't have happened. (tears) The ambulance had just left when I got there; it just keeps going through my mind and *I can't get over it.* Alexa had just come to the age, she was 12, that we kinda started talkin' about things, about sex and life, and for once I saw her as a growing young lady and not a spoiled little brat that could run to her daddy. And it's sorta like how Jim does with Donald. He sees things in Donald that he doesn't like in himself, so he tries to change it. I saw the same thing in Alexa. And so I was more strict with Alexa. |

From that point, there was an intriguing digression to Nikki's arguments with Jim's mother, Harriet. Harriet had been affectionately addressed as "Cissy" by Alexa when she was alive. This sudden shift did not escape the notice of the treatment team and the therapist was cued to check out the meaning of the juxtaposition between the two relationships—Nikki's arguments with her mother-in-law and those with her daughter.

| | |
|---|---|
| *Therapist:* | How did we go from arguing with Alexa to arguing with Jim's mother? |
| *Nikki:* | Harriet would buy things for Alexa but keep 'em at her house. I didn't understand it. Jim told me I was sensitive . . . she bought dresses I never got to see on Alexa. I had a lot of anger and resentment and then Alexa was killed. And I felt guilt. Why wasn't I stronger? Why didn't I battle things that would've helped her? I was too dumb; I was too weak. |
| *Jim:* | Too young. |

Jim and Nikki's grief over Alexa was compounded by grief they were already carrying over marrying too young. Because they had many conflicts with their parents and because they had never consolidated their marriage, their relationships with their children became forums to work out flaws in the family legacy. The relationship each parent had with the child who shared the same gender was under the most strain. Assessment at this point indicated that the family needed to be purged of their guilt and offered a new sense of competence. The treatment plan accommodated to the family's willingness to probe deeper. The "empty chair" technique, first introduced by Perls (1969) and adapted by Andolfi (1979) to family therapy, was incorporated to give the family a chance to say their good-byes to Alexa so they could move on. The following piece is especially poignant for the propinquity of verb tenses, from past to present.

| | |
|---|---|
| *Therapist:* | (getting up from her chair so that the empty chair directly faces the family, particularly Nikki) Anyone who can stand up all the way through is no weak woman. The strength it takes to cry is incredible . . . what we think is that there's a whole lot of unfinished business with Alexa. There's a lot of things that you need to say to her . . . |
| *Nikki:* | (sobbing) I really *did care*. I really *care* but I wasn't very good at showing it. I was too busy worrying about what was going on—why Harriet hated me so much. Oh, why Alexa had to suffer for me. Oh, God! I wasn't hurt . . . (uncontrollable crying). She didn't do anything to anybody . . . oh, God! I loved her so |

|  |  |
|---|---|
|  | much . . . they just kept tellin' me I wasn't any good. God, I hated Harriet so much. There's not a day that doesn't go by that I don't think about her . . . what I could've done different. I don't know. I just don't know. It hurts so much, for so long. I don't know. God, she was a good girl. |
| *Therapist:* | You can tell her that. Why don't you tell her that now? |
| *Nikki:* | Oh, God, Alexa. Alexa, I love you. You mean a world to me. Oh! Well, Alexa, your mom's in a sad way now. But God, I loved you. I didn't know it until after you were gone. I'm a mean old mom . . . but I always meant well. I always tried to protect you. Me—and Cissy—always won. Oh, well. It's over with now. God, just rest in peace, that's all. Oh God, Alexa. I wished it'd been me. God. I wished it'd been me. But it's final. So, Alexa, I'm trying with Donald and Jim, and damn Mom even gets along with the old bat Cissy now, and so I'm gonna make it. But God, Alexa, just remember I love you. I always did. No matter what. . . . (crying softly) (therapist leaves to consult with the team). |
| *Jim:* | I don't—I don't think you, uh—I don't think you realize that Alexa, Alexa knew that you loved her. She knew that. You're the one that took what—uh—a lot of others said and believed it more than anyone else. And it didn't ev—nothing you said or nothing you thought was wrong. And it never bothered me or Alexa. And I know 'cause you knew how close I was to her. Just because we were close doesn't mean she didn't understand. You know that? I *know* she did. . . . (therapist returns) |
| *Therapist:* | (to Don) You're a little caught in the middle, but you know something your mother doesn't know. She knew it once, but she's forgotten it and I think the thing that you're going to need to do is help her remember. Something that you knew about Alexa and something you know about you. And she's forgotten. And that is, that kids know their parents care, *because* they get on their case, *because* they make them do something, *because* they don't let them get away with things, *because* they protect them from getting spoiled and ruined and all of that. That's how kids know they're loved. And I remember you saying that last year, that you knew that even though your father was on your case all the time that it was 'cause he cared. |
| *Don:* | Yeah. |
| *Therapist:* | And your mother's forgotten that. But Alexa died knowing she was loved. She died knowing her mother loved her. 'Cause that's how kids know. And that argument didn't say, "I don't love you" anymore than you not being able to get the stuff that |

you want sometimes from your father says he doesn't love
you. It just says, "You're not getting this stuff." That's all. . . .

The beginning of the next session heralded a new era. Nikki acknowledged that she was finally able to sort through some of Alexa's things: "I
went ahead and let go of some things. I'm saying she's really gone. I haven't
been able to do that." Don had been very quiet in the last session and it
was difficult to know what responsibility he felt, being the only family
member home at the time of the accident. He was asked what he remembered
about the day Alexa died.

| | |
|---|---|
| *Don:* | I asked the babysitter if I could go out there and she said, "No, you're too young. I kept asking the lady, "Is she gonna be all right?" I thought she was fine. . . she was breathing . . . she (Alexa) was always there. She protected me. |
| *Therapist:* | Did you think you could've changed that? |
| *Don:* | (defiantly) Yeah, I could've. . . . |
| *Therapist:* | You're angry at the babysitter who kept you in. . . what would you like to say to Alexa? |
| *Don:* | I loved her. I'm sorry about what happened, but I couldn't change it. |

The final piece of the family legacy that still was too far distanced from
healing was Jim's ultra-strength and rationality. If his wife and son were to
be imbued with "symptomatology" while he remained removed from
such openness, he would never be able to accept their common human
failings, or his own. Down the road Don and/or Nikki might once again
present with symptoms. The third session was punctuated at the end with
this question from the team: What part did you play in Nikki's overspending and Don's procrastination at school? The question was jolting for him
and he reported having done much soul searching by the next week. He
had been profoundly moved by the question and engaged spontaneously
in an emotional "confession" to both of them, sharing with them that he
felt he had let them down by not seeing what they needed from him. The
burden of having to be above all emotionality had been lifted.

## SIGNS OF TREATMENT
## COMPLETION/EFFECTIVENESS

Once the family confronted their worst fears with each other, the range
of emotion shared between them permitted spontaneous laughter and

bantering for the first time in treatment. They went from being stilted "tin soldiers" to learning to portray themselves as competent, teasing human beings. Even the subject of Alexa afforded a whole gamut of feelings. Rather than fleeing from a haunting ghost, the family was laying Alexa and much of their history to rest. This time termination was mutually determined, without any caveat.

## CONCLUSION

The case study depicted throughout this chapter should be examined for both its unique and its universal aspects. Not every child or adolescent problem will require the breadth and depth of a contextual family therapy approach. Not every set of parents will yield to treatment themselves. But wherever there are parents, children, and relationship problems, there is a family history that becomes the backdrop for any successful treatment to take hold over time. Catastrophic life events such as parental unemployment or death of a family member can become the nodal points for straining that family legacy to the limit. Crises present the most opportune time for families to reach an impasse and, out of desperation, for them to become open to treatment. Children can often unwittingly provide the family therapist clues as to where to probe. The challenge for the clinician is to ease the cross-generational burden for the offspring without overtaxing the parents. The case study presented is just one effort in learning when to follow the lead of families and when to lead them where they dare not go on their own.

## REFERENCES

Ackerman, N. J. (1980. The family with adolescents. In E. A. Carter and M. McGoldrick (Eds.), *The family life cycle: A framework for family therapy* (pp. 147–169). New York: Gardner Press.
Andolfi, M. (1979). *Family therapy: An interactional approach.* New York: Plenum Press.
Bebbington, P., Harry, J., Tennant, C., Strut, E., & Wing, J. K. (1981). Epidemiology of mental disorders in Camberwell. *Psychological Medicine, 11,* 561–579.
Boor, M. (1980). Relationships between unemployment rates and suicide rates in eight countries, 1962–1976. *Psychological Reports, 60,* 562–564.
Boszormenyi-Nagy, I., & Spark, G. M. (1984). *Invisible loyalties: Reciprocity in intergenerational family therapy.* New York: Brunner/Mazel.
Boszormenyi-Nagy, I., & Ulrich, D. N. (1981). Contextual family therapy. In A. S. Gurman & D. P. Kniskern (Eds.), *Handbook of family therapy.* New York: Brunner/Mazel.
Brenner, M. H. (1971). Economic changes and heart disease mortality. *American Journal of Public Health, 61,* 606–611.

Carranza, E. (1972). A study of the impact of life changes on high school teacher performance in the Lansing school district as measured by the Holmes and Rahe schedule of recent experiences. Unpublished doctoral dissertation, Michigan State University.

Cobb, S. (1974). Physiological changes in men whose jobs were abolished. *Journal of Psychosomatic Research, 18*, 245–258.

Cook, D. G., Cummins, R. O., Bartley, M. J., & Shoper, A. G. (1982). Health of unemployed middle-aged men in Great Britain. *Lancet, 5* (1), 1290–1294.

Donovan, A., & Oddy, M. (1982). Psychological aspects of unemployment: An investigation into the emotional and social adjustments of school leavers. *Journal of Adolescence, 5*, 15–30.

Feather, N. T. (1982). Unemployment and its psychological correlates: A study of depressive symptoms, self-esteem, Protestant Ethic values, attributional style and apathy. *Australian Journal of Psychology, 34*, 309–323.

Feather, N. T., & Barber, J. G. (1983). Depressive reactions and unemployment. *Journal of Abnormal Psychology, 92*, 185–195.

Feather, N. T., & Davenport, P. R. (1981). Unemployment and depressive affect: A motivational and attributional analysis. *Journal of Personality and Social Psychology, 41*, 422–436.

Fischer, J. L. (1980). Reciprocity, agreement and family style in disturbed and nondisturbed families. *Journal of Youth and Adolescence, 9*, 391–406.

Fleming, S. J., & Adolph, R. (1986). Helping bereaved adolescents: Needs and responses. In C. A. Corr & J. N. McNeil (Eds.), *Adolescence and death* (pp. 97–118). New York: Springer.

Frank, C. (1984a). Contextual family therapy. *The American Journal of Family Therapy, 12* (1), 3–6.

Frank, C. (1984b). Major constructs of contextual therapy: An interview with Dr. Ivan Boszormenyi-Nagy. *The American Journal of Family Therapy, 12* (1), 7–14.

Friedlander, F. (1966). Importance of work versus non-work among socially and occupationally stratified groups. *Journal of Applied Psychology, 50*, 437–441.

Garbarino, J., Sebes, J., & Schellenbach, C. (1984). Families at risk for destructive parent-child relations in adolescence. *Child Development, 55*, 174–183.

Ginsburg, S. W. (1942). What unemployment does to people. *American Journal of Psychiatry, 99*, 439–446.

Gore, A. (1978). The effect of social support in moderating the health consequences of unemployment. *Journal of Health and Social Behavior, 19*, 157–165.

Gurin, G., Veroff, J. & Feld, S. (1960). *Americans view their mental health.* New York: Basic Books.

Haley, J. (1976). *Problem-solving therapy.* San Francisco: Jossey-Bass.

Haley, J. (1980). *Leaving home.* New York: McGraw-Hill.

Harris, I. D., & Howard, K. I. (1984). Parental criticism and the adolescent experience. *Journal of Youth and Adolescence, 13*, 113–122.

Hauser, S. T., Vieyra, M. A. B., Jacobson, A. M., & Wertlieb, D. (1985). Vulnerability and resilience in adolescence: Views from the family. *Journal of Early Adolescence, 5*, 81–100.

Hill, M. J., Harrison, R. M., Sargeant, A. V., & Talbot, V. (1973). *Men out of work: A study of unemployment in three English towns.* New York: Cambridge University Press.

Hill, J. P., & Holmbeck, G. N. (1987). Disagreements about rules in families with seventh-grade girls and boys. *Journal of Youth and Adolescence, 16*, 221–245.

Humphrey, J. A. (1977). Social loss: A comparison of suicide victims, homicide offenders and non-violent individuals. *Diseases of the Nervous System, 38*, 157–160.

Jacob, T., & Seilhamer, R. A. (1985). Adaptation of the areas of change questionnaire for parent-child relationship assessment. *The American Journal of Family Therapy, 13*, 28–38.

Jahoda, M., & Rush, H. (1980). *Work employment and unemployment: An overview of ideas and research results in the social sciences literature.* (Occasional Paper No. 12). Science Policy Research Unit, University of Sussex, England.

Johnson, J. H. (1986). *Life events as stressors in childhood and adolescence.* Newbury Park, CA: Sage.

Kasl, S. V., & Cobb, S. (1982). Variability of stress effects among men experiencing job loss. In L. Goldberger & S. Breznitz (Eds.), *Handbook of stress: Theoretical and clinical aspects.* New York: The Free Press.

Kasl, S. V., Gore, S., & Cobb, S. (1975). The experience of losing a job: Reported changes in health, symptoms and illness behavior. *Psychosomatic Medicine, 37,* 106–122.

Kaufman, H. G. (1982). *Professionals in search of work.* New York: John Wiley & Sons.

Kidwell, J., Fischer, J. L., Dunham, R. M., & Baranowski, M. (1983). Parents and adolescents: Push and pull of change. In H. I. McCubbin & C. R. Figley (Eds.), *Stress and the family, Volume 1: Coping with normative transitions.* New York: Brunner/Mazel.

Koch, A. (1985). "If only it could be me": The families of pediatric cancer patients. *Family Relations, 34,* 63–70.

Lehman, D. R., Williams, A. F., & Wortman, C. B. (1987). Long-term effects of losing a spouse or child in a motor vehicle crash. *Journal of Personality and Social Psychology, 52* (1), 218–231.

Leventman, P. G. (1981). *Professionals out of work.* New York: The Free Press.

Mattessich, P., & Hill, R. (1987). Life cycle and family development. In M. B. Sussman & S. K. Steinmetz (Eds.), *Handbook of marriage and the family* (pp. 437–470). New York: Plenum.

May, J. L., & Brown-Standridge, M. D. (in press). Restructuring the context of unemployed professionals and their spouses: A couples' seminar for prevention of marital dysfunction. *The American Journal of Family Therapy.*

McCubbin, H. I., Needle, R. H., & Wilson, M. (1985). Adolescent health risk behaviors: Family stress and adolescent coping as critical factors. *Family Relations, 34,* 51–62.

McNeil, J. N. (1986). Talking about death: Adolescents, parents and peers. In C. A. Corr & J. N. McNeil (Eds.), *Adolescence and death* (pp. 185–201). New York: Springer.

Minuchin, S. (1974). *Families and family therapy.* Cambridge, MA: Harvard University Press.

Montemayor, R. (1983). Parents and adolescents in conflict: All families some of the time and some families most of the time. *Journal of Early Adolescence. 3,* 83–103.

Montemayor, R. (1986). Family variation in parent-adolescent storm and stress. *Journal of Adolescent Research, 1,* 15–31.

Montemayor, R., & Hanson, E. (1985). A naturalistic view of conflict between adolescents and their parents and siblings. *Journal of Early Adolescence, 5,* 23–30.

O'Brien, G. E., & Kabanoff, B. (1979). Comparison of unemployed and employed workers on work values, locus of control and health variables. *Australian Psychologist, 14,* 143–154.

Olson, D. H. L. (1976). Bridging research, theory and application: The triple threat in science. In D. H. L. Olson (Ed.), *Treating relationships.* Lake Mills, IA: Graphic.

Orzack, L. H. (1959). Work as a central life interest of professionals. *Social Problems, 7,* 125–132.

Perls, F. S. (1969). *Gestalt therapy: Excitement and growth in the human personality.* New York: Julian Press.

Peterson, G. W., & Rollins, B. C. (1987). Parent-child socialization. In M. B. Sussman & S. K. Steinmetz (Eds.), *Handbook of marriage and the family.* New York: Plenum.

Richardson, R. A., Galambos, N. L., Schulenberg, J. E., & Petersen, A. C. (1984). Young adolescents' perceptions of the family environment. *Journal of Early Adolescence, 4,* 131–153.

Sainsbury, P. (1955). *Suicide in London: An ecological study.* (Mandsley Monograph No. 1). London: Chapman & Hall.

Schulman, G. L. (1985). Treatment of the disturbed adolescent: A family system approach. *International Journal of Family Therapy, 7,* 11–25.

Silverberg, S. B., & Steinberg, L. (1987). Adolescent autonomy, parent-adolescent conflict and parental well-being. *Journal of Youth and Adolescence, 16,* 293–312.

Smith, K. A., & Forehand, R. (1986). Parent-adolescent conflict: Comparison and prediction of the perceptions of mothers, fathers and daughters. *Journal of Early Adolescence, 6,* 353–367.

Sterling, S., Cowen, E. L., Weissberg, R. P., Lotyczewski, B. S., & Boike, M. (1985). Recent stressful life events and young children's school adjustment. *American Journal of Community Psychology, 13,* 87–99.

Tuckman, J., & Lavell, M. (1958). Study of suicide in Philadelphia. *Public Health Reports, 73,* 547–553.

Uhlenberg, P. (1978). Changing configurations of the life course. In T. K. Hareven (Ed.), *Transitions: The family and the life course in historical perspective* (pp. 65–97). New York: Academic Press.

Voydanoff, P. (1983). Unemployment: Family strategies for adaptation. In C. R. Figley & H. I. McCubbin (Eds.), *Stress in the family, Volume 2: Coping with catastrophe.* New York: Brunner/Mazel.

Weber, J. A., & Fournier, D. G. (1985). Family support and a child's adjustment to death. *Family Relations, 34,* 43–49.

Weiner, I. B. (1980). Psychopathology in adolescence. In J. Adelson (Ed.), *Handbook of adolescent psychology* (pp. 447–471). New York: Wiley & Sons.

Wetzel, J. R. (1987). *American youth: A statistical snapshot.* Washington, DC: The William T. Grant Foundation Commission on Work, Family and Citizenship.

White, B. J. (1977). The criteria for job satisfaction: Is interesting work most important? *Monthly Labor Review, 100* (5), 30–35.

Windshuttle, K. (1980). *Unemployed.* Melbourne, Australia: Penguin.

Youniss, J. (1983). Social construction of adolescence by adolescents and parents. In H. D. Grotevent & C. R. Cooper (Eds.), *Adolescent development in the family* (pp. 93–109). San Francisco: Jossey-Bass.

# 10

## Rape and the Family

### CASSANDRA A. ERICKSON

*Anne Harris was waiting with anticipation for Barbara to come home from her class at the nearby university. She had some good news to share with her daughter. Barbara had received a letter stating that she was accepted into her first choice of the graduate programs she had applied to. Barbara arrived considerably later than usual and it soon became apparent that something was wrong. Her clothes and hair were disheveled and she had a frightened look on her face. When Anne asked what was wrong Barbara shouted at her, "I was raped on the way to my car!" She refused to say anything more and ran into her room.*

*When Barbara's father, Michael, and her younger sister, Catherine, came home shortly afterwards, Anne immediately told them what happened. They went to Barbara's room to talk to her, but Barbara said she didn't want to talk and asked to be left alone. Anne told her they had to call the police. Barbara was taken reluctantly to the hospital for examination and the police met them there. Even with prompting Barbara offered only sketchy information and finally refused to answer any more questions.*

*Over the next few weeks the family noticed that Barbara had stopped going out with friends and had lost her enthusiasm for school. They expressed their concern by attempting to talk to her about the rape, but she always said she was fine and just wanted to forget the whole thing. Her family became increasingly worried. Anne and Michael found they could no longer concentrate on their work and they began fighting more often. Catherine became anxious whenever she had to leave for school and finally refused to go altogether. At this point, Anne realized that Barbara and the family needed to seek outside help and she called the family therapy center in town.*

The crisis of rape is shared by the victim and her family (Feinauer & Hippolite, 1987; White & Rollins, 1981). Post-rape intervention should include not only the victim but also important members of the victim's social network (Silverman, 1978). The goal of this chapter is to present a treatment approach for rape victims and their families. This approach is adapted from Williamson's (1982a) theory of the termination of the generational boundary. His step-by-step consultation process is applied to systemic therapeutic intervention with rape victims and their families; however, it is generic for traumatic events occurring externally to the family system.

## DESCRIPTION OF STRESSOR

*Rape Defined*

The word *rape* is derived from the Latin *rapere*, meaning to steal, seize, or carry away (Warner, 1980a). The legal definition of rape in many states is vaginal intercourse between male and female, and anal intercourse, fellatio, and cunninlingus between persons regardless of sex in which the offender compels the victim by force or threat of force and/or impairs the victim's judgment or control through the administering of drugs or intoxicants (Koss, Gidycz, & Wisniewski, 1987, p. 166).

*Prevalence and Incidence*

Accurate estimates of the prevalence and incidence of rape are difficult to obtain since the majority of rapes are not reported (Kilpatrick, Veronen, & Best, 1985). Estimates suggest that for every rape reported, one in three-to-ten go unreported (Kilpatrick, Veronen, & Best, 1985; Law Enforcement Assistance Administration (LEAA), 1975; Nelson, 1980; Russell, 1984). Researchers suggest that victimization surveys involving interviews with a sample of the general population provide the most accurate rates for prevalence and incidence (McDermott, 1979; Skogan, 1981; Sparks, 1982); however, even these are likely to be underestimated since they cannot identify all victims.

Research findings on prevalence of rape show that women surveyed by telephone or interview disclose rates of 14.5% (Kilpatrick, Veronen, & Best, 1985), 24% (Russell, 1984), and 27.5% (Koss, Gidycz, & Wisniewski, 1987). Nelson (1980) estimates that one in eight women will be a victim of rape in her lifetime, while Russell (1984) suggests a nearly 50% chance.

Incidence rates indicate the number of rapes occurring during a specified period of time. Although studies assessing the incidence of rape are rare, Koss, Gidycz, and Wisniewski (1987) found in their sample of 3,187 women that 207 different women were involved in 353 rapes during a 12-month period. Their findings show that 7.6% of their sample experienced a rape over a year's time.

Rape rates are highest for women ranging from 16-19 years of age, with the second highest rate occurring in the 20-24 age group (Koss, Gidycz, & Wisniewski, 1987; Nelson, 1980). Rates are one-third higher for black women than for white women (Nelson, 1980). Married women report being raped at nearly one-fourth the rate of those who have never been married (Nelson, 1980). Women who are attending school or looking for work demonstrate the highest rates, with the lowest rate found among retired women (Nelson, 1980).

## Debunking Myths About Rape

Cultural and societal conceptions about rape are often inaccurate. These misconceptions have serious implications for the reactions of the victim and her family to the rape. Several researchers have attempted to repudiate the myths associated with rape (Burge, 1983; Burt, 1980; Groth, Burgess, & Holmstrom, 1977; Halpern, Hicks, & Crenshaw, 1978; Norsigian, 1979; Rodabaugh & Austin, 1981; White & Rollins, 1981). Many of the most commonly accepted stereotypes are contradicted by the realities:

1. Rape is a crime of violence, not of sex. The primary motive of most rapists is to act out feelings of aggression, dominance, power, and hatred. Sex is the means of venting their anger and exercising control over their victims.
2. Rape occurs in "safe" and private places as well as in the open. Between one-third and two-thirds of all rapes occur in the victim's home or in another private residence.
3. Rape can happen at any hour of the day, not just under the cover of darkness.
4. In the majority of cases, rape is planned in advance, not impulsive. The rapist often waits for the most opportune time to attack or for the most opportune victim to appear.
5. Rape often cannot be avoided, even if the victim resists. Sexual assault is a life-threatening act and fear often immobilizes the victim. Even if the victim were to resist, she becomes more vulnerable to brutality or homicide. Submission, therefore, does not imply consent.

6. There is no "typical" victim. Victims are chosen because they appear to be vulnerable. They may be any age and come from any background.
7. Victims don't "ask" to be raped. Rape victims are usually neither provocative nor promiscuous. Despite a victim's dress, behavior, or whereabouts, the rape and the violence are precipitated by the rapist's interpretation of the victim, not by the victim's intentions.
8. Seductive sexual fantasies are not the same thing as a secret desire to be raped. Fantasies are always under the control of the woman's imagination—she chooses the time, place, circumstance, and man. Fantasies are desirable and pleasurable, rape degrades and humiliates.
9. There is no "typical" rapist. Rapists may be young, attractive, and personable. At least two-thirds have regular sexual outlets and are not "sex-starved."
10. Rape is committed as often by someone the victim knows as by a stranger. The offender may be a trusted neighbor, colleague, boyfriend or relative of the victim.

Despite clear evidence to the contrary, many current beliefs about rape stereotype the victim, the perpetrator, and the nature of the act. Intervention with rape victims and their families needs to include efforts to dispel these misconceptions through education.

## VICTIM REACTIONS TO RAPE

Rape is a crisis which precipitates intense emotional reactions for the victim (Burgess & Holmstrom, 1974; White & Rollins, 1981). Both the rape and its aftermath impose extremely difficult coping tasks and involve highly threatening issues (Abarbanel, 1980). During the assault, the victim's coping strategies fail. After the assault, these strategies are immobilized or inadequate to handle the intensity of the sequelae. The victim's affect, cognitions, behavior, and personality are affected.

Abarbanel's (1980) and Burgess and Holmstrom's (1974) descriptions of victim reactions to rape may be combined into three phases. The first phase, initial reactions, occurs immediately following the rape. The second phase, subsequent reactions, occurs in the days and weeks following the rape. The third phase, long-term reactions, describes the more lasting effects of the trauma. These phases characterize the "rape trauma syndrome," the emotional disorder manifested by specific behavioral, somatic, and psychological symptoms in response to the crisis of rape (Burgess & Holmstrom, 1974).

It is important to keep in mind that "individual differences among victims may moderate the intensity, duration, and manifestation of these common reactions. Certain issues will be more important for some victims than for others" (Abarbanel, 1980, p. 145). Thus, victims will not necessarily experience all the symptoms nor will they experience them in the same sequence (Burgess & Holmstrom, 1974). The process of coping and reorganization will also begin at different times and progress at different rates for each victim (Gilbert & Erickson, 1988).

*Initial Reactions*

The first emotional reaction to rape is often a period of shock and disbelief (Abarbanel, 1980; Burgess & Holmstrom, 1974). For some victims the psychological trauma is relatively invisible (Abarbanel, 1980; Burgess & Holmstrom, 1974). They are numb and may have difficulty concentrating and making decisions, thus appearing confused and distracted. These victims block out and deny the experience and will resist talking about the rape. This denial can be initially adaptive because it gives the victim time to prepare for dealing with the cognitive, affective, and behavior disruption. Other victims show more visible emotional upset and may be agitated, hysterical, volatile, and/or angry (Abarbanel, 1980; Burgess & Holmstrom, 1974). These victims often express such behavior as crying, sobbing, smiling, restlessness, and tenseness.

*Subsequent Reactions*

During the first few days and weeks following the rape, victims will begin to feel the physical effects of the assault, including soreness and fatigue (Abarbanel, 1980; Burgess & Holmstrom, 1974). They may develop such physical symptoms as tension headaches, stomach pains, loss of appetite, and nausea. They may also experience such somatic responses as difficulty falling or staying asleep and startle responses, becoming jumpy over minor incidents.

Victims often begin to express a wide range of emotional reactions, including fear, humiliation, vulnerability, guilt, anger, revenge, and self-blame (Burgess & Holmstrom, 1974; Janoff-Bulman, 1979, 1985; Katz & Mazur, 1979). They may also express pragmatic and realistic concerns over such issues as pregnancy, venereal disease, whom to tell about the assault, how others will react, retaliation by the rapist, future safety, and the extent and duration of lifestyle disruption (Abarbanel, 1980). Victims often withdraw from sexual activity because it triggers painful flashbacks of the rape (Abarbanel, 1980; Burgess & Holmstom, 1974; Katz & Mazur, 1979; Woodling, Evans, & Bradbury, 1977). They may continue to choose not to talk about the rape as a way of attempting to restore equilibrium and a sense of normalcy (Sutherland & Scherl, 1970).

*Long-term Reactions*

The long-term reactions of victims may result in their making active changes in their lives (Abarbanel, 1980; Burgess & Holmstrom, 1974). Many victims change their residence and telephone number. Many also turn for support to family members and close friends. The effects of the rape, however, may still be felt. Some victims report upsetting dreams and nightmares of the rape, recurring flashbacks, and/or preoccupation with thoughts about the rape (Abarbanel, 1980; Brodsky, 1976; Burgess & Holmstrom, 1974). Many victims begin to search for a reason or explanation for the rape, repeatedly reviewing the event and its circumstances (Abarbanel, 1980). This may be seen as an adaptive response through which the victim attempts to undo the event and regain control of her life (Abarbanel, 1980; Bard & Sangrey, 1986.)

Victims may express emotional reactions for a long period of time, including anxiety, mood swings, crying spells, outbursts, agitation, and depression (Abarbanel, 1980). Many report that they also lose their sense of humor (Abarbanel, 1980). Irrational fears may develop, such as fear of indoors, fear of people behind them, and sexual fears (Burgess & Holmstrom, 1974; Girelli, Resick, Marhoefer-Dvorak, & Hutter, 1986; Katz & Mazur, 1979; Kilpatrick, Veronen, & Resick, 1979; Wilson, 1978). These fears may relate to a particular aspect of the rape (e.g., the rapist approached the victim from behind) or may become generalized (e.g., feeling vulnerable to harm or danger in crowds).

All of the reactions described above result from disruption to the victim's lifestyle and functioning as a result of the rape. The nature and extent of the lasting effects of the trauma are unpredictable. White and Rollins (1981) identify some of the variables contributing to the effects of rape on the victim: the types of coping behaviors and strategies used during the actual rape; the age, life situation and personality of the victim; the level of involvement between the victim and rapist; and whether the rape was reported and how authorities responded.

Most researchers do agree, however, that the availability of supportive relationships will strongly enhance the victim's ability to resolve the issues raised and the losses sustained by the rape (Abarbanel, 1980; Burgess & Holmstrom, 1974; Woodling, Evans, & Bradbury, 1977). If victims are given appropriate support, they may begin to open up their feelings related to the assault. Some victims, however, may remain withdrawn and experience difficulty talking with others. It is for those victims that the intervention described in this chapter is particularly beneficial.

## FAMILY REACTIONS TO RAPE

As previously mentioned, the impact of rape is shared by the victim and her family. Sudden changes in the victim may interrupt routines, coping patterns, and the balance of interpersonal relations of the family system, thus becoming a source of enormous stress (Burge, 1983). Family members, in turn, must begin a process of healing by adjusting their own roles, attitudes, and behaviors to deal with the effects of the trauma. Thus, family responses are influenced by the impact of the rape on the victim (White & Rollins, 1981).

### Differential Recovery Process

Several different processes may be occurring simultaneously as the victim and family members cope with the reality of a life changed by the rape (Gilbert & Erickson, 1988; White & Rollins, 1981). These different processes may serve to facilitate or retard the healing process for each family member, including the victim. Family members, much like the victim, may hold different aspects of the rape as significant and experience varying emotional reactions. Family members, however, are affected by the interaction of adjusting roles, attitudes, and behaviors. They continually reevaluate their changes in relation to those of other family members. This can become complex since the victim and family members are likely to be at different stages in the healing process at any given point in time. Thus, the way individual family members interact and respond affects how they and the victim will continue to process the rape experience.

### Reactions of Family Members

"Just as rape represents a traumatic event that precipitates a crisis in the life of the victim, it may also assault the psychological equilibrium of the victim's couple and family systems" (Silverman, 1978, p. 166). Family members may suffer as seriously as the victim in their attempts at adaptation (Orzek, 1983; Salasin, 1981; White & Rollins, 1981).

White and Rollins (1981) outline several affective responses that are likely to occur after the rape of a family member. The husband or boyfriend is likely to experience intense feelings of anger and rage (Burgess & Holmstrom, 1974; Silverman, 1978). The victim and her family may share a sense of devaluation and guilt as well as feelings of anxiety and depression. They may also share the view that the rape has changed their lives in debilitating and irreversible ways.

Spaulding (1980) outlines some additional responses. Family members may experience uneasiness, frustration, and a sense of helplessness in that they may not know what to do or say to the victim. Family members may also feel guilt at not having been able to prevent the rape. This is often characterized by "if only" statements (Burgess & Holmstrom, 1974). The family's anxiety about the victim's safety may result in interfering and overprotecting with such questions as "Where are you going?" and "What time will you be back?" Family members, much like the victim, may deny that the rape occurred, preferring to refer to the incident as an "attempt." Male mates may have difficulty understanding the victim's avoidance of physical contact.

Warner (1980b) and others (Everstine & Everstine, 1983; Silverman, 1978; White & Rollins, 1981) suggest that family members may express some of the same physical and emotional responses as the victim. For instance, immediately after the rape, the victim's husband, parents, and siblings may experience a sense of shock and helplessness. Male members in particular may also manifest such symptoms as insomnia, loss of appetite, diarrhea, skin reactions, irritability, spontaneous outbursts of anger or crying, and withdrawal. In addition, family members may find they have a need to blame someone or something for the rape. The outlets for this blame often include the perpetrator, other family members, or the victim herself.

## FAMILY COPING

White and Rollins (1981) suggest that "crisis situations provide a context in which both strengths and problems in family relationships are brought more sharply into focus" (p. 105). Family members' abilities to utilize their strengths and overcome their deficiencies after a crisis often contribute to whether they will cope functionally as individuals and as a family system.

Coping is an active process in which family members take direct action in mobilizing their resources to deal effectively with a stressor and its associated hardships (Patterson & McCubbin, 1983). Family members attempt to achieve a balance in family functioning through the interaction of resources, perceptions, and behavioral responses (Patterson & McCubbin, 1983).

## Factors Influencing Family Coping

*Prevailing cultural views.* The ability of families to cope is affected by their attitudes and beliefs concerning rape (Orzek, 1983; Young & Erickson, in press). White and Rollins (1981) suggest that cultural views and definitions of rape greatly influence the way a family defines rape and the changes precipitated by it. The risk of families implementing dysfunctional coping strategies increases with their acceptance of the societal myths and stereotypes associated with rape, the victim, and the rapist. For instance a husband's reactions to his wife's rape are strongly influenced by whether he views rape as an act of violence or, as cultural views dictate, a sexual act.

*Nature of the crisis.* The sudden, arbitrary, and unpredictable nature of rape often does not allow the family time to prepare themselves for coping with the associated stresses (Bard & Ellison, 1974; White and Rollins, 1981). When a crisis evolves more slowly, families have some opportunity to anticipate the crisis and are therefore better able to adjust their patterns of functioning to cope with it.

*Prior functioning.* Families characterized by chronically disturbed relationships are impeded in their ability to mobilize functional coping strategies (Holmstrom & Burgess, 1979; Silverman, 1978; White & Rollins, 1981). The addition of another stressor, such as a rape, only adds stress to already vulnerable relationship issues (Orzek, 1983; Silverman, 1978). For instance, couples whose sexual relations were problematic prior to the rape are likely to experience added stress in this area after the rape.

Silverman (1978) further describes situations in which interpersonal difficulties can lead individuals to place themselves at greater risk of rape before it even occurs. For instance, a woman might be raped while taking a late-night walk after storming out of the house following a heated argument with her husband about his staying so late at work. In such a case, the rape may reflect self-destructive attempts to deal with ongoing relationship problems.

Families characterized by healthy relationships, however, are better able to recover from a crisis (Burr, 1973). Burr (1973) identifies integration and adaptability as two important variables that enhance the quality of family relationships. The extent of organization and flexibility that has evolved in a family prior to the occurrence of a crisis are also critical resources for coping with a crisis (Burr, 1973; Olson, Sprenkle, & Russell, 1979; White & Rollins, 1981). Burgess and Holmstrom (1974) suggest that in the case of rape, organization and flexibility are likely to be reflected in sex-role attitudes, sexual relations, and beliefs about sexual access.

## Functional Family Coping

*Role flexibility.* During the process of healing from the trauma of the rape, each family member may find that he or she needs to redefine his or her role in terms of each other family member (Olson, Sprenkle, & Russell, 1979). The ability of family members to shift roles as needed may be an important adaptive response to a crisis such as rape (Burge, 1983; Hill & Hansen, 1962). For example, different family members may require caregiving, attention, or reassurance at different times.

*Externalized blaming.* Families that are able to externalize blame for the rape are less vulnerable to long-term negative consequences from the rape (White & Rollins, 1981). For instance, a rape victim's mother might choose to blame the occurrence of the rape on the way men and women are socialized rather than on her daughter or other family members.

*Mobilizing resources.* Family members are best able to cope with the trauma of rape when they can access their own resources (e.g., interpersonal, material) as well as those outside the family (e.g., friend networks, family-oriented support services) (Patterson & McCubbin, 1983; White & Rollins, 1981). Although family members may find themselves temporarily overwhelmed by the rape, they soon begin to turn their energy into action.

*Open communication.* Many researchers agree that one of the most critical resources of the family for dealing with a crisis such as rape may be the patterns of and opportunities for open communication (Gilbert & Erickson, 1988; Holmstrom & Burgess, 1979; Silverman, 1978; White & Rollins, 1981). Communication among family members that is supportive, flexible, and nonjudgmental facilitates discussion of emotions and cognitions surrounding the event (Gilbert & Erickson, 1988). For instance, Burgess and Holmstrom (1974) found that when the family discusses the rape, the victim's phobic responses are more likely to be resolved.

*Appropriate social supportiveness.* Appropriate and positive social support is often essential to restore stability to the family system after a crisis such as rape (Figley, 1983; Silver & Wortman, 1980). Appropriate support satisfies and meets the needs and expectations of the victim (Erickson, 1988). For instance, family members express appropriate support when they provide an environment that is open to the expression of feelings without pushing the victim to talk.

## Transitional Family Coping

Not all coping responses are clearly definable as either functional or dysfunctional. Some responses may begin as functional coping strategies but become dysfunctional if they continue over a long period of time. These strategies may initially prepare the family members to deal with the impending emotional fallout, but become dysfunctional when they serve as an exercise in avoidance or self-destruction.

*Denial.* Some victims and their families initially block out and deny the experience (Abarbanel, 1980; Sutherland & Scherl, 1970). This defense can be adaptive and protective in that it gives them time to prepare for the emotions that are to come. Family members may perform routine tasks, continuing as if nothing happened. This represents a way to reaffirm a sense of normalcy and to begin regaining mastery and control.

*Withdrawal.* The victim and family members may also withdrawal from each other for a period of time. They may refuse to talk about the event in an attempt to restore equilibrium (Sutherland & Scherl, 1970; White & Rollins, 1981). Again, this provides an opportunity for family members to begin galvanizing their energy for the time when their experiences and reactions will need to be shared.

*Behavioral self-blame.* The victim and family members may each go through a period of blaming themselves for the rape. Blaming oneself for what one did or did not do can serve to frame the event as modifiable and controllable (Janoff-Bulman, 1979, 1985). This enables the family to believe that similar events can be avoided in the future. Behavioral self-blame becomes maladaptive if it shifts over time to characterological self-blame, attributing blame to one's enduring personality characteristics. Characterological self-blame focuses on traits that are stable and relatively unchangeable. Thus, behavioral self-blame remains adaptive as long as it does not shift from "I did a stupid thing" to "I did a stupid thing because I'm a stupid person."

## Dysfunctional Family Coping

*Misguided attitudes.* Those who are close to the victim may be subject to the same myths and misconceptions about rape held by the general public (Burt, 1980; Feild, 1978; Silverman, 1978). For instance, male mates or other family members may hold the view that "nice women don't get raped" or "any women who is raped must have asked for it." These kinds of thoughts often lead to feelings of resentment and anger toward the victim. Because this anger is usually unconscious, it becomes manifested indirectly. Thus, the victim's husband may criticize her for not having been more careful or ask her whether she enjoyed the experience. These types of responses from family members, however, increase the risk that victims will be "revictimized" (Silverman, 1978) and experience a "second rape" (Burge, 1983).

*Internalized blame.* In an attempt to find some sort of explanation for the event, family members sometimes turn blame toward the family system (Burge, 1983; White & Rollins, 1981). Blame may be directed at the victim through angry statements such as "Why didn't you try to get away?" These statements often reflect family members' attempts to preserve an illusion of control when confronted with the reality of loss of control (Salasin, 1981). Blame may also be directed toward other family members or toward self. Accusations and recriminations may provoke interpersonal or personal conflict for family members. They may also further burden the victim with guilt and self-accusations (Bard & Sangrey, 1986).

*Guilt.* Family members often experience guilt and a sense of responsibility for the rape (Silverman, 1978). Issues of self-concept or role expectations may be manifested through feeling that they failed in their duty to protect the victim (Burge, 1983). This is often expressed through "if only" statements (e.g., If only I had not left her alone) (Burgess & Holmstrom, 1974).

*Anger.* Historically, a woman has been viewed as the property of her man (Silverman, 1978; Warner, 1980a). This attitude is still sometimes reflected today through the victim's husband feeling personally wronged and attacked by the rape of "his woman." Her husband may express anger and indignation that she "allowed herself" to become "damaged merchandise" (Silverman, 1978). This response only reinforces the victim's sense of humiliation and devaluation.

*Revenge.* Family members, particularly men, may also express their anger through thoughts of "extracting violent retribution from the rapist on behalf of the victim" (Silverman, 1980, p. 170). This often takes the form of detailed descriptions of what the man would do to the rapist if he ever caught him. Although anger and blame in this case are directed externally to the family system, in actuality these thoughts often serve to protect rather than to appropriately channel the man's own sense of helplessness (Silverman, 1978). The victim may find that she has to bear the extra burden of calming and reassuring her "protector."

*Helplessness.* Family members may become frustrated because they are at a loss for knowing what to do or say to the victim and each other. They cannot "undo" the event nor can they prevent the changes that will occur in their lives as a result of the rape. They may feel vulnerable and out of control. The expression of blame, guilt, anger, and/or revenge often reflects feelings of helplessness.

*Distraction/avoidance.* Family members sometimes attempt to keep the victim occupied with a variety of activities in order to "undo" or deny the effects of the rape (Silverman, 1978). The victim may also be encouraged by a family member to keep the rape a secret under the guise of protecting other family members (Silverman, 1978). This conspiracy of silence may reflect such issues as family discomfort with sexuality, hidden alliances and long-standing family problems, or fear of being blamed. Family secrets, however, tend to become great burdens and may destroy potentially adaptive behaviors (Silverman, 1978). In any case, these responses deprive the victim of the opportunity to mourn the personal losses experienced by the rape, deny her much-needed support from family members, and confirm her worst fears that the rape might, in fact, be "too terrible to discuss."

*Patronizing/overprotecting.* Families commonly respond to rape by patronizing and overprotecting the victim (Silverman, 1978; Spaulding, 1980). For instance, the mother of a rape victim might insist on driving her daughter wherever she needs to go even though she has lived alone for several years. This may represent family members' attempts to relieve feelings of guilt and responsibility for having failed to protect the victim.

The danger of these responses for the victim is that they may reinforce her feelings of helplessness and vulnerability. The victim will have difficulty reestablishing a much-needed sense of control.

*Inappropriate social supportiveness.* Family members who are trying to help a victim deal with the rape may unintentionally make matters worse (Janoff-Bulman, Madden & Timko, 1983; Rook, 1984; Silver & Wortman, 1980). Their attempts at being supportive may be inappropriate (Erickson, 1988). For example, in their desire to help the victim, family members may attempt to rally together all those people the victim might consider supportive (Silverman, 1978). They may call upon her friends, coworkers, teachers, supervisors, and so forth. The victim, however, may experience this as invasive since she may want to share her experiences with only a chosen few. Family members and others should appropriately respect her needs for privacy and confidentiality.

## Case Example—The Harris Family

During the weeks before Anne sought counseling for her family, it seemed to her that her family was beginning to fall apart. Anne noticed that not only had Barbara lost touch with her friends, but she had stopped eating and wasn't sleeping well at night. Barbara complained of severe headaches and nausea and seemed to jump at the slightest noise. One night Anne and Michael awoke to hear her crying in her bedroom, but when they went to talk with her she shouted at them to get out.

Tension was building in the home. Michael became uncharacteristically enraged at the smallest incidents. He often locked himself up in his study after coming home from work and refused to emerge even for dinner. Catherine was taking over many of the responsibilities that Michael was neglecting. She seemed to be doing better than any of them. She maintained her enthusiasm over her old activities and seemed to be enjoying herself. And yet, why was Catherine suddenly so afraid of going to school? In fact, the last few days she had refused to go altogether.

Anne herself was beginning to feel anxious. She found that she couldn't concentrate because her mind was becoming preoccupied with reproachful thoughts about having let Barbara take a night class on campus. She didn't argue much with Catherine about going to school and just tried to stay out of everyone's way. The disruption continued until Anne finally decided they needed outside help.

## GENERAL APPROACH TO TREATMENT

White and Rollins (1981) suggest that "for the majority of families, intervention may be necessary to facilitate open expression of responses to the crisis of rape" (p. 106). This chapter borrows the step-by-step consultation process found in Williamson's (1981; 1982a,b) theory on personal authority and termination of the intergenerational hierarchical boundary and applies it to systemic therapeutic intervention with rape victims and their families.

### Overview of Williamson's Consultation Process

Williamson's (1981; 1982a,b) theory suggests that a young adult develops personal authority with respect to his or her family of origin through the process of terminating the intergenerational hierarchical boundary. The therapeutic task is to eliminate the young adult's continuing emotional dependency upon his or her parents by resigning from the position as "child" and declaring his or her peerhood.

Williamson's (1982a) step-by-step consultation process for this boundary termination is described as short-term, strategic, experiential, intergenerational family therapy (Bray, Williamson, & Malone, 1986). After careful assessment of the family's readiness for treatment, therapy begins by gathering information from the young adult in order to develop an agenda for direct work with the parents. The young adult relates his or her story to the therapist and writes an autobiography, presenting evidence for the nature of his or her present relationship with the parents. Therapy then moves to a process of preparing the young adult for direct confrontation with his or her parental system. The young adult prepares first an informal and then a formal letter or speech inviting the parents to join him or her in dealing with some relationship issues. The letter/speech is presented to the parents in private face-to-face conversation. The therapist and young adult then decide on specific agenda items to present in the Three-Day Consultation.

During the first day of the consultation process the young adult begins working on the least intense of the issues with each parent. On the second day the young adult addresses the most difficult of the issues. He or she officially resigns from any positions of triangulation and covert loyalty between the parents and then declares that he or she is no longer their "child." The hierarchical intergenerational boundary is terminated. On the third day both generations express intense grieving over the losses they have endured and then move to an exploration of implications for their future relationship. The young adult has assumed a status of peerhood with his or her former parents and has achieved a higher quality of personal authority.

This process of developing personal authority is in many ways similar to the process of "working through" associated with a traumatic event such as rape. A rape victim and her family achieve personal authority with respect to the rape when they can assimilate and incorporate the experience into their lives. The overall dilemma for the young adult, as with the rape victim and her family, is "how to embrace and assimilate one's history . . . in an explicit way, and simultaneously to transcend the emotionality" (Bray, Williamson, & Malone, 1986, p. 424).

## Modification to Williamson's Consultation Process

In recognition of the family's integral role in the victim's rape experience, the one modification made to Williamson's consultation process will be to intervene with the family system from the beginning. Figley (1986) suggests, however, that it is premature to include all family members in treatment together before the victim has to some degree confronted and worked through the trauma. The victim may, for instance, create a barrier for the free-flow expression of feelings by family members (Felix, 1980).

Initially, then, the victim and her family will be seen separately to prepare her for sharing the traumatic experience with the family. As the therapist works with the victim, he or she also works with the family to gather information, offer support, and educate them concerning the symptoms and behaviors they may expect from the victim. When all family members are reunited for the Three-Day Consultation, the emphasis is on integrating the rape experience into the family system (Figley, 1986).

## Goals of Treatment

The ultimate goal of treatment is to facilitate the family's integration of the trauma of the rape experience into the family system. If this goal is reached, therapy has strengthened family cohesion and adaptability through the fostering of effective communication and supportiveness skills and the building of individual and family strengths. The "family" may include members from the victim's family of procreation, family of orientation, and/or any significant others. Although the treatment approach is described here in the context of the family of procreation, it is equally appropriate for couples, extended family, close friends, and so on.

The therapist encourages adaptive familial responses through tasks that help family members to:

1. recognize that rape is a family crisis that requires shared efforts to mobilize energy and resources;
2. recognize and attempt to resolve the specific needs and conflicts of each individual member, including
   a. developing cognitive understanding of what the experience of rape represents to the victim and other family members;
   b. developing cognitive understanding of the nature of the healing process;
3. encourage and appropriately channel self-disclosure and affective responses;
4. understand that although rape is a traumatic event, the harm and disruption need not be irreparable or permanent.

The treatment approach described here consists of a combination of individual and family sessions. These may be modified according to the specific needs of the family. In addition, the therapist now refers to the "victim" as a "survivor" to emphasize the focus on adaptive strength, change, and growth (Figley, 1985).

This approach is most appropriate for those families who were functioning adequately prior to the rape and whose dynamics and interaction can incorporate the kind of self-disclosure and supportiveness demanded. Thus, the therapist must carefully assess the family's appropriateness for treatment of this nature.

## ASSESSMENT AND DIAGNOSIS

### Initial Interview

During the initial interview the clinician assesses the family's appropriateness for the treatment approach described. The clinician must first determine the presence of an identifiable external traumatic stressor — in this case, rape. This approach is not appropriate for families who have been traumatized from within the family system since this requires more traditional family therapy to deal with structural issues. The clinician must also determine the extent to which the family is coping functionally with respect to the rape. In particular, the clinician assesses all family members' symptomatology as well as their attitudes and acceptance of stereotypes associated with rape in general. Finally, the clinician assesses family adaptability and cohesion as well as the nature, extent, and satisfaction of family social supportiveness.

Through information obtained during the initial interview and assessment process, the clinician should also evaluate the specific needs and strengths of the family system (Crosby & Jose, 1983; Orzek, 1983); age-specific issues related to life-cycle stage of the family system and individual members (Hilberman, 1976; Rodabaugh & Austin, 1981); and commitment to maintaining family relationships (Crenshaw, 1978). Assessment, however, remains an ongoing process, and the clinician should always be open to new and relevant information.

*Assessment Measures*

*The Impact of Event Scale* (IES). This measure reliably detects symptoms found in the diagnostic criteria for Post-traumatic Stress Disorder (PTSD) (Horowitz, 1986; Horowitz, Kaltreider, Wilner, & Alvarez, 1979; Horowitz, Wilner, & Kaltreider, 1980). The clinician assesses the extent of symptomatology to evaluate the current impact of the rape on each family member. The clinician uses this information to educate the survivor and her family concerning the reactions they may expect from her and other family members.

*DSM-III-R Post-traumatic Stress Disorder (PTSD) diagnostic criteria.* These criteria more specifically diagnose the presence of PTSD symptomatology (American Psychiatric Association, 1987). PTSD symptom categories include persistent reexperiencing of the event, avoidance of stimuli associated with the trauma or numbing of general responsiveness, and increased arousal. Related symptoms include depression, impulsive behavior, organic mental disorder, survivor guilt, and substance abuse. PTSD incorporates the symptoms associated with the survivor's Rape Trauma Syndrome, but that may also affect other family members through secondary catastrophic stress reactions (Figley, 1983). A diagnosis of PTSD indicates that one or more family members are not functioning adequately as a result of the rape and need in-depth individual therapy to work through their experience and reactions.

*Rape Attitude scale.* This instrument consists of statements measuring four rape-relevant attitude variables—sex role stereotyping, sexual conservatism, adversarial sexual beliefs, and acceptance of interpersonal violence (Burt, 1980). Each statement is rated on a 7-point agreement-disagreement Likert scale. The clinician uses this instrument to assess individual family members' beliefs and attitudes concerning women, sexuality, and violence. This information alerts the clinician to attitudes and emotions that could further disrupt the family system. The clinician can then mobilize these into direct expression and gently help family members to reformulate those that are most potentially damaging.

*Rape Myth Acceptance scale* (RMA). This instrument consists of 19 items measuring the acceptance of commonly held myths about rape (Burt, 1980). Each item is rated on a 7-point Likert scale ranging from "strongly agree" to "strongly disagree." The clinician uses this information to educate the survivor and family members on appropriate facts about rape, the victim, and the rapist.

*Family Adaptability and Cohesion Evaluation Scales (FACES III)*. This instrument measures cohesion and adaptability within the family system (Olson, 1986; Olson, Portner, & Lavee, 1985). The 20-item scale is taken twice, once for perceived and once for ideal descriptions of the family. The scores are then plotted onto the Circumplex model to indicate the type of system they perceive and ideally desire. Family satisfaction is indicated by the discrepancy between ideal-perceived scores. The clinician uses this information to identify chronically disturbed families located at the extremes (disengaged or enmeshed, chaotic or rigid). These families may require more traditional family therapy intervention.

*Purdue Social Support Scale* (PSSS). This scale measures individual perceptions of five components of social support: emotional support, encouragement, advice, socializing, and tangible aid (Burge & Figley, in press). Individuals list up to seven supporters and rate their expected satisfaction with each person's help on a 5-point scale from "very satisfied" to "wouldn't seek this." The clinician requests that each individual list each of the family members and any significant others who will be in treatment. The clinician determines the family to be appropriate for this treatment approach if they show a strong social support network, counterindicating the need for long-term intervention.

## TREATMENT APPROACH

The following approach will follow the Harris family through the treatment process. As the therapist works with Barbara to prepare her for sharing the impact of the rape experience, the therapist also works with Anne, Michael, and Catherine to gather information, offer support, and educate them concerning the symptoms and behaviors they may expect. When all family members are reunited for the Three-Day Consultation, the emphasis is on integrating the rape experience into their family system (Figley, 1986).

Each step in the preparation process, adapted from Williamson (1982a), will address separately the therapeutic interventions appropriate for Barbara and her family. The reader should keep in mind, however, that the following description is somewhat idealized. The therapist must remain flexible since the actual process may not have such clearly delineated steps or agendas.

### Informal Story

*Survivor.* The treatment process begins with the therapist working to establish trust and rapport with Barbara. After a few initial sessions she may begin to open up about the rape experience. Informal conversation centers around the rape and the therapist discovers what parts of the experience are "psychologically dead or alive." His or her goal is to assess the degree to which Barbara has worked through the trauma of the rape.

*Family.* The treatment process for the rest of the family begins with Anne, Michael, and Catherine relating each of their perceptions of the story surrounding the rape and its aftermath. The therapist also obtains everyone's perception of the degree to which Barbara has worked through the event. Informal conversation centers around the rape, and the therapist looks for those parts of the trauma that are "psychologically dead or alive" for each of them.

### Small Groups

*Survivor.* The therapist begins to prepare Barbara for direct confrontation with the rape experience. She is placed in a small group of other rape survivors to create the expectation and provide the encouragement necessary to begin exploring the experience. This is especially important for clients such as Barbara who are hesitant or withdrawn.

In group therapy the survivor is often able to begin sharing feelings and perceptions with other fellow survivors that she might be reluctant to share in another context. The atmosphere is one of support and understanding and often serves to reduce feelings of isolation (Donaldson & Gardner, 1985).

*Family.* Anne, Michael, and Catherine are also placed in a group with other families of rape survivors. Group therapy provides two important functions for the family. First, it provides a context within which family members learn about traumatic stress reactions so they know what to expect and can develop strategies for effective interaction with their traumatized family member. Group therapy often helps family members to understand their role in helping the survivor and each other work through the trauma (Figley & Sprenkle, 1978; Herndon & Law, 1986), particularly their potential for maintaining and eliminating the effects of the trauma (Stanton & Figley, 1978).

Second, group therapy serves as a context for providing understanding and psychological support for the family members themselves in order to bolster morale, normalize their own reactions, and help them discover personal and shared perceptions of the event. This may be the family's first opportunity to recognize and share their own pain. Some family members, including Anne, Michael, and Catherine, have developed symptoms of their own related to the event and may require special attention. The therapist empathically frames the catastrophe as a shared event and describes the family members as *co-survivors* of trauma.

## Autobiography

*Survivor.* The therapist asks Barbara to write an unstructured and informal autobiography of her experiences which highlights the sequence of events and perceptions associated with the rape. Barbara presents the autobiography in the office, affording a "spontaneous affective interpretation as [she] reads [her] own cognitive constructions" (Williamson, 1982a, p. 26) of the rape. The therapist invites Barbara to explain further what she has just read, allowing continued self-revelation of her frame of reference.

The therapist begins to help Barbara understand that she is a person in context — affecting and being affected by her family and others. The therapist presents her with the choice of attending the family's autobiographical session, explaining the rationale and rules. The purpose of the invitation is to ease the transition of joining Barbara with her family and to allow her a unique and nonthreatening opportunity to observe how her family perceives the rape. If Barbara chooses to come, she is asked to participate minimally since this is her family's time to share (her time will come later).

*Family.* The therapist asks Anne, Michael, and Catherine to write and present a brief, unstructured, and informal autobiography of his or her perspectives and experiences which highlights the sequence of events and perceptions associated with the rape. The therapist then invites each of them to explain further what he or she just read and invites the other family members to respond. If Barbara has decided to attend, she is only allowed to respond with questions or observations that are related to others' experiences. The therapist notes functional and dysfunctional patterns of interaction.

### Contemporary Patterns

*Survivor.* Barbara presents to the therapist physical or experiential evidence for how the rape affects her life now. At this point, she and the therapist should have developed a fundamental picture of the character of the rape and its impact on her, including patterns of functional and dysfunctional coping.

The therapist also obtains information about Barbara's patterns of interaction within the family system. Interventive questions might include asking who she can count on in the family, how much she can count on that person, who she could most easily talk to about the trauma, who would have the most difficulty hearing about the trauma, and so forth. This provides the therapist with additional insight into interactional patterns and reinforces for Barbara the systemic and contextual nature of her experience.

*Family.* Anne, Michael, and Catherine each presents physical or experiential evidence for how the rape affects his or her life now. The therapist asks them to discuss their present level of functioning and coping as a family. An intervention might include asking them to discuss the differences between family functioning prior to and subsequent to the rape. The therapist continues to note functional and dysfunctional patterns of interaction.

If the therapist believes at this point that dysfunctional patterns may undermine Barbara's ability to share her story and the family's ability to incorporate and begin working together on the trauma, the therapist should pursue brief interventions and/or assign homework to begin to disrupt these patterns. Particularly dysfunctional families may require traditional family therapy sessions prior to continuing the treatment process.

Up until this point, Barbara has been seen primarily in individual sessions. The purpose has been to empower her in preparation for confronting the trauma in more detail and for sharing the event with her family. The family has also been empowered through recognition of their integral role and their own suffering. Barbara is now ready to invite the family to join her in mutual sharing and helping in dealing with the event. A formal ritual for allowing the family to become a part of her trauma experience is presented.

### Preparation for Joining Survivor and Family

*Informal letter/speech.* Barbara prepares an informal letter or speech in which she invites the family to join her in directly confronting the traumatic experiences. She is asked to include conversation about how the trauma is affecting her at the moment and to express her readiness and desire to share the experience. The importance of her family in helping Barbara to deal with the event is identified. She is also encouraged to discuss with the therapist any difficulties foreseen by sharing the experience, including possible effects to the structure, boundaries, power, sanctions, myths, and so on, of the family.

*Formal letter/speech.* Barbara then prepares a formal letter or speech to the family with the guidance of the therapist, addressing some of the issues which previously emerged. Barbara informs the family that she is ready to risk taking some important steps in dealing directly with the trauma of the rape and would like them to share the experience with her. The therapist helps her prepare for dealing with emotionality or intensity from the family.

*Presentation of letter/speech.* Barbara then contacts all important family members by letter or phone and invites them to come to a Three-Day Consultation to address the impact of the event on her family and on herself. Family members are encouraged to share their own experiences as well. The therapist privately asks each member of the family to act as a consultant for Barbara and the other family members and solicits their support and advice.

*Face-to-face conversation.* Barbara meets with her mother, father, and sister privately to talk briefly about the rape and its impact on each of them personally. This is a more intimate and reciprocal exchange covering some of the issues that emerged from the family autobiographical presentation. While discussing the effects of the rape, Barbara also encourages her family to talk about anything else they wish, including other events in their earlier lives that have shaped and affected them. This should be a time of *gentle exploring* of both the highlights and the low points in the history of the family and each family member. The therapist encourages Barbara to share some of her own perceptions and experiences as well, both related and unrelated to the rape.

*Debriefing.* If all is going well, Barbara and her family are becoming aware of the unresolved grief issues and unmourned loss experiences associated with the rape. Before beginning the Three-Day Consultation, Barbara is allowed to decide which rape issues she is willing or not willing to talk about based upon her own desires and the reaction of her family to the invitation and intimate discussions. Because of the intense emotionality, interactions between Barbara, the therapist, and her family should be carried out in an aura of playfulness with a focus on the absurdity and hypocrisy of human experience. This allows each family member to "wean himself or herself away from his or her own personal tragic story in life" (Williamson, 1982a, p. 30).

The therapist determines readiness to begin the Three-Day Consultation. Since doubt and reservations may be expected from Barbara and/or other family members, the therapist should carefully judge whether their hesitancy actually indicates that they are not ready to confront the trauma of the rape and its impact. The timing for the consultation is considered right when all family members express conscious and willful commitment to this final stage of confronting and working through the trauma.

Once the therapist determines that the family is ready for the consultation process, he or she meets separately one final time with Barbara and her family to prepare an agenda of items to be reviewed. This includes concerns that have emerged during previous sessions and contains those issues of continuing emotional and cognitive significance to Barbara and her family. Barbara and the therapist organize these items into three categories: those issues related only to her, those issues related only to the other family members, and those issues related to the family as a whole. These issues are then ordered in terms of emotional intensity so that a gradual escalation of high-voltage issues will emerge over time.

## Three-Day Consultation

The Three-Day Consultation should provide a context in which Barbara and her family can share *in detail* their experience of the trauma of the rape and their associated emotions and cognitions. The goals of this consultation are to focus on understanding the aftereffects of the traumatic experience for Barbara, the other family members, and the family system (Moffat & Moffat, 1984); empowering Barbara, the other family members, and the family system (Balis & Harris, 1982); developing support and communication strategies (Moffat & Moffat, 1984); and initiating changes in family roles, rules, perceptions, and patterns of interaction (Moffat & Moffat, 1984). The ultimate task of the Three-Day Consultation for Barbara and her family will be to turn the rape from an experience relived over and over to "just thoughts" and memories (Schultz, 1984). The rape becomes integrated into the family's experience and the family learns how to manage the associated stressors and utilize them as resources for the future.

During most of the Three-Day Consultation the therapist dissociates from Barbara's and her family's emotions and thoughts. The therapist acts as a moderator who provides direction to the consultation process. If the family is in fact ready, the support previously provided by the therapist should have been internalized so that they can handle their agendas within the confines of their own strength, personal authority, and resources. This mild form of "therapeutic abandonment" (Williamson, 1982a, p. 31) should be accepted if the therapist simultaneously fills the room with the expectation that the clients can and will do the work they are there to do.

The therapist's role as moderator is to continually read family members, keeping an eye on their emotional and cognitive thermostats. Each family member has his or her own hierarchy of readiness to deal with these difficult issues. The therapist attempts to direct the consultation process by discretely determining what matters are important to address and when. The only time the therapist becomes actively involved is if power struggles, coalitions, or dysfunctional coping strategies emerge (e.g., one family member reverts to blaming Barbara for the rape). The therapist usually defuses these in a firm but supportive manner.

The structure of the Three-Day Consultation consists of two two-hour therapy sessions followed by one three-hour session, occurring within a maximum five-day period with at least one overnight between sessions. This provides opportunity for the family to sleep on, dream about, and discuss informally their experiences in the sessions.

The main focus of the first day is on Barbara and her emotional and cognitive experience of the rape and its aftermath. The second day focuses on clarification of Barbara's experience as well as the sharing of the other family members' emotional and cognitive experiences. The third day focuses on the effects of the rape on the family system and its present interactional style and structure. The family discovers new coping strategies for dealing with the short-term and long-term stress.

*First day.* The first day begins with low-key socializing in which the therapist forges a bond with the family as a whole, defining their relationship as a team effort. The ground rule is set that all family members are free to respond or not to respond to any issues or questions brought up in the consultation process.

The family then briefly discusses what they hope to accomplish in the next three sessions, including their fantasies and misgivings. Barbara uses this opportunity to set the scene and to state clearly her own underlying desires and agendas for the consultation. The discussion should be fully reciprocal between all family members; however, the main focus remains on Barbara's experience. This serves to empower her and to provide her with some of the much-needed control that is often lost due to the rape experience. The therapist sets the tone of the session as one of empathy and caring.

Barbara is then asked to share the traumatic experience in as much detail as she is willing with her family. The therapist asks the family to listen quietly and with understanding—to open their hearts and minds and to "be with" and "be for" Barbara for a while.

Barbara now physically faces her family and begins to talk in detail about the actual rape experience. She leads the family through the events, describing what she felt and thought at the time. The therapist encourages Barbara to share her experience only to the extent that she is willing. The therapist sits by Barbara so that "no lethal damage is done as the steam escapes and as difficult matters are made explicit" (Williamson, 1982a, p. 32). Barbara presents her personal issues and perceptions emerging from the experience.

This sharing experience will likely be profoundly emotional for both Barbara and her family. When the story is done, the therapist checks to see that all family members are okay. If they are not, more preparation or debriefing may be needed. The therapist may add an air of humor or playfulness to begin winding down the session. The family is instructed to have a relaxing and enjoyable evening and to discuss the issues presented only if they wish. The therapist conveys his or her appreciation for their willingness and courage to share and be understanding.

*Second day.* The second day begins with a debriefing of the previous day, including conversations, private reflections and dreams, and each person's response to the events of the first session. During this session the family is given the opportunity to react to and ask questions of Barbara concerning the trauma of the rape.

The family members begin by exploring those areas of Barbara's experience which continue to mystify them due to inadequate, distorted, or unavailable information. She clarifies these questions and concerns and discusses with her family the ways in which she is still affected by the rape (e.g., sleep disturbances, fears of recurrence). Barbara expresses to her family her wish to work through the leftover traumatic stress reactions and to resign from her special position as a victim of catastrophe. Finally, she shares some of the growth experiences that emerged from the rape and suggests that the family can help her in further growth.

The family members now become the focus of the session. Anne, Michael, and Catherine share their perceptions of the rape and how it has affected their lives in the past and present. Each discusses his or her emotional and cognitive reactions associated with the rape and its effects on Barbara and the other family members. This is the time for the family members to share with each other how their lives have changed as a result of the rape and to share their reactions to these changes. Both the areas of negative impact and the areas of growth are discussed. The therapist invites Barbara and each of the other family members to respond.

This may be an emotional, poignant moment for both Barbara and her family, particularly since this may be the first time that some family members acknowledge their feelings and thoughts related to the rape and its impact. Other issues may also emerge, such as sudden awareness of the reality and inevitability of aging, dying, and death. This is an opportunity for all family members to get in touch with their humanness and vulnerability as well as their strength and inner resources. If all has gone well, the family has come to understand the magnitude of the effects of the rape and the importance of supporting each other through the aftermath. The power of the trauma of rape and the hold it has on the family is beginning to diffuse.

*Third day.* The third day of the consultation begins by debriefing the family's reflections and responses to the previous two days. During this final session, the family explores new strategies for dealing with the impact of the event on the family system, particularly the current interactional patterns and structural alignments that were affected by the trauma. The goal is to help the family to successfully integrate the rape into their family system by rebuilding the system's functional interactional patterns.

The therapist becomes somewhat more involved in this session, actively offering support to all family members. The author recommends that this final session be extended to three hours (with a break halfway through) in order to provide ample opportunity for modifying dysfunctional interactions and for acquisition of more functional coping strategies.

At this point in the consultation process, some family members may need to express grief over the losses suffered in association with the event. The therapist attends to this grief by trying to understand internal frames of reference and emotional reactions to these losses. He or she further suggests that there will be times in the future when the specter of the rape will reappear and assures the family that this is a normal reaction and does not indicate emotional imbalance.

The therapist asks the family to review the changes in the way family members relate to each other as a result of the rape trauma. With the information that he or she previously obtained on interactional patterns and structure of the system, as well as any new information that emerges from this or previous sessions, the therapist now actively intervenes to further alter dysfunctional interaction styles or structure. Some prior work on these issues has already been performed with the more dysfunctional families following the Contemporary Patterns session and prior to the beginning of the Three-Day Consultation. For those families with rigid patterns of interaction, the therapist may recommend further family therapy sessions.

The second half of this session focuses on helping the family to learn new methods of coping through strategy and skill development. The therapist introduces this goal by suggesting that this final phase of the consultation process be oriented toward practical methods for inspiring future growth. The therapist works with the family on developing functional coping methods, including skills for assessing individual and family vulnerability to stress as well as for dealing with the short-term and long-term stress associated with the rape (Moffat & Moffat, 1984). The therapist emphasizes the need for maintaining an open communication network to provide a healthy, nonjudgmental environment for discussing leftover thoughts and feelings related to the trauma, as well as other family issues that may emerge (Hogancamp & Figley, 1983). This further serves to provide an atmosphere for self-validation and redefinition of relationships (Montgomery, 1981). Most of all, family members are encouraged to provide support by framing each other's successes and providing constructive suggestions for areas of growth (Schultz, 1984).

The therapist affirms the strength, inner resources, and personal authority of the individual family members and of the family as a system, reinforcing their courage and hard work. Finally, the therapist expresses caring by encouraging family members to keep in touch if they wish.

## TREATMENT COMPLETION, EFFECTIVENESS, AND FOLLOW-UP

Treatment is complete when the family is able to function on a new level that incorporates the traumatic experience. Because of the potentially permanent disruption caused by the impact of rape, Whiston (1981) suggests that this is more appropriate than returning the family to a preassault level of functioning.

Treatment may be considered effective if it maintains family integration, cooperation, an optimistic definition of the situation (Patterson & McCubbin, 1983), and functional coping strategies. Effective treatment can "stimulate a total reevaluation of the quality of the relationships, a new-found closeness and common sense of purpose in response to the external crisis the [family] shares" (Silverman, 1978, p. 169). The rape experience has become integrated into each family member's world views and into the family system's interaction.

A brief follow-up interview is suggested within about six months. The therapist assesses the family's progress in person or over the phone. Some temporary regression to traumatic stress reactions may be normalized while the therapist should recommend family therapy for those families who are not able to maintain their strengths and resources for change and growth.

## CONCLUSION

The goal of this chapter was to adapt and apply Williamson's (1981; 1982a,b) theory of personal authority and the termination of the generational boundary to the process of healing from the trauma of rape. Williamson's (1982a) consultation process for this boundary termination was modified and adapted to step-by-step treatment with survivors of rape and their families. This consultation process was theoretically based and requires future research to substantiate or refute the ideas presented.

The process of integrating a rape experience into the survivor's life and into the family system is complex. Ultimately, however, the survivor's potential for triumph over the trauma of rape lies in developing stronger and more meaningful bonds within the family system and in turning the experience into one of personal growth. Survivors of a rape experience and their families also have a message to share with the world — a message born of the loss of innocence and the achievement of wisdom and experience. The theme of the message portrays the importance of meaning, purpose, and dignity of life (Moffat & Moffat, 1984).

## REFERENCES

Abarbanel, G. (1980). The roles of the clinical social worker: Hospital-based management. In C. G. Warner (Ed.), *Rape and sexual assault: Management and intervention* (pp. 141–165). Germantown, MD: Aspen Publications.

American Psychiatric Association. (1987). *Diagnostic and statistical manual of mental disorders* (3rd ed., revised). Washington, DC: American Psychiatric Association.

Balis, E., & Harris, J. (1982). Re-empowering a disabled family network. *International Journal of Family Therapy, 4*(1), 42–59.

Bard, M., & Ellison, K. (1974). Crisis intervention and investigation of forcible rape. *Police Chief, 41*, 70–75.

Bard, M., & Sangrey, D. (1986). *The crime victim's book* (2nd ed.). New York: Brunner/ Mazel.

Bray, J. H., Williamson, D. S., & Malone, P. E. (1986). An evaluation of an intergenerational process to increase personal authority in the family system. *Family Process, 25*, 423–436.

Brodsky, C. M. (1976). Rape at work. In M. J. Walker & S. L. Brodsky (Eds.), *Sexual assault*. Lexington, MA: Lexington Books.

Burge, S. K. (1983). Rape: Individual and family reactions. In C. R. Figley & H. I. McCubbin (Eds.), *Stress and the family, Volume 2: Coping with catastrophe* (pp. 103–119). New York: Brunner/Mazel.

Burge, S. K., & Figley, C. R. (in press). The social support scale: Development and initial estimates of reliability and validity. *Victimology, An International Journal.*

Burgess, A. W., & Holmstrom, L. L. (1974). Rape trauma syndrome. *American Journal of Psychiatry, 1*(8), 981–986.

Burr, W. R. (1973). *Theory construction and sociology of the family.* New York: Wiley.

Burt, M. R. (1980). Cultural myths and supports for rape. *Journal of Personality and Social Psychology, 38*(2), 217–230.

Crenshaw, T. L. (1978). Counseling the family and friends. In S. Halpern (Ed.), *Rape: Helping the victim* (pp. 51–65). Oradell, NJ: Medical Economics Company, Book Division.

Crosby, J. F., & Jose, N. L. (1983). Death: Family adjustment to loss. In C. R. Figley & H. I. McCubbin (Eds.), *Stress and the family, Volume 2: Coping with catastrophe* (pp. 76–89). New York: Brunner/Mazel.

Donaldson, M. A., & Gardner, R. (1985). Diagnosis and treatment of traumatic stress among women after childhood incest. In C. R. Figley (Ed.), *Trauma and its wake, Volume 1: The study and treatment of post-traumatic stress disorder* (pp. 356–376). New York: Brunner/Mazel.

Erickson, C. A. (1988). The relationship of source and satisfaction of social support to negative perceptions of support received. Submitted for publication.

Everstine, D. S., & Everstine, L. (1983). *People in crisis: Strategic therapeutic interventions.* New York: Brunner/Mazel.

Feild, H. S. (1978). Attitudes toward rape: A comparative analysis of police, rapists, crisis counselors, and citizens. *Journal of Personality and Social Psychology, 36*(2), 156–179.

Feinauer, L. L., & Hippolite, D. L. (1987). Once a princess, always a princess: A strategy for therapy with families of rape victims. *Contemporary Family Therapy: An International Journal, 9*(4), 252–262.

Felix, K. (1980). Management of sexual assault victims in a community health agency. In C. G. Warner (Ed.), *Rape and sexual assault: Management and intervention.* Germantown, MD: Aspen Publications.

Figley, C. R. (1983). Catastrophes: An overview of family reactions. In C. R. Figley & H. I. McCubbin (Eds.), *Stress and the family, Volume 2: Coping with catastrophe* (pp. 3–20). New York: Brunner/Mazel.

Figley, C. R. (1985). From victim to survivor: Social responsibility in the wake of catastrophe. In C. R. Figley (Ed.), *Trauma and its wake, Volume 1: The study and treatment of post-traumatic stress disorder* (pp. 398–413). New York: Brunner/Mazel.

Figley, C. R. (1986). Traumatic stress: The role of the family and social support system. In C. R. Figley (Ed.), *Trauma and its wake, Volume 2: Traumatic stress theory, research and intervention* (pp. 39–54). New York: Brunner/Mazel.

Figley, C. R., & Sprenkle, D. H. (1978). Delayed stress response syndrome: Family therapy indications. *Journal of Marriage and Family Counseling*, July, 53–60.

Gilbert, K. R., & Erickson, C. A. (1988). The development of a family definition of the event: Information exchange among family members after a catastrophe. Submitted for publication.

Girelli, S., Resick, P., Marhoefer-Dvorak, S., & Hutter, C. (1986). Subjective distress and violence during rape: Their effects on long-term fear. *Violence and Victims, 1*(1), 35–46.

Groth, A., Burgess, A., & Holmstrom, L. (1977). Rape: Power, anger, and sexuality. *American Journal of Psychiatry, 134*(11), 1239–1243.

Halpern, S., Hicks, D. J., & Crenshaw, T. L. (1978). *Rape: Helping the victim.* Oradell, NJ: Medical Economics Company, Book Division.

Herndon, A. D., & Law, J. G. (1986). Post-traumatic stress and the family: A multimethod approach to counseling. In C. R. Figley (Ed.), *Trauma and its wake, Volume 2: Traumatic stress theory, research and intervention* (pp. 264–279). New York: Brunner/Mazel.

Hilberman, E. (1976). *The rape victim.* New York: Basic Books.

Hill, R., & Hansen, D. (1962) Families in disaster. In G. Baker & D. Chapman (Eds.), *Man and society in disaster* (pp. 185–221). New York: Basic Books.

Hogancamp, V., & Figley, C. R. (1983). War: Bringing the battle home. In C. R. Figley & H. I. McCubbin (Eds.), *Stress and the family, Volume 2: Coping with catastrophe* (pp. 148–165). New York: Brunner/Mazel.

Holmstrom, L. L., & Burgess, A. W. (1979). Rape: The husband's and boyfriend's initial reactions. *The Family Coordinator, 28*, 321–330.

Horowitz, M. J. (1986). *Stress response syndromes* (2nd ed.) New York: Aronson.

Horowitz, M. J., Kaltreider, N., Wilner, N., & Alvarez, W. (1979). Impact of event scale: A measure of subjective stress. *Psychosomatic Medicine, 41*, 209–218.

Horowitz, M. J., Wilner, N., & Kaltreider, N. (1980). Signs and symptoms of post-traumatic stress disorder. *Archives of General Psychiatry, 37*, 85–92.

Janoff-Bulman, R. (1979). Characterological vs. behavioral self-blame: Inquiries into depression and rape. *Journal of Personality and Social Psychology, 37*(10), 1798–1809.

Janoff-Bulman, R. (1985). The aftermath of victimization: Rebuilding shattered assumptions. In C. R. Figley (Ed.), *Trauma and its wake, Volume 1: The study and treatment of post-traumatic stress disorder* (pp. 15–31). New York: Brunner/Mazel.

Janoff-Bulman, R., Madden, M. E., & Timko, C. (1983). Victims' reactions to aid: The role of perceived vulnerability. In A. Nadler, J. D. Fisher, & B. M. DePaulo (Eds.), *New directions in helping, Volume 3: Applied perspectives on help-seeking and -receiving* (pp. 21–42). New York: Academic Press.

Katz, S., & Mazur, M. A. (1979). *Understanding the rape victim: A synthesis of research findings.* New York: John Wiley.

Kilpatrick, D. G., Veronen, L. J., & Best, C. L. (1985). Factors predicting psychological distress among rape victims. In C. Figley (Ed.), *Trauma and its wake, Volume 1: The study and treatment of post-traumatic stress disorder* (pp. 113–141). New York: Brunner/Mazel.

Kilpatrick, D. G., Veronen, L. J., & Resick, P A. (1979). Assessment of the aftermath of rape: Changing patterns of fear. *Journal of Behavioral Assessment*, *1*(2), 133–148.

Koss, M. P., Gidycz, C. A., & Wisniewski, N. (1987). The scope of rape: Incidence and prevalence of sexual aggression and victimization in a national sample of higher education students. *Journal of Consulting and Clinical Psychology*, *55*(2), 162–170.

Law Enforcement Assistance Administration. (1975). *Criminal victimization surveys in 8 American cities* (Publication No. SD-NCS-C-5). Washington, DC: U.S. Government Printing Office.

McDermott, M. J. (1979). *Rape victimization in 26 American cities.* (Analytic Report SD-VAD-6). Department of Justice, Law Enforcement Assistance Administration. Washington, DC: U.S. Government Printing Office.

Moffat, L., & Moffat, J. (1984). *Families after trauma.* White Bear Lake, MN: Minnesota Curriculum Services Center.

Montgomery, B. (1981). The form and function of quality communication in marriage. *Family Relations*, *30*, 21–30.

Nelson, C. (1980). Victims of rape: Who are they? In C. G. Warner (Ed.), *Rape and sexual assault: Management and intervention* (pp. 10–26). Germantown, MD: Aspen Publications.

Norsigian, J. (1979). Rape. In the Boston Women's Health Book Collective, *Our bodies, ourselves.* New York: Simon & Schuster.

Olson, D. H. (1986). Circumplex model VII: Validation studies and FACES III. *Family Process*, *25*, 337–351.

Olson, D. H., Portner, J., & Lavee, Y. (1985). *FACES III.* St. Paul, MN: Family Social Science, University of Minnesota.

Olson, D., Sprenkle, D., & Russell, C. (1979). Circumplex model of marital and family systems: Cohesion and adaptability dimensions, family types, and clinical application. *Family Process*, *18*, 3–27.

Orzek, A. (1983). Sexual assault: The female victim, her male partner, and their relationship. *The Personnel and Guidance Journal*, November, 143–146.

Patterson, J. M., & McCubbin, H. I. (1983). Chronic illness: Family stress and coping. In C. R. Figley & H. I. McCubbin (Eds.), *Stress and the family, Volume 2: Coping with catastrophe* (pp. 21–36). New York: Brunner/Mazel.

Rodabaugh, B. J., & Austin, M. (1981). *Sexual assault: A guide for community action.* New York: Garland STPM Press.

Rook, K. (1984). The negative side of social interaction: Impact on psychological well-being. *Journal of Personality and Social Psychology*, *46*(5), 1097–1108.

Russell, D. E. (1984). *Sexual exploitation: Rape, child sexual abuse, and workplace harassment.* Beverly Hills, CA: Sage Publications.

Salasin, S. E. (1981). Services to victims: Needs assessment. In S. E. Salasin (Ed.), *Evaluating victim services* (pp. 21–38). Beverly Hills, CA: Sage Publications.

Schultz, S. (1984). *Family systems therapy: An integration.* New York: Jason Aronson.

Silver, R., & Wortman, C. B. (1980). Coping with undesirable life events. In J. Gardner & M. Seligman (Eds.), *Human helplessness.* New York: Academic Press.

Silverman, D. (1978). Sharing the crisis of rape: Counseling the mates and families of victims. *American Journal of Orthopsychiatry*, *48*(1), 166–173.

Skogan, W. G. (1981). *Issues in the measurement of victimization* (NCJ-74682). Department of Justice, Bureau of Statistics. Washington, DC: U.S. Government Printing Office.

Sparks, R. F. (1982). *Research on victims of crime: Accomplishments, issues, and new directions* (DHHS Publication No. [ADM] 82-1091). Washington, DC: U.S. Government Printing Office.

Spaulding, D. (1980). The role of the victim advocate. In C. G. Warner (Ed.), *Rape and sexual assault: Management and intervention* (pp. 199–212). Germantown, MD: Aspen Publications.

Stanton, M.D., & Figley, C. R. (1978). Treating the Vietnam veteran within the family system. In C. R. Figley (Ed.), *Stress disorders among Vietnam veterans* (pp. 281–289). New York: Brunner/Mazel.

Sutherland, S., & Scherl, D. J. (1970). Patterns of response among victims of rape. *Journal of Orthopsychiatry, 40,* 213–229.

Warner, C. G. (1980a). Rape and rape laws in historical perspective. In C. G. Warner (Ed.), *Rape and sexual assault: Management and intervention* (pp. 1–7). Germantown, MD: Aspen Publications.

Warner, C. G. (1980b). Family and friends: The other victims. In C. G. Warner (Ed.), *Rape and sexual assault: Management and intervention* (pp. 213–219). Germantown, MD: Aspen Publications.

Whiston, S. K. (1981). Counseling sexual assault victims: A loss model. *Personnel and Guidance Journal, 59*(6), 363–366.

White, P. N., & Rollins, J. C. (1981). Rape: A family crisis. *Family Relations, 30*(1), 103–109.

Williamson, D. S. (1981). Personal authority via termination of the intergenerational hierarchical boundary: A "new" stage in the family life cycle. *Journal of Marital and Family Therapy, 7,* 441–452.

Williamson, D. S. (1982a). Personal authority via termination of the intergenerational hierarchical boundary: Part II. The consultation process and the therapeutic methods. *Journal of Marital and Family Therapy, 8,* 23–37.

Williamson, D. S. (1982b). Personal authority in family experiences via termination of the intergenerational hierarchical boundary: Part III. Personal authority defined, and the power of play in the change process. *Journal of Marital and Family Therapy, 8,* 309–323.

Wilson, P. R. (1978). *The other side of rape.* St. Lucia, Queensland, Australia: University of Queensland Press.

Woodling, B. A., Evans, J. R., & Bradbury, M. D. (1977). Sexual assault: Rape and molestation. *Clinical Obstetrics and Gynecology, 20*(3), 509–530.

Young, M. B., & Erickson, C. A. (in press). Cultural impediments to recovery: PTSD in contemporary America. *Journal of Traumatic Stress.*

# Appendix: Glossary of Major Terms

**Adaptability dimension:** ability of the system to respond to developmental or situational stressors with appropriate shifts in the power structure, relationship roles, and rules.

**Adaptation phase:** family response to a major transition or change (e.g., divorce, serious illness, death) that creates a family crisis; characterized by a shift in the family's structure, rules, and/or patterns of behavior.

**Adjustment coping strategies:** short-term responses, consisting of avoidance, elimination, and assimilation, used separately or in combination by the family to bring about adjustment to family life changes, demands, and transitions.

**Adjustment phase:** family response to a minor transition or change that is characterized by minimal disruption of the family's established rules and patterns of behavior and structure.

**Assimilation:** a family adjustment coping strategy characterized by the family's efforts to accept the demands created by the stressor into its existing structure and patterns of interaction.

**Attributions:** characteristics, possessions, qualities, causes, or judgments one perceives or makes about an object.

**Avoidance:** a family adjustment coping strategy characterized by efforts to deny or ignore the stressor in the hope that it will go away.

**Bonadaptation:** improvement in an individual's overall set of coping resources so that future stressors will be more efficiently handled.

**Boundary:** an abstract demarcation which separates family subsystems according to function or hierarchy.

**Catastrophe:** an extreme emergency that is a sudden, unexpected, often life-threatening (to self or significant others) event or series of events, and renders the survivors feeling an extreme sense of helplessness; with sufficient magnitude the event will (1) disrupt the lifestyle and routine of the survivors; (2) cause destruction, disruption, and loss; along with (3) a permanent and detailed memory of the events which may be recalled voluntarily or involuntarily.

**Chaotic adaptability:** the tendency for a family to overrespond to a particular stressor by changing too much or too quickly.

**Contextual family therapy:** a comprehensive, transgenerational approach to treatment which takes into account familial identity, intrapsychic processes, relational transactions, and the "ethics" or balance of interactions across generations.

**Coping behaviors:** specific efforts (covert or overt) by which an individual (or a group of individuals such as the family) attempts to reduce or manage a demand on the family system.

**Coping patterns:** group of coping behaviors representing more generalized ways of responding that transcend different kinds of situations used by an individual or family. An example of an individual coping pattern would be "maintaining psychological stability"; a coping pattern for a family unit could be directed at "maintaining family integration and cooperation."

**Covert rules:** behavior patterns within a family that are not explicit but are nonetheless consensual.

**Crisis-traumatic stress reactions:** a set of behaviors and feelings associated with coping with the crisis/stressor/traumatic event.

**Defensive collusion:** an unconscious mechanism which serves to unite family members around family issues, while at the same time fending off intrusion or inquiry from outside the family.

**Demands:** expectations (usually unspoken) about what the environment "ought" to provide (family demands for security, flexibility, solidarity, identity/boundaries).

**Denial-numbing response:** a defensive method of coping with a catastrophe by either denying (or being incapable of perceiving) that there is any danger/demands/stressor or becoming numb to/denying the danger.

**Developmental life crises:** a shift in system pattern, common to most similar social systems, due to normal growth and maturation. Some examples are marriage, birth of first child, and adolescence.

**Developmental tasks:** age-appropriate behaviors which, when mastered, result in an increased sense of inner unity, an increase in good judgment, and an increase in the capacity to do well.

**Disengagement:** decrease in family bonding over time; increasing individual autonomy and decreasing family interdependency.

**Distancing:** engaging in activities that are primarily done individually, such as reading or studying; these activities promote a feeling of separateness (or distance) between people.

**Elimination:** a family adjustment coping strategy that is an active effort by the family to rid itself of all demands by changing or removing the stressor or altering the definition of the stressor.

**Empty chair technique:** a Gestalt intervention developed by Fritz Perls to allow therapy clients to talk to a key person who is absent, but whose presence can be represented by the immediacy of the "empty chair." A variation on this theme is to have the empty chair represent some aspect of the client's own self.

**Endogenous life crises:** discrete traumatic events, such as incidents of child abuse or wife battering, inherent to a unique yet characteristic set of internal family patterns that produce them.

**Enmeshment:** high family bonding; decreased individual autonomy and high family interdependency.

**Environment:** a concrete, immediate physical setting (microsystem) or settings (mesosystems) or more global ones less easily observed context (macrosystems).

**Equifinality:** a systems concept that holds that similar outcomes may result from different origins.

**Exosystem:** the external organization of a particular microsystem (e.g., associations, societies, collectives, consortia).

**Family adaptation:** a long-term response of a family that is adequate to resolve a crisis and involves both restructuring of established roles, rules, goals, and/or patterns of interaction and consolidating efforts by family members into a coherent unit and in support of the newly instituted changes; includes three basic coping strategies of synergism, interfacing, and compromising.

**Family adaptation interdependence strategy:** family efforts of system maintenance to achieve increased integration, morale, member self-esteem, and other goals that make family life valuable to its members.

**Family adaptation interfacing strategy:** family efforts, following internal restructuring, to achieve a new "fit" or complementarity with community members (e.g., neighbors, friends, coworkers), institutions (e.g., work, school, religious institutions, government), and other systems outside the family.

**Family adaptation synergism strategy:** family efforts to coordinate and pull together as a unit to accomplish a shared lifestyle and orientation that cannot be achieved by any member alone but only through mutuality and interdependence.

**Family adaptation/working through the trauma:** absence of restoration of order, routine, and predictability within the family system organization

**Family adaptive resource:** an ability to deal with any type of demand/stressor; a collection of skills, experiences, and economic, personal, social, and intellectual reserves available to the family through its members.

**Family adjustment:** a short-term response that is adequate to manage many life changes, transitions, and demands.

**Family adjustment and adaptation response (FAAR):** a model that builds upon the Double ABCX model in an attempt to account for how certain characteristics of family systems influence the extent to which the system is vulnerable and adjusts and adapts to life stressors (event, series of events, transitions, hardships, prior strains/pileup).

**Family adjustment assimilation strategy:** active family efforts to accept the demands created by the stressor into its existing structure and patterns of interaction; absorbs the demands by making only minor changes within the family unit.

**Family adjustment avoidance strategy:** family efforts to deny or ignore the stressor and other demands in the belief and hope that they will go away or resolve themselves.

**Family adjustment elimination strategy:** active effort by the family to rid itself of all demands by changing or removing the stressor, or altering the definition of the stressor.

**Family appraisal:** family's definition of the situation at three levels: the family's appraisal of the specific stressor event or transition; situational appraisal or the family's subjective definitions of the demands and capabilities placed upon them and how these two relate to each other; and global appraisal or how the family views the relationship of the family members to each other and the relationship of the family to the larger community.

**Family bonadaptation:** improvement in a family's overall set of coping resources so that future stressors will be more efficiently handled.

**Family bonding:** the degree of cohesiveness, sense of closeness among family members; the tendency for mutual interdependence for social support.

**Family coherence:** a specific level of family appraisal involving acceptance, loyalty, pride, faith, trust, respect, caring, and shared values in the management of tension and strain.

**Family cohesion (or integration) dimension:** a family adaptive resource which is the emotional bonding members have with one another and the degree of individual autonomy persons experience in the family system.

**Family coping responses:** action that makes it possible for the family members to understand, shape, and master the environment, as well as themselves; enables the family to recover from the stressors and to reorganize, promoting a better fit between environmental and family demands.

**Family crisis:** a transitional state of family system disorganization characterized by the family's situational inability to restore stability, by its cyclical trial-and-error struggle to reduce tension, complemented by efforts to make changes in the family structure and patterns of interaction. The latter also contribute to the family's instability.

**Family definition factor:** (the cC factor in the Double ABCX Model) the collective family view/meaning/perception/theory connected with a stressor situation/crisis.

**Family distress:** a negative state that results from the family's defining the demands-resources imbalance as unpleasant (e.g., fear, boredom).

**Family eustress:** a positive state that results from the family's defining the demand-resources imbalance as desirable and a challenge family members enjoy (e.g., joy, happiness, fun).

**Family hardiness:** the family's internal strengths and durability characterized by an internal sense of control over life events and hardships, a sense of meaningfulness in life, involvement in activities, and a commitment to learn and to explore new and challenging experiences.

**Family hardships:** those demands on the family unit specifically associated with the stressor event.

**Family hyperstress:** a state that arises from an actual or perceived imbalance when the stressor/demand far exceeds the family's capabilities/resources.

**Family hypostress:** a state that arises from an actual or perceived imbalance when the family's capabilities/resources far exceed the stressor/demand.

**Family intimacy:** a family environment characterized by each family member evaluating his or her balance of distance, coaction, and intimacy as within acceptable limits.

**Family legacy:** the specific configuration of expectations that stem from family identity, ethnicity and rootedness, plus concomitant implications for the family offspring.

**Family maladaptation:** ineffectively coping with a stress to the extent that additional problems and conflicts emerged; development of new dysfunctional patterns (e.g., keeping family secrets) that have an ongoing negative effect on family interactions.

**Family perceptions:** current views of the family and its members about the stressor that are formed simultaneously with becoming aware of the stressor and frequently change (viewing the stressor in more or less serious terms) as resources are applied.

**Family post-traumatic/post-crisis perceptions:** the consensus family views about the causes and consequences of a particular family stressor.

**Family resources:** behavioral, family interaction patterns utilized in coping with the stressor; resources are immediately applied to the stressor.

**Family schema:** a specific level of family appraisal involving a set of beliefs or assumptions that a family holds about the family members in relation to each other and about their family in relationship to the community and systems beyond their boundaries. This form of family life orientation guides the family's responses to stressful life events and crises.

**Family stress:** a state that arises from an actual or perceived imbalance between demand (e.g., challenge, threat) and the family's capability to deal with the demand (e.g., family's resources and coping repertoire).

**Family stressor:** a life event impacting upon the family unit that produces or has the potential of producing change in the family social system (boundaries, goals, patterns of interaction, values).

**Family trauma:** a state of crisis, disorganization, and general unrest within the family during which time there are frequently desperate and dysfunctional efforts to cope and restore order, routine, and predictability to the family.

**Family traumatic stress/crisis reactions:** patterns of family interaction associated with coping with the crisis/stressor/traumatic event, drawing upon the emerging family resources and points of view about the ongoing crisis.

**Family type:** a set of basic attributes about the family system which characterizes and explains how a family system typically appraises, operates, and/or behaves.

**Family vulnerability:** interpersonal and organizational condition of the family system shaped, in part, by the pileup of demands placed upon the family and the family's life cycle stage.

**Families of catastrophe:** families that are experiencing either the unfolding of a catastrophe or its aftermath, which evolved either within the family or through the experiences of one or more family members.

**Feedback:** a term derived from cybernetic theories indicating that a part of a signal is added back into an original signal to produce increasing amplification of the original signal (positive feedback) or decreasing intensity of the original signal (negative feedback); in family disagreements, positive feedback results in ever-increasing conflict and negative feedback results in conflict resolution.

**Fight-or-flight response:** reactions by individuals caught in a catastrophic situation, to freeze, flee the situation, or stay and fight.

**First order change:** a change within the accepted premises and patterns of a system. These are changes in intensity, frequency, duration, etc.

**First order reality:** a commonly agreed upon and relatively useful definition of the way things are in a given context.

**Fit:** the particular relationship between the demands of an individual or family and those of an environment; stress is the *lack of fit* and adaptation is the *existence of a good fit*.

**Generic response patterns:** a patterned and often sequenced set of responses to a given life crisis which have been found to be typical within a given culture or subculture.

**Healing recapitulation:** resolving anxiety and stress associated with the memories of a catastrophe by discussing it in detail and thereby acquiring a sense of mastery, understanding, and acceptance of what took place.

**Helplessness:** a sense of inability to influence or stop the situation/catastrophe, especially the danger.

**Hierarchy:** a concept indicating that organized systems have different levels of organization.

**Ignominy:** the degree to which the catastrophic experience was degrading, humiliating, or embarrassing.

**Incidental life crisis:** a system variation resulting from an unpredictable external event. This is not common to all like systems. Examples are rape, job loss, mugging, and premature family member death.

**Indebtedness:** the sum total of obligations incurred upon the family by a given family member.

**Individual perceptions:** cognitive appraisal of the seriousness of the stressor, the array of options for coping, and her or his descriptions of the stressor and states of coping (i.e., no problem versus crisis).

**Individual resources:** behaviors, emotions, and tangible goods utilized to cope with the stressor.

**Individual traumatic period:** a relatively brief period of crisis characterized by a sense of helplessness, hyperalertness, aimlessness, disorganization, or general unrest and distress that may last only a short time but is extraordinarily stressful for the person.

**Individual working through of the trauma:** resolving the crisis and the cognitive disorganization introduced by the stressor that resulted in the trauma/crisis.

**Invisible loyalties:** implicit family expectations and injunctions (rules) which become internalized by each family member, and which get played out in conformity to family norms.

**Macrosystem:** the overarching institutions of the culture, such as its religious life, political system, or economic organization that give meaning and character to daily life as enacted at the microsystem level.

**Maladaptation:** ineffectively coping with a stress to the extent that additional problems and conflicts emerged; development of new dysfunctional patterns (e.g., addiction, abusive behavior, criminal behavior) that have an ongoing negative effect on future coping efforts.

**Mesosystem:** a collection of microsystems within which an individual interacts in a given period of time (e.g., employment, educational, religious, food market).

**Microsystem:** immediate physical context in which family members come face-to-face with each other and with other people as part of their roles within the system.

**Moderator variables:** factors which, when present, influence other factors by increasing or decreasing their value.

**Nonsummativity:** a concept emphasizing that summation of the parts does not result in the same outcome as taking the whole on its own, frequently stated as "the whole is different than the sum of its parts."

**Nonuniformity hypothesis:** the hypothesis that different treatments will be differentially effective for clients with different presenting problems and situations and at different times of life.

**Normalizing:** a therapeutic intervention which places a person's or family's responses in the context of normal response patterns, given the nature of the stressor.

**Normative family transitions:** brief, ubiquitous, expected changes in patterns, relationships, roles, or other elements within the family system over the life of the family system.

**Overt rules:** behavior patterns within a family that are governed by explicit agreements.

**Paradox:** a contradiction which follows correct reasoning from a given set of premises.

**Paradoxical-looking intervention:** an intervention which appears contradictory to an external set of accepted premises on the nature of therapy or the helping role.

**Pileup:** accumulation of stressors and strains placed on the family system that can include the stressor event and its associated hardships, normative transitions, prior unresolved strains, consequences of the family's efforts to cope, and intrafamily and social ambiguity.

**Positioning:** a therapeutic intervention wherein the therapist adopts a position with respect to a client or his or her problem which is distinctly different and often opposite to that of helpful others. This is done to attribute health and strength to the client and elicit explanations about strength in the face of adversity.

**Post-traumatic family resources:** those human resources (e.g., social support system, social skills) that survived the crisis/trauma, along with additional ones acquired (e.g., medical first aid skills, utilization of crisis center staff) as a result of coping with the crisis/trauma.

**Post-traumatic family stress reactions:** patterns of family interaction associated with coping with the collective and constantly evolving memories (post-traumatic stress reactions) of the current crisis and more distant (and poorly worked through) crises/traumata, drawing upon the emerging family resources and points of view to do so.

**Post-traumatic family stressors:** continuing demands on the family associated with the traumatic event/crisis.

**Post-traumatic family therapy:** helping families change unproductive ways of relating to each other that have emerged during and following the traumatic event/crisis as are associated with their current problems and reasons for seeking treatment.

**Post-traumatic perceptions:** those cognitive patterns that arise following the crises/trauma, along with any new and emerging ones. Individuals constantly reframe or modify their perceptions of their predicament, which may or may not promote healthy recovery.

**Post-traumatic stress reactions:** a set of reactions and emotions associated with dealing with the memories of the crisis/trauma (e.g., startle reactions, sleep disorders, depression, flashbacks, survivor's guilt, cue sensitivity), in addition to memories of any other traumatic experiences.

**Post-traumatic stressors:** continuing demands on the individual associated with the traumatic event/crisis.

**Power rules:** a balance achieved within a family through numerous decisions in which the family members expect different types of decisions to be made by certain persons in predictable ways; there may be more or less agreement about power rules.

**Predicting:** a therapeutic intervention used to help clients anticipate typical or generic system responses to the current crisis and to inoculate them against possible problematic reactions.

**Prescribing:** a therapeutic intervention wherein the therapist is often directing clients to engage in some form of the problem behavior, yet in new ways or for new reasons.

**Process:** change in a system over time.

**Recursive:** an organizational aspect of events which evaluates relationships based on a circular causality model.

**Reframing:** a therapeutic intervention which recasts or redefines the meaning of a role, relationship, action, context, or intervention to facilitate understanding or behavior change.

**Resistance resources:** a family's capabilities and strengths that can be called upon to meet the pileup of demands placed upon the family.

**Restraints:** therapeutic interventions which are designed to reduce anxiety around the pressure to change and enable clients to more easily take the side of new ideas or actions.

**Rigid adaptability:** the tendency for a family to underrespond to a particular stressor by resisting to change at all.

**Role strain:** the stressful effects of feeling that one must perform too many prescribed behaviors.

**Second order change:** a change of a system's primary premise, rule, or pattern, usually yielding strikingly different or opposite patterns than occurred prior to the change.

**Second order reality:** an alternate, yet equally or even more useful definition of the way things are in a given context.

**Secondary traumatic stress reactions:** experiencing traumatic stress indirectly or victoriously when a family member is exposed to a catastrophe/traumatic event.

**Social support:** the exchange of well-being-enhancing resources between two people, including emotional support, advice, companionship, tangible aid, and encouragement.

**Sociality factor:** the extent to which there is communication among fellow victims at the time of the catastrophe and immediately afterwards.

**Solution-generated problems:** a problem pattern initiated and perpetuated by attempted solutions to perceived life crises.

**Specific response patterns:** crisis response patterns which are a product of the unique assumptions and interaction patterns of a specific system.

**Splitting:** a therapeutic intervention wherein a therapist continues to offer direct support while delivering a strong challenge attributed to an external source, such as an alternate theory or a colleague.

**Stimulus regulation family coping/adaptation:** family efforts to selectively let in, delay, or shut out demands to minimize family disruption and exhaustion of its resources; setting priorities.

**Stress:** a state of physical or psychological strain that imposes demands for adjustment upon the individual.

**Stressor pileup:** the accumulation of prior strains, unresolved hardships, unresolved transitions, dysfunctional coping, boundary/social ambiguities that, together, can become a source of stress requiring immediate attention.

**Stressors:** event or series of events that demand immediate attention to control.

**Structure:** the manner of organization of a system; the way the parts are arranged.

**Subsystem:** an element that carries out a particular process in a system.

**System:** "a set of elements standing in interaction" (von Bertalanffy) so that what affects one part affects others.

**Task assignments:** interventions designed to require specific behaviors from clients in the interim prior to the next therapy session.

**Triggering event:** some reminder of the catastrophe that is strong enough to cause the victim to remember in varying degrees the details of the catastrophe and its accompanying stress.

**Typology Model of Adjustment and Adaptation:** a model developed as a specific evolution of family stress theory that depicts the pileup of demands, family vulnerability, family type, resistance resources, family appraisal, and problem-solving and coping strategies as critical factors in determining how families adjust and adapt to normative and situational stressor events.

**Uniformity myth:** the belief that a therapy should be capable of successful treatment of clients with almost any disorder.

**Wholeness:** seeing patterns in behavior rather than reducing entities to their constituent parts in a reductive fashion.

**Vicious cycle:** an insidious, escalating pattern of interaction wherein the more a given solution is applied, the worse the problem gets.

# Name Index

305

# Subject Index